VOIC OUR VISIONS

WRITINGS BY WOMEN ARTISTS

EDITED BY MARA R. WITZLING

The Women's Press

FRONT COVER

Faith Ringgold, *Dancing on the George Washington Bridge*, 1988
Acrylic on canvas, dyed, printed and pieced fabric. 68" x 68"
Collection: Roy Eaton, New York
Courtesy Bernice Steinbaum Gallery, NYC

THE FOLLOWING WERE TRANSLATED FROM THE ORIGINAL BY THE AUTHOR:
Rose Bonheur, Sa vie, son oeuvre (Paris: Flammarion, 1908)
Marianne Werefkin, Lettres À Un Inconnu, 1901–1905 (Museo Communale, Ascona)
Kay Sage, Selected Poetry
From *Demaine Monsieur Silber* (Paris: Pierre Seghers, 1957)
From *Faut Dire C'Qui Est* (Paris: Debresse-Poésie, 1959)
From *Mordicus* (Paris, December 1962)

First published in Great Britain by
The Women's Press Ltd 1992
A member of the Namara Group
34 Great Sutton Street
London EC1V ODX

Published in the United States of America in 1991 by Universe
300 Park Avenue South, New York, NY 10010

Copyright © 1991 Mara R. Witzling

Designed by Douglas &Voss Group, New York

91 92 93 94 95 / 10 9 8 7 6 5 4 3 2 1

Printed in the United States of America

CIP data available from the British Library

Dedicated to my parents and my children

CONTENTS

PREFACE

ELIZA **C**ALVERT **H**ALL'S Aunt Jane of Kentucky said that "piecin' a quilt is like livin' a life." For me, writing this book has been like making a quilt. Pieces and scraps were collected, cut up, sewn together, and rearranged to create a new pattern. As in quilt-making, much of the work was done between many interruptions, over a long period, the fragments pieced into numerous individual squares, worked several at a time. The process was arduous, even tedious, and at times the project looked (in Aunt Jane's words), "pretty much like a jumble o' quilt pieces before they are put together." It wasn't until I was quite far along that the pattern became visible and I could begin to see how these separate units did, in fact, form a whole.

From the very beginning, I felt myself privileged to be intimately connected to the voices of so many women. The lives, the art, and the words of those women included in this volume — and even those who for one reason or another were not — quite literally, called to me, spoke to me, touched and affected me profoundly. It has been my desire to allow each writer to speak for herself, to directly connect with other listeners. Unfortunately, I was unable to obtain permissions in two instances. The Gwen John Estate would not allow us to reproduce a series of letters from Gwen John to Rodin, and we could not come to an agreement on the use of various other material. The Estate of Eva Hesse was also unable to comply with our request to reprint a selection of entries from Hesse's diaries.

Many friends and colleagues have supported and encouraged my seemingly interminable work on this book. The idea was originally conceived almost a decade ago in a conversation with the late Jean Brown of the Department of Theater and Dance. At a crucial juncture later on, Melody Graulich and Elizabeth Hageman of the English department, and Laurel Ulrich of the History department, generously shared their insights and expertise with me, and helped me to focus the direction of my work. In the Department of Art and Art History, Margot Clark has been my steadfast comrade-in-arms over the years, as has Joan Esch, more recently. I also owe a debt to my many students whose new eyes have enhanced my own ability to see.

While there is no way I could begin to express my gratitude to my circle of friends, both in the New Hampshire seacoast area and beyond, I am compelled to thank Carol Aronson and Jean Silverman for our regular get-togethers that have kept me sane and balanced over the years and my sister, Catherine Witzling, whose phone calls have been a life line. I need to acknowledge, also, that my ongoing conversations with Candice Leonard and Jill Morgan have provided the nourishing subsoil of all my thinking.

Dean Stuart Palmer of the College of Liberal Arts at the University of New Hampshire supported this work most generously through a College of Liberal Arts Summer Faculty Fellowship and through two Liberal Arts Faculty Research Grants. Receipt of the Gustafson Fellowship through the Center for the Humanities at the University of New Hampshire gave me the gift of time through a course release when it was sorely needed.

A special thanks is due the staff of the Interlibrary Loan department at the UNH Dimond Library, particularly to Karen Fagerberg, whose diligence gave me access to a wide range of materials. Many thanks, too, to all those at other collections who generously made their holdings available to me.

At Universe, the manuscript profited greatly from Dorothy Caeser's careful editing, and from my lengthy dialogue with Adele Ursone concerning every aspect of this endeavor. Finally, my friend and companion, Bix Hamby, was with me through it all.

INTRODUCTION

THIS BOOK, AN introduction to writings by women artists, has been conceived as a contribution to the ongoing process that is making it possible for us to "hear women's voices." [1] Because all the voices included here are those of visual artists, listening to them may enable readers to "see" the authors' visions with greater clarity. The aim here has been to bring together the written words of nineteenth- and twentieth-century women artists, for the first time, rather than to compile a definitive edition of the written works of any one artist. Both previously published and virtually inaccessible materials are included here, in this first publication to gather the writings of important women artists of the last two centuries into a single volume.

The written works of twenty nineteenth and twentieth century visual artists have been included in this volume. Each artist is introduced by a brief biographical sketch in which her goals and achievements are assessed and her place in the history of art is examined. Major themes in both her artwork and her writings are also identified and discussed.

Although these women defined themselves as visual artists, each was also a writer, and despite their diversity, the process of verbalizing had more than a passing importance for each. Their writing was neither casual nor occasional, but was sustained over some period of time.

The artists included all saw themselves as professionals and made art according to the rules of the dominant tradition. Despite the fact that most of their historical precedents and contemporary colleagues were men, these women ruptured the conventional structure and defined themselves as artists. How they were able to do that, often against all odds, is elucidated by the extracts of their writings, selected to provide examples of each artist's discussion of such subjects as her work, her aesthetic self-actualization, and her gender. Lengthier extracts have been favored over short ones, to enable the reader to find significance in and make connections between text and image. An isolated quotation might help us to understand an artist's visual work, but excerpts that are too narrowly focused lose their richness and impose too forcefully the editor's interpretation on the reader. Longer quotations allow the works to speak for themselves.

Often women artists wrote in order to explore the conflicting demands of their profession and gender. The question Can a woman be an artist?, further refined as How can a woman be an artist?, and finally focused to Can *I* be an artist? is asked — and answered — by many artists in numerous ways: to confidantes in their letters, to themselves in their diaries, to the public in autobiographies. Georgia O'Keeffe writes to Anita Pollitzer, "I don't see why we ever think of what others think of what we do — isn't it enough just to express ourselves?" Berthe Morisot confides in her sister, "I think that no matter how much affection a woman has for her husband, it is not easy for her to break from a life of work." Marianne Werefkin despairs in her diary that she has been cook, kitchen maid, and seamstress, and has thus wasted her talent. Barbara Hepworth tells us that she does not think that motherhood is incompatible with being an artist, "as long as one does at least a half hour's work per day."

This book has a dual purpose, to provide a resource for informed readers and students and to point scholars in fruitful directions for further explorations. Its additional goal is to bring muted voices to speech, to gather together a chorus.

EXCLUSION OF WOMEN ARTISTS AND THEIR WRITINGS FROM ART HISTORY

Although artists' writings have long been considered helpful resources in understanding the pursuit of the artistic endeavor, those by women artists have been largely overlooked. Both scholars and students have found artists' writings especially useful in analyzing the artists' visual works, and numerous collections of such writings have been published during the past twenty-five years. Based on the contents of these collections, one would assume that women artists did not leave a substantial written record, for they are scarcely represented at all.[2]

Women artists were prolific writers, however, extending back at least as far as the seventeenth century, from which time a number of letters by Artemisia Gentileschi have been preserved, in which she "speaks openly of her great ambitions for personal achievement and fame."[3] She wrote to her patron Don Antonio Ruffo, "You will find the spirit of Caesar in this soul of a woman."[4] Less than a century later, between 1720 and 1721, Rosalba Carriera kept a daybook of her stay in Paris, in which she made brief annotations regarding her sitters, commissions, sightseeing activities, and even a mention of some "dark days." This diary is only a small part of her abundant written record, including also letters to an international circle of patrons, which together reveal the centrality of work in her life and the importance of her situation within the public rather than domestic realm.[5] Later in the eighteenth century, Angelica Kauffman left letters to her father and to the Royal Academy in London, as well as a compendium of her paintings.[6] Early in the nineteenth century Élisabeth Vigée-Lebrun wrote the first autobiography by a woman artist, begun as a series of letters to her patron, Princess Kourakin.[7] The number of women artists who wrote extensively from the middle of the nineteenth century to the present day is staggering, and one could not even list their names in a brief paragraph.

The omission of written material by women artists from the art historical record corroborates Tillie Olsen's theory regarding the silencing of women's creativity. According to Olsen, for every twelve males whose work is included in collections of great literary endeavors, only one woman is allowed to be heard. The underrepresentation of women's ideas reinforces their exclusion by communicating the message "of women's innately inferior capacity for creative endeavor." Art historical writing includes even fewer women than does literature. Olsen's outrage is aroused by a female representation of 8.3% of all writers whose work is included in literary anthologies,[8] yet a major anthology of writings about modern art includes only 2 women out of 113 artists, a proportion of 1.8%.[9]

The underrepresentation of the words of women artists reflects their lack of recognition in the art historical canon in general. The virtual exclusion of women from the ranks of the art historically great, from such survey texts as *Gardner's Art Through the Ages* and H. W. Janson's *History of Art*, has only begun to be redressed in the last twenty years. Only in recent editions have these two pillars of the canon been expanded to include women artists; neither discussed a single one for many years.[10] As recently as 1971, the question Why have there been no great women artists? could be posed by a feminist art historian.[11] Linda Nochlin's essay of that title, which helped provide the impetus for subsequent feminist revisions of art history, called for a feminist critique that would reformulate "the crucial questions of the discipline as a whole."[12] It is significant, however, that the very language of Nochlin's initial question implied that she accepted the critical assessment that there were "no female equivalents of Michelangelo or Rembrandt."[13]

During the past twenty years feminist art historians have followed Nochlin's lead and posed a variety of questions with richer and more revealing potential. Numerous books have been exclusively devoted to the history of women artists, in response to the question, Who *were* some women artists?[14] Many of the artists first introduced in general surveys have now been considered in greater depth in monographs, biographies, and journal articles. The contributions of women artists to several mainstream modernist movements have also been reassessed.[15] While these studies have attempted to insert the record of women artists into history, in the past twenty years many art historians have also questioned the impact of gender on the making of art and the writing of art history.[16] Some have questioned whether or not there is a "feminine" mode of creativity. Others have considered gender's effects as a social construction and investigated its impact on art by both women and men. Still others have questioned the very concept of "great art," suggesting that its defining characteristics have automatically excluded women due to their limited access to certain artistic sources.

Despite all this critical activity, it would be a mistake to conclude that the reversal of women's exclusion from art history is so well established that it no longer needs discussion. We are still at the beginning, not the end, of the process of making women artists and their work visible. Statistical analyses of gallery exhibitions show that only a very small percentage of women's work is shown at major galleries. Comparisons of prices fetched for work by living artists indicate that men's work is worth more than that by women.[17] Many museums contain only a few works by women, and these often remain in storage, inaccessible to the viewing public. General exhibitions frequently do not include a single work by a woman. Art history courses in which no women artists are even mentioned are still taught. Even though more women artists are included in some recent documentary histories, it is hardly an equitable representation. The visions of women artists are only now beginning to be seen, and the impact of gender on the art historical tradition has just begun to be assessed.

THE IMPORTANCE OF WRITING TO WOMEN ARTISTS

In part because of women's exclusion from the art world, writings by women artists had special significance to both the artists who wrote and to their readers. Women artists have been isolated, from other artists, from other women artists, from the concept of artist itself, and one major reason that they have written has been to validate their functioning as professional artists. Paula Modersohn-Becker's diary provided her with a steady and stable source of encouragement in the face of profound loneliness and doubt.[18] Marianne Werefkin constructed an alter ego in her diary whom she addressed as "dear friend," the confidante and supporter she needed to resume her path as an artist.[19] Although journal writing seems especially conducive to this kind of self-support, personal corrrespondence often served the same purpose, as in Mary Hallock Foote's letters to Helena deKay Gilder or those of Georgia O'Keeffe to Anita Pollitzer during 1915–17, an especially formative period of O'Keeffe's career.[20] Memoirs such as those of Vigée-Lebrun, Cecilia Beaux, or Emily Carr, written after the artists ceased to be professionally productive, are partly attempts at self-justification, a way of saying, "I wasn't always an idle old woman — I accomplished something in my life." Although artists of both genders ask similar questions of themselves and others in their writings (What is an artist? Am I an artist?), women's approach is always complicated by the male-oriented assumptions inherent in the societal definition of an artist, some of which will be discussed below.

For the same reasons that women artists have needed to validate their own vocation, their writings are especially meaningful to current readers. Many readers find biography (including autobiography) fascinating, searching it for implications concerning their own life and work. We want to learn how a particular artist was able to persist in the face of adversity, how this person fielded the vicissitudes of daily life and its numerous pressures, often compelling and seductive, that so often lure talented people away from their creativity into the realm of the mundane. For creative women today, the words of their forebears hold more than a response to idle curiosity; rather, they are a necessary corrective to the cultural silencing of women. Elaine Showalter has written that "women students are estranged from their own experience and unable to perceive its strength and authenticity, in part because they do not see it mirrored and given resonance in literature."[21] The female voice in writings by these artists can be a mirror for the contemporary woman looking to understand her own experience. As Sandra Gilbert and Susan Gubar have pointed out, nineteenth-century women writers often experienced an "anxiety of authorship," a sense that because of the obvious lack of female "greats," they too could never have an impact on the tradition in which they worked.[22] This concept is still relevant today, for contemporary women artists are often ignorant of their antecedents, despite advances in feminist scholarship. The words of those still-obscure women of past centuries who have dared to become artists need to be heard in order to help women artists of this and future generations.

Autobiographical writings provide readers with numerous examples of ways in which women artists have coped with the external pressures of their lives. For example, we learn that Barbara Hepworth worked amid the clutter and noise of her children, whom she allowed to roam freely around her studio.[23] She wrote that, although she did not feel compelled to produce a certain amount of work on a daily basis, she did seek to accomplish some creative activity each day. On the other hand, we learn from Cecilia Beaux's autobiography that she had a very different life-style, at least while she lived with her family in Philadelphia. She described how they shielded her from the pressures of everyday existence. Upon her return home each day from her uptown studio, they encouraged her to retire to her room, to emerge at dinnertime, rested and refreshed, to a meal that had been prepared for her. Käthe Kollwitz insists that she could not have raised two children, kept house for her physician husband, and continued to work at her art without the help of her housekeeper. She wrote about her realization that creativity often comes in waves, according to cycles which cannot be scheduled at one's convenience . We also see that, even without the distraction of children, an artist can be deflected from her creative course by mundane concerns. Emily Carr's time was so filled with the tasks associated with caring for her animals and running a boarding house that she failed to produce any notable work for a period of fifteen years. This was especially ironic since she had chosen to support herself by this means in the belief that it would be compatible with and allow her time to achieve her artistic goals. Once she finally resumed painting on a regular basis she became remarkably productive.

In reading and studying the words of these women we search for whatever it was that made them persist in the face of adversity, and despite the distractions, rejections, and periods of physical incapacity that marked most of their lives. They overcame forces that would silence their voices, and we hope to find some inspiration from their experiences that we can take to heart, that can help us in our own struggles with everyday existence. Their ability to achieve reduces, by its example, our own anxiety of authorship.

FINDING A VOICE AND A VISION

The metaphor of "voice," so evident in women's writing of the past century, gives meaning to the relationship between writings by women artists and the artwork that they produced. A creative woman's attempt to find her voice involves searching for a medium through which she can effectively communicate her experience. To gain one's voice implies that one is able to speak authentically, that is, to express one's inner feelings without being constrained by social conventions or expectations. Failure to achieve this means being condemned to silence. "Tell all the Truth but tell it slant," wrote Emily Dickinson in the 1860s, expressing the compromise that many women artists used to negotiate the conflict between what they wanted to express and the language available to them to articulate it.

Several works of nineteenth-century American fiction with female artist figures as protagonists addressed this issue. Avis, in Elizabeth Stuart Phelps's *The Story of Avis*, envisions her painting unlocking the voice of the mute sphinx and revealing the previously unspoken secrets of women throughout the ages. Ironically, by the end of the novel, Avis's own voice has been silenced and she is unable to create.[24] An opera singer in Mary Hallock Foote's "The Fate of a Voice" actually loses her voice, retrieves it, but then allows it to be diminished when she chooses marriage over a singing career and ultimately sings only in obscure mining camps.[25] Foote described the words of a letter she wrote to her lifelong friend Helena deKay Gilder, as "the cries that one woman utters to another," something that is not usually voiced outside the private sphere.[26] In the twentieth century, Virginia Woolf took up the theme of women's unheard voice and their need to use it in *A Room of One's Own* (1928). In this germinal essay, Woolf concerned herself with defining the circumstances that enable a woman to write. She exhorted her audience to give voice to their real experience, "to write exactly what we think" in order to reverse the muteness of a hypothetical woman writer, "Shakespeare's sister," who died young, never having written a word, but who "lives in you and me and in many other women who are not here tonight for they are washing up the dishes and putting the children to bed." [27]

For a visual artist there is an analogous process of articulating her authentic vision, of painting exactly what she sees (to paraphrase Woolf), similarly subverted within the Western tradition. Often, voicing her thoughts provided one way to clarify her inner vision. This was surely the case in the genesis of Georgia O'Keeffe's mature style. The period during which she was actively searching for an artistic idiom that expressed her internal vision is well documented in her prolific correspondence with Anita Pollitzer. O'Keeffe vividly described the process by which she not only became aware of her artistic vision but also of the importance of following it. "I said to myself, I have things in my head that are not like what anyone has taught me — so natural to my way of being and thinking that it hasn't occurred to me to put them down. I decided to start anew — to strip away what I had been taught — to accept as true my own thinking."[28] The point that O'Keeffe described, when she decided to "forget what she had learned" and follow instead the inner necessity of her "own thinking" is really the crucial moment in the career of any artist in any medium, regardless of gender. However, while every artist may experience a tension between traditions transmitted and the special quality of his or her own insights, that tension is much more a dichotomy, an absolute division, for a woman artist.

It is especially difficult for a woman artist to trust the validity of her own thinking, in part because of Western culture's representation of women as the Other, the individual whose experiences have been granted only marginal status. While claiming to be universal, the Western tradition not only excludes the feminine but also denigrates it. As Whitney Chadwick has pointed out, "the binary oppositions in Western thought . . . have been replicated within art history and used to reinforce sexual difference as a basis for aesthetic valuations. . . . Qualities associated with femininity . . . have provided a set of negative characteristics against which to measure 'high art.'"[29] Ideally, an artist will learn to trust her vision no matter how despised it is and despite the cultural pressures to deny it. But women artists, like many women successful within the dominant patriarchal context, have tended to internalize phallocentric standards. Like their male colleagues, they feel uncomfortable when they come in contact with another woman's "femaleness," her inability or refusal to follow the rules of the game, her differentness. Like the men who trained them, they often seek to maintain the status quo, even though it means repressing aspects of their persons to do so.

The lack of role models for women to use their own voices has resulted from their exclusion from cultural history, itself due to standards that dictate that there is something fundamentally wrong with the way women are. "Wrong is not my name," wrote the poet June Jordan in the process of claiming her own voice and casting out that of the white male establishment by which she had been raped, both literally and through the marginalization of her experience.[30] The challenge of eliminating the imperatives of an artistic tradition that defines the feminine as "the mutilated other" was well documented by Judy Chicago in *Through the Flower*, in which she takes the flower to symbolize the unfolding of her true artistic vision, the butterfly as the freeing of her soul. Her "struggle as a woman and an artist" (as the book is subtitled) was undertaken to gain legitimacy as an artist while also remaining "true to her femaleness."[31] Chicago developed the "vaginal" visual structure that characterizes her mature work as an attempt to articulate her experience as a speaking female subject. It is necessary even for women artists who might not think overtly in terms of gender and sexuality, or do not conceptualize their visions with a sexual motif, to negotiate between phallocentric cultural constrictions and their own visions.

One final point to be made concerning this polarity of masculine and feminine speaks to the current debate among both literary and art-historical feminist critical theorists. Some critics reject anything that suggests either that there is a concrete "feminine" aspect or that women might have some particular claim to it.[32] The source of their caution is a desire not to fall once more into a biology-as-destiny trap, but the resulting antagonism between the so-called cultural and post-structural feminists obfuscates the issue. Regardless of whether or not one believes that women are essentially different from men, there is general agreement that Western culture has despised and denigrated those sexual and social attributes that have been defined as feminine. Women's actual body experiences — menstruation, pregnancy, lactation, penetration, all traits that are biological — have been considered unclean and imbued with negative value.[33] The female body itself has been associated with nature (deemed bad) and male society has asserted that only through the suppression of the body can the so-called ultimate good — culture — be achieved. The full and positive implications of the female body and its metaphors have been lost to the entire culture. Thus, Judy Chicago's use of the vagina as a positive symbol, derided by some as a debasement of the achievements of women and a reduction of their images to their sexuality, was in fact her attempt to reverse cultural negativism by imbuing that which has been despised with positive symbolic value. Likewise, Paula Modersohn-Becker painted herself "as if pregnant," not to communicate an adulation of motherhood but to show the metaphorical possibilities of her "spiritual pregnancy," her artistic ripeness.[34] In these works, Modersohn-Becker and Chicago seem to be following Hélène Cixous's dictum that "women must write through their bodies" in order to break out of cultural marginality.[35] In other words, the private and unspeakable must be spoken in public if women's knowledge and its positive value is to be claimed for the entire culture.[36]

Social constructs and behaviors that have been identified as female, such as caring, nurturing, and accommodating, have also been devalued within society at large. An individual of either gender who possesses these traits is seen as weak, less competent than the normal adult, a term synonymous with the male.[37] Whether or not women have an essential capacity for caring or nurturing, these roles are an intrinsic part of women's actual lives, many of which are supportively devoted to caring for children, parents, spouses, companions, and friends. Yet this strength is still considered a liability in our culture. What has been called "maternal thinking," based on the interactive and empathic way in which a mother handles her children's crises, provides an alternative model for managing interpersonal relationships and conflicts that could help resolve issues that plague the culture at large.[38] Rather than celebrating oppression, as some have claimed it would do, accepting the positive values of caring and maternal thinking would expand the cultural definition of a fully actualized human being and facilitate the ability of all artists, women and men, to find and use their voices and their visions.

Beyond the Myth of the Artist-Hero

The term "artist" has been equated in society with *male* artist, implying qualities and privileges exclusively associated with maleness. Woman, on the other hand, has meant denial of artistic agency and relegation to the role of object or muse. Many women drawn to an artistic vocation have been forced to reconcile the conflicting cultural demands of their womanhood and their artisthood. Some, like Judy Chicago, have dealt with this process overtly. But even when the conflict and its resolution are not articulated directly, women artists have had to deconstruct the male aspects of artisthood in order to claim their vocations as artists. Very often it has been their writings which have provided a safe space in which to negotiate these conflicts.

The myth of the artist as a heroic (male) figure who struggles to create, much as Hercules and Lancelot labored to achieve their goals, evolved during the Renaissance in a form that precluded women's full participation. Giorgio Vasari, in his *Lives of the Artists*, reinforced at that time the new concept of the artist as a genius of mythic proportions, a titan, whose life was dedicated to the creation of great art.[39] The human creator was then defined as a reflection of God, the Ultimate Creator; an artist was male almost by definition. Vasari described women artists according to Boccaccio's fourteenth-century precept that women artists were "atypical of their sex," reinforcing "the idea that women and art are incompatible."[40] Vasari specifically concentrated on those attributes of women's art that had more to do with "diligence rather than invention, the locus of artistic genius."[41] When Angelica Kauffman's biographer wanted to separate her from previous women painters and legitimize her status as a history painter, he followed "the conventions for describing typical male artists rather than female ones, . . . differentiating her life from those of other female artists to represent her in the same manner as the most celebrated male painters."[42] Although over the years the image of the artist has evolved to include additional aspects, such as that of the lonely outsider and of a mercurial figure "born under Saturn," the core of the artist's image has remained true to those early, male-oriented conceptualizations.[43] During the nineteenth century, women were again excluded by definition from the view of the artist as the epitome of a "bourgeois masculine persona."[44] In Western culture, art making and art history have remained phallocentric notions.

Women have always made art although it has been granted lesser worth than that made by men, particularly when done in genres that lie outside the high art tradition. Although the many forms of needlework exhibit a continuum of female creative endeavor, sewing itself could be a double-edged sword, a form of oppression as well as expression, interminable busywork used to keep women in their place.[45] That place was the private sphere, which was viewed as lesser when compared to the "great humanistic endeavors" that inhabited the public sphere. Prior to the nineteenth century, when a woman artist attempted to create art in the public realm she faced institutional discrimination, being given access only to the so-called minor art forms. The socially anomalous status of women artists also allowed their being written out of history to go unchallenged.

Women artists have devised numerous strategies in order to reconcile their identities as both women and artists. Not surprisingly, many have involved attempts to internalize some aspect of masculinity in order to gain power in the public realm. As Carol Gilligan wrote concerning the idea of women pursuing a quest, "If a woman is to embark on such adventures she must at least dress like a man."[46] In some cases that meant recasting a traditional script with a female protagonist. In the eighteenth century, Angelica Kauffman presented herself in a painting in the guise of Hercules at the crossroads, depicting her choice of artistic vocation as a hero's choice.[47] Elizabeth Stuart Phelps concludes *The Story of Avis* with Avis reading to her daughter the story of the quest for the Holy Grail, which will be achieved by Lancelot's son, Galahad, just as the daughter will succeed where her mother has failed.[48] More recently, Leonora Carrington has recast that quest as a feminist tale with a ninety-two-year-old woman.[49] As these examples indicate, the restatements are often much more than simple translations, adding levels of irony or subversion to the original stories.

Many women artists have taken on the privilege of the male via the power of the men in their lives. It has often been seen that daughters of artists became artists themselves, at least partly due to their access to the appropriate education.[50] In addition, their fathers' approval and support has been extremely significant in providing accessible models of masculine power. Some women artists have been personally drawn to strong male artists, their relationships frequently reflecting both the social and psychic advantages reaped by daughters of artists. Such associations could open up channels that facilitated the progress of a woman artist's career. Alfred Stieglitz showed Georgia O'Keeffe's work at his gallery yearly, although she was still defining her style. The first public exposure of Frida Kahlo's work occurred due to the instigation of Diego Rivera, and Leonora Carrington's was initially presented based on her relationship with Max Ernst. These strong and prestigious men had an even greater impact on the psyches of the women artists who were attracted to them. Proximity to their force, charisma, and power enabled these women to assume the power of agency, the ability to speak for themselves. Kahlo painted Rivera's portrait as her third, inner eye; Carrington depicted Ernst holding a lantern that contains a white horse, a symbol of her creativity.

Sometimes the internalization of masculinity resulted in androgyny, the attempt to encompass in one person the traits that have been associated with both genders.[51] Rosa Bonheur literally "dressed like a man" and in her correspondence often referred to herself in the masculine and to her companion, Nathalie Micas, as her wife. However, the world that Bonheur created for herself at By was overwhelmingly feminine, *le château de l'amitié parfaite* (the chateau of perfect friendship). In particular, Bonheur's revision of the Roman Catholic Credo corroborates her belief in an androgynous ideal, comprised of both father and mother.[52] Emma Jung has suggested that "women experience the masculine within themselves" as the *animus*, a male figure who gives "lightning flashes of knowledge" to the woman artist, analogous to the *anima* who inspires the male artist.[53] The works by Kahlo and Carrington referred to in the previous paragraph bear this out.[54]

Something akin to an animus seems to play a role in other women artists' self-conceptualizations. In Willa Cather's novel *O Pioneers*, the female protagonist has a recurring dream in which she is picked up and carried in the strong arms of an unearthly, powerful male, "yellow like the sunlight . . . who took from her all her bodily weariness."[55] Cecilia Beaux often referred to art as her Sun-God and, upon accepting an award from the American Academy of Design inscribed with an image of Apollo, she remarked that she had "always felt the influence of the Sungod." Irene Rice Pereira addressed light as a male in her poetry, and in her diary wrote that "this fire god himself glows with divine love." She also commented that "this god-like man that comes up in dreams must be an animus figure."[56] After her nervous breakdown, when Max Ernst was no longer her guide, Leonora Carrington wrote, "I felt that through the agency of the sun I was an androgyne." Marianne Werefkin sometimes described the alter ego that she created in her diary as her "beau," her muse, a masculine figure, "handsome, with flashing eyes," who loved only her.

On the other hand, some women artists abandoned their internalized male guides in favor of a source of female creativity, in order to better actualize their visions.[57] A painting by Remedios Varo, *Woman Coming Out of the Psychoanalyst's Office* (1961), vividly illustrates this process. In this work, a woman is shown leaving her therapist's office, indicated as such by the door plaque reading "Dr. F. J. A." (Freud, Jung, Adler), dangling his decapitated head by its beard over a well.[58] Judy Chicago similarly resolved her struggle as a woman and an artist only when she stopped trying to be "one of the boys" and began to identify women artists and writers as her mentors. Like Mary Daly's "metapatterning woman," these artists were able to retrieve their creative source because their "perception and commitment concerns Reality beyond paternal parameters."[59]

Often when a woman artist abandons male guides she "thinks back through her mothers."[60] A major part of Chicago's evolution included the search for both literary and artistic foremothers, whose legacy had an almost immediate impact on her work. She also became involved in exploring the aesthetic possibilities in what was defined as "traditional" women's culture. For Faith Ringgold, the process of finding an appropriate visual vehicle involved rejecting the visual language of the Western high art tradition and simultaneously connecting to art based on her African and her maternal roots. Ringgold and Chicago, looked "both high — and low," like Alice Walker in her written search for her mother's garden, her attempt to identify the way in which her mother expressed her creativity.[61] Hélène Cixous suggests something quite similar when she speaks of "writing in the feminine," passing on "the voice of the mother, what is most archaic."[62] Karen Elias-Button makes the point that a woman artist must "confront and incorporate matriarchal powers by reclaiming the face of the Terrible Mother" as her own.[63] For her, as for Cixous, this force is represented as Medusa who "is not deadly. She's beautiful and she's laughing."[64] Susan Suleiman has postulated that the "playing and laughing mother," who plays with the bounds of selfhood, is "a necessary part of artistic creativity" to which women artists need to be receptive in order to become speaking subjects.[65]

As more women claim the identity of artist, the gender associations with that term are beginning to be subverted.[66] Like laughing mothers, some women artists now follow routes that contradict the concept of the quest as the only possible path for achievement. In so doing they challenge the rhetoric that forms the basis of the traditional art historical model concerning the artistic genius who makes masterpieces. The active mode in which one moves toward a goal assertively, in a straight and linear path, has been associated with masculinity and achievement. The waiting mode, representing a loose, more expansive sense of time and direction, has feminine connotations and has been culturally derogated. While recognizing that the waiting mode can result in paralysis, Kathryn Rabuzzi sees this open-ended approach to time and space as one with redemptive powers for humanity.[67] Hélène Cixous makes a similar point when she contrasts masculine economy that is "governed by a rule that keeps time with two beats, three beats . . . exactly as it should be" with "feminine disorder, its laughter [that does not] take the drumbeats seriously" just as the movement in a "feminine text [is an] outpouring that doesn't follow a straight line."[68]

Several artists seem to reflect such an approach. Gwen John described herself as "god's little artist" and said that "doing housework and painting are about the same, only sometimes I learn something from painting." Käthe Kollwitz wrote, "I have never made a work cold" and she created an iconography in which the individual transcended biological motherhood to protect all the world's children. Barbara Hepworth said, "I sculpt from my body" and created work that expressed the relationship between interior and exterior, like fruit and its skin. Elizabeth Catlett wrote, " I do know that I followed an alternate path as an artist. I was not interested in making money and becoming famous. . . . When I physically transform a raw material into an aesthetic expression of the life of my people, I feel complete as a human being." These women artists offer a possibility of an alternative path in both their lives and their art. Whereas the nonlinear aspects of the feminine have been seen as potentially destructive both to the individual and to our culture, women artists have found that this approach can be both instructive and liberating.

GENDER AND GENRE IN WRITINGS BY WOMEN ARTISTS

Writing about her life is a significant act for a woman artist.[69] Although artists' texts can be interpreted simply as additional frames of reference, resources that enhance our understanding of the artists' visual works, which is indeed how they are usually considered, they also can be seen as the link between she who visualizes and she who verbalizes, of particular interest in a culture that has discouraged both activities for women. Despite the cultural proscriptions against women as artistic creators and articulators of their experiences, these women have dared to be both, to make art and to speak.

Women artists have voiced their visions in a variety of literary genres that are both revealing and concealing. The genre itself often provides helpful clues as to how the text should be read, but regardless of the genre, we need to read "behind" the words. An autobiography written for publication in an artist's old age, such as Cecilia Beaux's, may have been written as a reaffirmation of her youthful creativity, intended as a public record and to be read accordingly. On the other hand, a diary written during an artist's creative years was often more of a private conversation with herself, never meant for the perusal of others (as for instance, Paula Modersohn-Becker's diary, a vehicle for maintaining her sanity and creativity).[70] Some artists articulated their thoughts in more than one format; in these cases, our readings of one may be informed by the other. In Emily Carr's anecdotal, autobiographical sketches the persona she created to represent herself is a scrappy, feisty, good-natured trouper. Her voice in her journal, on the other hand, is more consistent with the intensity expressed in her paintings.

Several women artists have written formal autobiographies. At one time, critics did not attempt to distinguish between autobiography, in which a person shapes the telling of the events of his or her own life, and other biographical writing.[71] In any biography the author's desire to tell the truth is counterbalanced by his or her interpretation of the subject's life. Where the author is also the subject, the truth often proves elusive. As Roy Pascal points out, autobiographies are constructed by "design"; the author takes memories and tries to meld them into a story or, in the words of James Olney, to find a "metaphor of self."[72] The reader of autobiography in any event needs to take into account the distinction between the narrator's self and the one that she constructs in her narrative.

Most late twentieth-century autobiographies (like earlier ones that described an individual's spiritual development) are written with a purpose, often the story of travel toward and achievement of an identifiable goal.[73] Specifically, when artists write their life stories it is usually the "story of a calling."[74] Both Georgia O'Keeffe and Cecilia Beaux followed this pattern in their autobiographies, each revealing an important early visual experience that marked them as artists, then proceeding to detail their education. Pascal has commented on the "singularly unenlightening" anecdotal nature of the autobiographies of visual artists, stemming perhaps from the artists' inability to reduce visual experience to words, or to articulate the sources of their particular visual responses.[75] Artists' autobiographies can also be somewhat stilted in style, like many formal portraits.[76] In their projection of an "official" self, they omit the emotional equivalent of unflattering blemishes, revealing only rarely "intense feelings of hate, love, fear, the disclosure of explicit sexual encounters, or the detailing of painful psychological experiences."[77]

Most women artists' autobiographies follow, like those of their male counterparts, the prototype established by Giorgio Vasari in the sixteenth century. Vasari's biographical schema is quite consistent with the idea of the "story of a calling," since in his biographies he sought to establish the inescapable genius of the artist discussed. This approach has been dubbed "androcentric fiction" by Sidonie Smith, and would seem to conflict with the actual, cultural marginality of the lives of women artists.[78] Estelle Jelinek has suggested the existence of two separate, female and male, forms of autobiography, women choosing not to emphasize the public aspects of their lives nor to aggrandize the obstacles they have overcome. Most of the autobiographies included (in excerpt) in this volume conform to Jelinek's male, rather than female, model.[79] Even Judy Chicago, who tells of her struggle to find a style that enabled her to be true to her nature as both a woman and an artist, imposes a masculine shape on her story. Because the story that women artists tell — the story of an artist's success — is a man's story, they have had to "shun their own inner peculiarities and fit themselves into patterns of behavior and character suggested by the idea and ideals" of the male mode.[80]

In order to construct the image of a publicly successful artist, women artists have sometimes felt it necessary to suppress aspects of their voices that would be considered inappropriate. Comparison of Cecilia Beaux's correspondence with her autobiography is instructive in this light. While they do not contradict each other, the reader is not prepared for the intimate, lyrical, and passionate tone in her letters after reading only her more constrained autobiography. Carroll Smith-Rosenberg has commented that she would prefer to work only with unpublished materials or those not intended for publication, realizing that it is only in private speech that women feel free to speak from the heart.[81] Yet women artists *were* able to speak, albeit from the margins of culture. Sidonie Smith believes that a vital amalgam evolves from the tension women autobiographers experience when they attempt to shape their experiences according to a phallocentric model. She identifies the "subversive rearrangement of the dominant discourse and the dominant ideology of gender" that occurs when women "seize the language and its powers to turn cultural fictions into their very own stories."[82]

Diaries, in contrast to autobiography, are usually private writings not written for public presentation. In many ways they are a more reliable source of their writers' authentic thoughts and feelings. The journal has been referred to frequently as the prototypically "feminine" format. Holly Prado claimed: "The feminine principle . . . is inclusive and cyclical rather than single-minded. If there's any form of writing which reflects this principle, it's the journal. Everything fits, just as everything fits into women's daily lives."[83] Whereas an autobiography is written at one point in time and attempts to give coherence to disparate experiences, diaries grow organically, embodying the processes and uncertainties of life. In a compilation of women's diary entries, Mary Jane Moffatt wrote, "The form has been an important outlet for women partly because it is an analogue to their lives; emotional, fragmentary, interrupted, modest, not to be taken seriously, private, restricted, daily, trivial, formless, concerned with self, as endless as their tasks."[84] The contrast between the focused autobiography and the open-ended nature of journals can also be related to the contrast between the active and waiting modes identified by Kathryn Rabuzzi, who writes that "when recognizable temporal progression ceases in story, narration, as we typically use the term, ceases as well. Without plot, the lyric mode dominates and we end up with the paradox of storyless stories — stories in which nothing happens, just as 'nothing happens' in traditional women's mode of being, the waiting mode."[85] The journal is devoid of plot; rather, it is a witness to the particular "nothing" that happens in a person's life.

Among the writings by women artists included here, journal entries provide some of the most eloquent and revealing insights. Paula Modersohn-Becker's diary is her compatriot in her struggle to find a way to embody her internal vision. She writes of her admiration for a nursing mother and of her search for a "runic form" with which to express something primitive about human nature. In fact, the impact of these thoughts can be seen in her art as the important stylistic breakthrough she made in the years immediately preceding her death. As the private writings of women, journals also allow us to hear the artist's personal voice, her *cri du coeur*. Modersohn-Becker talked in her diary about the isolation of marriage and the sense of freedom she experienced alone in Paris. Käthe Kollwitz expressed her anguish at the death of her son and her sense of the rhythm of her creativity. In the case of Irene Rice Pereira, whose published writings are heady philosophical tracts and whose art was built on geometrical abstractions, her private journals provide the only key to her personality. Many women diarists, like Marianne Werefkin, created in their journals "an imaginary realm of freedom . . . always in excess of the permitted and possible world."[86] For many women artists, like Werefkin, diaries were particularly significant for the process of self-validation, providing the opportunity for the safe integration of many conflicting selves.

Critical journal reading requires awareness of several factors. First, not all journals were intended as private documents. Marie Bashkirtseff, for example, whose journal influenced numerous late nineteenth- and early twentieth-century women art students, decided in the course of writing her diary that she would publish it. The reader of such a document, written with an audience in mind, would need to search for the "kernel of truth" much as would a reader of an autobiography. Second, even though journals are written in "private language" that reveals "the secret thoughts of individuals, [this] mirrors the public language in a thousand ways."[87] Thus, a person might conceal her real feelings even when confiding in a diary, expressing instead conventional thoughts and assumptions. Third, a journal can never be an exact record of reality because, even if distortion is not deliberate, the process of selectivity means that the writer omits certain incidents, or stresses anecdote at the expense of feeling or vice versa. Finally, journals have often been "revised" prior to their publication, sometimes by surviving family members eager to maintain or enhance the family's reputation, or by supposedly impartial editors. Bashkirtseff's family, for example, expurgated significant passages from her journal.[88]

Because they were almost always intended as private documents, letters are also important tools for re-creating the lives of women. They share with journals some of the same advantages and problems. Like journals, they are an open-ended form, seen sometimes in the structure and content of a single letter and often in a series of letters, an ongoing correspondence. Mary Jane Moffatt's comments above regarding the intimate, personal, and fragmentary nature of journals also apply to letters. Their most salient difference is that letters presume a particular audience, an intended recipient. Thus, we are able to observe the author within a relationship, particularly so in the case of the many women who were involved in a lifelong correspondence with each other,[89] including Berthe Morisot and her sister Edma, Gwen John and Ursula Tyrwhitt, and Georgia O'Keeffe and Anita Pollitzer. The critic needs to bear in mind the two-person aspect of letters, evaluating how the relationship between sender and recipient affects a letter's content.

Many artists included here, like their male counterparts, have written essays for the express purpose of explaining some aspect of their visual art. Since the mid-nineteenth century, artists have commonly written about the aesthetic issues in their art, such statements forming the bases of most collections of artists' writings. Such essays are particularly useful in assessing each artist's work because they communicate the ideas that form its theoretical basis. Harriet Hosmer, for example, wrote a defense of her method of producing sculpture (and that of many neo-classical sculptors). Barbara Hepworth published statements concerning the Constructivist aesthetic, which helped to explain the common language of her contemporaries and to articulate the meaning of abstraction in her own work. Irene Rice Pereira wrote treatises on the infinite nature of space that reveal the deeply philosophical intent of her paintings. Judy Chicago explained the historical background and iconography of her environmental sculpture, *The Dinner Party*. Although gender would seem to have less impact on aesthetic statements than on other written genres, the very fact that a woman artist writes down her aesthetic philosophy indicates that she takes her artistic agency seriously.

This volume also contains short stories and poetry. When encountering these literary works, it is helpful to consider the relationship between the artist's visual and verbal images, asking such questions as, To what extent do they reinforce each other?, How do they differ?, and What does the artist express through each? Kay Sage, who published four books of poetry, wrote, "When I'm tight / I write / To paint I must be sober," implying a different level of involvement with the two media. Yet her poetry is compelling both on its own terms and in its uncanny resemblance to the vision in her paintings. Many surrealists besides Sage were writers as well as painters. Leonora Carrington published two novels, two plays, and several collections of short stories, all compatible with the dream world she created in her paintings.[90] Irene Rice Pereira's poems convey the cosmic mysticism postulated in her philosophical tracts with far greater intensity and vividness. The arrangement of her studio book suggests that she conceptualized her paintings and poetry simultaneously.

NOTES

1. The concept of voicing women's previously unarticulated experience is discussed in Carroll Smith-Rosenberg, "Hearing Women's Words: A Feminist Reconstruction of History," *Disorderly Conduct: Visions of Gender in Victorian America*, (New York: Alfred A. Knopf, 1985), pp. 11–52.

2. See Herschel Chipp, *Theories of Modern Art* (Berkeley.: University of California Press, 1970); Robert L. Herbert, *Modern Artists on Art* (Englewood Cliffs, N. J. 1964); Barbara Rose, *Readings in American Art Since 1900* (New York: Praeger, 1975); and Harold Spencer, *American Art* (New York: Charles Scribner's Sons, 1980). Herbert's book does not contain a single statement by a woman, and the others have little more. Chipp includes two brief selections by women in more than six hundred pages of text (a paragraph by the Surrealist Hannah Höch and a page by the American artist Elaine de Kooning). Both Rose and Spencer deem Georgia O'Keeffe the only woman worthy of inclusion in their volumes; in both cases she is represented by incomplete examples.

3. Mary Garrard, *Artemisia Gentileschi: The Image of the Female Hero in Italian Baroque Art* (Princeton, N.J.: Princeton University Press, 1989), p. 373.

4. Ibid. p. 397.

5. See Bernardina Sani, *Rosalba Carriera: Lettere, Diari, Frammenti* (Florence: Leo S. Olschki Editore, 1985).

6. Wendy Wassyng Roworth, "Biography, Criticism, Art History: Angelica Kauffman in Context," in *Eighteenth-Century Women and the Arts*, ed. Frederick M. Keener and Susan E. Lorsch (New York and London: Greenwood Press, 1987).

7. Élisabeth Vigée-Lebrun, *Memoirs of Madame Élisabeth Louise Vigée Lebrun*, trans. Lionel Strachey (New York: Braziller, 1988).

8. Tillie Olsen, "One Out of Twelve: Writers Who Are Women in Our Century," in *Silences* (New York: Delacorte Press/Seymour Lawrence, 1978), pp. 22–46 (the quotation, p. 25). In the same book, see also "One Out of Twelve — The Figures," pp. 186–93, for Olsen's analysis of women represented in literature courses and anthologies up to 1976.

9. Chipp, *Theories of Modern Art*; see note 2.

10. Horst de la Croix and Richard G. Tansey, *Gardner's Art Through The Ages*, 5th ed., 1970 (New York: Harcourt, Brace and World) includes Käthe Kollwitz and Bridget Riley. In the seventh edition, 1980, the following artists were added: Rosa Bonheur, Mary Cassatt, Artemisia Gentileschi, Barbara Hepworth, Louise Nevelson, Georgia O'Keeffe, and Élisabeth Vigée-Lebrun. Angelica Kauffman is included in the eighth edition from 1986. There were no women artists included in H. W. Janson, *History of Art*, 2d ed. (Englewood Cliffs, N.J.: Prentice-Hall, 1977). The third edition, published in 1986, refers to the the same women as Gardner's seventh edition, with the exception of Kauffman, and with Hosmer and Käsebier included as well.

11. Linda Nochlin, "Why Have There Been No Great Women Artists?" *Art News* 69: 9 (January 1971), pp. 22–39, 67–71; reprinted in Elizabeth C. Baker and Thomas Hess, *Art and Sexual Politics* (New York: Macmillan, 1973), pp. 1–43, and Linda Nochlin, *Women, Art and Power and Other Essays* (New York: Harper and Row, 1988), pp. 145–78.

12. Nochlin, *Women, Art and Power*, p. 146; see also Griselda Pollock, *Vision and Difference: Femininity, Feminism and the Histories of Art* (London and New York: Routledge, 1988), p. 2.

13. Nochlin, *Women, Art and Power*, p.150.

14. The first of these was Karen Petersen and J. J. Wilson, *Women Artists: Recognition and Reappraisal* (New York: Harper and Row, 1976). Other early surveys include: Ann Sutherland Harris and Linda Nochlin, *Women Artists 1550–1950* (New York: Alfred A. Knopf, 1977); Elsa Honig Fine, *Women and Art* (Montclair, N. J.: Allanheld and Schram, 1978); Germaine Greer, *The Obstacle Race*, (New York: Farrar, Straus and Giroux, 1979); Charlotte S. Rubinstein, *American Women Artists* (Boston: Avon Books, 1982).

15. See Tamar Garb, *Women Impressionists* (New York: Rizzoli, 1986); Whitney Chadwick, *Women Artists and the Surrealist Movement* (Boston: Little, Brown and Co., 1985); and Shulamith Behr, *Women Expressionists* (New York: Rizzoli, 1988).

16. See Lucy Lippard's *From the Center* (New York: E. P. Dutton, 1976) and her *Overlay* (New York: Pantheon Books,1983); Rozsika Parker and Griselda Pollock's *Old Mistresses: Women, Art and Ideology* (New York: Pantheon Books, 1981), their *Framing Feminism* (London and New York: Pandora Press, 1987); Pollock, *Vision and Difference*; and Whitney Chadwick, *Women, Art and Society* (London and New York: Thames and Hudson, 1990). Also helpful are Norma Broude and Mary D. Garrard, eds., *Feminism and Art History* (New York: Harper and Row, 1982) and Arlene Raven, Cassandra Langer, and Joanna Frueh, eds., *Feminist Art Criticism, An Anthology* (Ann Arbor, Mich.: UMI Research Press, 1988).

17. For statistics, see "Gorilla Warfare, Women Battle Sexism in the Art World," *San Francisco Examiner*, February 25, 1990, *Image* insert, pp. 12–19. An anthology edited by Ellen C. Johnson, *American Artists on Art* (New York: Harper and Row, 1982), seems to show an improvement in the representation of women's writing, containing 12 statements by women out of a total of 52, although in terms of pages, only 38 out of 279 pages contain writing by women.

18. Gillian Perry, *Paula Modersohn-Becker* (London: Woman's Press, 1979), p. 10. Perry compares the content of Modersohn-Becker's journal entries with those of Gwen John and Marie Bashkirtseff.

19. Portions of Werefkin's diary have been translated from the original French into German and published as Marianne Werefkin, *Briefe an einen Unbekannten, 1901–1905*, ed. Clemens Weiler (Cologne: Verlag M. DuMont Schauberg, 1960). The extracts included in this volume are the first published translation into English.

20. See Nancy Scott, "The O'Keeffe-Pollitzer Correspondence, 1915–17," *Source* 3 (Fall 1983), pp. 34–41. A selection from this correspondence is published in Jack Cowart, Juan Hamilton, and Sarah Greenough, eds., *Georgia O'Keeffe: Art and Letters* (Boston: Little Brown and Co., 1987). For the Foote-Gilder correspondence, see Carroll Smith-Rosenberg, "The Female World of Love and Ritual: Relations Between Women in Nineteenth Century America," *Disorderly Conduct*, pp. 53–76.

21. Elaine Showalter, quoted in Olsen, "One Out of Twelve — Writers," p. 29.

22. Sandra M. Gilbert and Susan Gubar, *The Madwoman in the Attic: The Woman Writer and the Nineteenth-Century Literary Imagination* (New Haven: Yale University Press, 1979), p. 13. Gilbert and Gubar are using Harold Bloom's concept of "anxiety of influence" as their source for "anxiety of authorship."

23. For this and other references to specific observations and short quotations by artists included in this volume, see the writings in the appropriate chapters that follow.

24. Elizabeth Stuart Phelps, *The Story of Avis*, ed. Carol Farley Kessler (New Brunswick, N.J.: Rutgers University Press, 1985).

25. Mary Hallock Foote, "The Fate of a Voice," in *The Last Assemby Ball: A Pseudo-Romance of the Far West* (Boston: Houghton Mifflin Co., 1889).

26. Foote to Gilder, 1891, quoted by Melody Graulich in "The Cries That One Woman Utters to Another," paper delivered at Western American Literature Conference, Durango, Colorado, October 1986.

27. Virginia Woolf, *A Room of One's Own* (1928; reprint, Harmondsworth, Middlesex: Penguin Books, 1970), pp. 111–12. Tillie Olsen, "Silences in Literature," *Silences*, pp. 5–21, continues this line of thought in her discussion of both the external and internal circumstances which "silence" an author's voice. Although, according to Olsen, male writers have also been subject to "unnatural silence," for women in particular "the circumstances for sustained creation have been almost impossible"(p. 18). Joanna Russ further analyzes the various critical subterfuges that have been used to suppress women's writing in *How to Suppress Women's Writing* (Austin: University of Texas Press, 1983).

28. Georgia O'Keeffe, *Georgia O'Keeffe* (New York: Viking Press, 1976), unpaginated.

29. Chadwick, *Women, Art and Society*, pp. 8–9.

30. June Jordan, "Poem About My Rights," *Passion: New Poems, 1977–80* (Boston: Beacon Press, 1980), pp. 86–89.

31. See Mara Witzling, "*Through the Flower*: Judy Chicago's Conflict between a Woman-Centered Vision and the Male Artist Hero," in Suzanne Jones, ed., *Writing the Woman Artist* (Philadelphia: University of Pennsylvania Press, 1991).

32. A good summary of the debate is presented in Linda Alcoff, "Cultural Feminism versus Post-Structuralism: The Identity Crisis in Feminist Theory," *Signs* 13:3 (1988), pp. 405–36.

33. Andrea Dworkin's *Intercourse* (New York: Free Press,1987) provides a vivid discussion of how men have despised women's sexuality. On female bodily functions and how they can provide positive metaphors for knowing, see Stephanie Demetrakopolous, *Listening to Our Bodies* (Boston: Beacon Press, 1983). Nancy Chodorow, *The Reproduction of Mothering: Psychoanalysis and the Sociology of Gender* (Berkeley: University of California Press, 1978), also discusses the implications of women's permeable physical boundaries.

34. Nor Hall, *The Moon and the Virgin* (New York: Harper and Row, 1980), in the chapter entitled "Spiritual Pregnancy," speaks of the suggestive aspects of pregnancy as it relates to knowing and thinking.

35. Hélène Cixous, "The Laugh of the Medusa," *Signs* 1:4 (1976), pp. 886, 888.

36. Gloria Orenstein, in *The Reflowering of the Goddess* (Elmsford, N.Y.: Pergamon Press, 1990), pp. 73–74, seems to make a similar point when she says that the feminist matristic, the celebratory, has been misrepresented as essentialist, and suggests that "incorporating symbols from ancient Neolithic and Paleolithic culture . . . into the new feminist matristic iconography is actually a way to reverse essentialism, by recontextualizing the lives of women within an expanded historical framework including millennia in which their connection to nature was not demeaned but rather honored."

37. Carol Gilligan, *In a Different Voice* (Cambridge: Harvard University Press, 1982).

38. See Gilligan, *In a Different Voice*. For a discussion of caring as a philosophical stance, see Nel Noddings, *Caring: A Feminist Approach to Ethics and Moral Education* (Berkeley: University of California Press, 1984). For maternal thinking, see Sara Ruddick, *Maternal Thinking: Towards a Politics of Peace* (Boston: Beacon Press, 1989).

39. Giorgio Vasari, *Le Vite de' piu eccellenti pittori scultori e architettori italiani, da Cimabue insino ai tempi nostri . . .*, 1st ed., Florence, 1550, revised 1568. (A one-volume, paperback English translation was published in 1965 by Penguin, as *Lives of the Artists*.)

40. Pollock, *Vision and Difference*, pp. 41–42.

41. Chadwick, *Women, Art and Society*, p. 26. Vasari also made sure to stress that the women artists he discussed embodied traits appropriate to noblewomen (Pollock, *Vision and Difference*, pp. 41–43).

42. Roworth, "Biography, Criticism, Art History."

43. A classic discussion of the mercurial nature of the visual artist is found in Rudolf Wittkower and Margot Wittkower, *Born Under Saturn* (New York: W. W. Norton, 1969). Maurice Beebe's *Ivory Towers and Sacred Founts* (New York: New York University Press, 1964) treats some issues related to the male artist's psyche.

44. Pollock, *Vision and Difference*, p. 24.

45. The best analysis of sewing as both liberation and confinement is Rozsika Parker's *The Subversive Stitch: Embroidery and the Making of the Feminine* (London: Women's Press, 1984). Unfortunately this book is not generally available in the United States.

46. Gilligan, *In a Different Voice*, p. 13.

47. Kauffman's painting is discussed in Roworth, "Biography, Criticism, Art History," Parker and Pollock, *Old Mistresses*, and Marina Warner, *Monuments and Maidens* (New York: Atheneum, 1985).

48. Phelps, *Story of Avis*, pp. 240–50.

49. For analyses of *The Hearing Trumpet*, see Susan R. Suleiman, *Subversive Intent, Gender Politics and the Avant-Garde* (Cambridge: Harvard University Press, 1990), pp.169–79, and Orenstein, *Reflowering of the Goddess*, pp. 179–85.

50. Linda Nochlin, for example, has argued this point at length in "Why Have There Been No Great Women Artists."

51. Androgyny, once hailed as an ideal, see Carolyn Heilbrun, *Towards a Recognition of Androgyny* (New York: Alfred A. Knopf, 1973), is now repudiated by some feminists such as Adrienne Rich who feel it is an empty position, neither man nor woman. Carroll Smith-Rosenberg has written of its prevalence in the 1920s in "The New Woman as Androgyne," *Disorderly Conduct*, pp. 245–96.

52. Albert Boime speculates that this might be related to her Saint-Simonian background, which held an androgynous view of God and humans. See Albert Boime, "The Case of Rosa Bonheur: Why Should a Woman Want To Be More Like a Man," *Art History* 4:4 (December 1981), pp. 402, 404.

53. Emma Jung, *Animus and Anima* (Zurich: Spring, 1974), p. 28.

54. Estella Lauter, "'Visual Images by Women," in *Feminist Archetypal Theory*, ed. Estella Lauter and Carol Rupprecht (Knoxville: University of Tennessee Press, 1985), p. 66. Although Lauter discusses Kahlo's use of Rivera's image as a third eye, she suggests that we suspend the search for the animus in visual art by women.

55. Willa Cather, *O Pioneers* (Boston: Houghton Mifflin Co., 1913; reprint, 1941), pp. 206–7.

56. Irene Rice Pereira, 23 January 1963, Archives of American Art, Washington, D. C., Roll D222, frame 304–5.

57. Lauter, "Visual Images by Women," p.69.

58.Ibid., pp. 69–70. Lauter relates this specifically to Varo's quest for a mythic framework that expressed feminine regenerative powers, represented by the well over which the figure (who looks something like the artist) holds the head.

59. Mary Daly, *Pure Lust* (Boston: Beacon Press, 1984), pp. 394, 411.

60. Woolf, *Room of One's Own*, p. 96.

61. Alice Walker, "In Search of Our Mothers' Gardens," in *In Search of Our Mothers' Gardens* (New York: Harcourt Brace Jovanovich, 1983), pp. 231–43.

62. Hélène Cixous, "Castration or Decapitation," *Signs* 7:1 (1981), p. 54.

63. Karen Elias-Button, "The Muse as Medusa," in *The Lost Tradition*, ed. Cathy Davidson and E. M. Broner (New York: F. Ungar, 1980), p. 204.

64. Cixous, "Laugh of the Medusa," p. 885.

65. Suleiman, *Subversive Intent*, p. 180.

66. Grace Stewart, *A New Mythos: The Novel of the Artist as Heroine 1877–1977* (St. Alban's, Vt.: Eden Press, 1979); see particularly p. 178.

67. Kathryn Rabuzzi, *The Sacred and the Feminine: Toward a Theology of Housework* (New York: Seabury Press, 1982). See especially Chapter 7, p. 145. See also Mary Catherine Bateson, *Composing a Life* (New York: Atlantic Monthly Press, 1989), who suggests that we "explore the creative potential of interrupted and conflicted lives, where energies are not narrowly focused or permanently pointed toward a single ambition . . . ."

68. Cixous, "Castration," pp. 43, 54.

69. This has special relevance in light of contemporary criticism's ongoing discussion of the act of writing. Much of this discussion centers around "l'écriture féminine" as postulated by Hélène Cixous in works cited herein. Two others who have engaged in this discussion are Julia Kristeva and Luce Irigaray. All three derive at least some of their premises from Jacques Derrida, *L'Écriture et la différence* (1967); *Writing and Difference*, trans. Alan Bass (Chicago: University of Chicago Press, 1978). Elaine Marks and Isabelle Courtivron, in *New French Feminisms* (Amherst: University of Massachusetts Press, 1980), have collected some of the most significant texts. Also see Toril Moi, *Sexual/Textual Politics* (London and New York: Methuen, 1985); Elaine Showalter, ed., *The New Feminist Criticism* (New York: Pantheon, 1985); and Teresa de Lauretis, *Feminist Studies/Critical Studies* (Bloomington, Indiana: Indiana University Press, 1986).

70. A reading of Modersohn-Becker's must take into account the fact that the existing text is not the original, but one that has been edited by her family.

71. For a summary of the critical study of biography, see Estelle Jelinek, *Women's Autobiography* (Bloomington: Indiana University Press, 1980), pp. 1–2.

72. Roy Pascal, *Design and Truth in Autobiography* (1960; reprint, New York and London: Garland, 1985); James Olney, *Metaphors of Self: The Meaning of Autobiography* (Princeton, N.J.: Princeton University Press, 1972). Besides Estelle Jelinek's *Women's Autobiography* cited above, two other discussions of women's use of autobiography are Shari Benstock, ed., *The Private Self: Theory and Practice of Women's Autobiographical Writings* (Chapel Hill: University of North Carolina Press, 1988) and Sidonie Smith, *A Poetics of Women's Autobiography* (Bloomington and Indianapolis: Indiana University Press, 1987).

73. Mary Grimley Mason and Carol Hurd Green, *Journeys: Autobiographical Writings by Women* (Boston: G. K. Hall, 1979).

74. Pascal, *Design and Truth*, p. 135.

75. Ibid., pp. 135–36.

76. William Howarth, "Some Principles of Autobiography," *Autobiographical Essays: Theoretical and Critical*, ed. James Olney (Princeton, N. J.: Princeton University Press, 1980), says that "autobiography is a self-portrait" (p. 85).

77. Jelinek, *Women's Autobiography*, p.13. Here Jelinek is discussing autobiographical writings in general, not just those by women.

78. See Smith, *Poetics of Women's Autobiogrpahy*. She postulates that autobiography and its history are "another two of those public narratives men write for each other as they lay claim to an immortal place within the phallic order" (p. 26). She continues by analyzing Judeo-Christian injunctions "against woman's claim to public discourse" and its "profound ramifications for her engagement in literary self-representations" (p. 28).

79. Jelinek, *Women's Autobiography*, pp. 5, 7–17.

80. William Matthews, *British Autobiographies: An Annotated Bibliography* (Berkeley: University of California Press, 1955), p. viii. Matthews's comments were made in a different context, but are applicable to some women artists' autobiographical writings.

81. Smith-Rosenberg, "Hearing Women's Words," p. 29: "Men have too often drowned out women's words and perceptions, that the rediscovery of women's unique language must be our first priority."

82. Smith, *Poetics of Women's Autobiography*, pp. 175–176.

83. Holly Prado, *Chrysalis* 7 (review of *One to One* by Christa Baldwin and *The New Diary* by Tristine Rainer), p. 116.

84. Mary Jane Moffatt and Charlotte Painter, eds., *Revelations: Diaries of Women* (New York: Vintage Books, 1975), p. 5.

85. Rabuzzi, *Sacred and Feminine*, p.167.

86. This point was made regarding Marie Bashkirtseff by Rozsika Parker and Griselda Pollock in *The Journal of Marie Bashkirtseff* (London: Virago Press, 1985), pp. viii–x. It is also apt to describe Marianne Werefkin's diary which she constructed as a series of "letters to an unknown." See Renate Berger, *Malerinnen auf dem Weg in 20. Jahrhundert* (Cologne: Dumont, 1982), pp. 247ff. for a discussion of Werefkin's diary as her alter ego.

87. Smith-Rosenberg, "Hearing Women's Words," pp. 44–45.

88. Parker and Pollock, Introduction, *Journal of Marie Bashkirtseff*. For a complete discussion, see Colette Cosnier, *Marie Bashkirtseff: Un Portrait sans Retouches* (Paris: Éditions Pierre Horay, 1985).

89. In fact, these correspondences form the basis of Carroll Smith-Rosenberg's discussion in "The Female World of Love and Ritual."

90. Other women Surrealists were also prolific writers. Some artists and their works are Dorothea Tanning, *Abyss* (New York, 1977); Ithell Colquhoun, *Goose of Hermogenes* (London, 1961) and *Grimoire of the Entangled Thicket* (Stevenage, England, 1973); Valentine Penrose, *Herbe à la lune* (Paris, 1935) and *Dons des Feminines* (Paris, 1951).

Does at Rest. Oil on canvas. 13⅛" x 25⅜".
The Currier Gallery of Art, Manchester, N.H.

ROSA BONHEUR

1822–1899

ROSA BONHEUR MAY well have been the most illustrious woman artist of the nineteenth century. Her gruff personality, extraordinary love of animals, and singular mode of dressing made her an especially recognizable character. Anna Klumpke, the companion of Bonheur's last years and writer of her memoirs (also a painter in her own right) remembered being given a Rosa Bonheur doll when she was a child growing up in San Francisco. Bonheur established her fame early in life through several monumental paintings of animals in motion, culminating in *The Horse Fair* (1853). She described herself as an *animalier*, but she transcended the limitations of most work in this genre through her sensitivity to the psychology of her animal subjects, as well as respect for their brute strength. In 1860, with her friend Nathalie Micas and Nathalie's mother, Bonheur moved to a chateau in By, France, near the Forest of Fontainebleau where she lived the rest of her life. Although she never stopped working, after her move to By, Bonheur no longer exhibited at the Salon, until her very last years. Nonetheless she remained a public figure, and was awarded prizes for her achievements and sought after for her company. Unlike some artists in this volume, Bonheur did not use the written word as another creative means; however, she maintained prolific correspondences with numerous friends and acquaintances. Examination of these letters as well as of other written documents reveals her singular personality and dedication to art.

Rosa Bonheur was the daughter of an artist and in that respect she resembles many other women artists of the nineteenth and earlier centuries. Rosalie Marie was the oldest of Sophie and Raymond Bonheur's four children, all of whom were artistically active at some point in their lives. M. Bonheur supported his family by giving art lessons, first in Bordeaux and, after 1828, in Paris at a school for girls that he founded and directed. Mme Bonheur was a musically talented woman who had been raised in a cultivated bourgeois environment, and was probably ill-prepared for the life of a struggling painter's wife. Rosa described her early years as unstable, claiming that the family "used to migrate like the birds." Her father was actively involved in the utopian St. Simonian movement and, during 1830, he lived in their monastery at Ménilmontant where his wife and children visited only on Sundays. Three years later, when Rosa was eleven, her mother died of "exhaustion," leaving the four young children in their father's sole care. Bonheur's accounts of her early life indicate her conflicting feelings about her father's utopianism. On the one hand, she held him responsible for her mother's early death, and spoke of him as a man who cared more about humanity than about the needs of the individuals closest to him. On the other hand, she was proud of his liberal views and accepted some of his St. Simonian ideas, such as belief in the female element of the godhead, into her evolving world view.

The second most significant event in Bonheur's early life, after the death of her mother, was her meeting with Nathalie Micas. The Bonheur family became acquainted with the Micas family shortly after Mme Bonheur's death, when Nathalie's parents commissioned a portrait of their then-ailing daughter. The two girls, of very different temperaments, became fast and lifelong friends. Association with the Micas family provided respite from her own chaotic family life. After her father remarried in 1842, Bonheur spent increasingly more time with them, finally moving into their home after her father's death in 1849 and, in 1860, into the By chateau that she purchased with Nathalie and Mme Micas.

When dictating her memoirs to Anna Klumpke, Bonheur described the chateau as *le domaine de l'amitié parfaite* (the realm of perfect friendship). This remarkable female environment allowed Bonheur to fill the void left by her mother's death and, at the same time, provided her with an alternative to conventional marriage. Her forty-year association with Nathalie Micas and her subsequent relationship with Anna Klumpke are significant aspects of Bonheur's biography.

Bonheur began her art studies early, with her father, and became a professional at a young age. According to Bonheur, she "had a passion for drawing" at age four and covered her walls with sketches. Both her dictated memoirs and fragmentary autobiography stress her artistic precocity (a common facet in artists' biographies in general). After unsuccessful stints at boarding school and as a seamstress's apprentice, Bonheur convinced her father to take her as a pupil. She worked first with pencils and moved from that to copying works in the Louvre. By 1841, when she was nineteen, Bonheur exhibited for the first time at the annual Salon; in 1845, she was awarded a third-class medal. Her work was represented at the Salon for the next fifteen years, always by paintings that included animals as their subjects. During this time, she began to work alongside her father in his studio. When he died in 1849, she and her sister Julie took over as heads of his drawing school for girls, a position Bonheur held until her move to By in 1860.

In the late 1840s Bonheur began to frequent animal markets and slaughter-houses to acquire models for her animal studies. To do her work she invented a costume consisting of loose trousers and an unbelted smock that was a modified version of the St. Simonian garb for women. She had to obtain *certificats de travestissement*, permission to wear male attire in public, which resulted in her becoming something of a cause célèbre. Bonheur often felt it necessary to justify this kind of dress — by wearing with her outfit small feminine shoes, by asserting that she wore it only for work, or by mentioning her closet full of female attire.

Plowing in the Nivernais, shown at the Salon in 1849, brought acclaim to Bonheur and was purchased by the government for the Musée du Luxembourg. According to an early critic, Bonheur received inspiration for this image on hearing George Sand's novel *La Mare au Diable* read aloud. Sand describes a "youth" driving a "magnificent team of four pairs of young oxen" who "still rebelled against the yoke . . . and trembled with anger as they obeyed the authority so recently imposed." This monumental, horizontal canvas showing brute animal strength became the foundation for Bonheur's next works, the ones for which she received the greatest recognition. *Plowing* differs from its textual source in that the painting makes human authority seem subsidiary to animal force.

Bonheur's visits to the horse market and her studies of draft horses developed into her successful *The Horse Fair* (1853). Like *Plowing*, this painting heroizes the power, strength, and energy of the animals and minimizes the presence of their human handlers. The exceptional renown of this one work insured Bonheur's reputation for the rest of her life. It was purchased by the dealer Ernest Gambart in 1855, toured England, was bought two years later by an American, toured the United States, and ended up in the Metropolitan Museum of Art. Bonheur was awarded a gold medal at the 1855 Exposition Universelle for another work, *Haymaking in the Auvergne*, after which it was purchased for the Musée du Luxembourg, where it hung as a companion to *Plowing*.

In the following decades Bonheur and Nathalie Micas traveled a great deal, both for Micas's health and Bonheur's inspiration. Their tour of England and Scotland, begun in July 1856, came close on the heels of *The Horse Fair*'s success. Perhaps because animal painting was particularly popular in England, Bonheur's work was received there even more enthusiastically than in France. During this trip Bonheur had the opportunity to meet with fellow animal painters Sir Edwin Landseer and Frederick Goodall, to argue aesthetics with John Ruskin, and, most important, to spend time in the untamed Scottish landscape to which she responded profoundly and to which she returned in her work throughout her life.

When Bonheur went to By with her two friends and large menagerie, she may not have intended the changes in her work that followed the move. Although she continued painting steadily until her death in 1899, her subsequent works were mostly smaller than before in scale and scope. As before, she painted many images of animals including her series of *les grandes fauves* — lions, tigers, panthers — she also drew continually. When Klumpke went through Bonheur's studio after her death, she was amazed to find thousands of well-sorted sketches, organized chronologically. Shortly after her arrival in By, Bonheur began work on a large canvas, analogous to *Plowing* and *Haymaking*, called *Wheat Threshing in the Camargue*, which remained unfinished for thirty-five years. (When Klumpke moved into the chateau Bonheur made plans to build a new studio where the two could complete the large canvas together. The studio was still under construction when Bonheur died.)

In her later years, the image of America as a wild, untamed place attracted Bonheur. When Buffalo Bill Cody performed at the 1889 Exposition Universelle with his Wild West Show, Bonheur made numerous sketches at their campgrounds and invited Cody to visit her studio, where he became the subject of one of her better-known later works (*Buffalo Bill Cody*, 1889). Bonheur's artistic life became more private during her later years; she did, however, receive many awards for her artistic achievement, including in 1865 the Cross of the Legion of Honor, the first woman to be so honored.

Stylistically, Bonheur's work is consistent with trends in realism that were current in the middle of the nineteenth century. Throughout her life she stressed the importance of faithfully recording the actualities of nature. Surprisingly, although her abode bordered the Forest of Fontainebleau she is not known to have had any contact with those other famous denizens of the forest, the Barbizon painters, whose work stressed the overall landscape rather than the creatures who inhabited it, as Bonheur's did. Bonheur identified with other sculptors and painters of animals; she developed a camaraderie with such British artists as Landseer, and particularly with the French painters Pierre Mène, Auguste and Henri Cain, and Paul Chardin, with all of whom she maintained long correspondences.

Her choice of theme — that is, animals in their natural habitats — could be considered masculine and certainly stood in contrast with nineteenth-century expectations that women artists' subjects would reflect the limitations of their activities to the domestic sphere. Indeed, Bonheur accentuated the masculine aspects of her occupation, particularly in her letters to fellow artists, whom she addressed as "you old thing" or "you old cuss" and to whom she described herself as a "general" or a "fellow."

Bonheur's profound involvement with animals as fellow creatures on this earth surpassed even their centrality in her art. Her accounts of her childhood emphasize her love for them and her letters describe in detail the antics of many creatures of all sorts. She kept numerous creatures in her Paris studios and courtyards; at By she created a complete menagerie, including dogs, birds, monkeys, horses, a herd of sheep, and two lions. When she first took Klumpke into her "sanctuary" and showed her the mounted heads of her animals, Bonheur explained that these were not only her models but her friends. While some critics have suggested that Bonheur's intense identification with animals is indicative of a pathological confusion, a more positive interpretation — that it was the expression of a "biophilic" consciousness — is appropriate. Bonheur viewed the world holistically, once telling a friend that she believed that it was "monstrous" that animals should be said to have no souls. In a telling revision of the Catholic mass that Bonheur inscribed on the back of an engraving of the Virgin and Child, she stated that she believed in "le Couple sauveur, Christ androgyne" and greeted the earth as "full of grace" and "mother of love."

It is in this context that it is most helpful to view her relationships with Nathalie and Mme Micas, and Anna Klumpke. At By, Bonheur created a matrifocal environment built on affection, affinity, and caring, and filled it with the earth's creatures. Like Rosalba Carriera and Mary Cassatt, each of whom lived with her sister and parents, Bonheur's living arrangement provided her with emotional support outside the constraints of traditional marriage. At By, Mme Micas and Nathalie took on the concerns of running the household, allowing Bonheur to concentrate on her work. In many ways the Bonheur-Micas household exemplifies the intense emotional connectedness of women, common during the nineteenth century, as described by Carroll Smith-Rosenberg in her essay "The Female World of Love and Ritual." Their involvement in each other's lives was primary and their mutual affection was apparent, illustrating an intense and abiding attachment. Bonheur referred often to "my dear Nathalie" and "my poor Nathalie," writing in 1846 that to experience a pleasure without her was to only half enjoy it because "you understand me, you, my Nathalie." When Nathalie died in 1889, more than forty years later, Rosa was devastated. Mme Micas played an essential role in their world, as the enveloping and protective mother who cared for both her daughters. (In her correspondence, in fact, Bonheur often referred to Mme Micas as "mother.") As her involvement with Anna Klumpke developed, Bonheur wanted to include her — and even her mother — in this world, as her letters to Mme Klumpke reveal. Nathalie would not be jealous, Bonheur said; but rather that it was "in memory of Nathalie that I am giving you [Klumpke] that which we called 'le domaine de l'amitié parfaite.'" Bonheur even wanted to continue the "perfect friendship" beyond the grave and, in fact, she, Nathalie and Mme Micas, and Klumpke are all buried in the Micas family vault in Paris, under the inscription *Amitié est une affection divine* ("Friendship is a divine affection").

While Bonheur's correspondence offers enlightening glimpses into her life, her two testaments — written just months before her death — are especially important documents in which she justifies her right to choose her own life-style and to dispose of the money she had earned and the property she had inherited from her relationship with Nathalie Micas. In the testaments Bonheur asserts that she earned her money by her own work and makes a case for her right to control it. (In the eighteenth century, Rosalba Carriera adopted in her last will and testament a similar though somewhat less aggressive tone.) Bonheur's testaments raise the issues of freedom of life-style and sexual orientation; in this, they represent a radical break with a culture in which women were bound by familial expectations, a break made larger for Rosa Bonheur by her relationships with Micas and Klumpke. These documents also show that women's lives have been lived in contravention of conventional, delimited scripts.

The diminution of Bonheur's fame after her death illustrates one of the ways in which the dominant historical tradition has silenced women: by trivializing their achievements. In her own time Bonheur was appreciated as a dynamic painter with a unique vision, but the canonical judgment of art history has invalidated her achievement as *retardataire*, the late expression of a limited genre. Fortunately, for those who still stand in awe of Bonheur's works, the feminist revision of art history is making it once more possible to see them.

SOURCES

Ashton, Dore, and Denise Hare. *Rosa Bonheur: A Life and a Legend.* New York: Viking Press, 1981.

Boime, Albert. "The Case of Rosa Bonheur: Why Should a Woman Want to Be More Like a Man?" *Art History* 4 (December 1981): 384-409.

Harris, Ann Sutherland, and Linda Nochlin. *Women Artists 1550-1950*. New York: Alfred A. Knopf, 1977.

Klumpke, Anna. *Rosa Bonheur: Sa vie, son oeuvre*. Paris: Flammarion, 1908.

Smith-Rosenberg, Carroll. "The Female World of Love and Ritual: Relations between Women in Nineteenth-Century America." Chapter in *Disorderly Conduct: Visions of Gender in Victorian America*. New York: Alfred A. Knopf, 1985.

Stanton, Theodore. *Reminiscences of Rosa Bonheur*. London, 1910. (Reprint. New York: Hacker Art Books, 1972).

Tufts, Eleanor. *Our Hidden Heritage*. New York and London: Paddington Press, 1974.

EXCERPTS FROM ROSA BONHEUR, "FRAGMENTS OF MY AUTOBIOGRAPHY" (*Magazine of Art,* 1902)

(*Entry marked with asterisk from Theodore Stanton, *Reminiscences of Rosa Bonheur* [New York, 1910. Reprint. New York: Hacker Art Books, 1972].)

I was born in Bordeaux, in the Rue Sainte-Catherine, on the 16th of March, 1822, and was the eldest of four children. My father, a drawing master, was only twenty-two years old then, and we lived with my mother's parents, *pépé* and *mémé*, as they are called in the Bordelais. I was allowed to run about everywhere, and I have kept the sweetest recollection of that happy time of freedom. Once, I ventured so far from home that a neighbour, finding me in the Square des Quinconces, brought me back to my house, where everyone was in despair. We used to spend our Sundays in the country, not far away. I ran after animals in the wood, and often lost myself. I was ungovernable. I positively refused to learn my alphabet, but had already a great passion for drawing before I was four years old. I covered the white walls with my shape-less sketches as high as I could reach, and also enjoyed myself very much in cutting out paper models. They were invariably the same; first I made long strips of paper, then with my scissors I cut out the shepherd, then the dog, then the cow, the sheep, and finally the tree, always in the same order. I remember spending many a day in that way.

❖

. . . In the same building where we lived was a school kept by a M. Antin, who was a Jansenist, and who became a good friend of ours, my father showing thus early a tendency to break with established things in spiritual matters, a tendency which grew with the years and which has always left its stamp on me. Old Father Antin, as we all called him reverentially, remarking that I was unoc-cupied, proposed to my father to take me as a pupil; so I entered the little boys' class with my brothers Auguste and Isidore. This was, I believe, the first pro-nounced step in a course which my father always pursued with us children and which in modern times has been named co-education. The influence which it had on my lifework cannot be exaggerated. It emancipated me before I knew what emancipation meant and left me free to develop naturally and untram-melled. I well remember that I was not at all shy because my only companions were boys. When, during the recess, we went to play in the garden of the Place Royale — today, Place des Vosges — I was generally the leader in all the games, and I did not hesitate now and again to use my fists. So from the very start, a masculine bent was given to my existence. This school life, which did so much for me in so short a time, continued till 1830.*

❖

... One evening, coming home after a trying day of work, he found me putting the finishing touches to my first picture from nature, 'A Bunch of Cherries.' 'This is very good indeed,' he exclaimed. 'You must work seriously now.' And I did. From that day I began to copy from casts and from engravings, without, however, neglecting to paint from nature. How much more fascinating it was to me, than to learn grammar and arithmetic!

It was also at about that time that I went to study at the Louvre, where, owing to my dress and manners, the gallery-keepers gave me the name of *Le petit hussard*. My lunch consisted of a halfpenny loaf of bread and one pennyworth of fried potatoes, with a mug full of the clear water from the fountain in the Cour du Louvre. I copied a few pictures by great masters, such as 'Henry IV,' by Porbus, which I immediately sold; 'Les Bergers d'Arcadie,' by Poussin, which my father gave to the Minister of the Intérieur; 'Les Moissonneurs,' by Léopold Robert, and some others. But it was in the Sculpture Gallery that I chiefly distinguished myself by a copy of 'Saint Jérôme.' The students came to watch me working, no longer with contempt. I do not know for certain what became of my 'Saint Jérôme;' it was probably bought for a church. I was so fascinated by the pictures of the old masters that I spent many hours in the vast galleries crowded with their *chefs d'oeuvre*, and copied many of them. I strongly advise beginners who wish to give themselves up to the difficult and arduous career of art, to follow my example and get thoroughly acquainted with the old masters. It is the true foundation of art, and time, thus spent, brings forth fruit sooner or later. ....

❖

I had to catch the rapid motion of animals, the reflection of light and colours on their coats, their different characteristics (for every animal has its individual physiognomy). Therefore, before undertaking the study of a dog, a horse, a sheep, I tried to become familiar with the anatomy, osteology, myology of each of them. I acquired even a certain knowledge of dissection; and, by the way, I must strongly advise all animal painters to do the same. Another excellent practice is to observe the aspect of plaster models of animals, especially to copy them by lamp light, which gives more distinctness and vibration to the shadows. I can assure those who do not doubt my sincerity as an artist, that I owe all that I know to those patient and conscientious exercises. ....

❖

... To perfect myself in the study of nature, I spent whole days in the Roule slaughterhouse. One must be greatly devoted to art to stand the sight of such horrors, in the midst of the coarsest people. They wondered at seeing a young woman taking interest in their work, and made themselves as disagreeable to me as they possibly could. But when our aims are right we always find help. Providence sent me a protector in the good Monsieur Emile, a butcher of great physical strength. He declared that whoever failed to be polite to me would have to reckon with him. I was thus enabled to work undisturbed. . . .

A few more words about my home life. I live as a simple peasant woman, rising early, but retiring late. In the morning I take a walk round my garden with my dog, and afterwards a drive in my pony-cart in the forest of Fontainebleau. From 9 till 11:30, sitting at my easel, I work steadily at my painting. Then I take a very simple lunch, and when it is over, smoke a cigarette and take a glance at the papers. At one o'clock I take up my brushes again, and at five I go out. I love to watch the sun slowly disappearing behind the lofty trees of the forest. My dinner is as simple as my lunch, and I spend my evening in reading, giving the preference to books on travelling, hunting, or history.

❖

EXCERPTS FROM ROSA BONHEUR'S CORRESPONDENCE, 1853–1899
FROM THEODORE STANTON, REMINISCENCES OF ROSA BONHEUR (NEW YORK, 1910. REPRINT. NEW YORK: HACKER ART BOOKS, 1972)

ROSA BONHEUR TO ISIDORE BONHEUR (BROTHER OF BONHEUR)
September 1853
I am seeing a good many things, Isidore, my old boy. There is here a big mountain with lots of animals on the top, where the cows do wonderful things when the fancy takes them. For instance, they will set off and gallop like mad, executing twists and turns, and carrying their tails high in the air when they have a fly behind them. The sheep of this country have a more lively way of wagging their caudal appendage than those I have seen elsewhere; and the result of all this is that the poor creatures let themselves tumble down what painters would call splendid, but the shepherds, frightful precipices, where they are dissected by vultures. . . .

My dog is getting enormous. I don't know how I shall manage to convey him from here, for he will be as big as a donkey. Dear me! What an unfortunate hobby mine is! What would you say if I were to confess what efforts I have made to resist the desire to bring back a sheep and a goat? I really can't help it. I have my failings as well as my virtues. I am so fond of little sheep. However, this dog is quite enough for the journey.

I have not done much work; but the time has not been wasted, since I have got a whole host of ideas. . . .

❖

ROSA BONHEUR TO MR. P. J. MÈNE
(FRENCH PAINTER)
January 24, 1864
My whole day is devoted to my stags. In the evening, after dinner, the ladies read to me, not to the stags, till eleven o'clock, after which I am too lazy to write letters. And yet, I am going to do so to-night, for I want to get something out of you! Here is what I want. Do you happen to have a plaster stag for a study, either to lend or give me? If so, it would be a godsend to your friend, Miss Rosa Bonheur, a most distinguished artist, as you know. You might send the thing to 24 Rue Haute-feuille, and I'll answer for the rest. . . .

❖

RosA Bonheur to Auguste Bonheur (brother of Bonheur) and
Mme Peyrol (Juliette Bonheur [sister of Bonheur])

By, June 15, 1864

I am happy to announce to you that yesterday I received the most gracious
visit that a sovereign can pay to an artist, and that I am most deeply touched by
it. Her Majesty came with all her Court to surprise me. You may fancy, my Juliette, how gladly I would, at first, have hidden myself in my mouse-hole. Fortunately, I only had to pull off my blouse and put on a jacket, but, in my confusion
and haste, I couldn't get my head out of my blouse collar. But at last I freed
myself, just in time to make my appearance, and somehow or other welcome
her very gracious, very good and charming Majesty. Luckily, Hippolyte happened to be in the studio, and he helped me, quite simply and nicely, to exhibit
my dust-covered sketches. . . .

❖

RosA Bonheur to Isidore Bonheur (brother of Bonheur)

February 7, 1867

Dodore, you old cuss, I have just received your letter, which I could hardly
read but which pleased me all the more as I'm in the same box as regards
handwriting. . . .

You old cuss! I asked you for the address of your modeller, and you haven't
sent it. You forget, I have a masterpiece to get modelled, or else it will be spoilt,
which would be a pity. So please send me this address, in the name of the pigs!
I will arrange with him.

Peg away, peg away, my dear Dodore! You must produce us something fine
in two months! As for your Sis, why, she is a body that hesitates at nothing. I
work as I did at twenty, only there are so many things to do at once that I am
like a donkey with 20 feeds of oats around him and trotting about to each of
them in turn. . . .

❖

RosA Bonheur to Paul Chardin (French painter)

August 23, 1867

One finally becomes so enervated and worn out by things of this life,
whether they affect one nearly or remotely, that unless one lets one's self drift,
it is necessary to react against the laws of physical nature which each day
deprives us of a little of those we love, and of ourselves, too, happily! One has to
become, if not hard, if not selfish, at least tough, and to brace in order to go on
to the end without allowing one's self to drop like a rag.

As for me, I must own that I am in the position of the old rat who, after
sniffing about over hill and dale, retires, quite satisfied, to his hole, yet, in reality, somewhat sad to have seen the world without taking a part in it. So I shut
my door in the face of all that is commonplace and keep only three or four sincere affections, after studying those who wished to do the same, a thing allow-
able to each; so that, after having chosen one's friends, one keeps those that
please and neglects those that don't. Now, my good Rapin, you of course belong
to the small number of those I really like, and you will find me always happy to

receive you but more and more buried in my small shell, with my door shut against the indifferent. For you, then, I will open it and for three or four other friends of my predilection. . . .

Rosa Bonheur to Paul Chardin (French painter)
By, October 15, 1869
I will tell you what I was saying to myself just now. Since All Saints' Day is near at hand, I was saying that about this time the famous Rapin used to come and call on his old General in order to go and sketch with her on the melancholy Long Rocher, both shivering with cold; then, in order to warm themselves at lunch time, they would descend into the Grotto, lighting a big fire that their varlet had gleaned wood for among the firs, at the expense of the State, and there toast their poor trembling bodies and blue faces; next they would stuff themselves with enormous hunks of bread seasoned with good victuals and an agreeable cup of coffee boiled over the big fire; and finally, they would smoke an exquisite cigarette while chattering about everything that passed through their head and then return each to his seat to go on daubing masterpieces. Lastly, the good Rapin would come in the evening and stretch himself in front of a large fire that blazed in the big chimney of the studio, and there muse and smoke.

This time has already gone by, and my letter is to tell you that the years succeed each other with their varying experience, and that about this season I usually think of the old friendship between the Rapin and the General. Now the General's voice has become hoarser and more cracked, when she smokes in the morning. She gets up late and grows fonder of being alone like the solitary boar. But she nevertheless remembers her friends and was glad as always to receive a kind, affectionate letter from her worthy Rapin. . . .

Rosa Bonheur to Mme Peyrol (sister of Bonheur)
February 25, 1870
Don't worry about me. I am all right now, though I have been really unwell — mentally, however, rather than physically. I was so upset to see poor Nathalie suffer; and she has been very ill. Such a life is a veritable martyrdom. You may imagine, consequently, that I was not much in the humour to do honour to a marriage. . . .

Besides, I have annoyances of an artistic character. You know yourself what it is to be tempted to kick a hole through the canvas, just as I am now, in order to give more depth to my landscape. What a profession! How much better I should like to charge a body of men, sabre in hand, and so allay my rage, instead of having to fret and fume before a bit of canvas, and to see some one else suffer into the bargain.

At present, Nathalie is somewhat improved; so don't be anxious about me. I hope Mammy will soon be well also, and that the devil will get tired of substituting evil for good. Say your prayers, and let fly at him with some holy water! When I have finished the picture that causes my fits of rage, I will run up to Paris. In the meanwhile — love.

Rosa Bonheur to Mme Peyrol (sister of Bonheur)
July 18, 1873

I had been really thinking of going to Paris lately. But I have been unwell, partly on account of my age, and partly because I injured the calf of one of my legs in trying to cure a cramp with my whip. It was only yesterday that I began to walk again. I fretted myself to fiddle-strings, for I am not used to being cooped up. . . .

Nothing goes on right when I can't carry out my ideas; and I don't care to work except when things are to my liking. The devil cannot conquer me, however. For the last three weeks he has been playing me his tricks, so that I haven't touched a brush. Consequently, I am like the bristling hair on the back of a mad dog.

I intend to go to Paris as soon as I can trot about again. In the meanwhile, love to you and Dodore. If you come over with your boys, you will give me much pleasure. Remember me to all.

❖

Rosa Bonheur to Auguste Bonheur (brother of Bonheur)
April 1, 1882

I am very happy to find, my dear brother, that you care little for the grandeurs of this world. We have quite the same ideas on this subject, as on many others. We are not brothers for nothing.

As for my art, the older I grow, the more I love it. Were I to paint only daubs, it would make no difference. You see I am even more of a philosopher than you; and, as we neither of us do worse than other folks, we can afford to be open-minded and go our own way.

❖

Rosa Bonheur to Paul Chardin (French painter)
By, January 4, 1886

Here at By everything is still the same except the years that pass over our whitened heads. I am still surrounded with my animals. My old Nathalie and I love them more than we do three-fourths of our own species. I am at present making experiments on wild beasts. We are rearing a lion and a lioness which are gentleness itself toward us. The painting is going on as usual. The forest is devastated more and more. In twenty years' time there will be nothing but sand, firs, and heaps of stones. But it is all the same to me, for I shall be in a better world, I hope, together with my old life's companion.

❖

Rosa Bonheur to Mme Auguste Cain (wife of French artist)
By, July 7, 1889

My health is very good. I am like iron in that respect. As for my mind, my dear friend, you can very well understand how hard it is to be separated from a friend like my Nathalie, whom I loved more and more as we advanced in life; for she had borne, with me, the mortifications and stupidities inflicted on us by silly, ignorant, low-minded people, who form the majority on this terrestrial ball, called the earth. She alone knew me, and I, her only friend, knew what she was worth. We both of us made ourselves humble, so as not to hurt the feelings of other people, while we were too proud to seek the confidence of idiots who doubted us. Keep this outpouring of my heart for yourselves alone, my old friends. I should be very sorry to pain anybody. . . .

❖

ROSA BONHEUR TO PRINCESS STIRBEY, MME FOULD (NÉE SIMONIN VALERIE, FRIEND OF BONHEUR)

September 3, 1889

For the last five months I have not felt in a mood to paint. You will understand what a struggle I have had and what strength is necessary to combat my low spirits, so that I can employ the short time that remains to me in this world in executing, if I can, some paintings which I have in mind. It seems to me that this would be the desire of my friend, who was so proud of what I can do and who would advise me to so act if she were in reality near me. . . .

❖

ROSA BONHEUR TO PAUL CHARDIN (FRENCH PAINTER)

December 30, 1891

I muse a good deal, only half living in this world. I count the days that pass. They glide by and I am rejoiced at it. I live alone and like it best. If, perchance, I see a human being, I am bored the more. Painting still pleases me, especially when I begin a picture. Before I finish it, I find it tiresome.

❖

ROSA BONHEUR TO ISIDORE BONHEUR (BROTHER OF BONHEUR)

February 21, 1892

I hope, my dear old brother, your cold is nothing serious. Just scrawl me another line, if only to help me while away the time; for I can't go up to Paris at this moment. I am sticking close to my lions, like you when you are getting to the end of some creation. At times, I go at it hammer and tongs, saying to myself: 'Now, my little Rosa Bonheur, my girl, you have just produced a masterpiece!' And in this satisfactory state of mind, I long for the morrow in order to add a few more finishing touches. Then, when morning arrives, I could box my own ears! It's too red! It's too green! It's too light! It's too dark! 'Come! We must alter all that, my poor girl! You are a confounded fool, all puffed up with pride! Let us make haste and remedy all that!'

So the days pass, the months and the years; for during this time the anchor has been weighed and the vessel scuds along. One needs to be wide awake. Now there's moon, now there's sun, and we revolve quickly.

When evening comes, I read the newspaper, which sends me into a rapture of wonder over my fellow-creatures' state of mind. Or else I make projections with my Diogenes lantern or touch up blue-paper proofs.

That's how the time is spent, my old greybeard, and that's why I can't very well desert my frigate, especially as my crew work better when I am personally in command, and also because I have promised Mr. Lefèvre to deliver him my merchandise by the end of the month; and you know in the navy a man must keep his word.

❖

ROSA BONHEUR TO RENÉ PEYROL (NEPHEW OF BONHEUR)

August 26, 1898

Thanks for your kind letter on my birthday. You must excuse me if I am rather late in acknowledging it. But I have been melting in perspiration —

some sixty pounds or more I should say I have lost — and have been obliged to fly from my two studios, both the upstairs one and the downstairs one. I have been incapable of doing anything. One must be an American, like my companion and portrait-painter, Miss Klumpke, to work when it is 90° in the shade. It is only during the last two days that my faculties as a painter and a writer have been somewhat restored. Please thank all the family for me. It will save me writing and so going to bed at eleven o'clock; for I was up at five, according to my custom.

I am awaiting the pleasure of seeing you again, which is rare enough now, like the fish. But I have only one room to offer you, each in turn, as America has made an alliance with old Europe and, in addition, is working to preserve for the family and for France the portrait of your aunt, Rosa Bonheur.

❖

ROSA BONHEUR TO M. VERDIER (FRENCH PAINTER, FORMER PUPIL OF RAYMOND BONHEUR, FRIEND OF BONHEUR)

September 21, 1898

I have just finished a picture which had to be ready for an exhibition in America. As I had promised it, I had to give all my time to it. So please forgive my delay in writing.

My health is good just now. I am thankful to say that change has occurred in my life. I have found a charming friend, a kind lady of great talent and most distinguished family. I am happy and proud of her friendship. I will tell you all about it when we meet, for I intend to introduce her to you soon, when we pay you a visit. It will be only for two or three days, for we both have to work. Miss Klumpke is the lady's name. She comes from Boston where she was established. But we have decided to work together for the rest of our days. She has just painted a very successful portrait of me. I hope you will like her, and that Mme Verdier will also. She is a good musician, which is a charm for me. In fine, my dear old friends, I feel quite young again, in spite of my seventy-seven years. I will write to you again, as soon as we can arrange our little trip.

❖

ROSA BONHEUR TO PRINCESS STIRBEY, MME FOULD (NÉE SIMONIN VALERIE, FRIEND OF BONHEUR)

January 26, 1899

A line simply to thank you for your gracious letter and to reassure you about my health, which has come back since I have found a kind, excellent friend who takes care of me and has cured me of my discouragement and misanthropy. I hope to introduce her to you one of these days.

. . . As for Princess Achille . . . she is right to prefer art to marriage, which more often than not takes a woman in. However, I don't despise this natural institution among all animals, and so useful to men, who would mope to death without wives.

Our artist household is getting on very well. My wife has much talent and the children don't prevent us from painting pictures. What annoys me is to have to wear spectacles.

Awaiting the pleasure of seeing you, I remain, your old grandson who celebrates next March his seventy-seventh birthday.

❖

ROSA BONHEUR TO THE MARQUISE DE GRASSE (CONSUELO FOULD, FRENCH ARTIST, DAUGHTER OF PRINCESS STIRBEY)
May 19, 1899

I made a point of going to see the Salon where my portrait is exhibited, painted by my dear friend Miss Klumpke, and a small picture of my own which had not been very well appreciated in America. This picture had accompanied to America an early portrait, and now, like a boat disturbing a lake, it is creating a commotion of which my artistic vanity makes me very proud.

I was very pleased to see your picture. You have made great progress, and I am glad to be able to tell you so. Near mine, I also saw Achille's picture and I beg you will compliment her on it for me. I can't write much myself just now, as my eyes are weak. . . .

❖

VERSION OF THE THE CATHOLIC MASS, WRITTEN ON BACK OF ENGRAVING OF THE VIRGIN AND CHILD
FROM ANNA KLUMPKE, ROSA BONHEUR: SA VIE, SON OEUVRE (PARIS: FLAMMARION, 1908)

Salutation: I greet you, oh earth full of grace, the living God is with you, you are blessed among all the planets, and the fruit from your bowels is savior. Holy earth, mother of love pour your grace upon our suffering, now and at our divine transformation.

Dominican Prayer: Our father who is in everything and everywhere, may your divine name be glorified; may your reign of love arrive on earth as your Christ is in the heavens.

Credo: I believe in God the all powerful Father, eternal creator of everything eternal; I believe in his Son, well-loved, the saviour couple, the androgynous Christ, unique sum of human transformation, sublime manifestation of the living God, who is in everything that there is; who was conceived in the breast of glorious nature, always mother and always virgin, who was born, who died to be reborn always more perfect, who has risen towards the future which he will open for us and where the living and dead will be judged.

I believe in holy love, God vitalizing all things, in the holy Church where all are called in body and spirit, in the communion of all men, sanctified by holy work, because all will be saved, in the forgiveness of shortcomings, in life eternal.

❖

EXCERPTS FROM TESTAMENT, 9 NOVEMBER 1898
FROM ANNA KLUMPKE, ROSA BONHEUR: SA VIE, SON OEUVRE (PARIS: FLAMMARION, 1908)

I the undersigned Rosalie-Marie called Rosa Bonheur, artist painter, healthy in body and spirit, freely explain here my last wishes, owing nothing to anyone, and not having the least debt, free in my wishes and of that which I alone earned through my work, never having had lovers or children.

I want to be buried in the same tomb as my friend Mlle Nathalie-Jeanne Micas, such as I have the right to, having been her universal legatee and sole heir, and as was thus agreed upon between us. . . .

I give and will to Mlle Anna Elizabeth Klumpke, my partner and painting colleague and my friend, all that I possess on the day of my death, making her my universal legatee. . . .

I declare here to those who have judged me to be very rich, that not having any fortune to distribute to my family for whom I have done my best before and after the death of my father, I have judged that I had the right, not owing anything to anybody, to ask Mlle Anna Elizabeth Klumpke, who has the same profession as I, and who holds by herself a very honorable position, as well as that of her family, to participate in my life and to remain with me. And thus to compensate her and insure her, since for her to live with me she sacrifices her own self-created personal position, and shares with me the expenses of improvements to my property and house; this testament is a duty of honor for me, and all honest people will be of my opinion, as well as my true friends. . . .

Following my wish and that of my friend Mlle Anna Elizabeth Klumpke, she will, after her death, be buried in the same tomb which belongs to me, which was left me by my friend Mlle Nathalie Micas.

Now I must thank God for the happy and exceptional life that he granted me and the protection in this world which I attribute to the soul of my dear mother.

❖

EXCERPTS FROM LETTER-TESTAMENT, 28 NOVEMBER 1898
FROM ANNA KLUMPKE, *ROSA BONHEUR: SA VIE, SON OEUVRE*
(PARIS: FLAMMARION, 1908)

I write this letter because I consider it a duty of honor to vindicate my conduct towards the Mesdames Micas, my friends, and to that which I have extended towards Mlle Anna Klumpke, who wants to accept my offer to live with to me. And so that people understand my integrity in making a point of securing the material interests of Mlle Anna Klumpke, who could possibly be compromised in living with me.

I have made Mlle Klumpke my universal legatee by a proper testament . . . desiring that people know the truth — that it is I who have persuaded Mlle Klumpke to stay with me; I do not want people to imply that she has accepted for material concerns, but truly for her affection for me. . . .

I want people to know that living alone, and often ill, since the cruel loss of my venerated friend Mlle Micas, no longer having a friend to concern herself with my interests and to help me keep my house in order, life has no longer been absolutely pleasant. . . . I have been at the sole care of my domestics, no longer having my dear Nathalie Micas.

Then, my family has judged me somewhat poorly all my life in my right to live freely. Since I first took care of my duty towards them, I had the same right afterwards to the independence that all adult people who support themselves have. . . .

I am obligated to say all that here, because it is quite necessary that the truth be known and that I have the duty to substantiate that I am free to do that which pleases me and to defend once and for all the honor of others, and my own.

I also had the right, after the death of my dear father, to leave my family to live with the Mesdames Micas, and to have an atelier of my own. . . .

❖

LETTERS

FROM ANNA KLUMPKE, *ROSA BONHEUR: SA VIE, SON OEUVRE*
(PARIS: FLAMMARION, 1908)

ROSA BONHEUR TO MICAS FAMILY

Mauriac, 6 September 1846

My dear friends, I have been here since Tuesday, nine o'clock in the evening. Excuse me for being late in sending you my news as I promised; but if you knew all that I have gone through in seeing this lovely countryside where they are so hospitable, where they have entertained me so much that I haven't had a single free moment. . . .

. . . I saw magnificent views, beautiful cascades that roll over rocks; the water is like crystal; it's savage and beautiful, a thousand times beautiful. Yesterday I was on the bridge at Ause, perched on a rustic cart drawn by oxen. Tomorrow I set out on a hunt with Jacques. Thus I am as happy as I can be. I embrace you.

Your friend, your child if you would like,

Adds these lines to Nathalie (whom she tutoyers):

My dear friend, you see that I don't lack distractions, it's so lovely here that my my spirit can only admire and imitate; something very difficult: imitation is so cold in rendering that which is. . . . But I will do my best. Ah! If only you were with me, I would lose my head with happiness, because to experience a pleasure without you is only to half enjoy it. You see, it is because you understand me, you, my Nathalie. It seems as if it has been a month since I have seen you; and then, life here is so different from that in Paris, that it seems to me to be even further away. I feel really strange in the morning; when I wake up I am astonished. . . . I await your news with impatience. . . .

I embrace you, my friend,

I embrace you as I love you.

ROSA BONHEUR TO MME MICAS (NATHALIE MICAS'S MOTHER)

12 August 1850

Dear good, mother,

I am taking up this morning the letter that Nathalie had begun. We have been in Luz which is quite near to here. It has been market day. We bought some Spanish grapes from a Spaniard who had a superb costume; I am snacking on a few while I write to you; I wish I could send you some because they are really good. I ate a few on an empty stomach. Right now Nathalie is waking up; we are going to see the doctor today for her aches; I think that is always the effect of the baths. There's the sun showing its face — that's good. . . .

At this moment Nathalie is combing her hair: she is making herself pretty to please the doctor: she has a weakness for that kind of behavior. We've done all sorts of things, dear big mother, your children are not without industry; in the mountains, next to a poetic stream we did our laundry. I soaped really well;

Nathalie is pleased with me; I received many compliments, quite deserved, besides. Because your children's beds were fairly dirty, and as in this country no one does the wash, and since one needs potash to get rid of dirt, we believed, with reason, to be more skillful than the laundresses of the region. . . .

Today we are going to see. As the temperature rises we are going to make an experiment. Don't be afraid . . . I will make Nana wear her jersey under her coat . . . I am in good spirits this morning, which proves to me that the temperature is going to rise. Nathalie is proceeding to drink her water; she is giving me a nice little kiss which I don't want to keep to myself: I give it to you, her good mother, who has been for me, without being conscious of it, a friend who will be the happiness of all my life, because I have happiness. One could never find a true friend like my Nathalie. I tell you that because she will not read my letter; post time has come. I am hurrying in embracing you as I love you, and that's good, good. . . .

ROSA BONHEUR TO ANNA KLUMPKE

By, 5 January 1898

I received your almanac for which I thank you and which gives me a strong idea of your original and vigorous cleverness. I was struck by the analogy between your imagination and that of the Spanish painter Goya, whom perhaps you do not know. Do you have some drops of Spanish blood in your veins, unbeknownst to you? . . . I thank you a thousand times and offer you my very affectionate good wishes for 1898.

I am furious at myself because I haven't yet found the time to finish Miss Walker's white horse, because apart from my habitual slowness, I am continually disturbed and at my age I am only able to work a little bit at a time. And now I have committed myself to exhibiting among my female companions, at the end of March, if I am able to make it. It is necessary then that Miss Walker waits until that time, and the first thing I will do afterwards will be her horse.

Don't torment yourself, please, about getting me the prairie grass. First, you have already sent me some. I only regret the life-like sketches which you had the goodness to paint during your trip to San Francisco. In the next place, your great American painter M. Bierstadt from New York was generous enough to lend me several of his studies.

I am planning many compositions about prairie subjects. Will I be able to execute them? I would like to live long enough for that, but by the grace of God!

Au revoir, dear and good mademoiselle, worthy sister of the paintbrush.

Receive with my affectionate wishes , a fraternal kiss.

ROSA BONHEUR TO MME KLUMPKE (ANNA'S MOTHER)

By, 18 July 1898

I take pleasure in coming to tell you how much I am attached to the heart and soul of your daughter Mlle Anna, who is an angel of goodness. Despite my age, because I am older than you are yourself, my heart has remained tender, as it has been since I lost my adored mother at the age of eleven.

I also lost a friend who was my guardian angel. Since then I have struggled between the desire to leave the earth and that of still leaving there several more proofs of the talent that God has given me. Then the noble souls whom I still love, even though they are no longer living in this world, have sent me a friend and at the same time your affection, I hope, and I am even certain. I am happy and proud that this affection brings me close to a family that I hold in such high esteem and a mother such as yourself, who has formed it for honor and work. Also, I respect you, and you should have confidence in the honor and sanctity of my profound affection for your daughter.

Allow me to embrace you as if I were the sister of your children.

Your old child, Rosa Bonheur

❖

ROSA BONHEUR TO MME KLUMPKE (ANNA'S MOTHER)

By, 8 August 1898

I am responding, in the manner that I must, sincerely and loyally, to your letter of 5 August.

My proposition to Mlle Anna, your beloved oldest daughter, is not made lightly: at my age — and I am far older than you yourself, dear Mme Klumpke — one knows all about life. I know that it is appropriate and probable that I will leave this world before Mlle Klumpke; I would not want, thus, for anything in the world, to put her in a compromising position.

If she decides to live with me, I reckon then, in loyal and honest friendship, to set up by a notary, a very clean situation for her in which she will be able to live with me under conditions with which she will consider herself at home. With my dear companion Mlle Nathalie Micas, we took all precautions, and with her mother too, because of each of our families, to escape all disagreements about material interests and to provide order in our private affairs.

As for me, I have a genuine fondness for your very noble daughter, and if I love her so much, it is after all because I understand her good nature, her lovely soul and even her childlike naiveté.

Would it not be happier for us to become united with each other, to lead a happy life, rather than living alone, each by ourselves, cultivating the same art and each having our own independence? Because I believe, thank God, to have too much pride and honor to impose myself on her. Miss Anna is free as the air and I am the first to think like you, dear good mother that you are; I am persuading your dear Anna to keep her studio in Boston and her distinguished connections.

Your dear letter could only increase my estimation of you, because a bit of a maternal feeling for your Anna has entered my old heart. It's fine that she consulted you as well as her sisters; I am in no way offended, to the contrary; it is very serious, and above all I love your dear Anna for her self, I give you my word of honor.

She will bring this letter to you herself the day after tomorrow, not wanting to determine anything before getting your advice. I know the worth of your family, as illustrated by your daughters who are all highly intelligent women and the best people; I, dear madame, am not at all worldly; but by my talent and honor, I am honored to be a friend of your family as well as of you, yourself.

This is all that I am able to say to you, I know that you are the best of mothers, and I feel affection and respect for you.

❖

ROSA BONHEUR TO MME KLUMPKE (ANNA'S MOTHER)

By, 31 March 1899

. . . Your Anna is an angel of goodness and the more that I know her the more I value her and love her.

At my age, given my experience of life and of humankind I have reason to assure her, because she could be easily duped by false fellows.

We are happy and I hope that wicked people will not disturb our honorable life of work.

I hope to see you come to stay with us. Your Anna adores you, and I share her feelings for the best of mothers. Set your mind at ease and know, dear Mme Klumpke, that although I am much older than you I have the highest affection and esteem for you and your family, and the most profound respect.

Zenobia in Chains, 1859. Marble. 49" h.
Wadsworth Atheneum, Hartford, Gift of Mrs. Josephine M. J. Dodge

HARRIET HOSMER

1830–1908

A **QUINTESSENTIAL EXAMPLE** of an independent woman artist whose life centered around her career, the sculptor Harriet Hosmer achieved renown and distinction during her lifetime. An American expatriate, "Hattie" was a major, well-loved figure in an international group of artists and writers living in Rome during the mid-nineteenth century and she was one of the first American artists to achieve distinction in that arena. Neoclassicism had predominated in Europe for almost a century by the time she reached artistic maturity, and Hosmer's work in that style even as its popularity began to wane might brand her a "follower" for pursuing an established visual system whose parameters she did not attempt to expand. She nonetheless manipulated the system quite successfully, both aesthetically and to her economic advantage. Like many other women artists who achieved fame in their own time, Hosmer's contribution to the history of art has been obscured by historical neglect.

Hosmer's letters provide an opportunity for reassessment of her place. Throughout her life, Hosmer was a prolific correspondent with many friends and acquaintances throughout Europe, England, and the United States. Her letters are chatty and anecdotal, and they convey a vivid sense of the personal dynamism that endeared her to a variety of patrons and artists, as well as the centrality of artistic pursuit in her life.

It is tempting to suggest that the freedom of her youth endowed Hosmer with the self-confidence needed to set out on and pursue her artistic path. Harriet Goodhue Hosmer was born in Watertown, Massachusetts, the child of a physician whose wife and three other children died of tuberculosis. Hiram Hosmer was determined that his surviving child would live and be strong, so his prescription for the petite Harriet was plenty of fresh air and exercise. From all descriptions Hosmer's personality was marked by spunk and daring. When she later lived in Rome, she continued her childhood love of horses with daily horseback rides on animals from her own stable and took notorious midnight rides through the city.

When she was sixteen, Hosmer was sent to Mrs. Sedgwick's boarding school — noted for its liberal atmosphere — in Lenox, Massachusetts, where she stayed for three years. The connections she made during these years greatly influenced her later life. Especially important relationships that she established at this time included those with Fanny Kemble, an actress with whom she maintained a lifetime friendship; Cornelia Crow (Carr), who edited and published Hosmer's letters after her death; and Wayman Crow, Cornelia's father, who became Hosmer's patron (referred to in numerous letters as "The Pater"). After graduation, Hosmer returned to Watertown convinced that she wanted to be a sculptor; she began studying in Boston and her doting father built her a studio behind their Watertown house. However, as a woman, she could not find anyone willing to teach her anatomy. A visit to Cornelia Crow in St. Louis solved this problem when Wayman Crow intervened on Hosmer's behalf for the first of many times, and persuaded Dr. Joseph N. MacDowell of Washington University Medical School to let Hosmer study anatomy with him. After nine months of study, Hosmer returned to Boston where she spent the next two years perfecting her craft. On her way home, she took a steamboat trip down the Mississippi: her willingness to travel alone is often cited as an example of her celebrated "spunkiness."

Like most American Neoclassical sculptors, Hosmer felt it necessary to pursue her studies in Italy, where the classical tradition had been well preserved and was still flourishing. In the autumn of 1852, not yet twenty-three years old and having completed only one sculptural bust (*Hesper*, 1852), Hosmer and her father set sail for Rome. They sought out John Gibson, an English sculptor considered the heir to Antonio Canova and Bertel Thorvaldsen, and convinced him to take Harriet as a student, on the basis of daguerreotypes of *Hesper*. She was given work space in Gibson's studio and went to live with the actress Charlotte Cushman, whom she had met during the previous year in Boston and who had been instrumental in persuading her to come to Rome. Hosmer's father returned to the United States alone, and Italy became Hosmer's primary residence until late in her life, when she spent her time traveling between the United States and England.

Hosmer's career became established soon after her arrival. She began by making several portrait busts, of Daphne and of Medusa, under Gibson's influence. Within a year or so, she received her first commissions for full-length sculptures from Wayman Crow and an associate. In fact, her most important work was to be completed during the next fifteen years. By the time she was thirty, Hosmer was well established as a Neoclassical sculptor with an international reputation. She had already completed her most distinguished piece — a larger-than-lifesize sculpture of Zenobia, Queen of Palmyra, in chains — and her most popular — an image of *Puck on a Toadstool,* originally executed in 1856, and of which she ultimately sold about fifty copies, first at $500 and later at $1000 each.

Hosmer became a principal figure among the group of English-speaking expatriates that congregated in Florence and Rome, including poets Elizabeth Barrett Browning and Robert Browning, the painter Lord Frederick Leighton, Fanny Kemble, and several members of the British aristocracy. In Rome she made herself the center of what Henry James somewhat condescendingly referred to as "a White Marmorean Flock," a group of American women sculptors in Italy that included Emma Stebbins, Louise Landers, and Edmonia Lewis. (Nathaniel Hawthorne presented a fictionalized view of this group in his novel *The Marble Faun.*) Elizabeth Barrett Browning wrote that "Hattie" was her and Robert's "great pet," and that many people were attracted to her. Also, according to Elizabeth Barrett Browning, Hosmer worked from "six o'clock in the morning till night." It seems that they were struck by the contrast between their expectations of a woman, particularly one of her diminutive size and jovial nature, and the seriousness with which Hosmer pursued her artistic profession. Although Fanny Kemble wished that "Hattie's" peculiarities "were less decided and singular," and worried that they would "stand in the way of her success with people of society and the world," these traits were endearing to many people, who began to buy her work on commission.

Although Hosmer's career never really suffered an outright reversal, after the mid-1860s, it ceased to move forward. She submitted proposals for several public monuments, including one dedicated to Abraham Lincoln for Springfield, Illinois, but received only one major public commission — for a monumental bronze statue of Thomas Hart Benton for the city of St. Louis. The waning popularity of Neoclassicism — particularly in post–Civil War America, where war had destroyed the spirit of republican idealism — may have been responsible for Hosmer's waning success. She never really changed her artistic style: her depiction of Benton, for example, was criticized because she presented a frontiersman garbed in a classical toga. Her last known commission, Queen Isabella offering her jewels to Columbus, unfortunately seems to have disappeared, existing today only in a photograph in the Schlesinger Library at Radcliffe College. This work was initially commissioned in 1889 by the Isabella Society for the 1893 World Columbian Exposition in Chicago, although it was ultimately exhibited in the fair's California pavilion, under the auspices of the California rancher Harriet Russell Strong and brought to Golden Gate Park in San Francisco, its last known location. In the latter decades of the nineteenth century, Hosmer spent increasingly less time in her Rome studio and more time visiting with friends and associates in England and the United States.

Several factors explain Hosmer's extended stay outside the United States. She was initially attracted to Rome because of its cultural advantages and she planned to remain abroad for about five years. Within her first two years there she reported to Cornelia Crow Carr that she had never been so happy, that she would never live anywhere but Rome, and that she certainly did not have such a sense of "quiet and content" in America. Contributing to her positive feelings must have been the freedom she was afforded as an artist, particularly as she became part of a select artistic coterie. (In this, her stay in Rome is comparable to Mary Cassatt's in Paris.) One cannot help but consider the contrast between her life in Rome and then-prevalent attitudes toward both artists and unmarried women in the United States. Hosmer, like most nineteenth-century women artists, did not combine marriage and career. She articulated her decision to follow her vocation in a letter to Wayman Crow in which she described herself as a "worshipper of Celibacy." In Rome she was not alone as a single woman with a profession; rather, she was surrounded by a group of achieving women, only one of whom, Elizabeth Barrett Browning, was married at the time.

Hosmer's method of work required that she remain in Italy. Like most sculptors of her day, Hosmer believed that the "art" of sculpture lay only in the creative act of modeling, the "thought" of the artist being written in clay and subsequently translated mechanically by workmen into marble, the artist doing only the finish work with his or her own hand. (Barbara Hepworth later rebelled against just this convention.) There was, as there still is, a thriving tradition of skilled marble carvers in Italy whose expertise Hosmer used to her advantage: a photograph shows her in the courtyard of her studio surrounded by more than twenty male workers. Hosmer supported herself by selling multiple copies of her works, which she modeled in clay and had the workmen execute in marble. This collaborative method poses problems for historians, both in authenticating her works and assessing her stylistic development. An artist might well have been tempted to turn out copies of old best-sellers, rather than produce new images. But when that too-typical accusation, that a woman artist's work is not her own, was launched against Hosmer, she wrote an essay describing and defending her work method, an extract of which is included in this volume.

Hosmer was particularly attracted to female subjects, although her approach to them is somewhat problematic. *Zenobia in Chains* (1859) expresses a more positive view of women's strength than any of her other surviving works. Although there were several copies made of this piece, the most admired of her works during Hosmer's lifetime, the Wadsworth Atheneum in Hartford owns the only known surviving copy, a reduced-scale version. A statue of a dignified, female figure shown in her captivity, its fame is justified for, in this, work Hosmer created a female image that broke with stereotypical norms of representing women — Zenobia remains undaunted, despite her chains. Furthermore, Hosmer does not exploit the erotic potential of Zenobia's situation nor offer her up to the possessing gaze of an implied male viewer, as, for example, Hiram Powers did in his *Greek Slave*, also an American Neoclassical sculpture of a woman in chains.

Zenobia is, however, like Hosmer's other female subjects, a victim. Other examples include Oenone, the shepherdess abandoned by Paris for Helen, and Beatrice Cenci executed for plotting patricide against her incestuous father. Hosmer's depictions of these other women are not nearly as forceful as that of Zenobia: Oenone is downcast and pensive, Beatrice Cenci is asleep and vulnerable. Although it might be naive to expect that Hosmer's images of women would always show their strength because she herself was an assertive woman, it is difficult to reconcile Hosmer's depictions of victimized women with her feminist orientation. She is known to have subscribed to Susan B. Anthony's women's-rights paper, *Revolutions*, and Phoebe Hanaford quotes Hosmer as saying, "I honor every woman who has strength enough to step out of the beaten path . . . strength to stand up to be laughed at if necessary." At least two of Hosmer's lost works may have presented images of this strength:

one of her friend, the ex-Queen of Naples, depicted in her Gaeta costume; the other of Queen Isabella conceptualized as the force behind Columbus. On the other hand, such pieces as *Fountain of the Siren*, that adorned patron Lady Marion Alford's conservatory and a copy of which the artist had in her own studio courtyard, were by Hosmer's own admission "so sweet that [they] ought only to play *eau sucrée*" (sugar water)!

Hosmer maintained correspondence with numerous friends, patrons, and associates. Her letters and papers now reside in the Schlesinger Library at Radcliffe College. In them her voice resounds, revealing her vibrant personality and the tenacity that enabled her to pursue an independent career, in a foreign city at a time when many American women were cloistered in domesticity. Hosmer frequently described the projects on which she was working, often referring to them as her "children," a figure of speech used by other women artists whose writings are included in this book. She continued to write discursive letters to her patron Wayman Crow until his death in 1885 and, like many nineteenth-century women, she maintained a lifelong correspondence with her school friend, Cornelia Crow Carr. The excerpts included in this collection have been selected for what they reveal about specific works or the insight they afford into Hosmer's mind and life.

SOURCES

Carr, Cornelia Crow. *Harriet Hosmer: Letters and Memories.* New York: Moffatt Ladd, 1912.

Cikovsky, Nicolai, Jr., Marie H. Morrison, and Carol Ockman. *The White Marmorean Flock: Nineteenth Century American Women Neoclassical Sculptors.* Poughkeepsie, N.Y.: Vassar College Art Gallery, 1972.

Comini, Alessandra. "Who Ever Heard of a Woman Sculptor?." In *American Women Artists 1830–1930*, edited by Eleanor Tufts. Washington, D.C.: National Museum of Women in the Arts, 1987.

Faxon, Alicia. "Images of Women in the Sculpture of Harriet Hosmer." *Woman's Art Journal* 2 (Spring-Summer 1981): 25–29.

Hanaford, Phoebe. *Daughters of America.* Augusta, Me.: True and Co., 1883.

Leach, Joseph. "Harriet Hosmer: Feminist in Bronze and Marble." *Feminist Art Journal* 5 (Summer 1976): 9–13.

Rubinstein, Charlotte S. *American Women Artists.* Boston: Avon Books, 1982.

SELECTIONS FROM LETTERS TO CORNELIA CROW CARR, WAYMAN CROW, AND ANNE DUNDAS, 1852–1869

HARRIET HOSMER TO WAYMAN CROW (PATRON OF HOSMER)

Rome, December 1, 1852

Can you believe that this is indeed Rome, and more than all that I am in it? I wrote you from Liverpool, and after that delayed sending you any word till I could say I was in this delightful place which I now consider my home. I will say nothing of Italy or of what you already know, but tell you at once of the arrangements I have made for the present in the way of art. Of course you know that Mr. Gibson, the English sculptor, is the acknowledged head of artists here. He is my master, and I love him more every day. I work under his very eye, and nothing could be better for me in every way. He gives me engravings, books, casts, everything he thinks necessary for my studies, and in so kindly, so fatherly a manner that I am convinced Heaven smiled most benignantly upon me when it sent me to him.

❖

HARRIET HOSMER TO WAYMAN CROW (PATRON OF HOSMER)
Rome, April 10, 1853

When an artist has received the first order, and such an order, he considers himself (or herself) placed, at least, on one artistic leg. As Mr. Gibson remarked, there are very few who can say the first benefit conferred on them was of such a princely nature. But now, my dear sir, I want to tell you that it will be some time before I can make anything which I should feel that I could send you as compensation, either in justice to yourself or as worthy of myself. Therefore for the present I shall derive no other good from your generosity than that which will arise from the possession of this "artistic leg," of which I speak, but which, I assure you, is a great thing. When I told Mr. Gibson the news, he said, "Brava, Brava, more splendid encouragement nobody ever received"; which is indeed true. And when I told Mrs. Kemble, she wouldn't believe it. I have received many congratulations on the strength of it, and every day feel more and more that I must strive to deserve the confidence you feel in me, and that by faithful study and devoted labor I must justify the interest expressed by my many friends.

. . . You will soon see a bust of my handiwork, for I am now engaged on one which was destined for you, from the beginning; that is, from the time Mr. Gibson told me I must put it into marble. I send it to you purely as a love gift, as a love offering to the whole family, and as a very slight return for the many kindnesses I received when I was with you. Her name is Daphne, and she is represented as just sinking away into the laurel leaves. It will not be with you before the winter, as I want to keep it in the studio a little while after it is finished. It is a great pleasure to me, as I work, to think where it is going, and that it will be before the eyes of those whom I love, and that they will have my first work sent from Italy.

❖

HARRIET HOSMER TO CORNELIA CROW CARR (SCHOOL FRIEND OF HOSMER)
Rome, April 22, 1853

I have not the least idea that I shall see America for five years at the inside. I have determined that, unless recalled by accident, I will stay until I shall have accomplished certain things, be that time, three, five, or ten years. My father will make me a visit in about three years, I suspect, or when he wants very much to see me, and then it will be my turn to visit him. As by that time you might forget how I look, I have caused to be taken a Daguerre of myself in daily costume, also one for the Pater. They are, like Gilpin's hat and wig, "upon the way."

You ask me what I am doing, and in reply I can say I am as busy as a hornet. First, I am working on your Daphne, and then making some designs for bassi–relievi. I reign like a queen in my little room in Mr. Gibson's studio, and I love my master dearly. He is as kind to me as it is possible for you to imagine, and he is, after Rauch, the first sculptor of the age.

Don't ask me if I was ever happy before, don't ask me if I am happy now, but ask me if my constant state of mind is felicitous, beatific, and I will reply 'Yes.' It never entered into my head that anybody could be so content on this earth, as I am here. I wouldn't live anywhere else but in Rome, if you would give me the Gates of Paradise and all the Apostles thrown in. I can learn more and do more here, in one year, than I could in America in ten. America is a grand and glorious country in some respects, but this is a better place for an artist.

HARRIET HOSMER TO WAYMAN CROW (PATRON OF HOSMER)
Rome, January 9, 1854

My father has made known to you his ill fortune, and had he made it known to me at an earlier period, I certainly should have sooner adopted the course I mean to pursue, viz: that of supporting myself. It now becomes my duty, as it is my pleasure, to relieve him of all expenses incurred by myself. On your goodness, then, my more than friend, I am forced to rely, and to accept the offer you have so generously made me. With such a start in the world, I think, nay, I am sure, I can make my own way, and perhaps the time may come when I can prove more sensibly than by words, that I am not unmindful of the obligations which I owe you. I am getting to know a little more of the world than I did once, and if I have gained this knowledge by costly experience, there is one comfort in thinking that it will never have to be paid for again.

As to my horse, I would gladly dispose of it, if I could. But the confinement of the studio during the greater part of the day makes it absolutely necessary for me to take some active exercise after my work is over. If Rome were Florence, one could walk, but you have seen enough of it to know what walks it offers, and the pure, fresh air is only to be found beyond the walls.

Now, dear Mr. Crow, in regard to your statue, by the time you receive this, I shall have begun the model. . . . Almost all artists have, and have had, a kind patron, and I am sure I may dub you mine. . . .

HARRIET HOSMER TO CORNELIA CROW CARR (SCHOOL FRIEND OF HOSMER)
Rome, April 22, 1854

. . . Do you remember what you said to me about becoming so fond of Italy that I should never want to go home to live? Oh! thy prophetic soul, it is even so! Here am I as merry as a cricket and as happy as a clam, finding the nights nothing and the days shorter. Never have eighteen months gone by so swiftly and happily, since I was born. I suppose it is, as Mr. Gibson says, because I have been always occupied; but there is something in the air of Italy, setting aside other things, which would make one feel at home in Purgatory itself. In America I never had that sense of quiet, settled content such as I now have from sunrise to sunset. . . .

There is the most charming circle of people here that you can imagine. Among them Mrs. Kemble and Mrs. Sartoris. Knowing these two, you will be able to judge how much they must contribute to anybody's happiness. They are like two mothers to me, and their house seems home all over. Then the Brownings are here, both so delightful, Mrs. Browning a perfect darling, and every Sunday and Wednesday evening there is a friendly party, as she calls it, at Mrs. Sartoris', consisting of Mrs. Kemble and the Brownings, two young artists and your humble servant. Mrs. Sartoris sings and Mrs. Kemble sometimes reads, and all in all, it is the perfection of everything that is charming. The Thackerays, too, have been here, and they are such dear girls. Every now and then there is an excursion projected for the Campagna, consisting of these same persons, and we go out for the day picnicking; thus I mingle amusement with study, and frolic with labor. Can you see how days could pass more rationally or agreeably?

I wish you could walk into my cozy little room in the studio, where all my days are spent, with the exception of the picnics. . . .

I want you so much to receive my first child (Daphne). I dare say you are tired of hearing about her and never seeing her, but the fact is, her little face was not quite clear, wanted a draught of Sarsaparilla to purify it, and so, as I desired of all people in the world that you and yours should have a fortunate fac–simile of her, I ordered another one to be cut, and as it is not a trifling job of a week or so, I have prevented from despatching her until now; but the workmen assure me it will be finished shortly, when, presto! it shall go to be kissed, and I hope, loved, by you all. At the same time I shall send another daughter to Boston, which you must make a point of visiting this summer.

HARRIET HOSMER TO WAYMAN CROW (PATRON OF HOSMER)
Rome, August 1854
By this time Bessie S. is Mrs. R. You see, everybody is being married but myself. I am the only faithful worshipper of Celibacy, and her service becomes more fascinating the longer I remain in it. Even if so inclined, an artist has no business to marry. For a man, it may be well enough, but for a woman, on whom matrimonial duties and cares weigh more heavily, it is a moral wrong, I think, for she must either neglect her profession or her family, becoming neither a good wife and mother nor a good artist. My ambition is to become the latter, so I wage eternal feud with the consolidating knot.

❖

HARRIET HOSMER TO WAYMAN CROW (PATRON OF HOSMER)
Rome, October 12, 1854
A painter . . . buys his canvas and his paints, which cost little and he is made; but from the time a sculptor begins, he finds that without funds he is at a standstill. Some seem to think that statues can be made like rail-fences. I do not agree with them. It is work, work, work, and if they would try their hands at it, they would become aware of the length of time one must study, before one can hope to do anything. Sometimes I cannot help thinking that too much is expected of me in so short a time as I have been here. Why, it is not three years yet, and what is that for learning so difficult an art in, an art which requires years and years to master? And when we consider that the first year I was kept copying the antique, it leaves rather a short time for me to have made my fortune in,

as I am afraid I was expected to do. My master is the one to know if I have made progress, and he is satisfied with me, and is not one easily satisfied either.

❖

HARRIET HOSMER TO CORNELIA CROW CARR (SCHOOL FRIEND OF HOSMER)
    Rome, October 30, 1854
    . . . I am taken to task for being an alien to my country, but do you know when one has lived in Rome for some time there is no place afterwards. It is a moral, physical and intellectual impossibility to live elsewhere. Everything is so utterly different here that it would seem like going into another sphere, to go back to America. Everything looks homey and the dear Italian tongue sounds as natural as English and everything is beautiful, I glory in the Campagna, the art is divine, and I dearly love the soft climate. I should perish in the cold winters at home, besides, I shall be positively tied here after this. I hope to have a studio and workmen of my own, and how could I be absent, for "*quando il gatto e fuori*," etc? Ah, there is nothing like it! I admire America, but (and I hear your reproaches) my heart's best love is for Italy. I wonder if Daphne has yet reached you? I hope you will like her and look upon her as a near relation. I am making a statue now that is to become yours one of these days. It makes me so happy to think that you will all have the very first things I send from Rome, — my first bust and first statue. I know they are going into kind, good hands, and I feel tenderly for them. You can't guess how busy I am from morning till night, nor how an artist must study and work to produce anything worthy of the name of art. Here have I been pegging away for more than two years, and I have learned just enough to feel that I know nothing; but *pazienza, col tempo tutto — forse.*

❖

HARRIET HOSMER TO ANNE DUNDAS (FRIEND OF HOSMER)
    September 27, 1856
    Nor have I been quiet either, while you have been on the wing, but have ridden to Florence by moonlight at the rate of fifty miles a night. Nothing was ever so fine as that journey. The entrance to Nepi, with its old towers and broken arches, the descent to the lake of Thrasimene, the climbing of the hill to Perugia, and the arrival at five in the morning at Florence, are all things to be set down in one's golden book. I remember particularly, too, the battleground of Hannibal, over which we rode at one o'clock on the loveliest night that was ever visited upon earth. In the silence and ghostliness of the hour, I could not help fancying I heard, above the clattering of our horses' feet, the rushing and neighing of steeds, the clashing of spears, and the shouts of the vanquished and conquering armies, but for two thousand years nature has been reclaiming her own and seems to have exhausted herself in making it one of the most beautiful spots in her kingdom, as if in a generous, forgiving spirit toward that humanity by which she was profaned. The ground was covered with fresh young vines and bright red poppies sown by some friendly Morpheus, perhaps, to make her forget in a long summer sleep the wrongs she had endured, and over all, the great, quiet moon, like a loving and pitying mother, watched as tenderly and as patiently as she did ages and ages ago. Oh! my A — — -, how

enchanted you would have been. There never was a more silent journey, for it was too beautiful to talk about. We wanted all our forces to think and to look, but thinking and looking were done to perfection. We came back by riding early in the morning and late in the evening, having made the three hundred and sixty miles in seven and a half days.

Yesterday I went into Rome to have photographs taken of my son and daughter; the latter was successful, the former only partly so, and we must try again. Master Puck's god-mother, you know, is to be that dear Mrs. Emily, to whom I am going to send the portraits of her devil-born god-child as soon as they can be printed. I shall send, too, the Œnone, which you must dispose of as you like best.

By the way, I have found a famous block of marble for the Cenci, and she is progressing in that material. I made several changes in her after you went away, for instance gave her a vast quantity more hair, putting very sizable locks over the raised shoulder, made a cushion of the upper stone (which was a great improvement), and put on (I'm sure you will say, 'Oh! horror!') a slipper!!! Perhaps you would be shocked if you saw that slipper, perhaps pleased; for my part, I liked it because it was more in costume, and from the arrangement of drapery I was afraid it might look like an affectation of the antique unless I had something to modernize it a bit. . . .

❖

HARRIET HOSMER TO WAYMAN CROW (PATRON OF HOSMER)
Rome, November 1857

I want to tell you of something which I think will please you, viz. a commission I have received to make a monument for the Church of *San Andrea delle Fratte* here. Madame Falconnet, who has just lost a daughter, has obtained permission to have a monument erected to her memory in this church, and has desired me to make it. It is to be a sleeping statue of the young girl, who (so much the better for me) was most lovely. The statue is to be placed upon a sarcophagus, and they have given us room enough to make an arch over it, so that we can have a background of darker marble, which will be a great thing for the figure. The place is good and the light magnificent. I shall endeavor to exhaust myself on the work, only saving enough of my corporeal and mental strength to drag my bones to St. Louis next year to behold you once more. I am very busy now, making a sketch of it (the monument, not the dragging of my bones), and my hands will be full for winter.

❖

HARRIET HOSMER TO ANNE DUNDAS (FRIEND OF HOSMER)
December 13, 1857

First of all, I wish to address myself to Mrs. Emily, and to thank her most sincerely for her tender affection for me. . . . Tell her, that I have a perfect little "Puck"; a little fellow I found and fell in love with in Albano, a wonderful pony whose only fault is in being too small, but strong as an elephant, full of wickedness, and is beginning to jump like a cat.

Of course you know all about poor Julie Falconnet's death, and perhaps you know that I am to make her monument. It is to be a sleeping statue of her, and I have this day finished the sketch, though Madame Falconnet has not yet seen it. I have represented her lying on a couch, the little feet crossed and a chaplet in one hand, while the other has fallen by her side. The dress is modern, of course, but very simple, with long flowing sleeves which compose well; that is all of it, and the beauty of the thing must depend on the fidelity with which I render the delicacy and elegance of her figure. A mask of her face was taken after death, which is very good, and that, with the bust, will enable me to get a good likeness of her. They have given me a capital place in the church (of *San Andrea delle Fratte*) with a beautiful light, and you may be sure I shall spare neither time nor patience on the work, but do the best I can for divers reasons, not the least of which is to prove to Madame Falconnet that I am grateful to her for the confidence she has shown in me; for it is not as if I were an old and experienced artist. Besides, I shall be very happy to have a work of mine in Rome, and such a *bella combinatione* cannot occur again.

I have begun a bas relief of "Night rising with the Stars," but was forced to suspend operations in that quarter till I had made the sketch for the monument, and while it is being set up in grand, I shall finish the former. . . .

❖

HARRIET HOSMER TO CORNELIA CROW CARR (SCHOOL FRIEND OF HOSMER)
Rome, January 8, 1858

I am busy now upon Zenobia, of a size with which I might be compared as a mouse to a camel. My mass of clay in its present humanized form is stunning. It certainly does make a larger piece of putty than I had anticipated, but I am consoled by, and rejoice in the fact, that it will be more grandiose when finished. To-morrow I mount a Zouave costume, not intending to break my neck upon the scaffolding, by remaining in petticoats....

Did I tell you that one day a lady visited my studio in company with another, a French lady. The stranger was charming in every way, I was delighted with her refinement and culture and in short fell quite in love with her. At the close of the visit, I accompanied the ladies to the gate. On their way the stranger stopped to admire some tulips and I plucked several and gave them to her. She received them very graciously and said, "When you come to Holland I will return the compliment." Some time after, I was in Holland on a very ceremonious occasion, and found my friend to be the late Queen of Holland. . . .

❖

HARRIET HOSMER TO ANNE DUNDAS (FRIEND OF HOSMER)
Rome, January 13, 1861

If you have not already been, pray go and see Rosa Bonheur and write me all about her. Mrs. Browning excepted, I do not know a woman for whom I have more respect and admiration than for her. I was greatly disappointed at not being able to find her when I was in Paris, but she was in the country, and so of course I couldn't even catch a glimpse of her studio. I wonder she doesn't come to Rome, at least for a time, for the whole Campagna would be her studio, and she would see it in all its wonderful beauty. Fancy the picture she might make of those regal gray oxen and those dragons of fidelity, the Campagna dogs! Browning told me she had half an idea of coming, and it is the most friendly advice one could give her.

I wish you were here to criticize my Fountain, the story of Hylas and the Water Nymphs, as perhaps I showed you in London.

HARRIET HOSMER TO [?]
   Rome, March 1861
   I had a discussion yesterday with Mr. May, he is a great woman's rights man, I find, just as much so as it seems to me is reasonable, that is, he thinks every woman should have the power of educating herself for any profession and then practicing it for her own benefit and the benefit of others. I don't approve of bloomerism and that view of woman's rights, but every woman should have the opportunity of cultivating her talents to the fullest extent, for they were not given her for nothing, and the domestic circle would not suffer thereby, because in proportion to the few who would prefer fighting their own way through the world, the number would be great who would choose a partner to fight it for them; but give those few a chance, say I. And those chances will be given first in America. What fun it would be to come back to this earth after having been a wandering ghost for a hundred years or so and see what has been going on in flesh while we have been going on in spirit!

HARRIET HOSMER TO WAYMAN CROW (PATRON OF HOSMER)
   Rome, May 26, 1865
   Just at this time I am having studio, house, and stable to look after, providing myself with all three at once, trying to get them in order, and to look after a dozen workmen besides. Oh, but you should see my studio, in order to see what things in the way of studios are capable of being made. I am going to have a copy of Lady Marian's fountain put up, complete, in the entrance room, not only complete, but playing, and I am going to have birds and flowers and every object of beauty, myself included, scattered about among the statues. In fact, I have no doubt people will come to see the appurtenances instead of the fine arts!

❖

HARRIET HOSMER TO WAYMAN CROW (PATRON OF HOSMER)
   Rome, March 1867
   . . . Turning from other things, here is my design. A subject for a chimney-piece ought to have something to do with wood or fire, so I have selected this, the Death of the Dryads. At the risk of telling you what you may already know, I will describe a little. According to mythology every tree had its own particular nymph, who dwelt in it; but when the tree died, the nymph died with it. Now I have represented these little lads busily engaged in cutting down the trees, and as they have cut off all but the last branches, there is nothing left for the Dryads but to die, which they are about to do. Below, two of the little fellows are warming themselves by the fire, which they are cutting wood to supply. That is the story. It is to be made of statuary marble and the figures are to be life size, so it will be something rather important. It is for Lady Ashburton, and is to be placed in the drawing–room at Melchet Court. . . .

❖

HARRIET HOSMER TO WAYMAN CROW (PATRON OF HOSMER)
Rome, January 4, 1869

I am making a statue of the Queen of Naples. I don't know that you ever saw that photograph of her with a cloak wrapped about her, called the Gaeta costume? She came to me the other day dressed exactly as she was then, spur and all. It will make an interesting statue, for the subject is invested with so much that is historic. I forgot to say there is a pile of cannon balls at her feet, and upon them I shall get her to write her name and Gaeta and the year. The costume is perfectly classic, and she is so beautiful and artistic looking that she lends herself wonderfully to art. . . .

❖

FROM HARRIET HOSMER, "THE PROCESS OF SCULPTURE" (*Atlantic Monthly*, 1864)

I have heard so much lately, about artists who do not do their own work, that I feel disposed to raise the veil upon the mysteries of the studio, and enable those who are interested in the subject to form a just conception of the amount of assistance to which a sculptor is fairly entitled, as well as to correct the false but very general impression, that the artist beginning with the crude block, and guided by his imagination only, hews out his statue with his own hands.

So far from this being the case, the first labor of the sculptor is upon a small clay model, in which he carefully studies the composition of his statue, the proportions, and the general arrangement of the drapery, without regard to very careful finish of parts. This being accomplished, and the small model cast in plaster, he employs some one to enlarge his work to any size which he may require; and this is done by scale, and with almost as much precision as the full-size and perfectly finished model is afterwards copied in marble.

The first step in this process is to form a skeleton of iron, the size and strength of the iron rods corresponding to the size of the figure to be modelled; and here, not only strong hands and arms are requisite, but the blacksmith with his forge, many of the irons requiring to be heated and bent upon the anvil to the desired angle. This solid framework being prepared, and the various irons of which it is composed firmly wired and welded together, the next thing is to hang thereon a series of crosses, often several hundred in number, formed by two bits of wood, two or three inches in length, fastened together by wire, one end of which is attached to the framework. All this is necessary for the support of the clay, which would otherwise fall by its own weight. (I speak here of Roman clay, — the clay obtained in many parts of England and America being more properly potter's clay, and consequently more tenacious.) The clay is then pressed firmly around and upon the irons and crosses with strong hands and a wooden mallet, until, from a clumsy and shapeless mass, it acquires some resemblance to the human form. When the clay is properly prepared, and the work advanced as far as the artist desires, his own work is resumed, and he then laboriously studies every part, corrects his ideal by comparison with living models, copies his drapery from actual drapery arranged upon the lay-figure, and gives to his statue the last refinement of beauty.

It will thus be seen that there is an intermediate stage, even in the clay, when the work passes completely out of the sculptor's hands and is carried forward by his assistant, — the work on which the latter is employed, however, obviously requiring not the least exercise of creative power, which is essentially the attribute of the artist. To perform the part assigned him, it is not necessary that the assistant should be a man of imagination or refined taste, — it is sufficient that he have simply the skill, with the aid of accurate measurements, to construct the framework of iron and to copy the small model before him. But in *originating* that small model, when the artist had nothing to work from but the image existing in his own brain, imagination, refined feeling, and a sense of grace were essential, and were called into constant exercise. So, again, when the clay model returns into the sculptor's hands, and the work approaches completion, often after the labor of many months, it is he alone who infuses into the clay that refinement and individuality of beauty which constitute his 'style,' and which are the test of the greater or less degree of refinement of his mind, as the force and originality of the conception are the test of his intellectual power.

The clay model having been rendered as perfect as possible, the sculptor's work upon the statue is virtually ended; for it is then cast in plaster and given into the hands of the marble-workers, by whom, almost entirely, it is completed, the sculptor merely directing and correcting the work as it proceeds. This disclosure, I am aware, will shock the many, who often ingeniously discover traces of the sculptor's hands where they do not exist. It is true, that in some cases, the finishing touches are introduced by the artist himself; but I suspect that few who have accomplished and competent workmen give much of their time to the mallet or the chisel, preferring to occupy themselves with some new creation, or considering that these implements may be more advantageously wielded by those who devote themselves exclusively to their use. It is also true, that, although the process of transferring the statue from plaster to marble is reduced to a science so perfect that to err is almost impossible, yet much depends upon the workmen to whom this operation is intrusted. Still, their position in the studio is a subordinate one. They translate the original thought of the sculptor, written in clay, into the language of marble. The translator may do his work well or ill, — he may appreciate and preserve the delicacy of sentiment and grace which were stamped upon the clay, or he may render the artist's meaning coarsely and unintelligibly. Then it is that the sculptor himself must reproduce his ideal in the marble, and breathe into it that vitality which, many contend, only the artist can inspire. But, whether skilful or not, the relation of these workmen to the artist is precisely the same as that of the mere linguist to the author who, in another tongue, has given to the world some striking fancy or original thought.

The Artist's Sister, Mme Pontillon, Seated on the Grass, 1873. Oil on canvas.
17¾" x 28½". The Cleveland Museum of Art, Gift of the Hanna Fund, 50.89

BERTHE MORISOT

1841–1895

FRENCH ARTIST **BERTHE** Morisot's inclusion among the Impressionist group is evident. She participated in all but one of the Impressionists' exhibitions, including the first, and had friendships and collegial relationships with many of the group's most celebrated members and their compatriots, including the painters Claude Monet, Pierre Auguste Renoir, Edgar Degas, and Édouard Manet and the poet Stéphane Mallarmé. A study of Morisot's work takes the viewer directly to the heart of the Impressionists' attempts to capture immediate visual experience. Respected by her peers, Morisot's work has nonetheless received less validation by art historians and critics than that of her more well-known (and male) colleagues.

As an active member of the principal avant-garde art movement of her time, Morisot distinguished herself from such other nineteenth-century women artists as the more artistically conservative Rosa Bonheur and Harriet Hosmer. Her personal biography also differed from many other women artists of her time, set apart as she was by marriage and child-rearing during her most productive working years. Morisot's prolific correspondence with her family and friends presents a picture of a dedicated artist, her work informed by the domestic milieu of a proper Parisian bourgeois woman and created within the artistic and social environment she shared with her male colleagues.

Although Morisot initially studied painting because it was considered a fitting accomplishment for a young woman, art soon assumed a prominent position in her life. The third daughter of a French civil servant and his wife, she spent her first decade in Bourges. In 1854, when her father was posted to Paris, the family moved to the Passy neighborhood where Berthe spent the remaining forty-odd years of her life. In the mid-1850s, Mme Morisot had all her three daughters take art lessons so that they could present their father with paintings for his birthday. Berthe and Edma, the middle sister, continued their studies with Joseph Guichard, who is said to have warned Mme Morisot that she might find the results "catastrophic" since the talents of both girls far surpassed the amateur level acceptable for the culti- vated bourgeois young lady. In 1861, the two sisters began to study plein-air painting with the landscape painter Achille Oudinot, through whose offices they encountered Camille Corot. Corot's influence appears in Berthe Morisot's early paintings, and it is believed that she may have been his student at one time. Begin- ning in 1864, both sisters exhibited at the annual Salon, Edma until she married in 1869 and ended her career, and Berthe until 1874, at which time she participated instead in the first Impressionist exhibition. That same year she married Eugène Manet (the painter Édouard Manet's younger brother) and, late in 1878, had her one child, Julie . Throughout her life Morisot worked steadily with no extended interruptions, writing to her sister Edma that "it is just as hard for a woman to break from a life of work as it is for a man."

Morisot was a founding member of the "Société Anonyme," the name the Impres- sionists gave themselves. (The label Impressionism originated with the press as a pejorative term.) Committed to the ideas of plein-air painting and unjuried exhi- bitions, she participated in all the Impressionist group exhibitions except the one in 1879, shortly after the birth of her child. Berthe Morisot's work falls into rough- ly three periods that parallel developments in the work of her male Impression- ist contemporaries. Even before she began exhibiting outside the Salon, Morisot was interested in finding a painterly structure suitable for expressing the imme- diacy of perception. Flat areas of color and form — far more static than in her later paintings — characterize most of her work from the late 1860s and early 1870s. We see the dominance of this formal structure in the way she uses a fan to con- nect the two figures in *Two Women* (a painting that also reveals the influence of *japonisme*). In a plein-air work such as *Harbor at Lorient*, Morisot uses patches of color and loose brushwork to convey the luminosity of water; touch is not near- ly as important here as it becomes in her mature work. The color in these early works is somewhat subdued, showing only occasional hints of the dramatic flair that marks her later pieces.

Morisot's mature Impressionist phase began around 1876 and continued for approximately ten years. Most Impressionists departed from the academic tradi- tion requiring the artist to hide all traces of the painting surface and his or her hand, using instead individual brush strokes as building blocks and allowing the white surface to show through. Contemporary critics perceived this aspect of Impres- sionism as a dissolution of form, and Morisot herself struggled with the issue of the painting process's visibility on the finished canvas, destroying, prior to the late 1870s, those canvases that she considered to be "unresolved." Her work of this peri- od is distinguished by fluid handling of paint with wildly broken brush strokes and a use of color which she first arrived at through experiments in watercolor. The colors are especially vivid: blues and greens predominate, punctuated by the lavender of a nurse's skirt or the orange hair of her daughter. The wild quality of her stroke and color schemes, and the frenetic energy they communicate, seem to be harbingers of the personalized, expressive use of brush strokes that characterizes work by later artists. She displayed her characteristic touch in such oil sketches as *Laundresses Hanging Out Wash* (1876) and in major canvases, including *The Lake in the Bois de Boulogne* (1879) and a portrait of her daughter Julie, *On the Verandah* (1884).

Around 1886 Morisot began to develop the style in which she worked until her death of pulmonary congestion in 1895. Morisot's working method changed during this last period of her life and, for the first time, she used preparatory drawings with regularity, perhaps because, like Renoir, she felt a need for more structural control. In these later works the direction of longer brush strokes is used to define the forms they represent. Despite the greater formal integrity of individual figures, these works have even more of an expressionist flavor than the earlier paintings and a more fluid, "unfinished" quality — as typified by such pieces as *The Cherry Tree* (1891–92) or *Girl With a Greyhound (Julie)* (1893). Some critics have suggested that the works from this period are not as strong as those from the previous phase of her career; however, Morisot remained at the height of her artistic powers until a cold that turned to pneumonia ended her life abruptly when she was only fifty-three.

Berthe Morisot held an integral position in the Impressionist movement on the basis of several factors. Among others, her work exemplifies the Impressionists' conscious attempt to redefine the nature of painting, and her stylistic development from plein-air realism to a more radical grammar of recording immediate perceptions parallels that of most of her male colleagues. Also, she was a professional and physical presence while the movement developed: she associated with other Impressionists, she exhibited her work in their exhibitions, and her work was handled by the dealers and collectors of Impressionist art. In other words, she was *there*, a member of the group. Morisot, however, has never been accorded the status of her stellar male colleagues, such as Renoir, Monet, and Degas. Although the contemporary documentary evidence makes it clear that she was accepted by both the press and other artists as a colleague, her career success was still marked by inconsistencies. For example, she did not have her first one-artist show until she was in her late forties — three years before she died — and, upon her death, Degas bemoaned her lack of reputation. Even today, reviews of Morisot's work acknowledge her achievements grudgingly, suggesting that she was a good, competent artist but surely not a great one. In fact, the excellence of her work may well have been overshadowed by her gender, resulting in a negative impact on her status as a member of the Impressionist group, on the perceptions of contemporary critics, and even on the current judgment of art historians.

Morisot does not appear to have been the victim of overt gender discrimination. She was not excluded from the study of art and, unlike her academic contemporaries, she was not consigned to studying anatomy from cows instead of humans. She sold a reasonable number of works during her life; and the fact that she did not more vigorously drive her career might have been more a function of her secure economic status than of her gender. Her social status enabled her to associate with other, like-minded artists and she held the respect of her confreres: in fact, Mallarmé and Degas were the executors of her estate, and Camille Pissarro wrote to his son that he was distraught at the death of their "comrade."

The content of Morisot's work is one area in which her gender may have exerted a subtle influence on her artistic success. Her subjects were primarily women in domestic, everyday situations. She painted them sewing, having tea, picking fruit, polishing silver, gazing at or nursing babies, playing with children, reading books, preparing for the theater. She showed her daughter reading, playing in the garden and with her dog, fixing her cousin's hair. Morisot's choice of subjects was markedly different from that of her male colleagues: she depicted the private "spaces of femininity" while they painted the more public life of the streets, cafés, and dance halls.

Many of Morisot's themes are similar to those of another woman Impressionist, Mary Cassatt. (See, for instance, Morisot's *The Cherry Tree* and Cassatt's *Two Women Picking Fruit* or Morisot's *Julie With Doll* and Cassatt's *Little Girl in a Blue Armchair*.) Their letters show that the women were acquainted with each other, although scarcely intimates, and aside from their shared social class, their lives and artistic styles differed greatly. Although some critics suggest that both artists' views were conservative, based on their acceptance of traditional gender differentiation, neither of them devalued the "female world of love and ritual" of which each was a part. In fact, both Morisot and Cassatt were artistically innovative in their expansion of the accepted iconography through incorporation of details from the domestic, private sphere into their public art.

The difference between the content of their work and that of their male colleagues illuminates women's problematic relationship to Impressionism and the art world in general. On the one hand, direct observation of domestic interactions would seem quite consistent with Impressionism, a movement that celebrated immediate perception of the everyday, whether seen in a haystack, a café scene, or a mother gazing at her child. On the other, as Tamar Garb and Kathleen Adler have suggested, the domestic content of Morisot's painting is at odds with the late nineteenth-century image of artist as *flâneur*, defined as a person who inhabited the public spaces of the modern city. Both art and literature have traditionally reflected the cultural devaluation and trivialization of women's private and intimate lives, and, hence, Morisot's subject matter was not considered correct material for "real art." This bias also had a direct impact on her status as an artist among artists. Her life — including marriage, a child, and close involvement with the lives of her sisters — did not follow the pattern of her male counterparts. She was no *flâneur* and, according to Griselda Pollock in *Vision and Difference*, as a proper lady she was excluded from the spaces that gave her male colleagues their freedom. And, although she was able to engage in their modernist conversation, she often felt awkward about participating in some of the Impressionists' functions. Anne Higgonet suggests that Morisot did not participate in the organizational meetings of the Société Anonyme, perhaps because they were held in cafés. Additionally, a letter to Mallarmé makes it clear that she refused his invitation to attend the Tuesday-evening literary discussions that he hosted, although he and many of the Impressionist painters regularly frequented the cultural soirées held each Thursday in the Morisot-Manet household.

Adding also to the critical devaluation of Morisot's work was its unique style. More fluid than that of Manet, Renoir, and Cassatt, it was almost proto-expressionistic and, like Cézanne, she was criticized for its "unfinished" quality. Her extremely sensitive approach to surface, touch, and finish was consistently described as "feminine," perhaps not intended pejoratively in the context of the times, but still a denigrating evaluation of Morisot's style.

A selection of letters, interspersed with biographical commentary, was first published by Morisot's grandson, Denis Rouart, in 1950. That selection is the source of the excerpts included in this volume. Garb and Adler's introduction to the 1987 edition of Rouart's volume points out that the Morisot persona he presented was his own construction. Although Rouart was proud of his grandmother's achievements, he bemoaned the fact that her letters "never touch upon the fundamentals." When read critically, however, the letters yield much important information about her life, her art, and the integration of the two. They show how dependent she was on the connection with her mother and sisters (particularly Edma, who had originally shared her artistic ambitions) and how, like Rosa Bonheur, she gained much support from the separate, feminine sphere. The letters also reveal her easy intimacy with such men as Renoir and Mallarmé, who were her true compatriots in art. Unlike Bonheur, who assumed a "masculine" voice in addressing her fellow artists, Morisot spoke to her male colleagues as the upper bourgeois woman that she was. While her earlier letters were mostly to her immediate family, in later correspondence she wrote more frequently to her artistic colleagues. Throughout, Morisot shows us her family as well as her professional world — her delight in her relationship with her daughter, Julie; her husband's efforts to facilitate her career; and his emotional support of her when he advised "Keep visitors out, see people only at night, and lock your door when you are working." Most significantly, perhaps, the letters reveal the persistence of work in Morisot's life — her contentment when it seemed to be going well and her despair when she felt she was working poorly. Morisot was intensely self-critical, and the moodiness in her writing creates an intriguing contrast with the more upbeat nature of her art.

Morisot's unpublished correspondence and four notebooks are held in private collections. Art historians can only hope for the eventual publication of these materials, which would provide an additional picture of the private context that can help us to understand Morisot's artistic achievements in the public realm.

SOURCES

Adler, Kathleen, and Tamar Garb. *Berthe Morisot*. Ithaca, N.Y.: Cornell University Press, 1987.

Morisot, Berthe. *Correspondence*. Edited by Denis Rouart. Translated by Betty W. Hubbard. Introduction by Kathleen Adler and Tamar Garb. Mt. Kisco, N.Y.: Moyer Bell, 1987.

Higgonet, Anne. *Berthe Morisot*. New York: Harper and Row, 1990.

Pollock, Griselda. *Vision and Difference: Femininity, Feminism and the Histories of Art*. London and New York: Routledge, 1988.

Stuckey, Charles, and William P. Scott, with Suzanne G. Lindsay. *Berthe Morisot, Impressionist*. New York: Hudson Hills Press, 1987.

EXCERPTS FROM BERTHE MORISOT'S CORRESPONDENCE, 1869–1895
FROM *CORRESPONDENCE,* EDITED BY DENIS ROUART,
TRANSLATED BY BETTY W. HUBBARD (MT. KISCO, N.Y.: MOYER BELL, 1987)

BERTHE MORISOT TO EDMA PONTILLON (NÉE MORISOT, SISTER OF MORISOT)

April 1869

I am not any more cheerful than you are, my dear Edma, and probably much less so. Here I am, trapped because of my eyes. I was not expecting this, and my patience is very limited. I count the days passed in inaction, and foresee many a calamity, as for example that I shall be spending May Day here with poultices on my eyes. But let us talk about you. I am happy to think that your wish may be fulfilled. I have no knowledge of these matters, but I believe in your premonitions. In any case, I desire it with all my heart, for I understand that one does not readily accustom oneself to life in the country and to domesticity. For that, one must have something to look forward to. Adolphe would certainly be surprised to hear me talking in this way. Men incline to believe that they fill all of one's life, but as for me, I think that no matter how much affection a woman has for her husband, it is not easy for her to break with a life of work. Affection is a very fine thing, on condition that there is something besides with which to fill one's days. This something I see for you in motherhood.

Do not grieve about painting. I do not think it is worth a single regret.

❖

BERTHE MORISOT TO EDMA PONTILLON (NÉE MORISOT, SISTER OF MORISOT)

May 2, 1869

The first thing we beheld as we went up the big staircase was Puvis' painting. It looked well. Jacquemard was standing in front of it and seemed to admire it greatly. What he seemed to admire less was my person. There is nothing worse than a former admirer. Consequently he forsook me very quickly. However, we next met Carolus Duran, who was with his wife, and who on seeing us blushed violently. I shook hands with him, but he did not have a word to say to me. His wife is a tall and handsome woman. He is showing a portrait of her, which, I think, is going to be a success, although it is quite vulgar. It isn't absolutely bad, but I find it mannered and flat. I don't have to tell you that one of the first things I did was to go to Room M. There I found Manet, with his hat on in bright sunlight, looking dazed. He begged me to go and see his painting, as he did not dare move a step.

I have never seen such an expressive face as his; he was laughing, then had a worried look, assuring everybody that his picture was very bad, and add in the same breath that it would be a great success. I think he has a decidedly charming temperament, I like it very much.

His paintings, as they always do, produce the impression of a wild or even a somewhat unripe fruit. I do not in the least dislike them, but I prefer his portrait of Zola.

❖

BERTHE MORISOT TO EDMA PONTILLON (NÉE MORISOT, SISTER OF MORISOT)

August 13, 1869

Manet lectures me, and holds up that eternal Mademoiselle Gonzalès as an example; she has poise, perseverance, she is able to carry an undertaking to a successful issue, whereas I am not capable of anything. In the meantime he has begun her portrait over again for the twenty-fifth time. She poses every day, and every night the head is washed out with soft soap. This will scarcely encourage anyone to pose for him!

❖

BERTHE MORISOT TO EDMA PONTILLON (NÉE MORISOT, SISTER OF MORISOT)
September 1869

I wanted to write yesterday, day before yesterday, in fact I have wanted to write all of these past days: painting alone is the reason for my silence. Roused by your example, I too wanted to do my plums and my flowers, the whole thing on a white napkin. This gave me an awful lot of trouble, with insignificant results. This mode of exercise annoys me deeply. . . .

I saw your friend Fantin, who inquired about you. He has become more ill-natured and unattractive than ever. While listening to his disparagements of everyone, I thought of what Degas says of him, and I concluded that he is not wrong in maintaining that Fantin is becoming as sour as an old maid. . . . We spent Thursday evening at Manet's. He was bubbling over with good spirits, spinning a hundred nonsensical yarns, one funnier than another. As of now, all his admiration is concentrated on Mademoiselle Gonzalès, but her portrait does not progress; he says that he is at the fortieth sitting and that the head is again effaced. He is the first to laugh about it. . . .

❖

BERTHE MORISOT TO EDMA PONTILLON (NÉE MORISOT, SISTER OF MORISOT)
September 1869

During the day I received a visit from Puvis de Chavannes. He saw what I had done at Lorient and seemed to find it not too bad. Tell Adolphe that when we examined the pier he complimented me on my knowledge of perspective, and that naturally I gave full credit where it was due. . . .

The Manets came to see us Tuesday evening, and we all went into the studio. To my great surprise and satisfaction, I received the highest praise; it seems that what I do is decidedly better than Eva Gonzalès. Manet is too candid, and there can be no mistake about it. I am sure that he liked these things a great deal; however, I remember what Fantin says, namely, that Manet always approves of the painting of people whom he likes. Then he talked to me about finishing my work, and I must confess that I do not see what I can do. . . . As he exaggerates everything, he predicted success for me in the next exhibition, though he has said many unpleasant things to me. . . . Since I have been told that without knowing it I produced masterpieces at Lorient, I have stood gaping before them, and I feel myself no longer capable of anything. . . .

Decidedly, I am too nervous to make anyone sit for me, and then the opinions of this one and that one worry me, and make me disgusted with things before they are in place. . . .

Manet exhorted me so strongly to do a little retouching on my painting of you, that when you come here I shall ask you to let me draw the head again and add some touches at the bottom of the dress, and that is all. He says that the success of my exhibition is assured and that I do not need to worry; the next instant he adds that I shall be rejected. I wish I were not concerned with all this.

❖

BERTHE MORISOT TO EDMA PONTILLON (NÉE MORISOT, SISTER OF MORISOT)
Winter 1870

Mother wrote to you at the time Puvis told me that the head was not done and could not be done; whereupon great emotion; I took it out, I did it over again. Friday night I wrote him a note asking him to come to see me; he answered immediately that this was impossible for him and complimented me a great deal on all the rest of the picture, advising me only to put some accents on mother's head. So far no great misfortune. Tired, unnerved, I went to Manet's studio on Saturday. He asked me how I was getting on, and seeing that I felt dubious, he said to me enthusiastically: "Tomorrow, after I have sent off my pictures, I shall come to see yours, and you may put yourself in my hands. I shall tell you what needs to be done."

The next day, which was yesterday, he came at about one o'clock; he found it very good, except for the lower part of the dress. He took the brushes and put in a few accents that looked very well; mother was in ecstasies. That is where my misfortunes began. Once started, nothing could stop him; from the skirt he went to the bust, from the bust to the head, from the head to the background. He cracked a thousand jokes, laughed like a madman, handed me the palette, took it back; finally by five o'clock in the afternoon we had made the prettiest caricature that was ever seen. The carter was waiting to take it away; he made me put it on the hand-cart, willy-nilly. And now I am left confounded. My only hope is that I shall be rejected. My mother thinks this episode funny, but I find it agonizing.

I put in with it the painting I did of you at Lorient. I hope they take only that. . . .

❖

BERTHE MORISOT TO EDMA PONTILLON (NÉE MORISOT, SISTER OF MORISOT)
May 1870

. . . I am still engrossed in this wretched painting. I certainly did show my two pictures; it is my principle never to try to rectify a blunder, and that is the main reason why I did not profit from my mother's intervention. Now I am thankful: having got over my first emotion, I find that one always derives benefit from exhibiting one's work, however mediocre it may be. On the other hand I am not receiving a great many compliments, as you think, but everyone is sufficiently kind enough not to make me feel any regrets, except of course Degas, who has a supreme contempt for anything I do. . . .

❖

BERTHE MORISOT TO EDMA PONTILLON (NÉE MORISOT, SISTER OF MORISOT)
Summer/Fall 1871

The water-colour looks very well now that it is framed. The dealer, who is, I am told, one of the most important in Paris, complimented me very highly, and said that it had attracted notice from all the artists who came to his establishment. I did not dare to ask him whether he would buy some of my work. I shall wait to do that until I have other pictures to offer him.

I hear that Fantin is making a fortune in London. Tissot is earning a lot of money, and little Clauss is delighted with her stay there. All these people are stealing my idea. Write to me in all seriousness what you would do if you were in my place. Yesterday my mother told me politely that she has no faith in my talent, and that she thinks me incapable of ever doing anything worthwhile. I see that she thinks me raving mad when I tell her that I must certainly have as much talent as Mlle Jacquemard.

I did not go to Manet's last Thursday. . . . On the preceding Thursday he was very nice to me. Once more he thinks me not too unattractive, and wants to take me back as his model. Out of sheer boredom, I shall end by proposing this very thing myself. I should like very much to see what you are doing. I am sure it is very good. The atmosphere of Cherbourg is favourable for painting. It seems that the water-colour of you in gray is my masterpiece — not the other. I am sorry you have not attempted this medium, which is much easier, because one can be successful without being aware of it.

I am doing Yves with Bichette. I am having great difficulty with them. The work is losing all its freshness. Moreover, as a composition it resembles a Manet. I realize this and am annoyed.

❖

BERTHE MORISOT TO EDMA PONTILLON (NÉE MORISOT, SISTER OF MORISOT)
St. Jean de Luz, Summer 1872

We shall stay here only three or four more days. I am not sorry, for frankly I am beginning to tire of being here. There is constant sun, good weather all the time, the ocean like a slab of slate — there is nothing less picturesque than this combination. We are going to Madrid, at least we think we are. I have written to Manet asking him for the address of Astruc who, I know, has been there for a fairly long time. He will be of great help to me, since he speaks Spanish and knows Madrid thoroughly, and he certainly will be able to point out to us the things worth seeing. He must feel about the Museum pretty much as I do. I am very sorry that you are not with us. I should enjoy the trip much more if you were in the party. We should give ourselves plenty of time to admire the Velasquez and the Goyas. That is for me about the only interest in going. . . .

❖

BERTHE MORISOT TO EDMA PONTILLON (NÉE MORISOT, SISTER OF MORISOT)
St. Jean de Luz, Summer 1872

. . . You will be surprised by the meagreness of my output when I return, but I am very philosophical. I work when I can, and when I feel like it, without being much concerned about the result.

❖

BERTHE MORISOT TO EDMA PONTILLON (NÉE MORISOT, SISTER OF MORISOT)
1872 or 1873

I sent my Cherbourg seascape to M—. He was to show it to Durand-Ruel. I have not heard anything about it since. I am eager to earn a little money, and I am beginning to lose all hope. Have you worked this week? You are far more fortunate than I am: you work when you feel like it, and that is the only way in which one can do good work. As for me, I work hard without respite or rest, and it's pure waste. . . .

❖

BERTHE MORISOT TO TIBURCE MORISOT (BROTHER OF MORISOT)
January 1875

My dear Tiburce: Eugène tells me that this is the day the mail goes off and for fear of missing another opportunity of writing to you, I am scribbling a few words in haste. The thought of you has obsessed me for several weeks, *mon pauvre ami*; where are you, what are you doing? I should give a great deal to know these things, and even more to be able to contribute in some way to your happiness. As for myself, I have been married a month now; it's strange, isn't it? I went through that great ceremony without the least pomp, in a dress and a hat, like the old woman that I am, and without guests.

Since then I have been awaiting developments, but up to now luck has not favoured us much. The trip to Constantinople, so definite, so certain at first, is no longer so. I must not complain, however, since I have found an honest and excellent man, who I think loves me sincerely. I am facing the realities of life after living for quite a long time in chimeras that did not give me much happiness — and yet, thinking of my mother, I wonder if I have really done my duty. All these questions are complicated, and it is not easy, for me at least, to distinguish clearly between the right and the wrong. . . .

❖

BERTHE MORISOT TO EDMA PONTILLON (NÉE MORISOT, SISTER OF MORISOT)
Cowes [England], Summer 1875

I regret very much, my dear Edma, that your wish should be a wish impossible of realization, and that you cannot come to join me here. It is actually no more difficult to get here than to go anywhere in France, but one makes a great to-do of this crossing. Cowes has become extremely animated; a few days ago the whole of the smart set landed from a yacht. The garden of the Yacht Club is full of ladies of fashion. At high tide there is an extraordinary bustle. But all that is not for us — we are only humble folk, too insignificant to mingle with this fashionable society. Moreover, I do not know how one would go about it, unless one had a fortune of several millions and a yacht, and were a member of the club. I am completely indifferent to all this; I do not care for new acquaintances, and this society, from the little I have seen of it, seems to be as dull as it is wealthy. At the Goodwood races I was struck by the elegance and the bored air of the women. On the other hand, the populace seemed very gay — there was an animation that contradicts the notions we have about people of the north.

I am horribly depressed tonight, tired, on edge, out of sorts, having once more the proof that the joys of motherhood are not meant for me. That is a misfortune to which you would never resign yourself, and despite all my philosophy, there are days when I am inclined to complain bitterly over the injustice of fate.

My work is going badly, and this is no consolation. It is always the same story: I don't know where to start. I made an attempt in a field, but the moment I had set up my easel more than fifty boys and girls were swarming about me, shouting and gesticulating. All this ended in a pitched battle, and the owner of the field came to tell me rudely that I should have asked for permission to work there, and that my presence attracted the village children who caused a great deal of damage.

On a boat one has another kind of difficulty. Everything sways, there is an infernal lapping of water; one has the sun and the wind to cope with, the boats changed position every minute, etc. . . . The view from my window is pretty to look at, but not to paint. Views from above are almost always incomprehensible; as a result of all this I am not doing much, and the little I am doing seems dreadful to me. . . . I miss the babies as models; one could make lovely pictures with them on the balcony. . . .

BERTHE MORISOT TO EDMA PONTILLON (NÉE MORISOT, SISTER OF MORISOT)
London, Fall 1875

I have received your letter here, my dear Mame. It was forwarded from Cowes. We left that little place very hurriedly; Eugène was depressed and I was in a bad temper, because I was doing only poor work. Here we have recovered our spirits a little. We walk a great deal, we look at many things, we even work. At least, for two successive days now we have made attempts to work on the Thames; the results are an unsuccessful water-colour and a pastel that according to Eugène is very good. You will be surprised that having so little time to spend in London we waste the hours on the water. But Eugène does not like to see the sights any more than I do. We live in London as Parisians live in Paris: we stroll about, we spend our days sometimes here, sometimes there.

I visited the National Gallery, of course. I saw many Turners (Whistler, whom we liked so much, imitates him a great deal), Wilkies, Gainsboroughs, and Hogarths. Unfortunately the museum is small; but the things I saw gave me a great desire to become thoroughly acquainted with English painting. We went to see Tissot, who does very pretty things that he sells at high prices; he lives like a king. We dined there. He is very nice, a very good fellow, though a little vulgar. We are on the best of terms; I paid him many compliments, and he really deserves them. . . .

BERTHE MORISOT TO YVES GOBILLARD (SISTER OF MORISOT)
Winter 1879

Well, I am just like everyone else! I regret that Bibi is not a boy. In the first place because she looks like a boy; then, she would perpetuate a famous name, and mostly for the simple reason that each and every one of us, men and women, are in love with the male sex. . . . Your Bibi is a darling; you'll find mine ugly in comparison, with her head as flat as a paving stone. Edma's photograph has dispelled all my illusions about her. . . . All poor Julie has to offer is her fat cheeks and her pretty complexion. . . . Another piece of news, less distressing: Eva Gonzalès is married. . . . Don't accuse me of being neglectful, my dear, I think of you and your children continually, but my life is becoming complicated, I have little time, and then I have my days of melancholy, my black days when I am afraid to take up a pen for fear of being dull. The death of the poor dear duchess made me pass through one of these bad phases. Mme Carré told me the other day, laughing at my looks: "I think you have lived too long." Well, this is true. Inasmuch as I see everything that I have known and loved disappear, I have lived too long. The loss of friends can no longer be replaced at my age, and the void is great.

BERTHE MORISOT TO EUGÈNE MANET (HUSBAND OF MORISOT)
March 1882

. . . I cannot get over everything you did for me in that first day; it seems to me that you are working yourself to death, and all on my account. This touches me deeply and vexes me at the same time. I am a little dumbfounded by your announcement that you have taken the picture of you and Bibi — this picture seems perfectly absurd to me. Please, look at it a second time. Besides, I am working on the picture begun in my room, I shall send it if I can, and that will make a good many Bibis, won't it? If my pictures are to be seen on easels, that is at very close quarters, one must not show things that might appear grotesque. However, you will see how they will impress the other exhibitors, and one can always make a change. . . .

❖

BERTHE MORISOT TO EUGÈNE MANET (HUSBAND OF MORISOT)
Spring 1882

It is impossible to set up one's easel because of the wind. I have worked in my room too much; with a model like Bibi one can advance only very slowly, unless one wants to risk ruining everything. It was going well, but it is not going well anymore; I am not despairing of getting it into shape again, although it will take longer than you think.

Am I not a failure at the exhibition? I have a feeling that I am, but I have become very philosophical. That sort of thing no longer depresses me as it had formerly. . . .

❖

BERTHE MORISOT TO EUGÈNE MANET (HUSBAND OF MORISOT)
Spring 1882

I received the newspapers last night and read them with great interest. Sisley and Pissarro seem to get all the glory. Why not Monet? This surprises me. I can see from here that my poor big *Marie* is a caricature. I don't think she has been badly reviewed at all. What does Edouard say of the exhibition as a whole? Has he been there? It seems to me that there are some good things despite Wolf's stupid article. . . .

Have you met Miss Cassatt? Why did she back out? Our friend Vignon seems to have a nice little success; not much mention is made of Guillaume though he has talent, and particularly a more clear-cut personality. Gauguin and I seem to play the part of the comic characters. Or am I mistaken? Do not be afraid to tell me, since being far away I am very philosophical.

❖

BERTHE MORISOT TO EDMA PONTILLON (NÉE MORISOT, SISTER OF MORISOT)
May 1883

My dear Edma, thank you for your affectionate letter, and thanks also to Adolphe, who wrote Eugène a note that touched him very much. These last days were very painful; poor Edouard suffered atrociously. His agony was horrible. In a word, it was death in one of its most appalling forms that I once again witnessed at very close range.

If you add to these almost physical emotions my old bonds of friendship with Edouard, an entire past of youth and work suddenly ending, you will understand that I am crushed. The expressions of sympathy have been intense and universal; his richly endowed nature compelled everyone's friendship; he also had an intellectual charm, a warmth, something indefinable, so that, on the day of his funeral, all the people who came to attend — and who usually are so indifferent on such occasions — seemed to me like one big family mourning one of their own.

I shall never forget the days of my friendship and intimacy with him, when I sat for him and when the charm of his mind kept me alert during those long hours.

❖

BERTHE MORISOT TO EDMA PONTILLON (NÉE MORISOT, SISTER OF MORISOT)
Summer 1884

It is very sweet of you to have sent me Jeannot's diary, which I find very nice and which touches me deeply. However, I know how much the admirations of our youth are dispelled with the years; after she has acquired all the lucidity of mature age, she will judge her aunt quite differently, that is to say, as she deserves. She is sweet, this little darling, and to record her thoughts every day is an excellent idea; nothing forms one's style more effectively. And by this I mean not the habit of turning out fine phrases but of putting one's thoughts into words. It even seems to me that we ought to be very lenient, to condone lack of correctness, provided that the feeling is real, and that the ideas are personal.

Correctness will be the natural result of practice and constant effort, especially when one devotes oneself to this study from early youth. I could never write four consecutive lines that made sense, owing to my laziness as a young girl, to the great difficulties I experienced — if I had made an effort it might have degenerated into originality. All this perturbs me because I have just been glancing through the diary of Marie Pau. Do you know it? I read the most laudatory articles about it, and I am deeply disappointed. What shocks me is to see this girl of fourteen write as grammatically as if she were twenty-five; all this in a monotonous correct prose which savours neither of life nor of youth, and which drags on listlessly from the beginning to the end of the volume. In truth, I think that the 'not bad' is further removed from the good than is the bad. Don't you think so?

In short, let Jeannot develop freely; if I were you I would be particular in the choice of reading — no drivel, nothing sentimental, nothing affected, as many good old French authors as possible. We are all born monkeys before we are ourselves; therein lies the danger of bad examples.

Paule too seems to have a certain fluency of style which I am urging her mother to cultivate. Why should there not be as much chance of success in a literary future as in an artistic one? In England all the women are going in for novel writing; I think there is a great future for the new generation in that; all these husbandless *bachelières* will want to take up their pens.

I don't know what makes me write all this, and in addition so illegibly that you won't be able to read it. Don't go blind on account of this, it is not worth the trouble.

❖

BERTHE MORISOT TO EDMA PONTILLON (NÉE MORISOT, SISTER OF MORISOT)
Spring 1885

I am working with some prospect of having an exhibition this year: everything I have done for a long time seems to me so horribly bad that I should like to have new, and above all better, things to show to the public. This project is very much up in the air, Degas' perversity makes it almost impossible of realization; there are clashes of vanity in this little group that make any understanding difficult. It seems to me that I am about the only one without any pettiness of character; this makes up for my inferiority as a painter.

❖

BERTHE MORISOT TO EDMA PONTILLON (NÉE MORISOT, SISTER OF MORISOT)
Rotterdam, Fall 1885

Ma chère amie, I received your letter just as I was leaving, having suddenly resolved to go to Holland instead of to Italy. I think you would like this country very much, particularly Amsterdam. I am enchanted with it, but the season is already too far along, and it is almost impossible for us to work outdoors. At the same time everything that passes before your eyes here makes you yearn to paint. The temperature is still very pleasant for walking, and the light and the sky have infinite charm.

Eugène was bored in Amsterdam, and we were spending a mad amount of money in a hotel too grand for us, so that we have fallen back on Rotterdam, and this I regret, for although the city is very beautiful, it is less characteristic, less Dutch. I have not yet seen The Hague; it is within walking distance; I do not know whether I shall like the museum, but that of Amsterdam was a disappointment. Rembrandt's famous 'Night Watch' seemed to me of the most disagreeable blackish brown, and, except for a charming portrait by Rubens, the other paintings are quite insignificant. . . .

At Haarlem I became acquainted with the work of Franz Hals, and there again I was disappointed. I had expected it to be better, judging from the figure in the La Caze gallery. His paintings show extreme skill, but they are commonplace. At least such was my first impression, and Bibi did not give me time to have a second one. Although she likes painting, museums bore her; she keeps tugging at me all the time to get it over with as soon as possible, and to be taken for a walk in the country.

❖

BERTHE MORISOT TO CLAUDE MONET (FRENCH IMPRESSIONIST PAINTER)
March 14, 1888

I think that you are very kind to reproach yourself on my account; the real truth is that the bad weather and my age are the only causes of my illnesses; I am becoming a bronchial old lady. At last I am on my feet again, and engaged in a pitched battle with my canvases. Do not depend on me to cover much wall space, I am not doing anything worth while despite my desire to do it, and the endless series of dark days we are having this year is an added obstacle. Your sun makes me envious as do other things too . . . even your "violence." You are being coy, but I well know that you are in good form, that you are doing delightful things, and I hope as much from Renoir, for it is you two who will make the exhibition.

The other day, at the older Goupil's, I saw pictures by Pissarro that are much less *pointillé*, and very beautiful; it seems to me that they might be liked. I went there to see the nudes of that fierce Degas, which are becoming more and more extraordinary.

We often talk about you with Mallarmé, who is very devoted and full of friendly feelings for you. He has lent me *Ten o'clock* by M. Whistler. I went to great pains to read his very literary English, without much profit.

❖

BERTHE MORISOT TO CLAUDE MONET (FRENCH IMPRESSIONIST PAINTER)
June 1888
Thank you very much for kindly remembering me and for your kind words about my wretched pictures at Durand's. I am all the more touched because, as you know, the show is a complete fiasco, and it seemed to me that each of us had his share of responsibility in this disaster, of course Renoir and Whistler less than the others; but all this the public cannot understand. As for you, you have conquered this recalcitrant public. At Goupil's one meets only people who have the highest admiration for you, and I find that there is much coquetry in your request to me to give you my opinion — I am simply dazzled! and you know it quite well. If you insist I shall tell you that the picture I like best is the one with the little red-brown tree in the foreground; my husband and I stood in ecstasy before it for an hour.

I saw Mallarmé on Thursday. I should be quite surprised if this charming man did not express all his admiration for you in a delightful letter. Both of us are still very eager to see you at Giverny, and I hope that next month the weather will be less unpleasant than this month.

❖

BERTHE MORISOT TO STÉPHANE MALLARMÉ (FRENCH POET)
September 1888
The answer is no, unfortunately, *cher ami* (I shall call you *cher maître*, if you prefer). We make this decision after much thought, having many reasons that are as sensible as they are dreary for remaining in Paris.

Mme Biard's proposal was very tempting, at least it seemed so despite my husband's prejudices against this poor woman. He had an unpleasant memory of quilts on beds (he could easily have taken them off).

In a word, we are leaving you entirely to your work and to your solitude, and you are less to be pitied than we who are living on our lovely recollections of last year.

I have still been planning to send you my masterpiece — not charming at all, though full of good intentions, but Lewis-Brown instead of meeting me at the printer's shop, as he promised, is being horribly lazy about it.

I am working fairly well, trying to take advantage of these beautiful days so rare this year; this is one of my sensible reasons for remaining in Paris.

Many regards from me to Miss Cassatt when you see her, and very affectionate regards from all of us to Mme Mallarmé and to Mlle Geneviève.

❖

BERTHE MORISOT TO SOPHIE CANAT
Cimiez, December 1888/January 1889
Your picture of our life here is all wrong. We are never on the Promenade des Anglais; our villa with its beautiful shade trees is all that we need. I am busy with Julie's lessons and also with my painting; we often walk in the mountains following the goat paths, though they are a little beyond my strength — my hair is as white as snow, and my legs are a little stiff.

As for society and parties, none at all, or at least as little as possible. I am enjoying my freedom thinking with some terror of the day when I shall have to take my daughter to dances.

❖

BERTHE MORISOT TO EDMA PONTILLON (NÉE MORISOT, SISTER OF MORISOT)
Cimiez, December 1888/January 1889
This place is delightful; I am working, I am doing aloes, orange trees, olive trees — in short, a whole exotic vegetation that it is quite difficult to draw. . . .

I have worked as much as I could; the result may seem meagre. . . . I should like to capture some of the charming effect of the surrounding vegetation. I am working myself to death trying to give the effect of the orange trees. I want it to be as delicate as it is in the Botticelli I saw in Florence, and this is a dream that I shall not realize. . . . I do not understand why this country here does not serve as a studio for all young landscapists: aside from its beauty one enjoys here an unchanging weather that makes possible the most careful studies. I won't say that work is easier here, for the landscape is fiendish, of an outline that does not permit of approximations and of colours that one never finds. It is extraordinary how much of Corot there is in the olive trees and the backgrounds. Now I can understand the title he loves — *Souvenir d'Italie.*

❖

BERTHE MORISOT TO CLAUDE MONET (FRENCH IMPRESSIONIST PAINTER)
Nice, March 7, 1889
My dear Monet, may I drop the 'dear Sir,' and treat you as a friend? Your letter has given me all the more pleasure because I was beginning to think that you had completely forgotten me. I have hoped throughout the winter that you would come somewhere in this region, or even, despite your prejudices against Nicé, to the villa Ratti. I am in a delightful place which you could have put to good use; I do not. I am working a great deal, but nothing comes of it. It is horribly difficult.

I know through Mallarmé that you have marvels at Van Gogh's, and indeed I regret that I am not there to see them. I shall make up for this by going to see you on my return. This will not be before the beginning of May. I am so comfortable here, and the country is so delightful, that the only thing I miss about Paris is my friends. My husband is very much better, my daughter looks like a peasant girl, and since we shall certainly not budge throughout the summer, I feel that it is better to take as much advantage as possible of the beautiful spring days.

❖

BERTHE MORISOT TO STÉPHANE MALLARMÉ (FRENCH POET)
Mezy, May 1890
. . . I have worked a great deal to prepare a room for you; nonetheless, my dear friend, you are forewarned. Wednesday I shall go to Miss Cassatt to see with her those marvellous Japanese prints at the Beaux-Arts. At five o'clock I shall be at the Gare Saint-Lazare, in the waiting room of the Mantes line. If you wish to join me there we shall travel together; you would spend Thursday with us and Friday morning you would take another express that will bring you to Paris at nine o'clock, that is to say, in time for the college, if you have classes.

All this, of course, if the fresh air of the country tempts you, if the weather is good; but you would give us great pleasure. The landscape will be less pretty later on. . . . No need to answer me if you come.

BERTHE MORISOT TO EDMA PONTILLON (NÉE MORISOT, SISTER OF MORISOT)
late 1890

I am well now but I have not yet got over the moral shock; I felt the embrace of death, and I am still terrified at the idea of all that might happen after I go, particularly to Julie. Have I ever told you that according to my will Mallarmé would be her guardian? But, how many buts. . . . If Eugène too went, or if he fell seriously ill, would you undertake to care for the child?

You ask me what I am doing. My attempts at colour prints are disappointing, and that was all that interested me. I worked all summer with a view to publishing a series of drawings of Julie. Worst of all, I am approaching the end of my life, and yet I am still a mere beginner. I feel myself to be of little account, and this is not an encouraging thought.

BERTHE MORISOT TO EDMA PONTILLON (NÉE MORISOT, SISTER OF MORISOT)
late 1890

Thank you for your affectionate letter; in a word, this is what I had — a rheumatic heart. Perhaps it is not as dangerous as it may seem to the patient, but the sensation is absolutely that your life is ebbing away, and since this will eventually happen one day or another, it is better to make arrangements concerning your loved ones.

I have always thought life to be a very precious thing, and I shall do everything in my power to live as long as possible. . . . Thank you for answering "Yes" so sweetly and for assuring me of your affection for Julie.

BERTHE MORISOT TO STÉPHANE MALLARMÉ (FRENCH POET)
Mezy, October 1891

My dear friend, we shall stay another week for the weather is marvellous. If you want to see the chateau, this is the time to come for we seem to be becoming seriously interested in buying it. . . .

Renoir has spent a few days with us, without his wife this time. I shall never succeed in describing to you my astonishment at the sight of this ungainly woman whom, I don't know why, I had imagined to be like her husband's paintings. I shall introduce her to you this winter.

I am in a hurry to return to Paris; I think that women never like the country wholeheartedly. At all events, I shall see you soon, and thanks for your letter; it is delightfully pretty, and almost touching.

BERTHE MORISOT TO LOUISE RIESENER
Summer 1892

Thank you, my dear Louise, for all the nice things you say to me about the exhibition, and also for your interest in my château. . . .

It was certainly a find, and I have a great satisfaction thinking that some day Julie will enjoy it and fill it with her children. But as for myself, I feel mortally sad in it, and am in a hurry to leave. During my husband's last days, his mind was haunted by this château, so that his memory is present here evoking all the sadness of his illness.

. . . I am very gratified to learn about what took place at Joyant's. I left Paris the day after the opening, which, needless to say, I did not attend. Renoir is in Spain, Mallarmé is busy, and, as you can imagine, Miss Cassatt is not one to write me about an exhibition of mine.

I came back one morning when I had business with my notary, and your charming cousin assured me that there were many visitors — but not at the time I was there. I was quite aware of that myself.

All in all, I shall tell you very frankly that the whole seemed to me less bad than I had expected, and that I did not dislike even the very odd pieces. Let us hope that in twenty years from now the new ones will have the same effect upon me.

❖

BERTHE MORISOT TO SOPHIE CANAT
October 7, 1892

You have understood perfectly, my dear friend: I do not write because my heart is filled with sorrow. But your letter was among those which I have put aside intending to answer. The affectionate memory that you have kept of Eugène touches me deeply: not everyone realized how kind and intelligent he was.

In brief, my dear friend, I am ending my life in the widowhood that you experienced as a young woman; I do not say in loneliness, since I have Julie, but it is a kind of solitude none the less, for instead of opening my heart I must control myself and spare her tender years the sight of my grief.

The situation of Yves is also heart-rending. Am I callous? For the past few days I have begun to be hopeful; the reports are somewhat better; the other day I showed a letter to Doctor Martin, and he thought on the basis of it that the progress of the disease was temporarily arrested.

I hope that your health is good, and I also hope that we shall meet again here. We now constitute a circle of old ladies of bygone days. Is not life strange? To think that we have already reached this point.

❖

BERTHE MORISOT TO JULIE MANET (DAUGHTER OF MORISOT)
March 1, 1895

My little Julie, I love you as I die; I shall still love you even when I am dead; I beg you not to cry, this parting was inevitable. I hoped to live until you were married . . . . Work and be good as you have always been; you have not caused me one sorrow in your little life. You have beauty, money; make good use of them. I think it would be best for you to live with your cousins, Rue de Villejust, but I do not wish to force you to do anything. Please give a remembrance from me to your aunt Edma and to your cousins; and to your cousin Gabriel give Monet's *Bateaux en réparation*. Tell M. Degas that if he founds a museum he should select a Manet. A souvenir to Monet, to Renoir, and one of my drawings to Bartholomé. Give something to the two concierges. Do not cry; I love you more than I can tell you. Jeannie, take care of Julie.

Reprinted from *Berthe Morisot: Correspondence*, edited by Denis Rouart, published by Moyer Bell Limited.

Five O'Clock Tea, c. 1880. Oil on canvas. 25½" x 36½".
M. Theresa B. Hopkins Fund. Courtesy, Museum of Fine Arts, Boston.

MARY CASSATT

1844–1926

AN **AMERICAN EXPATRIATE** whose entire career was spent in France, Mary Cassatt's name is familiar to the general public and her work is accepted within the art historical canon. Unlike the other American painters who transposed aspects of the Impressionist style to an American context, Cassatt participated in four Impressionist exhibitions. She was, however, also instrumental in bringing Impressionism to the attention of the American public through her advice to major collectors, particularly Louisine and H. O. Havemeyer. Like Harriet Hosmer's move to Rome, Cassatt's decision to remain in France — with the personal and artistic freedom it afforded — was vital to the success of her career. Cassatt's tenacious professionalism in the forefront of the public arena gave evidence of a career that could be described as masculine. Yet her choice of subjects and its emphasis on domestic, particularly maternal, themes represented a world view that is traditionally perceived as feminine. As an Impressionist, Cassatt was formally innovative and skilled at recording the spontaneous gesture. Her combination of the professional and the domestic helped in the acceptance of domestic interactions as serious artistic subject matter.

Writing was not as important to Cassatt as it was to some of the other artists included in this volume. Although the letters she wrote over her long life provide interesting documentation of her work and its context, she was not an obsessive writer nor a particularly vivid stylist. Her later correspondence is marred by illegibility resulting from her failing eyesight. Nonetheless, her letters help illuminate the content of her work, its social context and its importance in her life.

Cassatt's first exposure to European culture occurred during her childhood. She came from a privileged background — her mother belonged to an old Pennsylvania family, her father was a stockbroker — although, since the Cassatts spent little time at any one residence they were somewhat unconventional. At first their moves were within Pennsylvania, but in 1851 they left for Europe, stopping briefly in Paris before continuing on to Darmstadt, Germany, where they remained until 1855. After the death of a son, the Cassatts returned to Pennsylvania. In 1860, upon turning sixteen, Cassatt enrolled in the Pennsylvania Academy of the Fine Arts where she studied for the next five years, progressing from drawing from the models of antiquity through life drawing to painting. The women's curriculum differed at that time from the men's in that it omitted study from the nude model. All accounts suggest that Cassatt was part of a lively and committed group of young artists who were dedicated to becoming professionals.

As early as 1860, Cassatt felt it would be necessary to continue her studies abroad; her brother Alexander had written, "In three years Mary will want to go to Rome to study." Cassatt left for Paris late in 1865 and never again lived in the United States, with the exception of a short period of exile required by the Franco-Prussian War. During the next fifty-five years, she made only three other trips back "home," allegedly because acute seasickness prevented more voyages. It seems clear that her expatriation contributed to her achievement of professional status in a way that remaining in the United States would not have done. For example, during her penultimate stateside visit, a newspaper notice described Cassatt as the sister of the president of the Pennsylvania Railroad, rather than as an artist in her own right, and mentioned the exceptionally small size of her dog, rather than her own distinguished reputation.

Cassatt's first decade abroad was a period of apprenticeship in which she traveled frequently, exposing herself to diverse artistic influences, some of which included formal instruction. When she first arrived in Paris she took private lessons from Jean-Léon Gérôme; in 1868, she studied with Thomas Couture near Écouen, outside Paris, and in 1870 with Charles Bellay in Rome. The tight structure and substantial figures of her mature works show the legacy of these teachers. By the time of her brief return to the States her style had already begun to mature; two out of her four submissions had been accepted by the Salon in 1868 and 1870. Her letters to her friend and fellow artist Emily Sartain show how unhappy she was in the States and how she ached to return to Europe, particularly Spain, which she fantasized as an artist's haven. Her chance came in late 1871 when she received a commission from the Bishop of Pittsburgh to copy two works in Parma. She stayed there for eight months, studying with Carlo Raimondi and immersing herself in the plentiful Correggios. In 1872 she did finally reach Spain, where she pursued her studies by copying the paintings of old masters. The Spanish influence is evident in her submission to the 1873 Salon, *Young Girl and Toreador*, a good example of her pre-Impressionist style. Although all her Salon submissions between 1872 and 1875 were accepted, she was impatient with the Salon's artistic conservatism .

The next five years were pivotal: she made Paris her permanent home, became affiliated with the Impressionists, and came into her early artistic maturity. Cassatt chose Paris as her residence in order to "look after her own interests," a pragmatic decision based on economics rather than affection, as she had never particularly liked the city. It was a wise move. Paris was the center of artistic modernism and, after 1877, when Edgar Degas recognized her as a kindred spirit, Cassatt was accepted as one of the Impressionist group (then known as the "Independents"). Degas asked her to participate in their fourth exhibit, which took place in 1879, a year later than originally planned. Cassatt's contributions to that show, *La Loge* and *Little Girl in a Blue Armchair*, are prime examples of her early Impressionist paintings, with their careful recording of gesture and dramatic use of space and light. Cassatt received favorable notices as a result of her participation and, in 1882, her work was picked up by Paul Durand-Ruel, the most important dealer of Impressionist paintings. After 1879 her output had increased dramatically, possibly because she was now in touch with a group of like-minded artists. Certainly it must have been encouraging that her works had begun to sell. Some historians suggest that her relationship with Degas was the cause of her increased productivity. The nature of their relationship has fascinated many and been the source of much speculation. Before her death, Cassatt burned Degas's letters and characterized the possibility of romantic involvement with "that common little man" as a "repulsive idea."

Cassatt's mother, father, and sister Lydia came to live with her in 1877, occasioning a significant change in her everyday life. Some critics have emphasized the deleterious effects of this arrangement, notably Frederick Sweet, who described it as an "eighteen-year bondage." Cassatt certainly did become involved with the requirements of their failing health and subsequent deaths, beginning with Lydia, who died of Bright's disease in 1882. Despite her continued professionalism, it could be said that she assumed the role of the typical, good Victorian unmarried daughter, a view corroborated in her letters to her brother Alexander. It would be incorrect, however, to consider Cassatt's living situation in purely negative terms. The fact that her productivity increased shortly after her family's arrival speaks for itself. The group formed a household in which she was emotionally supported and, as an unmarried woman dedicated to her art, she was able to participate in family life without the pressure of a wife's responsibilities. Additionally, her parents enjoyed some relationships with her friends in the art world, sharing with Degas, for example, an active interest in horse-racing. Cassatt also remained in close contact with her brothers and their children, using various family members as artistic subjects, and accounting in part for her innovative treatment of domestic themes.

The subsequent years saw the consolidation of Cassatt's artistic success and the spread of her reputation. Durand-Ruel gave her one-artist exhibitions in 1891 and 1893; in 1895 the gallery arranged her first stateside individual exhibition in New York. A commissioned large mural representing "modern woman" was exhibited in the Women's Building at the 1893 World Columbian Exhibition in Chicago. (Mary Frances MacMonnies painted its companion, showing "primitive woman.") Cassatt described the work's feminist theme in a letter to Mrs. Bertha Potter Palmer, the organizer of the Women's Building, as depicting "young women plucking the fruits of Knowledge and Science." (Unfortunately this mural was lost at the end of the exhibition.)

The most significant new influence on Cassatt's artistic development during this period was her exposure to Japanese prints. Their intimate glimpse into women's private domestic environments was consistent with her own vision. In 1890 Cassatt attended a major exhibition of Japanese woodcuts at the École des Beaux-Arts with Degas and Berthe Morisot. The influence of these works with their love of pattern and plane can be seen in Cassatt's paintings from the 1890s and in the wonderful series of color etchings that she executed in 1891 (described in her letter of that year to Samuel P. Avery).

For the next twenty years Cassatt worked steadily. Although she was offered many prizes, she refused to accept any. As she wrote to Harrison Morris, she remained loyal to the credo of the "old Independents" and their "principles . . . no juries, no medals, no awards." Cataracts began to curtail her productivity after 1912 and several operations were not successful; her later years were spent in near-blindness. (It is ironic that two other women artists, Rosalba Carriera and Georgia O'Keeffe, suffered from blindness in their old age.) Cassatt's loss of sight and resulting inability to work, along with the world war, the deaths of her brothers and Degas, her diabetes, and her age in general, left her reclusive and depressed in her later years. Her isolation and bitterness are sadly and clearly communicated in her letters from that period to Louisine Havemeyer.

Cassatt was particularly innovative in her treatment of two themes: mothers and children and women's activities and interactions. While *Mother About to Bathe her Sleepy Child* (1880) is usually considered her earliest example of the former motif, most of Cassatt's works after the turn of the century focus on interactions between mothers and children. Some critics react negatively to Cassatt's frequent depiction of *maternités* and, though today's critics no longer accept the sexist devaluation of the subject matter, some assert that Cassatt was too conservative in her depictions of bourgeois, late nineteenth and early twentieth-century life. Cassatt's attention to specific detail distinguishes her work from that of her contemporaries and keeps it from slipping into the generalized sentimentality surrounding myths of maternity. The anxious face of the mother in *The Boating Party*, the restless twist of the baby in *Mother About to Bathe her Sleepy Child,* the groggy gaze of the mother in *Breakfast in Bed* offer only a few examples of Cassatt's ability to break from stereotypical views. By uniting the figures through pictorial abstraction, so that they often read as one solid form, Cassatt effectively expresses the closeness of the mother-child bond. She uses a similar device in her one work of *paternité,* in which her brother Alexander and his son Robert are formally united.

Cassatt's paintings of women and their interactions were also rich and distinctive. Women formed the major subject of her art, sometimes painted alone and monumental, as the figure in *At the Opera*, a visual discourse on seeing which represents a remarkable break with the usual depiction of women as the recipients of the male gaze. At other times she used composition to explore the intimate relationships between women, as in *Two Women Picking Fruit* or *Women Reading.* In the latter, as Griselda Pollock suggests, the space that the women inhabit becomes the locus of relationship. Like her contemporary Berthe Morisot, Cassatt used the Impressionist way of seeing to explore the domestic interior and the close yet diverse relationships among its female inhabitants. In her *Five O'Clock Tea*, composition and color epitomize what Carroll Smith-Rosenberg has identified as "the female world of love and ritual." In their use of the domestic interior, both artists differed radically from their male colleagues, who were often attracted to the Parisian demi-monde. Despite their similar use of iconography, however, Cassatt and Morisot developed different potentialities of Impressionist style.

Cassatt's letters provide useful information about her art and life, particularly her correspondence with Emily Sartain during Cassatt's apprenticeship years and with Louisine Elder Havemeyer over the last forty years of Cassatt's life. Both these relationships ended abruptly because of ill feelings precipitated by misunderstandings in which Cassatt felt her professional integrity had been compromised. Cassatt's friendship with Sartain, an engraver from a prominent Philadelphia family of artists, flourished while Cassatt was in the United States during the Franco-Prussian War. Although they sailed for Europe together in 1872, by 1875 they were no longer on speaking terms, their friendship unable to withstand their opposite stances on artistic modernism. Cassatt met Louisine Elder (later, Mrs. H. O. Havemeyer) through Sartain. Although "Louie" was ten years younger, they became fast friends with a notable mutual impact. Havemeyer later became Chairwoman of the National Women's Party and encouraged Cassatt's participation in feminist activities, enlisting her to contribute works to the 1915 Suffrage Loan Exhibition at the Knoedler Gallery in New York, a show organized by Havemeyer in 1915 and discussed in their correspondence. Cassatt guided the Havemeyers' art collecting, suggesting that Louisine, while still a teenager, use spending money to purchase her "first" Degas. In 1923 a misunderstanding about a series of drypoints, believed by everybody but Cassatt to be restrikes, made Cassatt bitterly eschew their friendship, although Havemeyer remained loyal to the end. Additionally, the frequent letters between Cassatt and the stateside members of her family provide an invaluable source of information about the texture of her daily life and its economic aspects, as does her correspondence with other friends and professional associates. One favorite correspondent, Theodate Pope, was one of the first American women architects.

As an artist, Cassatt was the consummate professional. Even while still a student, in a letter to her sister-in-law Lois, she distinguished between her sketching companion who was "only an amateur," and herself, one of the "professionals." She did not pursue art for its external rewards, yet she was utterly serious about its practice. Cassatt was affiliated with the artistic avant-garde of her time and the content of her works was innovative. She also exerted a great influence on American collectors to invest in the "new" art and was thus partially responsible for bringing this work to the American public's attention. While contemporary scholarship indicates that Cassatt should not be perceived as the only dedicated woman artist of her day, her current renown is entirely justified.

SOURCES

Hale, Nancy. *Mary Cassatt*. Garden City, N. Y.: Doubleday and Co., 1975.

Mathews, Nancy Mowll, ed. *Cassatt and Her Circle: Selected Letters*. New York: Abbeville Press, 1984.

Pollock, Griselda. *Vision and Difference: Femininity, Feminism and the Histories of Art*. London and New York: Routledge, 1988.

Smith-Rosenberg, Carroll. "The Female World of Love and Ritual: Relations between Women in Nineteenth-Century America." Chapter in *Disorderly*

Conduct: Visions of Gender in Victorian America. New York: Alfred A. Knopf, 1985.

Sweet, Frederick A. *Miss Mary Cassatt, Impressionist from Pennsylvania.* Norman, Okla.: University of Oklahoma Press, 1966.

EXCERPTS FROM MARY CASSATT'S CORRESPONDENCE, 1869–1924

MARY CASSATT TO LOIS CASSATT (SISTER–IN–LAW OF CASSATT; WIFE OF ALEXANDER CASSATT)

Beaufort sur Doron, Savoie, August 1, 1869

I have had such a variety of mishaps lately & have changed places so often that it is quite time I was hearing from you again. . . .

I am here with my friend Miss Gordon from Philadelphia, & we are roughing it most artistically. We made quite a trip before getting here. The first place we stopped at was Mâcon where we were perfectly disgusted & from there we went to Aix les bains a very fashionable watering place entirely too gay for two poor painters, at least for one, for although my friend calls herself a painter she is only an amateur and you must know we professionals despise amateurs. So as Aix was too gay we went on into the mountains of Bauge to a place called Les Chesseures our original destination. Unfortunately our hosts had but two beds & as we occupied them both they were obliged to sleep in the barn so we took pity on them & left & after further journeyings we came here. The place is all that we could desire as regards scenery but could be vastly improved as regards accommodations, however as the costumes & surroundings are good for painters we have concluded to put up with all discomforts for a time. . . .

❖

MARY CASSATT TO ELIZA HALDEMAN (FRIEND OF CASSATT AND FELLOW STUDENT AT THE PENNSYLVANIA ACADEMY)

Beaufort sur Doron, Savoie, August 17, 1869

I thought when I last wrote to you that by this time both Miss Gordon & I wd be on our way home, instead of that we have been settled here for several weeks, & home seems as far off as it did this time last year. I was afraid you had not received my answer to your letter, but Mother tells me that you did. I cannot therefore imagine why you have not written, & am afraid I said something to offend you, if so I did not mean it & hope this will meet with a response. Did mother tell you of my misfortune last spring? I did not get in the Salon! My picture Mr. Frère said was infinitely better than last years, but it was large & not sufficiently finished. I was very much pressed for time & therefore was not very much surprised at my fate, although of course I felt dreadfully about it. . . . Mr. Gerome was very kind to me for when I heard that I was refused I went to him but alas! it was too late, he told me if I had come twenty four hours sooner he would have got my picture through! . . . After I had heard my fate I went into Paris & staid there three months, but did but little work in fact none at all. I was not very well & of course very much discouraged, so I have only really been at work since I have been here, & even now I am taking it rather easy. . . .

❖

MARY CASSATT TO EMILY SARTAIN
Hollidaysburgh, May 22, 1871

. . . I was very glad to receive your letter this morning. I really thought you had completely forgotten me & were preparing to start for Spain with somebody else. Alas! we don't seem any nearer than we were some months ago, at least I don't, I have been abandoning myself to despair & homesickness, for I really feel as if it was intended I should be a Spaniard & quite a mistake that I was born in America. . . .

As to the matter of models I have not looked for them yet, but I have found a studio & shall move in tomorrow. The room is a large one high ceiling & a studio window built for a portrait painter rent $4 (four dollars) a month! We have only just got settled & are very well pleased with the town which is very pretty all the houses surrounded by gardens. . . .

MARY CASSATT TO EMILY SARTAIN
Hollidaysburg, June 7, 1871

. . . It has been so oppressively warm that we have not had the energy to settle anything as yet. I suppose I am getting acclimated but I find the process anything but palatable & wish myself in a more congenial climate, Rome last summer even with the fleas was as nothing compared to this place. I am very much obliged for your fathers kind offer about my pictures but for the present I will let them remain where they are. I am working by fits & starts at fathers portrait but it advances slowly he drops asleep while sitting. I commenced a study of our mulatto servant girl but just as I had the mask painted in she gave me warning. My luck in this country! I was amused at her finding that I had not made her look like a white person. . . . When I have struck a vein of models I will let you know & you must come up. I long to see you & have a talk about art. I cannot tell you what I suffer for the want of seeing a good picture, no amount of bodily suffering occassioned by the want of comforts would seem to be too great a price for the pleasure of living in a country where one could have some art advantages.

MARY CASSATT TO EMILY SARTAIN
Madrid, October 5, 1872

. . . I got here this morning at 10 o'clock at 12 I had had a bath was dressed and on my way to the Academie Museo or whatever they call it. Velasquez oh! my but you knew how to paint! Mr. Antonio Mor or Moro, whom you were introduced to at Parma has a word or two to say to you Emily. Titian also would like to introduce you to his daughter who is carrying the head of John the Baptist, holding it up on a platter with her beautiful bare arms. She says the one you saw in Dresden was a copy. Van Dyke's three children at Turin are beautiful, but he has a man in velvet and crimson satin that is a step beyond that in some respects. Oh dear to think that there is no one I can shriek to, beautiful! lovely, oh! painting what ar'nt you. I am getting wild I must eat some dinner if I can get any.

6 P.M. Just done dinner feel decidedly better, very tired though, & rather lonely. I dont see any women about, nothing but men. . . .

If I can tell you of prices not too high do you think you and Mrs. Tolles can come down? I don't hesitate to tell you that although I think now that Correggio is perhaps the greatest painter that ever lived, these Spaniards make a much greater impression *at first.* The men and women have a reality about them which exceed anything I ever supposed possible, Velasquez Spinners, good heavens, why you can walk into the picture. Such freedom of touch, to be sure he left plenty of things unfinished, as for Murillo he is a baby alongside of him, still the Conception is lovely most lovely. But Antonio Mor! and then Rubens! I won't go on, oh Emily *do* come you will never regret it. . . .

❖

MARY CASSATT TO EMILY SARTAIN
　　Madrid, October 13, 1872
　　. . . I have moved, have found a much cheaper hotel, kept by an Italian, the address was given to me in Varallo. The people are very kind, I have a bed room and sitting room and plenty of good things to eat and clean, but the entrance is through a pastry cooks shop and the staircase is very dirty. I pay six (6) frcs a day, and I have no doubt I could manage to live for much less. My journey from Parma here everything included cost 200 frcs. I only travelled 1st class in Spain and if I were you I think I would travel third class in France (I did) and second class in Spain. I am making a sketch from the Velasquez at the gallery, and I am quite if not more enthusiastic than before. I sincerely think it is the most wonderful painting that ever was seen, this of the Spanish school. Murillo has risen immensely in my opinion since I have seen his St. Elizabeth, it is a most tender beautiful thing, and I am told that his St. Anthony of Padua at Seville is even superior. . . . I have been looking over the photographs of the Seville gallery and I think it must be very fine indeed. Now my dear friends both of you please do come, come and I will wait for you here and we will go to Seville together and I will return to Italy with you in March. Don't mind about clothes or anything, for the people here are little more than barbarians. . . .

　　I think that one learns *how to paint* here, Velasquez manner is so fine and so simple. I also greatly admire Boccanegra but have seen only photographs as his pictures are in Seville I believe, but perhaps I may be mistaken and he has pictures here which I have not seen, there are so many pictures. Oh! If I could only tell you instead of this miserable scratching. An artist who has lived years in Italy tells me that nothing is to compare to Andalusia, now if you could only come while we are all in Madrid still, for of course I intend to push further South, where I can paint in the open air. I feel like a miserable little "critter" before these pictures, and yet I feel as if I could paint in this style easier, you see the manner is so simple . . . .

❖

MARY CASSATT TO EMILY SARTAIN
　　Seville, New Year's Eve, 1873
　　. . . Everything here goes on as usual. I am all day at Pilats house, and am known as the "Señora of the Casa Pilatos," Sundays and week days, Christmas and New Years day — I get up there sometimes at ten, or half past seldom as late as eleven, and work steadily to five. My present effort is on a canvass of thirty and is three figures life size half way to the knee — All the three heads

are forshortened and difficult to pose, so much so that my model asked me if the people who pose for me live long. I have one man's figure the first time I have introduced a mans head into any of my pictures. I had hoped to send something if only a head to the Vienna Exhibition, but I have not the most remote idea of when the pictures must be sent. You say that I have said nothing about the pictures here, but the fine ones are miserably lighted, and many of them inferior to their reputations, there is however a magnificent Zurbaran at the Museo. The great thing here is the odd types and peculiar rich dark coloring of the models, if it were not for that I should not stay. . . .

. . . Now that I have begun to paint from life again, constantly the thought of Correggio's pictures returns to my mind and I am thankful for my six months study in Parma. . . . I confess that if I did not live to paint life would be dull here, dreadfully dull, nothing absolutely nothing going on, as for the comic opera, it is comic indeed, my only surprise is how people live through it and some of them go every night. I will perhaps add a few lines in the morning, but it is very late, so for the present, good night — . . . .

❖

MARY CASSATT TO ALEXANDER CASSATT (BROTHER OF CASSATT)
Paris, June 22, 1883

I have a few minutes before the mail goes out to tell you about the picture business. Dreyfus told me finally that I might have the group of Mother & the children for you. I would rather keep it myself but I know he would not be pleased if I made him give it up to anyone but you. He won't take back the money for the picture, I am either to paint a portrait of his wife or if she won't consent to that I am to give them another picture; so as soon as the London exhibition is over I will send you Elsies portrait and the group. Please tell Lois I think the group will look well in a light room; that is light paper & perhaps over a door; it is painted to look as much like frescoe as possible so that it would be appropriate over a door as the Italian painters used to do, they are called "dessus de porte" here. About your portrait I am undecided, I am not satisfied with it, I think the one I did at Marly the best of the two; I will make up my mind when Gard comes, I am anxious to know whether he will think it like; whatever his opinion will be I know he wont conceal it, frankness is his virtue. . . .

❖

MARY CASSATT TO ALEXANDER CASSATT (BROTHER OF CASSATT)
Paris, October 14, 1883

. . . Annie & Mrs. Riddle were most hospitable to us in London, nothing could be kinder, Annie went with me to Whistler's studio where we were met by a pupil of his, he, himself was out of town, but he insisted upon this pupil being sent for to show me the studio. The portrait is not quite done yet I thought it a fine picture, the figure especially beautifully drawn, I don't think it by any means a striking likeness, the head inferior to the rest — The face has no animation but that I believe he does on purpose, he does not talk to his sitters, but sacrifices the head to the ensemble. He told Mother; she, you know went up to London before me & saw him at his studio; he told her that he would have liked a few more sittings, that he felt as if he was working against time; that I suppose is true enough. I told his pupil that you were very anxious to have the picture & that I hoped he would soon send it to you. After all I don't think you could have done better, it is a work of Art, & as young Sargent said to Mother this afternoon, it is a good thing to have a portrait by Whistler in the family. I hope you have Elsies portrait & the family group by this time; the box was sent the 10th of August to Richardson Spence & Co Liverpool to be shipped to you, but as it went by "petite vitesse" it may be a long time "en route." . . .

I did not send your portrait in the box because I really was not satisfied with it, I like much better the head I painted of you at Marly, & I could not bear to send you a poor thing. Monet is coming up, Petit the man you bought your Raffaelli from, has gone to Monets pictures with a will, bought forty of them from Durand, & it seems refused 10,000 frcs for one; if only your friend Mr Warren had known that; so hold on to your Monet's, I am only sorry I did not urge you to buy more. I met Mme Benard in the street the other day & she told me about the rise adding "We have ten it will be a little fortune some of these days." . . . Annie & Mrs Riddle are at St Germain, we went out to see them yesterday & I thereby made my cold so much worse that I have been in bed all day. They will be in Paris soon & have taken an apartement at the Hotel Liverpool, where they will stay until Christmas; I got a box from them, about a week ago, which contained a most lovely *old* Japanese tea & coffee set, which I had admired in London! . . .

MARY CASSATT TO ALEXANDER CASSATT (BROTHER OF CASSATT)
Tarragona, January 5, 1884
Here we are in Spain & what is not so pleasant waiting for the visit of a Spanish Doctor. Poor Mother is suffering with dreadful headaches, has not been able to leave the house hardly her bed since we have been in Spain. . . .

. . . My poor painting is sadly interrupted, I have no time now for anything & the constant anxiety takes all heart out of me; my only hope is that this change will set Mother right for a time. . . .

MARY CASSATT TO ALEXANDER CASSATT (BROTHER OF CASSATT)
Biarritz, April 29, 1884
. . . As for me I have been utterly upset, have had violent tooth ache & a swollen face, yesterday the dentist lanced the gum, but it seems worse to day; I think it is not only the tooth but all the worry and fatigue I have had. . . .

When I was in Paris I found Portier had sold two of my pictures for me & more were wanted but I have not touched a brush since we left home, have not been out of mothers room except for a walk, since I have been here. It will do me good to get to work again. Elsie's portrait was the first picture hung in the new apartement & looks much better there than in the old one. I am going to take the Salon for a studio & Father has a small salon arranged for him. . . .

MARY CASSATT TO SAMUEL P. AVERY
Paris, June 9, 1891
I thank you very much for your kind letter, it is delightful to think that you take an interest in my work. I have sent with the set of my coloured etchings all

of the "states" I had, I wish I could have had more but I had to hurry on and be ready for my printer, when I could get him — The printing is a great work; sometimes we worked all day (eight hours) both, as hard as we could work & only printed eight or ten proofs in the day. My method is very simple. I drew an outline in dry point and transferred this to two other plates, making in all, three plates, never more, for each proof — Then I put an aquatint wherever the color was to be printed; the color was painted on the plate as it was to appear in the proof. I tell you this because Mr. Lucas thought it might interest you, and if any of the etchers in New York care to try the method you can tell them how it is done — I am very anxious to know what you think of these new etchings. It amused me very much to do them although it was hard work. . . .

I received the Annual Report of the Metropolitan Museum you were so kind as to send me. I should like very much to give something to the Museum, but I don't feel as if I were well enough known yet at home to make it worthwhile. After my exhibition if I have any success with the artists and amateurs I will certainly present something to the Museum if you think they would care to have it. . . .

❖

MARY CASSATT TO BERTHA PALMER

Bachivillers, October 11, 1892

Your letter of Sept. 27th only arrived this morning, so unfortunately this will not reach you by the 18th as you desired. Notwithstanding that my letter will be too late for the ladies of the committee, I should like very much to give you some account of the manner I have tried to carry out my idea of the decoration.

Mr. Avery sent me an article from one of the New York papers this summer, in which the writer, referring to the order given to me, said my subject was to be "The Modern Woman as glorified by Worth!" That would hardly describe my idea, of course I have tried to express the modern woman in the fashions of our day and have tried to represent those fashions as accurately & as much in detail as possible. I took for the subject of the central & largest composition Young women plucking the fruits of knowledge or science & — that enabled me to place my figures out of doors & allowed of brilliancy of color. I have tried to make the general effect as bright, as gay, as amusing as possible. The occassion is one of rejoicing, a great national fête. I reserved all the seriousness for the execution, for the drawing & painting. My ideal would have been one of those admirable old tapestries brilliant yet soft. My figures are rather under life size although they seem as large as life. I could not imagine women in modern dress eight or nine feet high. An American friend asked me in rather a huffy tone the other day "Then this is woman apart from her relations to man?" I told him it was. Men I have no doubt, are painted in all their vigour on the walls of the other buildings; to us the sweetness of childhood, the charm of womanhood, if I have not conveyed some sense of that charm, in one word if I have not been absolutely feminine, then I have failed. My central canvass I hope to finish in a few days, I shall have some photographs taken & sent to you. I will still have place on the side panels for two compositions, one, which I shall begin immediately is, young girls pursuing fame. This seems to me very modern & besides will give me an opportunity for some figures in clinging draperies. The other panel will represent the Arts, Music (nothing of St. Cecelia) Dancing & all treated in the most modern way. The whole is surrounded by a border, wide below, narrower above, bands of color, the lower cut with circles containing naked babies tossing fruit, &&c. I think, my dear Mrs. Palmer, that if you were here & I could take you out to my studio & show you what I have done that you would be pleased indeed without too much vanity I may say I am almost sure you would.

When the work reaches Chicago, when it is dragged up 48 feet & you will have to stretch your neck to get sight of it all, whether you will like it then, is another question. Stillman, in a recent article, declares his belief that in the evolution of the race painting is no longer needed, the architects evidently are of that opinion. Painting was never intended to be put out of sight. This idea however has not troubled me too much, for I have passed a most enjoyable summer of hard work. If painting is no longer needed, it seems a pity that some of us are born into the world with such a passion for line and color. Better painters than I am have been put out of sight, Baudry spent years on his decorations. The only time we saw them was when they were exhibited in the Beaux-Arts, then they were buried in the ceiling of the Grand Opera. — After this grumbling I must get back to my work knowing that the sooner we get to Chicago the better.

You will be pleased, believe me, my dear Mrs. Palmer. . . .

❖

MARY CASSATT TO HARRISON MORRIS (MANAGING DIRECTOR OF THE PENNSYLVANIA ACADEMY OF THE FINE ARTS)
Paris, March 15, 1904
I have received your very kind letter of Feb. 16th with the enclosed list of the different prizes awarded in the Exhibition. Of course it is very gratifying to know that a picture of mine was selected for a special honor and I hope the fact of my not accepting the award will not be misunderstood. I was not aware that Messrs Durand Ruel had sent a picture of mine to the Exhibition. The picture being their property they were at liberty to do as they pleased with it. I, however, who belong to the founders of the Independent Exhibition must stick to my principles, our principles, which were, no jury, no medals, no awards. Our first exhibition was held in 1879 and was a protest against official exhibitions and not a grouping of artists with the same art tendencies. We have been since dubbed "Impressionists" a name which might apply to Monet but can have no meaning when attached to Degas' name.

Liberty is the first good in this world and to escape the tyranny of a jury is worth fighting for, surely no profession is so enslaved as ours. Gérôme who all his life was on the Jury of every official exhibition said only a short time before his death that if Millet were then alive, he, Gérôme would refuse his pictures, that the world has consecrated Millet's genius made no difference to him. I think this is a good comment on the system. I have no hopes of converting any one, I even failed in getting the women students club here to try the effect of freedom for one year, I mean of course the American Students Club. When I was at home a few years ago it was one of the things that disheartened me the most to see that we were slavishly copying all the evils of the French system, evils which they deplore and are trying to remove. I will say though that if awards are given it is more sensible and practical to give them in money than in medals and to young and struggling artists such help would often be welcome, and personally I should feel wicked in depriving any one of such help, as in the present case.

I hope you will excuse this long letter, but it was necessary for me to explain. . . .

MARY CASSATT TO JOHN W. BEATTY (AMERICAN ARTIST, DIRECTOR OF THE FINE ARTS, CARNEGIE INSTITUTE, PITTSBURGH)

Mesnil–Beaufresne, October 6, 1908

In reply to your form of Sept 16th asking for my photograph, I don't possess one, and it would be very disagreeable to me to have my image in a catalogue or in any publication.

It is always unpleasant to me to see the photographs of the artists accompany their work, what has the public to do with the personal appearance of the author of picture or statue? Why should such curiosity if it exists be gratified? . . .

MARY CASSATT TO THEODATE POPE (AMERICAN ARCHITECT)

Constantinople, December 23, 1910

. . . We hope to be in Cairo on January 3rd & have two months in Egypt — My brother & his family are enjoying it all as much as I am — It seems so odd not to be working all day, but seeing sights & enjoying the young friends of my nieces — I am glad you will be in New York & seeing Mrs. Havemeyer often I hope — She has had hard times, just think how much better if women know all about the men's work — At present men lead double lives — What we ought to fight for is equality it would lead to more happiness for both — Of course with that great big heart of yours, you lean towards socialism up to the present time it don't work, then too I believe if we are to be led to the promised land of more equal rights it will be by a silent leader there has been far too much talking & Roosevelt has been the sinner — I am not hard at least I hope I am not, but I am an individualist. . . .

MARY CASSATT TO THEODATE POPE (AMERICAN ARCHITECT)

Cairo, February 19, 1911

The climate & even the country is a great disappointment, & apart from some of the Temples there is nothing to see. Temples & Tombs still one learns — I am so glad to hear that you are enjoying your winter and are pleasantly situated at the St Regis, it isnt socialism, but that is far away, in the dim future — So you think my models unworthy of their clothes? You find their types coarse. I know that is an American newspaper criticism, everyone has their criterion of beauty. I confess I love health & strength. What would you say to the Botticelli Madonna in the Louvre. The peasant girl & her child clothed in beautiful shifts & wrapped in soft veils. Yet as Degas pointed out to me Botticelli stretched his love of truth to the point of painting her hands with the fingernails worn down with field work! Come over & I will go to the Louvre with you & teach you to see the Old Masters methods. You don't look enough at pictures. Paul Veronese had a jacket which he took about with him & constantly painted on all his models, I doubt if they were "cultured" how I hate the word, these are elemental things which no culture changes. Then who do you think makes the fashions? The uncultured girls, & they are launched by the "free lances" also uncultured but copied by the sheltered women — No you must learn more before snubbing me. I certainly won't paint you a picture, try one of the *refined* American ones produced in New York — Almost all my pictures with children have the Mother holding them, would you could hear them talk, their philosophy would astonish you. France has always been the home of Art & reason too as regards the race — When am I to see you to thrash this out together, it is always stimulating to talk things out with you! . . .

❖

MARY CASSATT TO LOUISINE HAVEMEYER (SUFFRAGIST AND FRIEND OF CASSATT)
    Villa Angeletto, January 11, 1913 [?]
    To go back to your letter, I don't see why women should pay taxes, except on their earnings, mostly they are living on their incomes made by the husbands therefore they are represented. I believe that the vote will be given freely, when women want it, the trouble is that so many don't want it for themselves and never think of others. American women have been spoiled, treated and indulged like children they must wake up to their duties. . . .

❖

MARY CASSATT TO ELLEN MARY CASSATT (NIECE OF CASSATT)
    Villa Angeletto, March 26, 1913 [?]
    Yours of the 17th is just here; and as the weather is storming and a pouring rain has been our portion all night and likely to be all day, I have plenty of time before me to answer some of your questions about cubists and others. No Frenchman of any standing in the art world has ever taken any of these things seriously. As to Matisse, one has only to see his early work to understand him. His pictures were extremely feeble in execution and very commonplace in vision. As he is intelligent he saw that real excellence, which would bring him consideration, was not for him on that line. He shut himself up for years and evolved these things; he knew that in the present anarchical state of things — not only in the art world but everywhere — he would achieve notoriety — and he has. At his exhibition in Paris you never hear French spoken, only German, Scandinavian and other Germanic languages; and then people think notoriety is fame and even buy these pictures or daubs. Of course all this has only "un temps"; it will die out. Only really good work survives. As to this Gertrude Stein, she is one of a family of California Jews who came to Paris poor and unknown; but they are not Jews for nothing. They — two of the brothers — started a studio, bought Matisse's pictures cheap and began to pose as amateurs of the only real art. Little by little people who want to be amused went to these receptions where Stein received in sandals and his wife in one garment fastened by a broach, which if it gave way might disclose the costume of Eve. Of course the curiosity was aroused and the anxiety as to whether it *would* give way; and the pose was, if you don't admire these daubs I am sorry for

you; you are not of the chosen few. Lots of people went, Mrs. Sears amongst them and Helen; but I never would, being to old a bird to be caught by chaff. The misunderstanding in art has arisen from the fact that forty years ago — to be exact thirty-nine years ago — when Degas and Monet, Renoir and I first exhibited, the public did not understand, only the "elite" bought and time has proved their knowledge. Though the Public in those days did not understand, the artists did. Henner told me that he considered Degas one of the two or three *artists* then living. Now the Public say — the foreign public — Degas and the others were laughed at; well, we will be wiser than they. We will show we know; not knowing that the art world of those days did accept these men; only, as they held "L'assiette de beurre," they would not divide it with outsiders. No sound artist ever looked except with scorn at these cubists and Matisse.

❖

MARY CASSATT TO LOUISINE HAVEMEYER (SUFFRAGIST AND FRIEND OF CASSATT)
Paris, November 11, 1914

I have yours about your musicale & your speech. Do lean Louie on the fact that German "Kulture" was purely masculine, and for that reason must disappear. That the victory of the Allies means liberty for Germans, a liberty which they had not temperament to acquire for themselves. Above all things there was no place for the intellectual qualities of women in their system. I was told the other day by Mme Acillas that this war has made men accept the fact of women voting with more tolerance, the womens movement has progressed. . . .

❖

MARY CASSATT TO LOUISINE HAVEMEYER (SUFFRAGIST AND FRIEND OF CASSATT)
Paris, July 5, 1915

I feel like a perfect brute having written you those letters, but indeed dear I was upset, you dont know all I do. Joseph [Durand-Ruel] was here, & as to the exhibition he said it was the cause which kept many people away, "society" it seems is so against suffrage. Many regretted to him that they missed seeing a fine exhibition but their principles forbade their going. Also he said that if women voted it would be for peace at any price. That B would be the next President & &. In fact a goose, not too great tho' [to] take advantage of Degas still. Enough, I am disgusted at all their ways & feel I never want to sell a painting again. We must meet before I can tell you all. Fancy having Degas pastels retouched by Dan Domeinzo!

I am so glad you spoke to all those people, surely it will do good. Do you think if I have to stop work on account of my eyes I could use my last years as a propagandist? It wont be necessary if the war goes on, as it must. Women are now doing most of the work. I never felt so isolated in my life as I do now. Your letters are the only things that made me feel not altogether abandoned. . . .

❖

MARY CASSATT TO LOUISINE HAVEMEYER (SUFFRAGIST AND FRIEND OF CASSATT)
Villa Angeletto, December 28, 1917

. . . In looking back over my life, how elated I would have been if in my youth I had been told I would have the place in the world of Art I have acquired and now at the end of life how little it seems, what difference does it all make.

I am nearer despair than I ever was, operating on my right eye before the cataract was ripe, was the last drop. I asked Borsch if it was ripe and he assured me it *was*! The sight of that eye is inferior but still I saw a good deal in spite of the cataract now I see scarcely at all. Oh Louie what a World we live in. I feel more and more that this is the end of civilization.

May this year see an end to some of the suffering. As to the millenium after the war I don't believe in it.

Heaps of love to you all. I can not see to read letters and soon won't be able to write.

❖

MARY CASSATT TO LOUISINE HAVEMEYER (SUFFRAGIST AND FRIEND OF CASSATT)
Villa Angeletto, September 8, 1918
. . . I had a letter from Rene Gimpel who was in New York on July 14th. . . . Rene went to see Monet and found him at work on large panels of water lilies. One would have to build a room especially for them I suppose. I must say his "Nemphas" [Les Nymphéas] pictures look to me like glorified wallpaper. You have some of [the] best work. I wont go so far as D who thinks he has done nothing worth doing for 20 years, but it is certain that these decorations without composition are not to my taste. Impossible to hang these with other pictures, & alone they tire one. The weather here is good it has rained, that is there have been storms. *Dont* overdo Louie the machine will give out. We are all machines. . . .

❖

MARY CASSATT TO AUGUSTUS SAINT-GAUDENS (AMERICAN SCULPTOR)
Villa Angeletto, December 28, 1922
I have taken refuge here from the gloom of Paris & I suppose you and Mrs. St. Gaudens are there & I regret I shall not have the pleasure of seeing you — I hope your Committee have found you some good things, but they are a Jury.

It may interest you to know what Degas said when he saw the picture you have just bought for your Museum [*Two Young Women Picking Fruit*]. It was painted in 1891 in the summer, & Degas came to see me after he had seen it at Durand-Ruels. He was chary of praises but he spoke of the drawing of the woman's arm picking the fruit & made a familiar gesture indicating the line & said no woman has a right to draw like that. He said the color was like a Whistler which was not my opinion, he had spoken of the picture to Berthe Morisot who did not like it. I can understand that. If it has stood the test of time & is well drawn its place in a museum might show the present generation that we worked & learnt our profession, which isnt a bad thing — I hope you had a pleasant time in Rome. My best wishes to you & Mrs. St. Gaudens for the coming year. May it bring you all this troubled world can give of good.

❖

MARY CASSATT TO WILLIAM IVINS
Villa Angeletto, January 17, 1924
Your letter is here, I must at once correct a wrong impression first as to my sight & then as to my memory. I can perfectly see my etchings & am not likely to forget those I have done, I see them every day when at home they are framed & line the walls — . . .

But I have had a joy from which no one can rob me — I have touched with a sense of art some people once more — They did not look at me through a magnifying glass but felt the love & the life. The greatest living optitian when he saw the etching of the naked baby burst out oh! the baby is living & told me he had spent two hours the evening before looking at the etchings two hours of delight — Can you offer me anything to compare to that joy to an artist — ....

I have had my joy I have once more stirred a feeling of art — and nothing you or any one else can offer me, could give me pleasure. Do not allow yourself to be upset. All the same the plates had never been printed before. I send your letter to Delatre he will understand.

Letter to Bertha Potter Palmer courtesy The Art Institute of Chicago.
Letters to Theodate Pope, courtesy the Hill-stead Museum Archives.
Letter to Eugenie Heller, Thomas J. Watson Library, The Metropolitan Museum of Art.
Lettters to John W. Beatty, Homer St. Gaudens and William Ivins, Archives of American Art, Smithsonian Institution.
Letters to Eliza Haldeman, Emily Sartain, Harrision Morris, Pennsylvania Academy of Fine Arts, Archives.
Letters to Lois Cassatt and Alexander Cassatt, Philadelphia Museum of Art Archives: Archives of American Art/ Carl Zigrosser Collection.
Letters to Louisine Havemeyer, Metropolitan Museum of Art, Courtesy the Estate of Lois Cassatt Thayer.

After the Meeting, 1914. Oil on canvas. 40¹⁵⁄₁₆" x 28⅛".
The Toledo Museum of Art, Toledo, Ohio. Gift of Florence Scott Libbey.

CECILIA BEAUX

1855–1942

By THE TIME she was thirty, Cecilia Beaux had committed herself to the professional, full-time pursuit of a painting career, never wavering from that decision throughout her long life. Unlike Harriet Hosmer or Mary Cassatt, American expatriates in Europe, Beaux established a successful career working in the United States. Beaux was a portraitist (like several earlier European women artists, including Rosalba Carriera and Élisabeth Vigée-Lebrun), a specialty that enabled her to support herself financially although for Beaux painting was always a creative activity more than a commercial venture.

Cecilia Beaux maintained an active correspondence with family and friends. Her letters reveal her determination and seriousness of intent, while also conveying the image of a woman with a passionate, sensitive and sometimes rhapsodic nature. Beaux wrote about her artistic career in an autobiography, *Background With Figures*, the first such formal text produced by the artists examined thus far in this volume. Beaux achieved moderate success during her lifetime, but posterity has not accorded her a position consistent with her accomplishments, although they certainly are comparable to those of several male contemporaries whose names are better known than her own.

In her autobiography, Beaux credited her family with fostering her artistic achievements. She believed that she had inherited her ability to work hard from her mother's Yankee stock and her lyricism from her French father. Her mother's death when

Beaux was twelve days old and her father's subsequent sorrowful return to France shortly thereafter actually proved fortuitous for Beaux's artistic development. Beaux and her older sister were left in Philadelphia, in the care of their mother's extended family. This matriarchal household was headed by their Grandmother Leavitt and included Aunt Eliza Leavitt, Aunt Emily Leavitt Biddle and her husband Uncle Will Biddle, as well as the young girls. The family structure was well-suited to fostering the high level of self-esteem and determination that made it possible for Beaux to become a self-supporting artist. Beaux often asserted that her family's emphasis on careful work and respect for the arts had a major impact on both her choice of career and her ability to pursue it. Like many nineteenth-century women artists and writers, Beaux never married. Although she lived alone after her mid-thirties, her extended family remained significant to her throughout her life. When she was in Europe she maintained contact in respectful letters to her elders and, later on, she established special relationships with her sister's children, and with their children in turn.

Although she received comparatively little formal training, Beaux's style was influenced by the late nineteenth-century academic tradition. She first studied drawing at home with her Aunt Eliza Leavitt, described in Beaux's autobiography as the "Aunt with the sketchbook," but her art education really began with drawing lessons in 1871 from a distant relation, Catherine Drinker. A year or two later she studied casts, bones, and lithographs with the Dutch artist Adolf van der Whelan, which perhaps provided her only training in anatomy. Initially, she had no intention of becoming an artist, for "such an ambition" seemed too remote; apparently while studying with van der Whelan her orientation shifted. There seems to be some question as to whether or not Beaux attended the Pennsylvania Academy of the Fine Arts: although her name appears in the Registry of Students for two seasons (1877–1879), she subsequently denied ever having attended classes there with the "rabble," as her Uncle Will Biddle referred to the students. Instead, she participated in a loosely organized studio class with fortnightly critiques by William Sartain, a realist trained in Munich who was the younger brother of Mary Cassatt's friend and fellow student, Emily Sartain. Beaux's only other formal art education occurred during her first European trip in 1888–89, when she enrolled in classes in Paris at the Académie Julian and at Colarossi's, two studio schools that attracted both male and female art students from around the world. (Marie Bashkirtseff and Rosa Bonheur's biographer and companion, Anna Klumpke, had studied at the Académie Julian just a few years earlier; Paula Modersohn-Becker and Emily Carr both subsequently took classes at Colarossi's.)

Beaux began to support herself through her art long before concluding her studies. Her first commission, received when she was only about twenty and before she began to study with Sartain, required her to produce drawings of fossils for a United States Geological Survey. At that time, too, she learned the technique of overglaze painting on porcelain and supplemented her income by painting children's heads on decorative plates, a purely commercial endeavor.

In 1883 she began her first major composition, *Les Derniers Jours d'Enfance*, which was brought to Paris (by her friend Margaret Lesley) and accepted at the 1887 Salon. A sensitive exploration of the changing relationship between Beaux's sister and nephew, it was the first of many such images focused on family members. In her autobiography, she provides an engaging discussion of the logistics involved in painting this work. A number of other well-received pieces followed, so that by the time Beaux left for France, she was an established artist who was pursuing further studies for artistic refinement rather than basic training.

This eighteen-month study trip, begun in 1888 when Beaux was thirty-three, was the single most important step of her career. Although she could have rested for the remainder of her life on her reputation as a competent portraitist, Beaux chose to put herself in the vulnerable position of student in order to stretch her talents. She immediately felt an affinity for France which she thought of as her spiritual home, a tie based upon her familial background as well as on her artistic interests. Her Parisian teachers recognized her talent, encouraging her to use fresher colors, a technique that was reinforced by a summer spent at Concarneaux in Brittany studying the effects of light. During this sojourn in France, Beaux also established important contacts with many other painters, including several affiliated with the Impressionist movement. During the course of her life she made seven more trips to France, although never again for the purpose of formal study.

Upon her return to the United States, Beaux continued to enjoy a successful career as a portraitist. She was appointed to the staff of the Pennsylvania Academy of the Fine Arts on whose faculty she remained for the next twenty years. She moved her studio to New York in the early 1890s, beginning in 1905 to spend her remaining summers at Green Alley, her home in Gloucester, Massachusetts.

Before leaving for Europe in 1888 Beaux had twice received the Mary Smith Prize from the Pennsylvania Academy. After her return, numerous prizes and portrait commissions punctuated her successful career, including one to paint Mrs. Theodore Roosevelt at the White House, an event that she vividly described. She was elected to the National Academy of Design in 1902, only the second woman to be so honored. (Anne Hall was the first in 1833.) In 1919, she painted the portraits of three European heroes — Cardinal Mercier, Sir David Beatty, and Georges Clemenceau — under the auspices of the United States War Portraits Commission. Although she felt honored to have received these commissions and wrote warmly about her experiences with the subjects, these works seem hampered by the stilted restraint of formal portraiture conventions when compared to the vitality of some of Beaux's other works of women and family members. Unfortunately, a fall in 1924 in which she broke her hip and from which she never fully recovered resulted in a subsequent marked decrease in the volume of her work.

It is not surprising that Beaux's development reveals two distinct peaks. Prior to her departure for France, Beaux had reached the first stylistic pinnacle of her career, as typified by such pieces as *Fanny Travis Cochran* (1887), a sensitive study of a young girl, executed in contrasting white and dark tones. In its tight composition and limited tonal harmonies, it is reminiscent of similar works by James Abbott McNeill Whistler (as is her earlier piece *Les Derniers Jours d'Enfance*). Thomas Eakins's pervasive artistic influence in Philadelphia is also visible in the stark realism of this portrait. Although Beaux's first works after her return from Europe do not reveal a major change in style, an evolution had begun which reached maturity four or five years later, resulting in the second "peak" of her career. In such works as *Ernesta and Nurse* (1894), she revels in exquisitely shimmering color harmonies that ripple through dark and light tonal contrasts. In subsequent works she lightened her palette and loosened her brush strokes. Together, these changes enabled her to achieve the symphonies of color and texture that characterize her most successful works throughout the remainder of her career.

Beaux pushed the limits of portraiture, a traditionally conservative genre dependent upon the production of recognizable likenesses, by merging color and structure in her brush strokes and through her abilities as a gifted colorist. Thus her later works are characterized by both sensual and immediate handling of paint, and rich, evocative color. Although her view of "modern" art was less than enthusiastic, one can see the impact of the Impressionists' unfettered technique on her work. In its technical bravura, Beaux's style has been compared to that of her fellow portraitist, John Singer Sargent. Beaux's portraits may be distinguished from Sargent's, however, by their greater psychological complexity. She had an uncanny ability to capture her sitters' moods through keen observation of gesture, and was especially skilled at using visual cues to communicate relationships. Beaux's double portrait of Mrs. Clement A. Griscom and her daughter Frances (*Mother and Daughter*, 1898), for instance, explores the complexity of the mother-daughter relationship through the contrasting placement of the figures and their gazes. Extending her powers of observation, Beaux also examined the relationship between humans and animals, as in the portrait of her brother-in-law Henry S. Drinker and his lookalike cat (*Henry Sturgis Drinker*, 1898, also called *Man with the Cat* or *At Home*).

Beaux's work raise some issues of social class. As a portraitist she was committed to recording the world of an upper-class clientele. The Griscom portrait discussed above, for example, commemorates the occasion of daughter Frances's social debut. On the other hand, Beaux worked to support herself by producing commissioned pieces, works whose creation could not be considered consistent with the popular contemporary credo of "art for art's sake." *Ernesta and Nurse* reflects the ambiguity of this situation: Beaux focuses on her young niece, who dominates the picture surface, while cutting off the figure of the nurse, Mattie, so that we see her only from the waist down. Does this, as some critics suggest, show Mattie's importance through the visible "dominant force of her guiding hand," or does the partial view imply that the actual nurse need not be part of the picture?

Beaux's autobiography, *Background with Figures*, was published in 1930 and is one of two main sources of her writings. Like the memoirs of Élisabeth Vigée-Lebrun and Emily Carr, Beaux's autobiography was written in response to a forced cessation of painting, after she had broken her hip. It is a formally written account of her life, containing a wealth of information about her early artistic development, trips abroad, and experiences while executing various works. Like most autobiographies it raises questions relating to the self-representation of the author-protagonist. Beaux shaped the events of her life into an "official version," in which she paints a flattering and somewhat stilted self-portrait. Current theorists such as Estelle Jelinek and Sidonie Smith have suggested that autobiographies by women and men tend to conform to different patterns, with Beaux's autobiography (like that of many other women artists) following the male model. Beaux's account of her call to vocation is devoid of references to gender, and focuses on the early perceptions and experiences that distinguished her vision. This is followed by lengthy discussions of her artistic education and works in the public realm.

The collection of Beaux's papers deposited in the Archives of American Art provides the opportunity to hear her private, less self-conscious, voice. This rich body of materials — mostly diaries, letters, texts of public lectures, and even some poems — allows insights into her personality denied by her autobiography. The diary entries, spanning forty years of her life, consist of short, informal notations about the comings and goings of each day, documenting the extent of Beaux's professional commitment and, like Rosalba Carriera's diary, showing that she worked almost continuously. They also reveal her moodiness when Beaux described "bad days," "bad nights," "boring dull days," and "lovely mornings," and asked, "How can I go on?" By 1913, entries were made only sporadically and, later, there are just a few notes and comments for each year.

The voice in her letters is chatty, breathy, and informal, a surprise if contrasted with the polished, formal tone of her autobiography. Like Georgia O'Keeffe, Beaux often used dashes to connect phrases that lacked appropriate nouns, a stylistic peculiarity that communicates spontaneity and intensity. Particularly fascinating are the frequent long letters she wrote to various family members at home when she was studying in Paris, most signed "your child." They reveal her continuing emotional involvement with the family, and also give a vivid picture of the life of an intense, dedicated and independent woman art student. She also sustained a long and intimate correspondence with Dorothea Gilder, the subject of several of her most vital paintings, including *After the Meeting*. Gilder was the daughter of *Century* magazine publisher Richard Gilder and his wife, Helena deKay Gilder, both part of Beaux's social circle after her move to New York. In some of the other writings, especially the texts of public lectures, she characterizes art as a "sungod," an animus figure that appears in the writings of Irene Rice Pereira and Leonora Carrington, also included in this volume. (In these and other writings, Beaux always refers to the artist in the male gender.)

SOURCES

Beaux, Cecilia. *Background With Figures*. Boston and New York: Houghton Mifflin, 1930.

Cecilia Beaux Papers, Archives of American Art, Washington, D. C. (microfilm, rolls 426-429; 600).

Harris, Ann Sutherland, and Linda Nochlin. *Women Artists 1550–1950*. New York: Alfred A. Knopf, 1977.

Jelinek, Estelle. *Women's Autobiography*. Bloomington: Indiana University Press, 1980.

Rubinstein, Charlotte S. *American Women Artists*. Boston: Avon Books, 1982.

Cecilia Beaux: Portrait of an Artist. Exhibition catalogue. Introduction by Frank Goodyear. Philadelphia: Pennsylvania Academy of the Fine Arts, 1974.

Smith, Sidonie. *A Poetics of Women's Autobiography*. Bloomington: Indiana University Press, 1987.

Smith-Rosenberg, Carroll. "The Female World of Love and Ritual: Relations between Women in Nineteenth-Century America." Chapter in *Disorderly Conduct: Visions of Gender in Victorian America*. New York: Alfred A. Knopf, 1985.

FROM CECILIA BEAUX, *BACKGROUND WITH FIGURES*
(Boston and New York: Houghton Mifflin, 1930)

EARLY MEMORIES

In childhood, attrition has not begun; the page is spotless, and in some natures, at least, is open to receive what will be remembered during a lifetime, as the moment or two, and the first, of ecstasy.

In the case which I am trying to record, these impressions are almost entirely visual; that is, they are not dependent on incident or other forms of sensation.

... Out of a delicate mist, shot through with morning sunlight, stand the masts of ships, and some drooping sails. It is the child's first realization of the light of morning on such — or, indeed, on any — scene. Where we went, the journey, the details of travel, all are a blank, but nothing in the years between has dimmed the peerless vision; the child's first meeting with the sun-god, or rather the first flash of his spear in rising mist. Little did she know that it was the hour, always destined for her to be the best, the reproductive, the creative hour; the hour of fearless hope, for in memory it is sheer beauty, at its opening, and nothing else, that remains.

❖

LESSONS WITH CATHERINE DRINKER

The spring term at Miss Lyman's ended in June, and it was thought that I had shown enough inclination and aptitude, in my home drawing-lessons, to warrant my having regular instruction.

I had not the slightest idea of being an artist. The gulf between me and such an ambition was too great. I could not see across it. When I thought of the Gibson Gallery, and the few other paintings I had seen, they were as remote from me, personally, as the Ark of the Covenant, and as much revered. The almost holy ecstasy I had felt at the sight of that head by Couture did not stir either ego or ambition. It was rather a winged flight outside of these and had nothing to do with any sort of performance of my own. I had never seen painting materials, canvas, colors, palette, etc. I had, I think fortunately, never seen first attempts in the use of these. In fact, my feeling for what lay about and around Nature and the life of my environment was really an unconscious perception of Art; my eyes eager for the enjoyment they were able to feel in every variety of perception made of me an absorbed spectator, rather than a performer.

Of course, I never had heard of 'self–expression.' Life to me was something to be relished. If I had dreams, they were of poetry, or of houses; not fairy palaces, but very real abodes; such, indeed, as would have been exactly right for our family if we, that is, our means, had permitted. ...

My uncle, who from this time forward became the directing power at every point in my development, had a relative, Miss Catharine Drinker, who soon after this became the wife of Thomas A. Janvier, the writer.

Cousin Kate Drinker's studio was at the top of an old house at Fifth and Walnut Streets, on Independence Square, so that that exquisite monument, standing in its grove of trees, was always near and visible to me as I came and went.

I am glad that the studio was typical, traditional, and not to be confused with any ordinary or domestic scene, for it was the first studio I ever entered. On its threshold, everyday existence dropped completely out of sight and memory. What windows there were, were covered with hangings, nondescript, as they were under the shadow of the skylight, which was upright, like a broad high window, and without glare. There was a vast sweeping curtain which partly shut off one side of the room, and this, with other dark corners, contributed to its mystery and suggestiveness. The place had long been a studio, and bore the signs of this in big, partly obliterated figures, outlines, drawn in chalk, upon its dusky wall, opposite the light.

. . . But the manifestation of what proved to be a lifelong first cause and study, that of the miracles of light and what they could develop and hide, were here first revealed to me in all their full volume and simplicity.

Painting "Les Derniers Jours d'Enfance"

Finding myself in a large barren studio, . . . I began to think of a picture. . . . The picture I saw to do was a large picture, and I saw it complete in composition, the figures, lighting, and accessories. I took an old piece of sketching-board and did the composition small, but containing all the important masses, lines, and color. The subject was to be my sister, seated, full-length, with her first-born son in her lap. The picture was to be 'landscape' in form, and the figures were to be seen as if one stood over them. The mother in black sat in a low chair, the brown-eyed boy of three almost reclining in her arms. He was to wear a short blue-and-white cotton garment, his bare legs trailing over his mother's knees. Her head was bent over him, and his hands lay upon her very white ones, which were clasped around him.

The whole picture was to be warm in tone and in an interior which did not exist, except in the mind of the designer.

Strangely enough, the presiding *dæmon* spoke French in whispering the name of the proposed work. 'Les derniers jours d'enfance.' And this title never seemed translatable or to be spoken in English. . . .

❖

I had pretty well arranged matters before my sitters came for the first time. None of the kitchen chairs I had would do; there would be no possibility of reaching the desired pose in any of them. There was an old steamer chair in our storeroom which, of course, could be relegated, though entirely wrong in accessory and design; in fact, like all steamer chairs these qualities were entirely absent except in action, but with the aid of two flat cushions, my models could take in it exactly the desired position. Harry possessed already the garment I wished him to wear, but my sister had nothing like my design for her; but this gave little trouble. Her frock was to be entirely black with slight variation in textures. An old black jersey of mine did very well for this, and, as the picture was to show only one arm fully, I made one black satin sleeve, fitting closely, with a little rich lace at the wrist. Around my sister's knees and lap, and exactly taking the lines of a skirt, we draped a canton crêpe shawl of my grandmother's. It had been dyed black, and had a rich, hanging texture, though delicate, and taking the form. . . .

The 'less than life' conception of the figures, as they sat, back in the picture, with no absolute foreground to 'place' them, would have usually required more experience than I possessed. But I had never heard of discouragement. Even after the picture was started, I changed the canvas and stretcher twice, and of course leaned heavily upon the original sketch, which contained every essential mass.

In the background, I followed the tones the sketch suggested. I felt the need of a strong horizontal mass across the canvas behind the group, and lower in value than the section above it, against which my sister's head and a little of the chair were to show. . . .

To me, nearly the highest point of interest lay in the group of four hands which occupied the very centre of the composition, the boy's fingers showing a little dark upon the back of the mother's white hand. The arm and back of the steamer chair I had to ignore and forget, as nothing was to be found that in the main would 'fit,' and I was obliged to invent a chair 'to taste.'

❖

STUDY AT THE ACADÉMIE JULIAN

I began, of course, with an 'Academy,' a full-length drawing. 'Tony' — that is Tony Robert Fleury — was to criticise that week, and at the hour entered a young-middle-aged and very handsome man, with a face in which there were deep marks of disappointment; his eyes, grey and deeply set, smouldered with burnt-out fires. How un-American they were! As I observed him from behind my easel, I felt that I had touched for the first time the confines of that which made France and Paris a place of pilgrimage. Into the room with him came something, not perhaps a quality of his own, but of what he had come from and lived in. The class, although accustomed to him, was in a flutter. I was still and icy with terror, fearing among other qualms that I might not understand him and blunder hideously.

My turn approached. He sat down. I knew only enough French to stammer out, as my defence, that it was my first attempt in Life-Class. He muttered something in a deep voice that sounded like an oath, and plunged me deeper in woe. The class, which understood better, looked around. I began to hear that he was quoting Corneille. He asked me where I had studied, and my story did not seem to account for my drawing. He rose, not having given me any advice, but bent his cavernous eyes on me with a penetrating but very reserved smile and turned to the next. The class had gathered round by this time, the English to the fore, and when le Maître had left, they rushed to me, and, if it had been the practice of the day in *cours* like ours, would have borne me on their shoulders.

Of course, I listened to all the criticism I could get wind of, and was to learn that analytical methods were not used in the French *cours*.

❖

. . . I am glad that my long hours in the Life-Class were untroubled by doubt. I was working my way into the mystery of Nature, like a chipmunk storing up what could be used later, every step revealing secrets of vision I burned to express; to cease from blundering and begin to conquer, to state what I saw as being a salvage of the best; discovery of integral truth, discovery of means to report it that would mate with my emotion. My powers, such as they were,

were too occupied for self-analysis or self-estimate. There was no virtue in this; I was simply too busy with what crowded the moments before me to think even of what I should do with my accumulation. I made one or two attempts at painting and found that, without space and power to move, I got nowhere. I could neither see nor feel, and I felt smothered among the canvases about me. I decided to give up painting in the class, and devoted all my time to drawing, the difference of scale taking the place of space. I tried only to learn the figure, amazing enough in the pose, but when the rest came, and I could see what movement revealed, I attempted only to get it by heart, to store up passages, articulations, weight. What I saw of color quality, surface light, which painting would express, I could not do violence to. I could not destroy my vision, turn it into leaden, meaningless pigment. I must *wait* for painting.

❖

Meeting with Claude Monet

I did not linger long on this visit. It was midsummer, the least characteristic period of the year in Paris. But before I left, one, to me, highly memorable event had occurred. Mrs. Tom Perry (Lilla Cabot Perry) was painting at Giverney, to be near Monet, and would take me to see him. No sun and weather could have been more fortunate for a visit to the specialist in light than we were blessed with. We found him in the very centre of 'a Monet,' indeed: that is, in his garden at high noon, under a blazing sky, among his poppies and delphiniums. He was in every way part of the picture, or the beginning and end of it, in his striped blue overalls, buttoned at wrists and ankles, big hat casting luminous shadow over his eyes, but 'finding,' in full volume, the strong nose and great grey beard. Geniality, welcome, health, and power radiated from his whole person. . . . Monet pulled out his latest series, views, at differing hours and weather, of the river, announcing the full significance of summer, sun, heat, and quiet on the reedy shore. The pictures were flowing in treatment, pointillism was in abeyance, at least for these subjects. Mrs. Perry did not fear to question the change of surface, which was also a change of *donné*. 'Oh,' said the *Maître*, nonchalantly, 'la Nature n'a pas de pointes.' This at a moment when the *haute nouveauté* seekers of that summer had just learned 'how to do it,' and were covering all their canvases with small lumps of white paint touched with blue, yellow, and pink. But they had not reckoned on the non-static quality of a discoverer's mind, which, in his desire for more light, would be always moving. For Monet was never satisfied. Even the science of Clemenceau, and his zeal for his friend, did not get to the bottom of the difficulty, which was purely physical. One could push the sorry pigment far, but not where Monet's dream would have it go, imagining that by sheer force of desire and *volonté*, the *nature* of the *material* he thought to dominate would be overcome. For the moment, when actual light gleamed upon it, fresh from the tube, it had the desired effulgence, but it could not withstand time and exposure, and maintain the integral urge of Monet's idea.

❖

Her family's support

It is needless to say that the environment of an artist, especially during the first years of struggle — for struggle is always present in one form or another —

has an immense influence upon his productivity and expansion. Many a youthful proclivity, perhaps power, has gone under before family or other prejudice, or careless interruption, or a lack of belief or understanding of the 'case.'. . .

. . . My family never flattered me, to myself or others; neither did they pretend to understand an art they had not applied themselves to. They understood perfectly the spirit and the necessities of an artist's life. . . .

The aunt with the sleek head (before mentioned), with her curving smile, used to quote a notice that had appeared in a penny newspaper: 'The Item does not hesitate to declare that Miss Cecilia Beaux is the best Female Portrait Painter in Philadelphia.' No wonder that I advanced with a thoroughly made-up mind on the subject of Sex in Art. But this aunt was the very one, who, in order that I might start fresh for my day's work, made my bed and 'did' my room, leaving the breakfast table — for I had to start early — to follow me to the front door, with my basket, containing a bottle of milk, and a large buttered roll that she had prepared. It was quite a long walk from our house in West Philadelphia to the trolley which bore me to town in about forty minutes. This was easy enough in the morning, and I generally reached my studio at nine. An hour was none too much for clearing the decks for action, preparing my palette, considering the canvas in progress, and my intentions concerning it, so that at ten I was no more than ready for the subject who was expected to be prompt also, and who finding me always waiting, easily got the habit.

I soon found that intensive work, for me, could not be carried over into the afternoon. Fortunately, I was aware when the moment came when there was nothing more, of the best, to give. But the later hours, though recognized not to be worthy of high pressure, could contain those operations and accumulations that characterize any studio, and upon which the golden hours should not be wasted. At this time, also, I was liable to the agreeable interruptions of friends, from some of whom I received fresh and stimulating influence.

After a struggle in the short winter days, with the weather, crowds, and long waits at street-corners at the rush hour (I rarely had a seat in the car), the walk home, on feet that had stood nearly all day, and with nerves that had spent all they had, what a refuge was mine! I need not speak to any one; I could go to my room until dinner time, and after it I frequently spent the whole evening on the parlor sofa, completely relaxed, and often asleep, or just conscious of my comfort, sometimes of my uncle's voice, reading, of quiet laughter, talk, and some challenge. Nothing was required of me. Although the life at home was or would have been monotonous, except for the mental quality of those who formed it, I was never expected to bring in life and entertainment to revive a dull evening; still less to do any of those small services that would naturally have been the part of the young, active member of the family. In all the years that followed my return from abroad, to the, alas, final breaking-up of our circle, I was never once asked to do an errand in town, some bit of shopping, or a call, that would have put the slightest pressure upon me. So well did they understand.

❖

EXCERPTS FROM CECILIA BEAUX'S, UNPUBLISHED WRITINGS
(Archives of American Art, Washington, D. C.)

CECILIA BEAUX TO ELIZA LEAVITT (MATERNAL AUNT)

Paris, April 12, 1888

... Mlle Klumpke is a short, quiet little thing and *lame* — feet all askew — and she speaks three languages equally well and plays on the zither — she is *very* nice to me and has invited me to come to her studio.'

You really need not be worried about any indiscretions of ours. We have almost no temptations — nor any chance for any — and we are not going to do anything imprudent in any way. I think Cecil takes pleasure in making out that things are improper to do.

... When we were leaving Mr. Stewardson's studio I made a laughing sort of apology about its being Bohemian ... and a slight but shocked expression passed across his face — and I was quite ashamed — The only other thing we have done that could possibly be called imprudent was our walking home with Mr. Rhinehart and Mr. Greyson from the Weeks' — and my taking a Sunday afternoon walk with little Billy Elliott, *the* stiffest little Philadelphia prig that ever lived who would perish before he would *do anything* not *comme il faut* ...

I am making a pretty good study this week at the Cours. The model stands like a statue and has bushy black hair. I am doing a life size head shoulder and arm on a big sheet of paper. Have begun the composition "Lot's Wife" but shant have time to finish it unless I do it this evening — We have Fleury next week and I shall try to do a good one for him. You ask how I do them. They are done in oil monochrome — brown or black or burnt sienna — on boards such as I used to sketch on last summer. . . . The one I did the *Supper at Emmaus* on was 8 by 10 inches.

❖

CECILIA BEAUX TO HER FAMILY

Paris, February 17, 1889

Dear Old Folks at home:

I address this letter to you Aunt Emily because you are always calling yourself 'old folks'. We have just done up our chores and settled down to write. I have semi-dusted the room and cleaned up — and I always try to wash the saucepan a little cleaner on Sunday morning. I also dusted out the closet shelves and threw away numerous drying things. . . .

We like Colarossi's very much. It is tough there but the class is a very nice one, mostly English and American and many of the girls are friends. . . .

It is very weird at Colarossi's going there at night. We went with Miss Forster and after passing through a hall of a house, descended into a large court gleaming with broken statues, and bas reliefs, models standing around with a little flickering light falling on them — then up and up long dark flights of stairs with only a small flaming lamp on the top step to light us — into a vast atelier where the ruler was fixing the gaslight not yet lighted. We didn't get started until half past seven. Had a darling little Italian boy for a model. . . . We shall probably only have Dignan once they say but must be thankful for that. Courtois came on Thursday evening — went through the room in about 15 minutes. Says only about one word to each girl but is very much to the point — at least he hit the mark on the head with me — I had made a horrid drawing. I knew it was common and clumsy and fussy. He told me it was too much *'tortillisés'* that I must study the main lines more carefully and be more *'simples.'* . . .

. . . I am much surprised that Mlle Klumpke should have received the Temple Gold Medal for that picture. It must have been a pretty poor exhibition — It was well having it in the Salon last year but the Figaro said about it that the kindest thing that could be said about it was that it would have been better left undone.

❖

CECILIA BEAUX TO DOROTHEA GILDER (BEAUX'S FRIEND, SOMETIME TRAVELING COMPANION, DAUGHTER OF RICHARD AND HELENA deKAY GILDER)
Washington, D. C., March 27 (1902)

I wrote, didn't I, that Ethel is in the picture? She is an enchanting child — She sits beside her mother in C.B. [Cecilia Beaux] costume on a sofa made of a W.H. [White House] monstrosity from the East Room, converted by means of a box addition, a comfortable and some green brocade, into a charming 'chaise longue' by C.B. The drama is — Mrs. R. [Roosevelt] (people in) cordially engaged with a visitor —Modestly fearless little daughter, impelled by mingled curiousity and affection enters and flings herself down besides Mama who takes her little hand into her own lap to insure quiet and communicate maternal sympathy. Little daughter not interested in visitor, looks eagerly eagerly across her mother's bows at something else for which I am an humble understudy. A pale blue velvet bow pins the eye to the middle of the canvas and around it these various animations vibrate and are finally lost in the ruby depths (no opposition) of the private dining room wall paper.

❖

EXCERPTS FROM ADDRESSES

BARNARD COLLEGE ANNIVERSARY DINNER, 29 APRIL (1911?), ON THE SUBJECT OF 'WOMEN IN ART'

I very earnestly believed . . . that there should be neither advantage nor disadvantage in being a man or a woman. I am pointing . . . to a millenium at least in a woman's view if I predict an hour when the term Women in Art will be as strange sounding a topic as the title Men in Art would be now.

There are now no obstacles in their way [for women in art]. All doors are open to women sculptors, painters, illustrators. In art it is unweaned strength alone that is truly productive.

There used to be a saying that Art is a jealous mistress. Let no woman be too proud to look upon her art as a jealous lord — a sungod who will have all or nothing. Who beams upon her real achievement but is cruelly scornful of less.

❖

SIMMONS COLLEGE, APRIL 30, 1907, ON THE PUBLIC AND MODERN ART

We should never separate the art of our time from the past. There is no fundamental reason. . . Art is what it has always been — a RESULT of Humanity — not a gift of the Gods to one period — and withheld from another.

The source of art is as remote as the source of Life — and as diverse as Life's manifestations. Our universe is made up of myriads of cycles, of myriad dimensions, each made up of infinitely divided periods of change. The cycle of the butterfly, the cycle of men, the cycle of the nations, — only a littlle longer — all these cycles may be measured easily — but the cycle of art is as large as the cycle of conscious life on our planet and how can we tell when that began? . . . The present moment is the only real one that can be touched and handled and all history is a succession of present moments.

We call a period modern but we must remember that Art has always been modern. For the public the artist is the seer — the interpreter. He makes beliefs tangible. He is like the poet, the voice of the inarticulate. To this expectant multitude he raises his voice. His word to them is the most majestic of all declarations — "Behold I show you a mystery."

This is the ideal condition.

❖

ON PORTRAITURE, MAY 14, 1907

To me it seems less important if we are seeking to understand the rock in its beauty to look at it historically . . . rather than to look at its beautiful union with nature, its hold on life around it, then its interlife and relation.

This seems more essential to me than to dig it out, weigh it and measure it. . . . For my part I would always rather look for what a subject is than for what it is not. I believe that every feeble, vulgar, spurious so-called Art production has a distinct and lasting effect wherever it is seen. . . . The artist has leaped a chasm. For he does not join soul with soul, mind with mind, but soul with body. The artist joins force of thought with the force of matter. From a few notes he must make great harmonies, out of reserve must come richness.

Fire and flood must accompany every touch of his hand.

The great works are all abstractions. The result of an alchemy so powerful that were the living subject to pass before us we should disbelieve in the evidence of our senses. The artist has turned matter into mind.

Estate of Cecilia Beaux.

Self–Portrait with Palette, c. 1883. Oil on canvas. 36⅛" x 28¾"
Musée des Beaux-Arts, Nice, France.

MARIE BASHKIRTSEFF

1858?–1884

MARIE BASHKIRTSEFF'S DEATH
in her mid-twenties makes uncertain any judgment regarding the artistic impact
she might have had, had she lived longer. Her journal, however, first published
three years after her death, greatly influenced several generations of young
women at the turn of the century (much as Anne Frank's influenced such readers during the second half of this century). Begun in her early teens, the journal
vividly depicts the process of coming into womanhood as it was experienced by
some in the late nineteenth century and offers insight into the way in which a woman
could claim her artistic vocation. Recent discovery of the extent to which Bashkirtseff's original diary was altered (probably by her family) for publication has
encouraged contemporary reevaluation of the journal and the persona presented therein.

A child of minor Russian aristocrats and a member of a chic international community, Bashkirtseff decided to study painting in her late teens; just seven years
later, she died of pulmonary congestion caused by tuberculosis. Born in Gavronzi
in the Ukraine, when she was about two, her mother left her father and returned
to the extended family of her birth, the Babanines. According to Colette Cosnier,
the uncensored manuscript of Bashkirtseff's journal reveals her mother as an attractive, high-living woman whose parents shared with her the responsibility for raising her children. Their household included, in addition to Marie, her younger brother,

and her mother, her mother's parents, sister, and profligate brother George and his daughter, Dina, as well as a family doctor. George was notorious for his scandalous affairs, possibly even arranging a marriage in bad faith for one of his sisters to a member of the Romanoff family. Mme Bashkirtseff censored most references to these occurrences after her daughter's death, but they may explain in part the social ostracism of the Babanine family. Attempting to gain recognition from members of the aristocracy, the extended family traveled to social centers within Russia, beginning in 1870 a tour of various European spas for the same purpose. Shortly after leaving Russia, they settled in Nice, their primary residence for the next seven years, and tried again to establish themselves in high society. Bashkirtseff returned to Russia only once before her death, spending the summer that she was about sixteen with her father at the villa in Gavronzi.

She began her journal in Nice, in October 1872, apparently intending it to be a private document. The earliest surviving entry, from January 1873, reveals her obsession with the Duke of Hamilton, an English nobleman also living in Nice, to whom she was never actually introduced. The romanticized description of this "daydream love affair" forms its first section. Infatuation with him (or possibly with another distantly admired nobleman) might well have been the factor that led her to begin keeping a journal. It is not unusual even now for a woman to use a journal to explore her responses to times of change in her life, and at first Bashkirtseff used her diary as a forum for exploring her emerging sexuality. Although to her dismay "the Duke of H." married someone else a year later, she recorded many of her actual liaisons (some of which were omitted from the published version to maintain her angelic image) and described as well the path of her intellectual development.

During the years in Nice, Bashkirtseff designed for herself a course of study based on that of the lycée. Her entries make clear that her elders did not hesitate to interrupt her studies for such activities as dress-fitting or entertaining. She also took private drawing lessons during this time and, in 1877, decided that she wanted to pursue a career as an artist. Believing that this required a move to Paris, Bashkirtseff persuaded her family to relocate. Although willing (and wealthy enough) to support the move, their respect for her professional commitment was not more serious than that for her earlier academic studies. At the Académie Julian, Bashkirtseff studied primarily with M. Julian himself and with Tony Robert-Fleury, who also taught Cecilia Beaux and Anna Klumpke, Rosa Bonheur's companion and biographer. Although her journals indicate that their critiques were not always glowing, it seems that both teachers respected her abilities. At first some of her fellow students perceived her only as a rich girl playing at being an artist, but again according to her journal, after seeing her talent and determination, they accepted her into their world with its camaraderies and rivalries. Cosnier claims that Bashkirtseff's family edited some of the more pungent descriptions of her student days prior to publication, presumably to erase traces of "unladylike" slang.

After only three years of study, in 1880, she made her first submission to (and acceptance by) the Salon, a painting of her cousin Dina, *Young Girl Reading* The Question of Divorce [a book by Dumas]. Thereafter she submitted work annually, with the exception of 1882, when she was ill. Much to her disappointment, her last entry, *The Meeting* (1884), did not receive a medal, although it did receive attention in the press. In the last three years of her life, the painter Jules Bastien-Lepage became her mentor.

Within six months of her last Salon submission, Bashkirtseff died of tuberculosis, possibly contracted at one of the many spas she visited with her family. Her health had been fragile for much of her life: in her girlhood she wanted to sing, but lost her voice; in 1880 she suffered a partial hearing loss; and, in 1881, she had a bad attack of the tuberculosis. Her premonitions of an early death, so evident in her writings, may have been engendered by her actual ill health and perhaps magnified by her penchant for the dramatic.

Bashkirtseff's artistic accomplishments, compiled in a *Catalogue des oeuvres de mademoiselle Bashkirtseff* published in 1885, listed well over one hundred works, although many were incomplete at the time of her death. Mme Bashkirtseff gave at least eighty-five of her daughter's works to the Hermitage Museum in Leningrad, and Cosnier has located nineteen others outside the Soviet Union. Considering that there were only seven years between Bashkirtseff's decision to study art and her death, her output was impressive, as was the acceptance of several works by the Salon. Whether she would have fulfilled her ambition will always be an open question. Despite her work's acceptance by others, Berthe Morisot bemoaned Bashkirtseff's artistic conservatism. Also, her seriousness of purpose has been questioned by feminist writers such as Simone de Beauvoir, who censoriously interprets her longing for fame and fortune as narcissism. This is an unfair categorization: art's central role in the last seven years of Bashkirtseff's life is clear, becoming during that time the main focus of her diary entries.

Bashkirtseff was conscious of her own social class's status in relation to others. Many of her later works, beginning with *Jean et Jacques* (1883), feature young street urchins. Although she claimed that she did not want to intrude on Bastien-Lepage's territory, in fact, her interest in this motif could have been stimulated by his work. Rozsika Parker and Griselda Pollock suggest that she found the subject of young working-class boys attractive because it allowed her to participate vicariously in their "fantastic" freedom, compared to her own very circumscribed existence as an aristocratic young lady. She writes of dressing down to pass inconspicuously among the bourgeoisie, but also writes condescendingly of the bourgeois inability to understand her artistic sentiments.

For many years Bashkirtseff was perceived as a type of late nineteenth-century heroine: a romantic, creative, and innocent young girl who died tragically of that fin de siècle scourge, tuberculosis. Shortly after her death, Bashkirtseff's mother had instigated the construction of a mythicized persona. Mme Bashkirtseff accentuated the sentimental aspects of her daughter's life and its premature end, creating a heroine mourned inconsolably by her loving, grief-stricken mother. She offered tours of a room in her apartment alleged to have been her daughter's last, although in fact Bashkirtseff had died before her mother's residence there, and she built an ostentatious tomb in Passy, designed by Bastien-Lepage's brother. Even the date of Bashkirtseff's birth was intentionally obscured (and continues to remain uncertain). The published journals give November 11, 1860, but examination of the original manuscript indicates that her age was altered to make her seem younger — hence, more precocious and tragic. Other apparent alterations and the discrepancy between the older Julian and newer Gregorian Russian calendars contribute to the confusion. The edited journal, first published only three years after Marie's death, was read by an entire generation, including Paula Modersohn-Becker, Berthe Morisot and Morisot's daughter, Julie Manet. After Mme Bashkirtseff's death in 1920, the papers found a new audience, but they were doctored once again to reflect someone else's view. The bowdlerized diaries were even satirized by humorist Stephen Leacock as *The Sorrows of a Super Soul: Marie Mushenough.*

As with any other journal, the reader is challenged to separate the narrator from the constructed protagonist, a particularly problematic issue in this case. Bashkirtseff herself speaks of the distinction between the two in her statement that "the woman writing, and her whom I describe, are really two persons." One complicating factor is that, after her first serious bout with tuberculosis, at least three years before her death, she had decided to publish the volume. Although she claimed in her preface that the prospect of publication made her especially truthful, the journal had ceased to be a private document. One cannot assume that she could be completely truthful even if she were writing her diary only for herself, but it was inevitable that her writing would be transformed by her awareness of a future audience. As with a formal autobiography the reader needs to approach with critical caution. Since the published journal was a highly expurgated version of the original eighty-four notebooks, the narrative voice may not accurately reflect that of the Bashkirtseff herself.

As Jane Marcus points out, Bashkirtseff attempted to gain the reader's complicity in her struggle for self-fulfillment, as she tried to persuade "us" to understand her as no one in her life was able to do. It is easy to dislike the protagonist of the early entries, who occupies her time with frivolities, who is obsessed with a man she has never met, and who engages in histrionics that the actual events of her life do not seem to justify. While these superficial interests may reflect the norms of her privileged class, they are also a function of her young age. At least at the beginning, Bashkirtseff's purpose in writing seems to have been to sort through the tensions involved in the process of becoming a woman. (Julie Manet's comment in her own youthful diary that Bashkirtseff's journal could best be understood by a young girl seems perceptive and accurate.)

Bashkirtseff's journal reveals her simultaneous struggles to become an artist and to become an adult. She began it in response to her newfound sexuality and continued it during the years of her developing maturity. Interested at first primarily in her social life — the clothes she bought and social events she attended — by her mid-twenties, her main focus was on becoming an artist, recording the long hours she spent in the studio and the release she gained from work. While her privileged background made it financially feasible for her to be an artist, it also constrained her. Her elegant clothes literally bound her. She bemoaned her lack of freedom "of coming and going." Her sexuality was also confined by the limitations and expectations of her class (even when the more explicit passages expurgated by Mme Bashkirtseff are mentally reinstated). Bashkirtseff voiced great conflict about marriage. On the one hand, it was expected of her, she was groomed for it, and she indulged in countless fantasies about her future mate. On the other, like so many other nineteenth-century women artists, she feared being trapped by marriage. As she wrote, "A famous man marries, he takes a woman whom he loves, . . . he organizes his house thus, and the woman is his. But me, I don't want to be that woman, because *I* am the famous man. So, therefore, what should I do? Remain free." The differing demands of her artistic vocation and her gender concerned her. She speaks of the contrast between her real self and her shell, saying "there is nothing of the woman about me but the envelope." There is also evidence to suggest that gender as a political issue was important for Bashkirtseff. Although her family omitted all references to the subject but one, she regularly attended meetings of a suffragist group and contributed to the feminist journal, *La Citoyenne*. Anna Klumpke recounted that Bashkirtseff circulated a petition at the Académie Julian demanding that women be allowed to work all day from the nude model, as were the male students.

Bashkirtseff's journal represents an excellent example of *les écritures féminines*. Parker and Pollock assert that through the "intense daily activity of writing," Marie Bashkirtseff created a text that covered "the lacks and the splits" in her daily life. To restore the speech of a woman who waited so long to be heard (as Cosnier says she tried to do in her recent biography), one must delve into many levels: the facts of Bashkirtseff's life, the words of her journal, the falsified accounts of her life, the response to the created myth. The published journal was twice translated into English, in 1889 by Mary Serrano and in 1891 by Mathilde Blind. The excerpts in this book are taken from the latter. Parker and Pollock present an intelligent rereading of the text in their introduction to Blind's translation; nonetheless, a new edition of Bashkirtseff's journal based on the original notebooks is long overdue. At least the process of reevaluation has begun.

SOURCES

Bashkirtseff, Marie. *The Journal of Marie Bashkirtseff.* Translated by Mathilde Blind. Introduction by Rozsika Parker and Griselda Pollock. London: Virago Press, 1985.

Cosnier, Colette. *Marie Bashkirtseff, Un portrait sans retouches.* Paris: Pierre Horay, 1985.

Langley Moore, Doris. *Marie and the Duke of H., The Daydream Love Affair of Marie Bashkirtseff.* Philadelphia and New York: J. B. Lippincott, 1966.

Marcus, Jane. "Invincible Mediocrity: The Private Selves of Public Women." In *The Private Self*, edited by Shari Benstock, 114–46. Chapel Hill: University of North Carolina Press, 1987.

EXCERPTS FROM MARIE BASHKIRTSEFF'S JOURNAL

Preface, May 1, 1884
. . . Why tell lies and play a part? Yes, it is clear that I have the wish, if not the hope, of remaining on this earth by whatever means in my power. If I do not die young, I hope to survive as a great artist; but if I do, I will have my Journal published, which cannot fail to be interesting. But as I talk of publicity, this idea of being read has perhaps spoilt, nay, destroyed, the sole merit of such a book? Well, no! To begin with, I wrote for a long time without a thought of being read, and in the next place it is precisely because I hope to be read that I am absolute-

ly sincere. If this book be not the *exact*, the *absolute*, the *strict* truth, it has no right to exist. I not only say all the time what I think, but I never contemplated hiding for an instant what might make me appear ridiculous, or prove to my disadvantage; for the rest I think myself too admirable for censure. Rest assured, therefore, kind reader, that I reveal myself completely, entirely. *I*, personally, may, perhaps, possess but a feeble interest for *you*; but do not think that it is I: think, here is a human being who tells you all its impressions from childhood. It cannot help being interesting as a document of human nature. Ask M. Zola even M. de Goncourt, or Maupassant. My diary begins at twelve years of age, and begins to have some meaning from the age of fifteen or sixteen. Therefore a hiatus remains to be filled up, and I will write a kind of preface which will enable the reader to follow this human and literary document. . . .

❖

Nice, January 1873

. . . I was made for emotions, for success; the best I can do, therefore, is to turn singer. If God would only have the goodness to preserve, strengthen, and increase my voice, I could achieve the success I long for. I could have the satisfaction of being known, admired, famous, and in that way I could secure him I love. If I remain as I am I have little hope that he will ever love me, for he knows nothing of my existence even. But when he sees me famous, successful! . . . Men are ambitious! . . . Then, too, I can be received in society, for I shall not be a celebrity sprung from God knows where! I am of noble extraction and there's no need for my making a living; this will ensure greater success and enable me to rise with more facility. Life will be perfect thus. I dream of nothing but fame, of being known all the world over. . . .

. . . And when he sees a young lady who has reached the highest pinnacle of fame a woman can attain, who is pure and virtuous, and has loved him faithfully from her childhood, he will be so surprised that he will wish to have me at any price, and marry me from sheer pride. But what am I saying? Why shouldn't I suppose him capable of loving me? Oh yes, with God's help! Has God not helped me to find out a way of securing him I love? . . . I return thanks, O God!

❖

Russia, August 29 1873

. . . I have begun arranging my hours of study. I shall have done to-morrow! I must study nine hours a day. God grant me energy and courage to apply myself; I have both, but would like still more.

❖

Russia, January 9, 1874

Coming in from my walk, I thought to myself, You'll never be staid and proper like other young ladies. I never could understand how this seriousness comes about. How one suddenly passes from childhood to maidenhood. I asked myself: How does it happen? Little by little, or in a single day? The causes which develop, ripen, or change you must either be brought about by some misfortune or by love. If I were a wit I should say the two things are synonymous; but I don't say it, because I think love is the most beautiful thing in the world. I may compare myself to a sheet of water which is frozen below and only agitated on the surface, for nothing interests or amuses me at *bottom*. . . .

❖

Russia, July 14, 1874

We have been speaking of Latin, of public schools and of examinations; this has inspired me with a burning desire to study, and when Brunet came I did not keep him waiting, but asked him for an account of the examinations. His account is such that I felt I should be able to present myself, after a year of study, for a scholarship. We will speak of it further.

I have been studying Latin since last February, and we are now in July. According to Brunet, I have accomplished in five months what they do at the college in three years. It's tremendous! I shall never forgive myself for having lost this year. It will grieve me dreadfully; I shall never forget it! . . .

❖

Nice and Rome, May 19, 1876

At midnight he (Pietro Antonelli) rose and bade me good-night, pressing my hand tightly.

"Good evening, Monsieur," I said.

Our eyes met, and I cannot describe what a simultaneous flash it was.

"Well, aunt, we shall leave early to-morrow; you had better go to your room, and I shall lock you in to prevent your disturbing me while I am writing; then I shall go to bed quickly."

"You promise?"

"Certainly."

I locked my aunt's room, and, after giving a glance in the looking-glass, I went down-stairs, and Pietro slipped through the half-open door like a shadow.

"So much may be said without words when we love! As for me," he whispered, "I love you."

It amused me to act a scene in a novel, and involuntarily I thought of Dumas. . . .

Did I really love him, or was it an affair of the imagination? Who can tell exactly? And yet, from the moment one doubts . . . doubt is no longer possible.

"Yes, I love you," I said, taking his two hands in mine and pressing them hard. He said nothing; perhaps he did not understand what importance I attached to my words, or perhaps he only considered them natural.

My heart had ceased beating. It was a delicious moment, for he remained as motionless as I did, without uttering a syllable. But I grew frightened, and told him to go. . . .

I began undressing, deep in thought all the time. If any one had seen me go into the drawing-room, near the staircase, at midnight, and leaving it at two o'clock, past two o'clock, after an uninterrupted *tête-à-tête* with one of the most profligate young Italians, this person would not believe the Almighty himself, if he should have a fancy for coming down from heaven in order to declare my innocence. . . .

❖

Nice and Rome, May 31, 1876

I am nervous about my eyes. I have been obliged to stop several times during my painting. I use them too much for I spend all my time in painting, reading, and writing.

I have spent this evening in going over my abstracts of the classics, as it gave me something to do, and then I discovered a very interesting work on Confucius, in a Latin and French translation. There's nothing like having one's mind occupied; work overcomes everything, especially brain work.

I can't understand how women can pass their time in knitting and embroidering, keeping their hands occupied and their heads idle. . . .

❖

Nice & Rome, July 2, 1876

. . . What is the good of my having studied, of having tried to know more than other women, of priding myself on knowing all the branches of learning that are attributed to famous men in their biographies? . . .

To marry and have children! Any washerwoman can do that.

Unless I could find a civilised and enlightened man, or one who is pliant and very much in love.

What do I want? Oh, you know well enough. I want GLORY. . . .

What then am I? Nothing. What do I want to be? Everything.

❖

Paris, May 30, 1877

. . . Indeed, the woman who is writing, and her whom I describe, are really two persons. What are all her troubles to *me*? I tabulate, analyse, and copy the daily life of my person; but *to me, to myself*, all that is very indifferent. It is my pride, my self-love, my interests, my envelope, my eyes, which suffer, or weep, or rejoice; but *I, myself*, am there only to watch, to write, to relate, and to reason calmly about these great miseries, just as Gulliver must have looked at the Lilliputians. . . .

❖

Paris, October 4, 1877

The day passes quickly when you are drawing from eight till twelve, and from one till five. Going backwards and forwards takes up nearly an hour and a half, and then I was a little late, so that I had only six hours' work.

When I think of the years and years I have lost, I feel tempted in my anger to wish it all at the devil. . . . But that would be worse still. Come, miserable wretch, be glad to have begun at last! And to think I might have done so at thirteen! Four years!

I should have painted historical pictures by now if I had begun four years ago. All that I have learned only hinders me. I must begin over again.

I have been obliged to begin the front view of the head twice over before it turned out to my satisfaction. As for the study from the nude, it came of itself, and M. Julian did not correct a single line. He was not there when I arrived; it was a pupil who told me how to begin; I had never seen a study from the nude before.

All I have done till now has been but a sorry jest!

At last I am working with artists, real artists, who have exhibited at the Salon, and who sell their pictures and portraits — who even give lessons.

Julian is pleased with the way I have begun. "By the end of the winter you will be able to paint some very good portraits," he said to me.

He says that sometimes his female students are as clever as the young men. I should have worked with the latter, but they smoke — and, besides, there is no advantage. There was when the women had only the draped model; but since they make studies from the nude, it is just the same. . . .

I am, oh! so happy!

❖

Paris, October 6, 1877

I have seen no one, as I have been at the studio.

"Don't be afraid," said Julian; "you will get on fast enough."

And when mamma called for me at five o'clock in the evening, he said something of this sort —

"I thought it was the whim of a spoilt child; but I must acknowledge that she really works, that she has determination, and is gifted. If she goes on in the same way, in three months her drawings may get into the Salon."

❖

Paris, October 11, 1877

. . . It is so cold that I caught cold; but I *forgive* that, if I can only draw. And why draw?

To . . . to get all that I have been crying for since the world began. To get all that I have wanted, and still want. To get on by my talent, or in any way I can, but to get on. If I had *all that*, perhaps I should do nothing.

❖

Paris, October 13, 1877

Saturday is the day for M. Tony Robert Fleury to come to the studio. . . .

I began last Wednesday, and he could not come on the Saturday of the same week, so that for me it is his first visit. When he came to my easel and began to pronounce judgement, I interrupted him —

"Excuse me, Monsieur . . . I only began ten days ago."

"Where did you draw before?" he asked, looking at my drawing.

"Nowhere."

"What do you mean by nowhere?"

"Well, I took thirty-two lessons in painting to amuse myself."

"That isn't working."

"I know, Monsieur . . . and . . ."

He smiled, and did not believe it at all, so that I had again to give my word of honour, and he again said, "It is marvellous, and gives extraordinary promise for the future. This study of the nude is not at all bad, and that part is even well done. Work away," &c. &c. . . .

Whilst writing this I stopped, thinking of all the work that it will require, the time, the patience, the difficulties. . . .

It is not as easy to become a great painter as it is to say the words; besides talent and genius, there is also that relentless mechanical labour. . . . And I heard a voice say, "You will feel neither the time, nor the difficulties, and you will reach the goal unexpectedly!" And I have a firm belief in this voice, which has never deceived me. It has foretold me enough misfortunes for it not to lie this time. I have faith in it, and I feel that I am right to believe. . . .

Paris, November 17, 1877

. . . The competition was decided. There were eighteen competitors. I am thirteenth; so there are five below me; that's not so bad. . . .

. . . And I must tell you that M. Julian and the others said at the men's studio that I had neither the touch, nor the manner, nor the capabilities of a woman; and that they would like to know if there is any one in my family from whom I have inherited so much talent and vigour, nay even brutality, in drawing, and so much perseverance in my work. . . .

Paris, April 12, 1878

Yesterday Julian met Robert Fleury at the café, and Robert Fleury said I was a really interesting and surprising pupil, and that he hoped much from my future.

It is to that I must anchor myself, especially in those moments when all my brain is invaded by that inexplicable and terrible fear, and when I feel myself sinking in an abyss of doubt and torments of all kinds, without any cause whatever. . . .

I begin to believe I have a true passion for my art, which reassures and consoles me. I want nothing else, and I am too disgusted with everything to think of anything else.

If it were not for that uneasiness, that fear, I should be happy. . . .

I get up at sunrise, and am at the studio before the model. If only I can free myself from this fear, this accursed superstition! . . .

Paris, April 13, 1878

At twenty-two I shall be either famous or dead.

You think perhaps that one works only with the eyes and fingers?

You who are *bourgeois*, you will never know the amount of sustained attention, of unceasing comparison, of calculation, of feeling, of reflection, necessary to obtain any result.

Yes, yes, I know what you would say . . . but you say nothing at all, and I swear to you by Pincio's head (that seems stupid to you; it is not to me) — I swear that I will become famous; I swear solemnly — by the Gospels, by the passion of Christ, by myself — that in four years I will be famous.

Paris, April 29, 1878

At work from eight in the morning to six in the evening, from which you must deduct an hour and a half for going out to lunch; there is nothing so good as regular work.

To change the subject, I must tell you that I believe I shall never be seriously in love. I always discover something comical in the man, and then all is over. If he does not seem ridiculous, he is awkward, or stupid, or tiresome. In short, there is always a something that discovers the ass beneath the lion's skin.

It is true that until I find my master I shall not let myself be caught by any charm. Thank heaven, the mania I have of finding out people's faults will prevent my falling in love with one and all of the Adonises on earth! . . .

How silly the people are who go to the Bois, and how unable I am to understand their empty stupid existence!

❖

Paris, September 30, 1878

I have done my first regular painting. I was to do still-life studies, so I painted, as you already know, a blue vase and two oranges, and afterwards a man's foot, and that is all. . . .

I have written to Colignon that I should like to be a man. I know that I could be somebody, but with petticoats what do you expect one to do? Marriage is the only career for women; men have thirty-six changes, women only one, as with the bank of the gaming table, but, nevertheless, the bank is always sure to win; they say it is the same with women, but it is not so, for there is winning and winning. But how can one ever be too particular in the choice of a husband? I have never before felt so indignant at the present condition of women. I am not mad enough to claim that stupid equality which is an utopian idea — besides, it is bad form — for there can be no equality between two creatures so different as man and woman. I do not demand anything, for woman already possesses all that she ought to have, but I grumble at being a woman because there is nothing of the woman about me but the envelope.

❖

Paris, January 2, 1879

What I long for is the freedom of going about alone, of coming and going, of sitting on the seats in the Tuileries, and especially in the Luxembourg, of stopping and looking at the artistic shops, of entering the churches and museums, of walking about the old streets at night; that's what I long for; and that's the freedom without which one can't become a real artist. Do you imagine I can get much good from what I see, chaperoned as I am, and when, in order to go to the Louvre, I must wait for my carriage, my lady companion, or my family?

Curse it all, it is this that makes me gnash my teeth to think I am a woman! — I'll get myself a *bourgeois* dress and a wig, and make myself so ugly that I shall be as free as a man. It is this sort of liberty that I need, and without it I can never hope to do anything of note.

The mind is cramped by these stupid and depressing obstacles; even if I succeeded in making myself ugly by means of some disguise I should still be only half free, for a woman who rambles about alone commits an imprudence. And when it comes to Italy and Rome? The idea of going to see ruins in a landau!

"Marie, where are you going?"

"To the Collseum."

"But you have already seen it! Let us go to the theatre or to the Promenade; we shall find plenty of people there."

And that is quite enough to make my wings droop.

This is one of the principal reasons why there are no female artists. O profound ignorance! O cruel routine! But what is the use of talking?

Even if we talked most reasonably we should be subject to the old, well-worn scoffs with which the apostles of women are overwhelmed. After all, there may be some cause for laughter. Women will always remain women! But still . . . supposing they were brought up in the way men are trained, the inequality which I regret would disappear, and there would remain only that which is inherent in nature itself. Ah, well, no matter what I may say, we shall have to go on shrieking and making ourselves ridiculous (I will leave that to others) in order to gain this equality a hundred years hence. As for myself, I will try to set an example by showing Society a woman who shall have made her mark, in spite of all the disadvantages with which it hampered her.

❖

Paris, February 5, 1880

I should always like to spend my time like to-day — working from eight o'clock till twelve, and from two till five. At five, the lamp is brought in, and I draw till half-past seven.

To dress from half-past seven to eight, dine at eight o'clock, then read, and to go to sleep at eleven.

I own, that from two till half-past seven, without stopping, is rather tiring.

❖

Mont Dore, August 17, 1880

I have never had the perseverance to complete any writing satisfactorily. The event happens, I get the idea, I write out a rough copy, and the next day I see in the papers an article which is like mine, and therefore makes mine of no use, which, to begin with, I had never completed, nor written out properly. Perseverance in art shows me that a certain effort is necessary in order to vanquish the first difficulty. The first step is all the difficulty.

This proverb has never struck me so forcibly.

Then, furthermore, and above all these, is the consideration of one's surroundings. In spite of the best will in the world, mine must be called brutalising. The members of my family are, for the most part, ignorant and commonplace. . . .

I assure you, too, that if I did not shut myself up so often by myself with my books, I should really be less intelligent than I am as it is. I seem to speak my mind freely, and occasionally no one has more difficulty in showing off. I often become quite imbecile, the words crowd my mouth and I cannot speak. I listen and smile vaguely, that is all.

❖

Paris, December 8, 1880

This evening the citizenesses Alexandrine Norskott and Pauline Orelle were present at the weekly meeting of the "Women's Rights" society which takes place in Hubertine's little drawing-room.

A lamp on the desk, at the left; on the right is the mantelpiece surmounted by a bust of the Republic; and in the centre with its back to the window, which itself is opposite the door, is a table covered with bundles of papers and boasting a candle, a bell, and a president, who looks very dirty and very stupid. At the president's left sits Hubertine, who looks down every time she speaks and rubs her hands all the time. At his right, a violent and withered old female Socialist is screaming: "That if there is any fighting to be done, she will be the first to do it." There were about twenty queer old types, a sort of female concierges, just dismissed from their lodges, and a few men — what rifraff you may imagine; some of those young fellows with long hair, worn in outrageous style, who cannot get a hearing in the cafés. I am wearing a very dark wig, and my eyebrows are blackened. The men ranted on socialism, collectivism, and the treacheries of the most advanced deputies. The red lady in the corner declared war against religion; whereupon Mme de D — — (Norskott) protested, and made several remarks which went off like shots and did good. However, Hubertine is very wise, and understands that it is not a question of proletaires or of millionaires, but of woman in general, who is claiming her rights. These are the grounds on which they ought to take their stand; instead of which they discuss shades of political opinion.

Our names have been entered, we have voted, paid our subscriptions, &c. There!

❖

Paris, January 2, 1882

My great passion just now is my painting, I cannot venture to say "my art;" to speak of art (and its aspirations or inspirations), one must have made one's name. Without that, you have the air of a conceited amateur, or, rather, there is in doing so . . . something of indelicacy which wounds the better feelings in my nature; it is like acknowledging some noble action . . . a false shame, in fact.

❖

Paris, January 6, 1882

Art, even amongst the humblest raises the mind, and gives us the feeling of possessing more than those who do not belong to the sublime brotherhood.

❖

Paris, June 30, 1882

I can't settle down, I wander about . . . and do nothing! There's the rub! The other day I discussed that point with Julian; he says that one way or another I have done nothing for a year and a half, save a month's work by fits and starts, and then nothing at all!

No continuance, no regularity, no real energy! It is true. I have not stuck to it; I ought to have conquered my work by doing a study every week; whereas, instead of that, I have been looking after fifty different things, and when anything pleases me I am disheartened because I am not able to do it. I have tried to go back to the studio, and I could not do so. Shall I be able to work by myself? I am confused, and no longer know where to go or what to do. I have not the strength to make a simple study; I must always be undertaking too much, and as I cannot get through it I am plunged in despair. And now I am in a state of nervous exhaustion. . . . And, after all, I shall never paint; I have never, never, never been able to do a good piece of painting. . . .

❖

Paris, August 7, 1882

The street! Returning from Robert Fleury's we walked through the avenues which surround l'Arc de Triomphe; it was about half-past six — a summer's evening; porters, children, errand-boys, workmen, and women, all at their doors or on the public seats, or chatting in front of the wine-shops.

Ah, what admirable pictures there were — really admirable! . . .

I came in marvelling at the streets; yes, and those who jeer at what they call naturalism do not know what it is and are fools. It consists in seizing Nature in the act, in *knowing what to choose* and seizing it. The power of selection makes the artist. . . .

❖

Paris, September 6, 1882

I am not an artist; I wanted to become one, and being intelligent I have learnt certain things. . . . Then what explanation can be given to what Robert Fleury said when I began: "You possess everything that cannot be learnt." He was mistaken. . . .

❖

Paris, August 3, 1883

Bastien-Lepage is disheartening. When one studies Nature closely, when one wants to imitate it perfectly, it is impossible not to think all the time of this tremendous artist. He possesses every secret of the texture of the skin; what others do is only painting; but his work is Nature itself. They talk of realists, but realists do not know what reality is; they are coarse and think they are true. Realism does not consist in reproducing a vulgar thing, but in the rendering, which ought to be perfect.

I do not want to do things which look like painting. I want it to look like flesh and blood, and to look like life! When you have taken an infinity of trouble all day, all you have gained is to reproach yourself cruelly for having worked badly, and for having produced a thing that looks dry and painted. And the remembrance of that monster of Damvillers crushes one. His work is broad, simple, and true, and all the details of Nature are there! Ah! misery.

❖

Paris, August 17, 1883

. . . When any one looks at my painting (I mean an artist, of course) I go away into the third room, so much am I afraid of a word or a look. But Robert Fleury has no idea that I am so little sure of myself. As I talk braggingly, he thinks that I think highly of myself, and give myself credit for great talent. Therefore, he has no need to encourage me; and if I told him my hesitations and my fears he would laugh; I spoke to him about it once and he took it as a joke. That is the formidable error which I give rise to. I think Bastien-Lepage knows that I am dreadfully frightened at him, and he thinks himself God Almighty.

❖

Paris, January 5, 1884

The opening of Manet's exhibition at the Ecole des Beaux-Arts!

I go there with mamma.

Manet has not been dead a year. I did not know much about his work. The general impression of this exhibition is striking. It is incoherent, childish, and grandiose. Some of his works are perfectly crazy, and yet there are splendid bits. Given a little more, and he would be one of the great masters of painting. His work is generally ugly, sometimes deformed, but always living. There are some splendid impressions.

And even his worst things have a something which prevents your feeling disgust or lassitude. There is so much *aplomb* — such appalling self–confidence, joined to an ignorance no less appealing. . . . It's like the childhood of genius. . . .

❖

Paris, March 11, 1884
It rains. But that's not it. . . . I feel ill. . . . Everything is so unjust. Heaven overwhelms me. . . .

Well, I am still at an age when there is intoxication even in death itself.

No one, it seems to me, no one loves *everything* as I do — the fine arts, music, painting, books, society, dress, luxury, excitement, calm, laughter and tears, love, melancholy, humbug, the snow and the sunshine; all the seasons, all atmospheric effects, the silent plains of Russia, and the mountains round Naples; the frost in winter, autumn rains, spring with its caprices, quiet summer days, and beautiful nights bright with stars. . . . I admire, I adore it all. Everything appears to me in an interesting or sublime aspect; I should like to see, possess, embrace it all, be absorbed in it, and die, since I must, in two years or in thirty — die in an ecstasy, in order to analyse this final mystery, this end of all or this divine beginning.

❖

Paris, May 3, 1884
Emile Bastien-Lepage comes at half-past eleven and I go down much surprised.

He has a lot of things to tell me. I have achieved a really big success.

"Not a success considered in relation to yourself or your fellow-students at the *atelier*, but a popular success. — I saw Ollendorff yesterday, who told me that if it had been a Frenchman's work, the State would have bought it. 'Yes, he is a very strong man that M. Bashkirtseff.' (The picture is signed M. Bashkirtseff.) Then I told him that you were a young girl, adding 'and a pretty one.' (Oh! he was quite taken aback.) All the world speaks of it as a great success."

Ah! I begin to believe in it a little. For fear of believing too much, I only allow myself to feel a limited amount of satisfaction, such as you would hardly give me credit for. In short, I shall be the last to believe that people believe in me. . . .

❖

Paris, June 25, 1884
Re-read my diaries of 1875, 1876, and 1877. I complain in them of I know not what; I have aspirations towards something indefinite. Every evening I felt sore and discouraged, spending my strength in fury and despair in trying to find *what to do*. Go to Italy? Stop in Paris? Get married? Paint? What was to be done? If I went to Italy I couldn't be in Paris and I wanted to be everywhere at once!! What vigour there was in it all!!!

As a man, I should have conquered Europe. Young girl as I was, I wasted it in excesses of language and silly eccentricities. Oh, misery! . . .

But if I am nothing, if I am destined to be nothing, why these dreams of glory since I can remember anything? Why these mad aspirations towards greatness which I formerly imagined to consist in riches and titles? Why, from the time that I had two consecutive ideas, from the age of four, this desire for things glorious, grand, confused, but immense? Ah, what have I not been in my childish dreams! . . .

❖

Paris, July 15, 1884

I come back to an old plan, which quite engrosses me, every time I see the good people on the public seats. It might be a grand study. It is always better to paint scenes in which the people don't move. Don't misunderstand me, I am not against action, but there can be neither illusion nor enjoyment in scenes of violent action to a refined public. You are painfully (though unconsciously) impressed by an arm which is raised to strike, and which doesn't, by those boys who are running yet remain in the same place. There are situations full of movement where it is nevertheless possible to imagine a few moments of immobility, which is enough.

It is always better to choose the moment following on a striking or violent action of any kind, than the one preceding it. The *Jeanne d'Arc* of Bastien-Lepage had heard voices, she has gone quickly forward, upsetting her spinning-wheel, and has suddenly stopped, leaning against a tree. But look at scenes where people are in the *midst of action*, with their arms raised; it may be very powerful, but complete enjoyment is never possible. . . .

❖

Paris, October 16, 1884

I have a terrible amount of fever, which exhausts me. I spend all my time in the *salon*, changing from easy-chair to the sofa.

Dina reads novels to me. Potain came yesterday, he will come again to-morrow. This man no longer needs money, and if he comes, it is because he takes some little interest in me.

I can no longer go out at all, but poor Bastien-Lepage comes to me; he is carried here, put in an easy-chair, and stretched out on cushions — I am in another chair drawn up close by, and so we sit until six o'clock.

I was dressed in a cloud of white lace and plush, all different shades of white; the eyes of Bastien-Lepage dilated with delight.

"Oh, if I could only paint!" said he.

And I —

Finis. And so ends the picture of this year!

The Country Road, 1907. Tempera on pasteboard. 26¾" x 41⅞ ".
Museo Communale D'Arte Moderna, Ascona, Switzerland

MARIANNE WEREFKIN

1860–1938

THIRTY YEARS AGO it was suggested that the history of the *Blaue Reiter* (the group of pre–First World War German modern artists known in English as the Blue Rider) could not be completed until the diaries of Marianne Werefkin were made public, so closely was she involved in its founding and development. Despite the retrieval in recent years of numerous texts and works by historically neglected women artists, Werefkin's diaries and artwork are still relatively unknown. Born in Russia, Werefkin emigrated to Munich just before the turn of the century; she remained in Germany until the outbreak of the First World War, when she was forced to flee to neutral Switzerland. In Munich, she established a successful salon and was a founding member of the Blue Rider, one of the major branches of German Expressionism. Werefkin's painting style integrated aspects of symbolism, expressionism, and abstraction. She was also a prolific diarist, using her journal to conceptualize the spirituality of artistic abstraction several years before her colleague Wassily Kandinsky published his well-known treatise *Concerning the Spiritual in Art*. Not only are her journals significant in their development of aesthetic theory, they are also a good example of the special way that women artists have often used the diary form. In them, Werefkin established a safe space where she was free to construct her artistic persona. She called the journal that she kept between 1901 and 1905 *Lettres à un Inconnu* (Letters to an Unknown), the title itself suggesting that she thought of her diary as an alter ego, a mirror in which she looked for what she described as her "larger self." For Werefkin, that search ultimately led to the "Unknown" as the source of both art and life.

The daughter of Russian aristocrats, Marianne Werefkin was born in Tula, Russia, in 1860. Her mother, Elizaveta Daragan, had aspired before her marriage to a career as a painter; her father was a general in the army, which necessitated a succession of moves for the family. At fourteen, Werefkin began private art lessons in Lublin, later continuing formal study at the Moscow School of Art. From the time she was nineteen, Werefkin had her own atelier, a work space that was separate from the family living quarters, an indication of commitment to pursuit of her artistic career. The realist Ilja Rjepin, whom she met in 1880 and with whom she studied for many years in St. Petersburg (now Leningrad), where her father was the head of the Peter and Paul barracks, proved to be her most significant teacher. A hunting accident in 1888 permanently disfigured her right thumb and index finger and almost ended her career as a painter, but she learned how to compensate for the loss with her other "working" fingers. She incorporated Rjepin's realistic style in her early work and wrote that she made a name for herself as "the Russian Rembrandt," painting the Jewish men from a village near her father's country estate. The course of Werefkin's life was changed in 1891 by her meeing Alexei Jawlensky, a fellow student of Rjepin, four years her junior, and a lieutenant in the Russian army. Werefkin later wrote to a friend that she had "loved his work and wanted to help him." Within the next five years, she had decided to devote herself to furthering Jawlensky's career by putting her own aside; at this time she gave up painting entirely. When her father died in 1896, she became the beneficiary of his rather large yearly pension, enabling her to move to Munich with Jawlensky, who resigned his army commission. The two remained unmarried, ostensibly because marriage would have precluded her receiving the pension income, from which she supported their household until payment was cut off after the 1917 Russian Revolution.

Even though the first half of nearly twenty years in Munich coincided with the self-imposed hiatus in her painting career, Werefkin exerted an influence on the art world through her association with other artists there. Upon their arrival, Jawlensky enrolled in Anton Azbé's school, where he met fellow emigré Wassily Kandinsky. Together with several other young artists, they began explorations of artistic abstraction, a new aesthetic which also became one of Werefkin's central concerns. The salon at the Werefkin-Jawlensky household at 33 Giselastrasse became the center of the Munich avant-garde, the site of theoretical discussions of abstraction in which Werefkin actively participated. The Neue Kunstler-Vereinigung München (NKVM, the New Artists' Association of Munich) was founded in their living room. By 1907 Werefkin had started to paint again, and she participated in the NKVM's three exhibits. The summers of 1908–12, Werefkin and Jawlensky spent in Murnau, Germany, primarily with Kandinsky and the painter Gabriele Münter, enjoying visits from various NKVM members and other avant-garde artists, including Franz Marc, August Macke, and Paul Klee. The Blue Rider group formed during these years, with Werefkin participating in its first exhibition in 1913.

The outbreak of the First World War in 1914 changed everyone's situation drastically. Marc and Macke went off to battle, where both lost their lives; Kandinsky returned to Russia, breaking Münter's heart; and Werefkin and Jawlensky moved to Switzerland, ending up in Ascona in 1918, after living for a time in Saint Prex and Zürich, where they had witnessed the birth of the Dada movement. Jawlensky and Werefkin also experienced the withdrawal of their means of support, Werefkin's father's pension, terminated as a result of the Russian Revolution. In 1922, Jawlensky returned to Germany, but Werefkin remained in Ascona for the rest of her life. By 1918, when they arrived in Ascona, it was already well established as an international community of intellectuals and occultists who congregated in Monte Verità, the Mountain of Truth, located above the city. Attractive to Werefkin, perhaps because of the proximity of others who sought contact with the Infinite, she does not, however, seem to have established any strong bonds with the members of the Monte Verità community.

Three distinct phases in Werefkin's style correspond roughly to her living circumstances. Until 1896, she painted realistically, using a fairly dark palette and surfaces built with layered glazes, typified by the last known work in this style, her 1896 portrait of Jawlensky. The next years in Werefkin's career are problematic for the historian. She stopped painting around the time she moved to Munich with Jawlensky, concentrating instead on furthering his career. The nature of their relationship and its negative impact on her work was extremely complex; she herself referred to it as a "drama." In her diary, she explained that she abandoned her art "when I believed that I . . . would be able to serve it better by abstaining so another could succeed." That she took this extraordinary step can be explained by her feelings about "the Artist" as an almost supernatural being, one that she felt herself precluded from becoming because she was a woman. Just how long Werefkin interrupted her career is uncertain. She writes that she first picked up a brush again shortly after she began her diary (in 1901), but the first sketchbooks after her work in Russia are dated 1906. As she never dated her paintings, they can only be assigned tentative ones, the earliest of which are around 1907.

When Werefkin started painting again, her style had been radically transformed. The discussions of modernism in her salon must surely have contributed to her dramatic change of vision. Another influential factor was several trips to France, beginning in 1903, during which Werefkin encountered the writings of Theodor Lipps and the work of the Nabis, the Fauves (with whom Jawlensky even exhibited in 1905), Paul Gauguin, and Vincent Van Gogh. The impact of their ideas is explored in her diary. Additionally, Werefkin was well-read in the works of Russian Symbolist writers, and had written some Symbolist poetry herself. From about 1907, her work gives evidence of all these influences in its flattened planes and heightened color. *Three Women in Landscape* (ca. 1907) is similar in its Neo-Impressionist mood to works by Edvard Munch in the north and Maurice Denis in France. Her participation in the formative meetings of the Blue Rider group also exerted a significant influence on her work. By about 1910, she had developed her mature style, similar to her earlier Expressionist works in space and color, but typified by the use of a more dynamic brush stroke. This period is exemplified by her famous, haunted *Self-Portrait* (1910), in which her amber eyes positively burn, or in *The Red Tree* (1910), in which the landscape vibrates with intensity.

Werefkin's paintings executed after her move to Switzerland constitute a third stylistic phase. Although somewhat similar to her works from the early 1910s, these later works seem more intensely visionary. Their space is more exaggerated and some appear to have a luminous glow. They also have a greater mystical and mythical resonance, as in *The Outrage* (1930,) showing a small figure that seems banished to wander amid towering mountains, or *La Grosse Lune* (1923), in which sailors seem to be setting out on a voyage. Both these works show as well the impact of the landscape around Ascona, situated on Lago Maggiore and surrounded on all sides by jutting mountains.

The convoluted relationship between Werefkin and Jawlensky needs clarification, particularly because of its impact on Werefkin's working life. Although Werefkin has often been referred to as Jawlensky's muse or mentor, in actuality their relationship was a good deal more complex than that would imply; in fact, they lived for many years in a ménage à trois. Werefkin's domestic servant, Helene Nesnakomoff, a young woman about fifteen years old at the time, accompanied Jawlensky and Werefkin in their 1896 move from St. Petersburg to Munich. In 1902, Nesnakomoff bore Jawlensky a son (whom he claimed as his "nephew," a deceit accomplished by the entire household's temporary removal to Russia to conceal the birth). They all continued to live together (including after 1902, Nesnakomoff's sister, Maria) for their entire stay in Munich and their early years in Switzerland. All that time, Nesnakomoff functioned as a servant, allegedly never sitting down at the table with the rest of the family. As her diary entries plainly show, Werefkin was extremely distressed by this situation. Elizabeth Erdmann-Macke, the wife of their colleague August Macke, described a visit to the household in 1911 and her belief that the child Andreas was Jawlensky's son, despite attempts to conceal the true nature of the relationship. When Jawlensky left Werefkin in 1922, he took Helene (whom he finally married) and his twenty-year-old son, to whom he finally gave his surname. After their departure, Werefkin refused to speak to Jawlensky again. It is difficult to understand the nature of their relationship; Jelena Hahl-Koch suggests that Werefkin was a sort of guru to Jawlensky, a spiritual guide in the tradition of the Russian Symbolists. Possibly Jawlensky needed support from a woman to function as an artist, and was only able to free himself from Werefkin after 1920, when the painter Emmy Scheyer gave up her own career to further his. It is more difficult to discern what positive aspects Werefkin may have found in the relationship, particularly in its later years.

Diaries are often begun at times of change in their writers' lives. Werefkin began hers in 1901, the very year that Nesnakomoff became pregnant. Werefkin was, at the time, forty-one years old, at a "middle age" often accompanied by reassessment of one's direction in life. (Käthe Kollwitz, for example, also began her journal soon after turning forty.) In the journal, she constructed an "Unknown," to whom she wrote letters in which she bemoaned the unsatisfactory nature of the facts of her life, seeking solace in "the abstract." She defined the Unknown as the "Me that is better than Me," the "best" in herself, an alter ego whom she invoked and conversed with in order to reclaim her artistic legitimacy. In many ways, the Abstract functioned as Werefkin's muse. Through the dialogue in her journal, she engaged in a self-actualizing process ("künstlerischen selbstfindungs-prozess"), in which she cleared her mind and reclaimed her vocation as an artist, a vocation she felt she had "wasted" in order to be "governess, cook, housekeeper" to Jawlensky. Additionally, her journal reveals that her personality was fragmented into many selves; using the term *moi*, Werefkin refers to several, including *moi-homme*, *moi-femme*, and *moi-artiste*. Through her journal letters, she began the process of self-integration that led to her being able to start painting again, to be an artist rather than a servant of the arts.

One measure of Werefkin's successful use of the journal format is the appearance in her more mature art work of the ideas about abstraction that she first explored in writing. Her theories about color, for example, particularly that "color defines form and then submits to it," are visualized in the first works after her return to painting, such as *Three Women in Landscape*. Also, specific themes, such as her description of watching "the sisters with the black capes and white borders" walk through town, were first observed in the journal and later in her painting.

Werefkin's journal's exhaustive exploration of the symbolic profundity of abstraction led Hahl-Koch to say that with Werefkin as with the Russian Symbolists, it is scarcely possible to distinguish between art theory and Weltanschauung (world view). In her examination of her own relationship to art, Werefkin developed a theory of art-making that was mystical and religious, a philosophy of life affording access to a higher reality. According to Werefkin, abstraction is the preferred route, for "the more reality has been transformed in a work of art into the unreal, the greater the work." She wrote that she was "insatiable in the world of abstraction," that she "loved the things that were not." In this, she connects herself to both the Russian Symbolist poets and such Western Symbolists as Charles Baudelaire and Edgar Allan Poe. Thus, it is significant that she wrote these letters not in Russian, her native language, nor in German, the language of her adopted home, but in French, the language of Symbolism. Werefkin's private writings are as important as Kandinsky's publications in providing the theoretical bases of abstraction; there is reason to believe, in fact, that he may have derived many of his theories from his conversations with her. (Kandinsky, for his part, did not acknowledge his intellectual debt to her, but instead condescendingly criticized her work as "confessions in a diary.")

Although Werefkin and other women associated with the Blue Rider played a major role in its inception, art history has relegated them to a more minor role than that of their male counterparts. Werefkin has been criticized for not going as far artistically as Kandinsky, or even Jawlensky, into the abstraction that she advocated. This assessment slights Werefkin's actual achievements. In its dreamlike use of flat color planes and spatial exaggerations, her work is closely aligned with that of Symbolist artists such as Munch and the Nabis, and the highly personal style of her work contributes to its appeal.

Werefkin's career resembles that of many other women artists both in being characterized by hiatuses and distractions during her lifetime and its current historical obscurity. Several recent European exhibitions of Werefkin's work indicate that it is currently being reassessed, giving hope that the women active in the Expressionist movement, like those involved with Impressionism and Surrealism, will be given full credit for their active participation and redefinition of an important branch of artistic modernism.

SOURCES
Berger, Renate. *Malerinnen auf dem Weg in 20. Jahrhundert*. Cologne: Verlag M. DuMont Schauberg, 1982.

Fäthke, Bernd. *Marianne Werefkin, Leben und Werk (Exhibition, Ascona, 1988)*. Munich: Prestel Verlag, 1988.

Green, Martin. *Mountain of Truth*. Hanover, N.H.: University Press of New England, 1986.

Hahl-Koch, Jelena. *Marianne Werefkin und der russische Symbolismus*. Munich: Verlag Otto Sagner, 1967.

Marianne Werefkin, Gemälde und Skizzen. Wiesbaden, Germany: Museum, Wiesbaden, 1980.

Roh, Juliana. "Marianne von Werefkin." *Kunst und das Schoene Heim* 57 (December 1959): 452-55.

Weiler, Clemens. *Alexej Jawlensky*. Cologne: Verlag M. DuMont Schauberg, 1959.

Werefkin, Marianne. *Briefe an einen Unbekannten, 1901–1905*. Edited by Clemens Weiler. Cologne: Verlag M. DuMont Schauberg, 1960.

MARIANNE WEREFKIN, *LETTRES À UN INCONNU*, 1901–05
(MUSEO COMMUNALE, ASCONA)

VOL. I, "My Beautiful One, My Unique!"

You for whom I have so looked hard without ever finding. You whom I have longed for, called after, without ever seeing you come, you who are always present without ever existing — I am writing to you now. You who are basically only myself, but a much bigger and more noble self, an ingenious self, a self far from me, as real as the whole distance between the dream and the reality. However, you alone are able to understand me, to believe in the necessity of these letters addressed to nothingness, to believe in the deceits of forms and feelings. My thought comes to me from you, to me are my actions and my way. From there the necessity of listening to you, although life has made us enemies. You are my thought, I am your realization. An image carries you and your large open wings.

Should I tell you the story of my life? I have looked for you — it is all there in these words. I have wanted to live double — my self reflected by my self. The universe around was only an incitement. The great matter was you, was me. Oh if I had been able to realize you with my hand. If the painted canvas were able to give me your dear image. The labor was you the work of art was me — I have kissed your head, I have looked elsewhere. I thought I would fathom you in the needs of charity, of affection. It was false. You are neither good, nor charitable. You do not know how to love. — You are only great and beautiful. I sacrificed to tenderness and still, my self, you do not know how to love. Oh how we struggled, you and I, before I learned to see you outside myself, outside of everything, of everyone, you the elusive, you the unique reality, the unique truth of my life. And now I am writing to you as if you were not me, as if my tenderness for you were not an obsession. . . . And that is how I want to love you, outside of myself, as if you were my work and not that which has granted me all the joys of the earth. I have called after you, I have cried tears of delirium, of passion in calling you to a bedside where human love has never been seated. You escaped me, you tormented me with all the torments included in the world. Me, I live among very human interests, I have a household, friends, business affairs, the same dimensions as everyone. But to live like that, I need to immerse my gaze in your eyes, it is in their mirror that I see myself as I would like to be, and it is only in seeing myself as I feel I should be. I think, therefore I am, my Beautiful One, to both of us, everyday we recreate the world, every day a paradise falls in our hands, to darken in the dust of many other similar paradises. . . . The paradises will fall in our hands, will sink in the dust and will be born again according to our will.

Many times I believed I found you outside of me. I remained like a prayer before those beings whom I believed to be you. I bowed to their service believing I was serving you. I opened my heart to them believing I would see you return in me, so that we would again become one. Yes, it was your blue wing . . . which made me run after them all. You picked up your wing and the poor sad faces of men . . . look at me from the depths of my heart where I have hidden them. They stay there nourished with pity but already your blue wing calls me from afar and their sad view is no longer anything other than the memory of a dream.

Valiantly I have looked for you at the bottom of myself. But there I knocked against all sorts of daily things, things that could not be you. I preferred to believe that you were outside of me. And that is how I am writing to you in friendship. In order to serve you I have betrayed you, in adoring you I have turned away from you. Let me believe however that my life such as it is, is all in you, for you, from you, that it *is* you, my Beautiful one, my Unique.

❖

VOL. I, 1ST LETTER, "un jour . . . "

And now to us, Unknown. I have looked for you in vain, but you, you are nothing of the Real. You are a supposition. . . . You are good, fine, very refined even, artistic, intuitive. You cut a good figure, you are someone. But especially you are very sympathetic to me, you catch in flight the playful thought, you follow the ingenious idea, you always cry and laugh at the right moment. You have the beautiful eyes of an intelligent dog and the caressing hand of a mother. Your white teeth laugh in a serious mouth, you love nature and art, trips, the countryside, music and books. And you adore me. When described this way you are banal, very banal, a hero of a romance for young girls. But you have a trait which makes you unequaled. You are mine, body and soul. You are thus again, me. And for me you are Love. As soon as my heart fails, as soon as my thought tires, as soon as I feel like a child and a woman I look for you. . . .

❖

"allegro"

. . .I want to give them [the men she loves] new horizons, new gods, a new and young faith, the creative force. They who want to love me do not know love, they want me to love them with a love that I do not know. Never do we understand each other. And I have taken you, you the unknown, for the unique love, as I have taken myself for the unique dream. . . .

❖

VOL. I, 3RD LETTER, "chamber pot"

One day I happened to assist a doctor at a gynecological examination. When the speculum was in place, the doctor showed me the bottom of the diseased womb. She was a woman in childbed, she had just bled in order to give life; after having given birth she had unexpected complications. The horror that I experienced was based in pity. The poor creature without any more shame, spread her fat legs and showed her purulent womb. A nauseating odor rose to my nose; the linens stained with blood and pus moved my heart. . . . I cared for the sick woman, approaching her each time with a retch. On the third day this woman cried out to me in sorrow that her husband "took" her that very night. Since then physical love has been a monster to me.

Yes, I have seen women in childbed in the countryside who, with all their blood drained, breathless, and white, . . . the newborn at their breast, exhausted again, while the husband told me about their unhappiness at seeing the laboring woman out of service for so long. . . .

Oh my unknown, it is not love, it is not even the coupling approved by nature. Of that which we give the name, I abhor that business. No religion, no poetic deceit can make me believe that that is love. We who love art and who defend it against the public, we will defend love against this filth. Let us leave the gymnastic joys of love to those who put oleographs on their walls. We who are able to tremble before the masterpiece, let us tremble so that we are not made to lose love. When they procreate it is the only way for them to affirm themselves. We have the choice of creations, the affirmations of our self. We are able to make the flowers flourish everywhere, the world of beauties is ours, the world of mysteries is ours also, we have admiration, we have divination, we have all the great people of the world as our brothers. . . . We are able to detach ourselves and plunge ourselves in the joy of life entirely. All in us is artistic, the people who see beauty, the heart that feels beauty, the spirit that invents it and the hand that creates it. Why should we do as those who do not have other joys than to believe, as night falls, in their double beds, after a day of heavy work and ennui that it is to be great and sanctified by love to jostle the companions of their bed. Our passion must be like our love — illusory and artistic, having no other end than the desire to be beautiful. To remain beautiful in unsated passion . . . Where the caress of the body exists to echo the lightness of the heart. That the coupling be a sanctification, that the woman thrown across the bed rises up greater — that she is still a virgin that the satisfied man stutters prayers. Oh, then love each other. Otherwise sanctify the chaste love, the illusory love of the artist.

For four years we have slept side by side. I have remained virgin, he has become virgin again. Between us sleeps our child — art. It is he who gives us the peacefulness of sleep. Never has desire sullied our bed. We have both wanted to remain pure. It is because not one bad thought came to disturb our nights that we are so close to each other. And yet we love each other. In the long years that we have been pledged to each other we have not exchanged a single indifferent kiss. He is everything for me, I love him like a mother, particularly like a mother, like a friend, a sister, a wife, like an artist, a comrade. I am not his mistress and never has my tenderness known passion. He, out of love for me has made himself a monk. He loves in me his art, he would be lost without me — and never has he possessed me. — We sleep in the same bed chastely, like two children pressed tightly against each other and at the time that others are addicted to rutting, we tell each other, heart to heart, our great hopes, our sublime desires. And both of us, we are healthy and light. I hold so much to his dear presence, so close to me in the somber hours of the night, when my spirit's genius is more alive. Thus he has all the first fruits of my thought, he sees the marvelous flowers of my imagination hatch. When my arms gently embrace him, it seems to me that the treasures of the heart, of sentiment, of thought, of sublimity, that I saw in him, have returned to me. He is the speech of my thought, he is the body of my soul. In the night's silence, across his sleep, my hand in his hand, I feel myself, I hear myself. These hours of the night are sacred hours, more than ever I feel myself the priestess of a great cult to which I am avowed. My kisses carry inspirations, my caresses are calls. When I say I love you I say — cry, Be an artist, be great. . . .

❖

Vol. I, "Minuit"

Life goes on, dear unknown, time begins to pass. The old agonies seem far away. We are there again in the calm of our perch. Work begins again, for him the paintbrush in the hand, for me, in the tension of all my being towards the proposed purpose. My faith is my life. The rest of it is only the framework. We hope. We work. Through him I am going towards your conquest, my Unique, for you I have put my being in him. We work. We hope. And now I again pick up the pen to begin again our chats, my dear unknown. To not disturb the others it is to you that I aim all that trots by my head. A lost illusion ties me more than ever to you alone. I have created a life of illusion. All there is mirage, vision. I tell myself stories, I invent for myself sympathies, interests. My unique, true interest is that which I have excluded from my life, at least from my personal activity. And each time that a part of my odd construction falls I remain wearied because I begin to catch a glimpse of reality. All bores me in the world of facts, I see an end, a limit to all things and my heart thirsts for the infinite and for eternity. How to speak of the feeling, so serious, that has seized me? . . . Human activity and its greatest efforts always fall back on broken wings. Oh, thus I close my eyes, I do not wish to see, to hear, to love, or to act. Only artistic creation, infinite, unlimited, work of god in man, appears desirable to me. It only is the truth and only it is the illusion. . . .

❖

Vol. I, "December or perhaps May"

. . . I have absolutely no desires, lusts, vanity in the material world. I am insatiable in the world of abstraction. . . I want a lovely life; in order for it to be, harmony and style are necessary. I avow mine to the key of aesthetic sentiment — the constant permanent creation everywhere and in every one. All is false there, all is true. The truth is the desire to see falsely. I do not want the naked truth; it is the principle of my life. It is that which makes my life one which is artistic and complete. Feelings, events, people and things, such as they are, are nothing to me. I wish them invented, illusory, false in so far as true life and in so far as art. I ascribe there, all the ridiculous things, I leave there the platitude, above the common, I do not entrust the unique view of which I am in awe. The companions of my dreams all remain steadfast on the way. . . . The others with whom I do not associate are not able to follow. . . . I remain always with you, my unknown. And now you look at me with eyes so large, so loving. You are so young today that I preserve the illusion. . . .

There is one thing that my nature cannot stand, that can only be expressed by the German word Knechtschaft. All rights of possession over my physical or moral person makes me shudder. Freely, of my own will, I give myself without hesitating. But as soon as I feel a hand that wants to seize me I bite it. Never will I allow physical love because it is a right of the man over the woman. The woman possessed is a slave. It is completely personal, but never would I be able to survive this enslavement. . . . Liberty is at the core of my me. Free I serve, taken I tyrannize. This ardor for liberty I have had in me since the first days of my life. . . . Never have I wanted to belong to anyone. . . . Physcial approach I detest because it is a form of possession. . . .

❖

VOL. I

I want to work. It is an obsession. I am gnawed at the heart by an excruciating desire to manipulate color. I see figures, with an incredible intensity, pass before my eye. Let us analyze this — if it is possible to toss it. Why do you no longer work? Why work again? Faith has left me — the habit of putting myself into the background, has done the rest. Am I a true artist? Yes, yes, yes. Am I a woman? Alas. Yes, yes, yes. Are the two able to work as a pair? No, no, no. Who will take up the desires — ? The two yield to a third: to the thinker. A woman does not take desires because she doesn't believe in love, the artist yields because he doesn't believe in his work. And now, after four years of abstinence this renewal of faith. Why? Why? All is against me. The work of my life, this talent that I protect with all my interest, with all my affection, it must be alone in the dwelling. Reason says, calm yourself. But the great passion in me, and my call to work, destroys all the calm acquisitions of my life. . . .

❖

VOL. I (1902)

. . . I am a vigorous, intelligent being, an artist, I have a creative soul and I have fallen into laziness, into doing nothing. I daydream a lot as my mother said. Now that she has sent me moral help — why can't I pull myself together? The state where I am at is holding me tightly. I have lost faith in myself and that is why my life has gone to the devil. Why: I have been strict with myself. I love art with a passion so selfless that when I believed that I saw that I would be able to serve it better by abstaining myself, so that another could succeed — I did it. And that faith was so great that it has endured, against all the tempests. You, you, in loving me like an imperceptible current, you have destroyed the calm, the serenity of my life. It was difficult, but so intact. And now it appears to me like an enormous false disgrace, an irreparable crime. It is not love which has dictated my conduct, it's a conviction. That's why I have carried all the deceptions of the heart without ever stumbling. I believed I did well, I felt big-spirited. And you told me that I was afraid of the beautiful solitary life dedicated to work, to the pangs of creation, that I cowardly hid myself behind a semblance of affection. The belief in my self that gave me your affection came too late. My poor life, mutilated by so many realistic chagrins is behind me, and in front there is only old age and death. . . . White like ermine, I passed unsullied across the mud because I have as my mantle my faith in the truth of my abnegation. I played the tart, the kitchen maid, the nurse, the governess, to be of service to a grand art, a talent which I believed worthy of carrying out new work. The horror of my real torments increase with each memory, with each thought. . . . You are the call to the ideal, a voice against which it is impossible for me to resist, to which everything in me responds, my being and my life. . . . A woman like me is not born everyday, and this woman lost herself in idleness, in the nothingness of a petty existence. The idea which threw its veil on everything, you have driven it out, revealing it as nothing, useless. And the man to whom I have given all: my spirit and my heart, my inspiration and my affection, my cares and my concerns, my energy, my faith and my confidence, to whom I have opened all the treasures of my genius and of my soul, who enjoyed understanding and help — this man looks upon me with indifference and prefers kitchen maids to me. I am alone — much more alone than if I hadn't done that, and I don't have the joy of being who I am. You — you have brought me the torments of love, of regret, of memories, of despair and you have left. In you I found myself again, and so that you will not perish as I did, I let you go free. . . .

❖

VOL. I

. . . In thoughts I am on the summits, in reality I am foundering in the mud. I believe myself a muse and I am only the housekeeper, the porter. I give my life for a creation à deux, and one only asks me to pay my accounts and to not get in the way. And when, in despair, I ask for the peace of love one is sharp with me and sends me about my business. . . .

At an age when there is no going back I have lost my moral equilibrium, my reason for being — that's what kills me, that's the evil. . . . I am not able to take back my self, neither in good nor in evil. I no longer see anything in me, and the desire for work, of renewal by it, of moral health by it, is great — raging in me. . . . Is it better to not find a way out, quite frankly, at the risk of breaking one's neck. Is it good to consent to stifle in oneself, the revelatory thought, desire. By the light of your eyes, my white flower, I see all that is lacking in my life: work and love. My despair is enormous, if only at least it would illuminate me. But one has closed his eyes to me, one has deafened his ears. I must continue to live as a blind person. Lord God, give me peace, sentient peace so that I could know what is good and what is evil. I have been strong in my faith, in the necessity of my courage. Your last terrible words broke that. I hope that God will pardon you, since I love you. But it is not about having lost you that I despair, it's about having lost my self. You always said: speak French, you will be more frank. What could be more frank than this confession of my moral downfall?

❖

VOL. I

. . . I know that fulfilled duty is the only true contentment in life. And I have always looked to do that duty. Never have I put it under the yoke of my own desire. And it is the duty to do that escapes me — for which I search, which breaks me apart. There is the duty towards others and the duty towards one's self, towards one's soul. The duty towards others is always clear and that one I have always scrupulously fulfilled, without letting myself ever by influenced by sympathy or antipathy, by its easiness or difficulty. I was and I am always what I am obliged to be to others: good friend, devoted daughter, I was always help- ful and true and active. It's the duty towards myself that amounts to less. I have an individuality rich in gifts. Have I shown these off as it was my duty to myself? Have I not let myself be too entranced by the lives of others? Have I not changed into even less instead of being of a true, great worth. It is the most sor- rowful point in my soul: my love for my self, with the idea of having squan- dered it.. . . .

❖

VOL. II, 7/XI

Before the blank canvas, the unrealized work, completely in the artist's head, must seem to him equal to the greatest. To say that which has never been said — is the reason for all artistic work. But only outside of the work should the artist worthily get down on his knees before the great artists of the past. It is not necessary to go to their school in the vain desire to apprehend their books, but there is a constant lesson that the work of the masters carries, because, it marks the road. It is necessary to learn their manner of acting with nature, their aware revelation of artistic personality. It is foolish to want to make them relive by analogous works. It is correct to penetrate their spirit. Art is not made only one way, art is a point of view. By its light, life in its ensemble is different from the common way. That is why only true artists can understand and advance. Rembrandt in our days would be Rembrandt again, because the work of the master is his self. But in order to be Rembrandt in our days he would have used new ways that would give a new culture.

❖

VOL. II, 11/XI (1903)

The details of life are a misery to me. God how I suffer from all these ques- tions of the household with the detestable coarseness of my servants into the bargain. All this screaming, all these slammed doors, all the rain of injuries which make up the daily routine of the kitchen give me twitchings of the nerves. Oh my dear friend, you whose voice called me towards my beautiful past, oh how I love you because you are young, you serve the idea, you under- stand the beauty of a life devoted completely to abstraction. Oh the evil you have done me, and the good of this evil. There is an atrocious page in my exis- tence. One can't do anything about it. It is me abdicating my self. I am not a woman. Neither love nor the family satisfies me. I don't like the baby, I detest the houshehold. I love all works of the human genius, I adore art, the beauties of nature and of the heart. The beautiful, the beautiful in all such as love and such as life. The quarrels of kitchen maids. Thank you for having understood me, thank you for having loved me. . . .

❖

VOL. II, 16/XI

Life is a sum of organic, chemical, physical, and mechanical events. Sci- ence demands of it, the why, the how, it orders them, it classifies them. Humanity accepts life in its entirety and lets itself go with the current of things. Man . . . setting himself against life, can't do anything but name the things that he sees, that he feels. Most of our appreciation is the definition of good and of evil — that is to say of the agreeable and the disagreeable, that in erroneous language translates into beautiful and ugly. The artist is the only one who detaches himself from life, opposes his personality to it, he is the only one who orders things as he wishes them to be in place of things as they are. Thus for him life is not a fait accompli, it is something to remake, to do again. He takes possession of his gifts in order to continue, to change. He makes his choice, it is he who creates the conceptions of beautiful and ugly, those are the things to preserve, the things to change. At the seat of the things that it is necessary to change he puts his desires, his aspirations, in one word, his personality. . . . . Religion, philosophy, music, literature, painting, architecture, sculpture — are only some ways for the artist to express that which displeases him in life, that which one would like to change there, that which is ugly which must become beautiful.

❖

VOL. II,17/XI

I am distracted. My nerves are beginning to make me feel bad. I love J. [Alexei Jawlensky] more than ever. I would like to multiply myself to be useful to him. I love him grandly, entirely. I am happy to be near to him. Each time that his thought returns to me I enjoy it as if it were a caress. The least agreement of our hearts is a celebration for me. But he has so little tenderness for me, but he only takes me in so far as I am necessary to him, but never on a large scale, never for my own sake. Never a single thought of my life, of me. And my eyes turn towards the other whom I also love so strongly, so tenderly, with such youth, towards that love where there is only us both, where all is so personal, where me, I am me, without any reasonable reason. I listen to the tender words, I see the eyes that adore me, I feel a caress that was never dared to be given. My self is divided in two. My self struggles. And to restore my harmony, I throw myself recklessly into my art. And my thought works, works while my heart loves its two loves. . . .

❖

VOL. II, 26/XII

Art is not hysteria. Art is as natural to man as is thought, it is a normal function of his brain. Art is observation and consciousness. It is not an instinct, vague, indecisive, sickly. Art is an eternal source — life, and an unlimited expression, the individual. These two elements, well-adapted, make masterpieces. Although in principle, life is always the same, it is always different in the impression the individual carries away from it. The individual, always the same in principle, is infinitely varied in his clash with life. Art is the sparks which are born from the chafing of the individual against life. Life being always the same, it is the force and the character of the individual which determines art. All speech that a human being finds to give a new impression is of art. Why believe that the speech must be epileptic to become art?

Two electric wires produce a spark. This spark possesses, then, the two wires which produce it. But one time the spark is a completely different thing than the wires. Such is art. It is the product of life and the individual. It is born from their clash, from the received impression. But this impression is made once, for then it is no longer, neither life nor the individual. It is art, something that has its life for itself, from that time to itself. Art is neither life nor the individual. . . . So that strength and unity remain in the artistic impression it is necessary that its expression carries a similar character [to life]. It is necessary that they adapt themselves each to each, as the cry adapts to sorrow, the laugh to joy, the tear to chagrin. Hypocritical, false cries, laughs and tears disgust us. Similarly, the false-intentioned expression will torture the artistic impression. This does not concern realism — it concerns sincerity. The work of art must be sincere with a sincerity sometimes naive, more often with an intentional, conscious sincerity. It is this sincerity which makes us raise arms against tradition . . . . It is this sincerity which makes the artist so severe in the choice of his modes of expression. It is not life which wants to make the work of art, it is the impression received by an artistic individual. It is not even the individual who makes the work of art, it is the impression given by life. Truth in art is only in the correspondence between the impression and its expression. . . . .

Refined art is not a grimacing art, writhing in an epileptic fit. . . . In all these definitions and conceptions about art there is no room for the grimace or for catalepsy. Art is an intellectual function, healthy, strong, true and it is only another form of the faculty of thought. It is not a delirium — it is a philosophy.

❖

Vol. II, 1904

I love the things that are not. It could well be the motto of my life. Things that are imaginary, desirable, dreamed, invented. As much as I believe to have loved it, it is one of those impossible things at the eye of reality, existing as all who create art.

❖

Vol. II, 10/II

J. [Jawlensky] is the knight serving my servants. He always defends them, always exonerates them. I feel myself so much out of their life. I know that in the kitchen the man that I love, and my servants who hate me in the way one often hates those to whom one owes everything, plot against me. I have overheard foul words, of a coarseness and rudeness not to be believed. . . .

❖

Vol. III, 1904, V–VI

Centuries and centuries will pass. And always, always my soul will look for yours, so pure, so big. I await it — that day when my soul will meet yours in nirvana — instead of rest, of pure pleasure, before the new journey, long and a hundred times more heavy, on the earth, which will follow this repose. And my soul near yours, I will walk, and again I will meet your soul again more beautiful and again more big in nirvana, and the centuries will pass. It is why I love you. I used to love you. I love you now — and I will love you across the centuries. O you — star of my soul — how happy am I to catch a glimpse of you, soul, so beautiful, so pure, so big and I await the supreme hour when mine will be worthy of yours.

— happy happy am I.

❖

Vol. III 1904, 24/VI

An art that is truly young and fresh must be based on a precise observation of nature. The ways of making the new impression must be personal and independent of existing forms. Thus it is false to think of one's work and then to copy it from nature. It is necessary for nature to inspire you with a purely physical impression. The ways of making that impression are completely in you and not in nature. But the work itself, it is life, it is nature. The artistic creation thus is made from without to within. All that which is created from within to without is the rhetoric of art, cold and intellectual. Art is *one* sensation, a sentiment; sensations and sentiments come to us from outside. But artistic thought made from the temperament of the artist, from his personality, from his received sensation, animates an appropriate form.

Art is a philosophy, it is an appreciation of life, a commentary on life. If art were only the creation of pictures, of pieces of music, of poems, art would be a futile occupation, sometimes only excusable. But art is one of the fires that illuminates life. Without it there would be less hope, more despair. Art is thus something in itself, by itself, without regard to who practices it. It has its laws, its principles, its evolution, its purpose. Art is artistic thought. . . . Science gives its "how" to the facts of life, art poses a "why?" True art is that which renders the soul of things. . . . It is the artist who makes the soul of things, it is his eye that puts it there. That is how art is personal and science is not. Philosophy, religion, love are arts. That which we call art is the same principle bound by the power to be realized by precise form: speech, sound, line, color. I give my "why" to the things that life has shown me — that is the artist's credo.

The history of art is the history of the artist in his fashion of comprehending life. He who is able to be an artist only when it is convenient is not one, because it is impossible for man to have two pairs of eyes, two souls, two intelligences. One is either an artist, or one isn't one. And if one is an artist, only then, in each movement of life, in us and around us, responds the echo of artistic thought, the transformation of experienced reality into the wished for irreality. The artist is someone who sees the world as a beautiful rug with many colors, as a song without words, or as a mystery. An artist is also one who sees in life the constant realization of some personal taste or the manifestation of a force of an invisible sentiment. In all these cases the artist is he who opposes to the reality of perceived things the unreality of his artist's soul, his taste, his passion, his melancholy, his joy, his verve, his foolishness. The work copied from life — that is not a work of art. The work imagined outside of life is a sick work. The work of art is life, and it is the artist. To study art it is necessary to study life and it is necessary to understand the artist. There is only one way of appreciating the work of art, it is in how the artist has become master of life. The more that the principles of the real change into the principles of the unreal, the greater is the work. He who makes a visual impression by a song of color is master of vision. He who makes a visual impression by a word of poetry is master of the soul. . . .

❖

Vol. III, January(?) 1905

I live in a cold environment that has no equal. The man to whom I am tied never gives me the least thought. All his attentions are for my servants and for women who seem to be servants, who often are far from being superior women. I am only there to pay the monthly allowance, and to take care of the concerns of the household, to care for the illnesses and to sustain his artistic incapacities. . . . My personal life is ignored. The passion that I see is only desire without caresses, without song of love. At the same time a hateful, depreciating speech follows all that could hold me to joy, all that could bring me a bit of warmth, of friendliness. . . . I am not complaining. I made my existence myself, and then love passed away. But it is strange that I who did not want to live except for art and love, who doesn't care about all vanities, it is strange that I must abdicate at both love and art. . . . I love love, I detest passion, especially since I have never felt it myself. I do not have love, and I have so much disgust and the chill of a wretched frigidity which has left my body indifferent and my heart revolted . That which holds me is my sentiment, the desire to remain honest despite and against all. The need to not renounce my past, to keep my life straight and whole.

❖

VOL. III, 6/III

Dear Unknown: My poor soul uncertain and tormented, seeks refuge in visions. It does not dare to remember or to think. It tries to dream as an artist, to look for forms of the expression of seen and understood things. It wants to escape to the sky. . . .

❖

VOL. III, 13/IV

. . . All art is in the individual. The greatest masterpieces are not the result of the progress of art. They are the expressions of outstanding individuals whose feelings only act as revelations and not as progress for the rest of humanity. There is neither old nor new in art, nor common nor banal, as these do not exist in human sentiments. It is the expression of something always the same in its essence, which does not vary according to individuality. Thus all the qualities, all the faults of art are in complete dependence on the feelings of the artist and his individuality. All judgment in art can only proceed from the individual. The most beautiful expressions in art are not more advanced art, just as individuals of developed sensibilities do not advance human capacities of sensitivity. Love, hate, agony, sadness, joy, have been part of man the animal, since he first peopled the earth, and not a new feeling has ever joined the sum of the common ones. But each individual has his manner of expressing them, of indulging in them. And the sentiments, always the same are eternally new, like man, always the same, is always new in his individuality. Art adapts itself like a glove to this law of feeling, it is the word which yields the thought. The laws of art are the laws which regulate feeling: the eternal form lives anew in the individual, the stable element in feelings is always the same. . . . The greatest works of art do not make art greater. Art does not succeed itself just as one is not able to transmit beautiful sentiments. Art lives and dies in the unique heart of he who carries it, just as all feelings only live and expand in the souls of those who feel them. There is no history of art — there is the history of artists.

❖

VOL. III, 9/VI

The realities of my life are completely in disaccord with the aspirations of my soul. Where is the life — free, frank, joyous, devoted to art, filled with work, relieved by love, filled with beautiful impressions, removed from the banal — of which I dreamed, which I wanted, for which I have given everything? That which saves me is my recoil from all that makes my life attractive. I did not want marriage because I did not feel the calling of children. Being an artist above all, I did not want the banalities of marriage. I have all of these without any of their joys. A child who is not mine shrieks in the house, three kitchen girls yell from morning to night, the studio is transformed into a nursery, and a child's chamber pot lays about where I would go. The man who is not my husband, who has given me neither social position, nor consideration, nor goodwill . . . this man gives me his bad moods, his uneasiness, his tiredness, his impotency in his work, the trouble of conversing with him, of protecting him, of caring for him. His happy moments he carries away, his attention he gives to my kitchen maid, the successes and joys of his art he keeps for himself. . . . I am alone, alone and alone — and I am neither free nor alone. One tosses me a word of affection like a tip, or a bone to a famished dog. I have given everything. I have kept to myself only my personal character. And that I will defend until my death, until my last breath and nothing will make me acquiesce to all that I suffer.

❖

VOL. III, 29/VIII–10/IX

. . . Inability to love, inability to act, inability to want and to believe — that is what the most ardent words, the most noble forces hide. The best of humanity capsizes in impotence. I have broken myself up heart and body to give and to instigate strength. All that came back to me, leaving the others more base than ever. My life has been spent in struggling with the weaknesses of others. In my dream I am healthy and strong, and the gulf between my strength and the weakness of others becomes larger, more impassable from day to day. I yield under my strength which arms itself against me, laughing at the vanity of my efforts, showing me the horror of my isolation. They — remain who they were. The meaninglessness of my life appears to me thus: to have served a false god. He failed to struggle for himself, for a work that belonged to him. It is there that I am weak too, I doubted myself, that's why I perish.

It is my birthday. As the only thought from the man to whom I have given everything — "Sincere greetings and regards to all — Alexis."

❖

VOL. III, 12/IX

Color dissolves form — it is a law of nature that only artists forget. Color directly influences impressions of size; thus a black point appears smaller than a white or yellow point, even if they are of the same size. Variety of colors disturbs the unity of the impression. The more monotone the impression, the more it acts like form. As soon as color becomes the principal purpose of the observation — the accurate, the real, notion of form disappears. Colored planes juxtaposed to each other have mutual influence on their different values. They lack, extend themselves, disappear, one in the others according to the laws of the marriage of colors. The lesson is that colored form is different from monotone form, that nothing is stable in the impression of form as nothing is stable in the impression of color, that the polychromed impression must, in order not to be false, find itself a form that is analogous to its chromatic essence, and must not borrow from the monotone impression, by an effort of logical thought. This is what Gauguin explained in his Tahitian paintings — color directly influences relief. A strong body in color always acts tame compared to a body modeled in black and white. . . .

The more an impression is polychromed . . . the less real form is possible. The polychromed impression must find a form which keeps it in the realm of the possible without disturbing its essence. That is the road to follow for those who sacrifice to color. Color dissolves existing form. It is necessary to find for its own form. Since color is outside of logic, the colored form is no longer subject to logic. Colored form is dominated by the laws of color. A lively tone consumes the others, the form which carries it dominates the others. To see color with temperament and to extend it on the forms moderated by logic is to have two souls, or at least an unbalanced soul. Color decides form and form submits to it. In order to ignore this law artists founder in eternal discussions about the necessity of drawing, forgetting that in art such words as drawing, color, form, line, tone, are not at all stable, but that only the laws that regulate them have a constant value. All the rest is always created by the one who creates.

❖

VOL. III, 2/X

One evening, in the raw light of electric lanterns, in the desert of streets depopulated by cafes and theaters, against the gray of walls, the Sisters passed by, all in black with a thin border of white on their capes. In the emptiness which surrounded me, in the emptiness that I carried inside me, their somber figures appeared to be enormous. It was a moral act which passed, filling with its grandeur the nothingness which exists around triumphant egoism. My thought followed the sisters along the torturous streets which led to their community. It marched next to their silence, it listened to their hearts beat. My thought came back to me so cold. . . .

❖

VOL. III, 8/X

It is a great contortion to believe that art is an escape from a complexity of sensations, emotions, feelings, and thoughts, which life represses and shuts up. Art has a role unto itself, it is neither a logical argument nor a cry of the heart. It is a philosophy, that is to say an explication of the events of life, conditioned by the events seen and the completely personal antecedents of the life of the artist. Art is born from the contact of the self of the artist with the external world. Art is neither outside of us — like scientific truth, nor in us, like the feelings of love. Art is born from the love which we bring to life outside of us. Take away the scientist — the truths, the facts of science remain preserved in the evolutions of the material and psychic world. Take away all reason for being from love, and love even so takes its place at the bottom of our heart, because love is ourselves, and science is the world outside of us. Art is neither ourselves, nor the world outside us. Art is a hyphen between that which is outside of us and that which is in us, it translates itself by a form which is neither in us or outside of us. It is a thought taking form. Neither the illogic of love nor the logic of investigation, are able to direct artistic thought. It is born exclusively to a sun to which it is predestined, which is artistic personality, taken in emotion by a vital impression. One is born an artist, or one is not one. One is not able to become an artist, as it is impossible to give someone a different body. To be an artist is to have the ability to change all emotions suffered, all impressions received in an appreciation exclusively personal, and to find the form in it. If this ability does not make up the basis of a person's self, there is nothing in the world, neither in us nor outside of us that would be able to give it to us. All those who have fallen in with artists as a consequence of looking for an outlet for exuberant feeling, or as a consequence of a knowledge of acquired learning, all these have taken a false road. They are the true public of the artist. But the artist does not become, he is born that way. Happy or unhappy, cultured or unsophisticated, his place is ready-made. The impressions of life passing by his soul take color and form and become that which they were not. That is to say, truths become invented and pertain by that to all that is not and that is art.

❖

VOL. III, (CA. 30/X)

I am not cowardly and I keep my word. I am faithful to myself, ferocious to myself, and indulgent to others. That is me, the man. I love the song of love — that is me, the woman. I create myself consumingly of illusions and of dreams — that is me, the artist. I am the best of comrades, the most honest friend, an artist in the widest sense of this word. I am cruel in my most tender affections. I have disgust for the things that are the most dear to me. Nothing sweeps me away because everything is so clear to me. I dream large, I see small, I do not know how to bend. I am strong because I possess myself, I am weak because I need to be, in order to be me, even in the heat of love. That which one gives me, I give it back in strength, but it is necessary that one give me the heart's warmth. I have not found my equal because someone who would understand me as I understand myself, would be a strong person, one who does not need me. And those who I find on my way are too small to appreciate all that would be able to come to them from me. I am pledged to moral solitude. How mistaken are those who believe that I need love. I need love to increase myself, because under its hot breath all my faculties take wings, and detach themselves from the daily and seek the ideal. I am a man more than a woman. The desire to please and pity alone make me a woman.

I listen and I take notes. All the judgments fall into place. . . . I am neither man nor woman — I am me. . . .

❖

VOL. III, EARLY NOVEMBER(?)

It is on this page that I finish these letters to the Unknown. If it was vague at first, it took human form and during three years it comprised all my joy. Now the Unknown has returned to its first state. It is my self outside of myself. I want to continue to write to it. But what a difference between the letters that are going to come and those that were.

No, these three books carry a name. And since that name is erased from my heart, my whole heart has changed.

There is a new characteristic between me and the Unknown — skepticism. These letters so full of naive faith, of blue dreams are no longer. I look in my heart and I see calm there.

I am able to close this book.

Self-Portrait with a Pencil, 1933. Charcoal on brown laid paper. 18¾"x 25".
National Gallery of Art, Washington, Rosenwald Collection.

KÄTHE KOLLWITZ

1867–1945

IN BOTH HER art and her personal life, Käthe Schmidt Kollwitz challenged the expectations of her times and rejected several assumptions fundamental to the art world's dominant tradition. Kollwitz worked primarily in graphic media, creating stark black-and-white multiples instead of the more usual, traditional but precious, painted pieces. Furthermore, at a time when aestheticism predominated, Kollwitz eschewed the idea of art for art's sake, instead seeing art as a means of fulfilling an individual's social responsibility. Exceptional also in the way she achieved a balance between the professional and personal aspects of her life, Kollwitz is only the second artist discussed so far in this volume who married and raised a family. Family life seemed to nourish and enrich Kollwitz's art, and may have been partly responsible for her great skill at expressing personal interactions in universal terms. Kollwitz might not have described herself as a writer; for close to thirty-five years, however, she kept a journal in which she explored major creative and personal issues. The entries in this eloquent document elucidate the unique way in which she linked her work and life through the bonds of caring.

The fifth child in a family of free-thinking religious leaders, Kollwitz (born Schmidt) acquired her sense of social responsibility early. Her grandfather, Julian Rupp, was the spiritual leader of the Free Congregation, a religious community in Koenigsberg (now Kaliningrad, U.S.S.R.) in the second half of the nineteenth century. Its basic tenets fostered a kind of idealistic socialism, with an emphasis on moral and ethical behavior. When Kollwitz was nine, her father gave up his work as a builder and took over as the community's leader. Although she never was especially religiously observant, Kollwitz remained influenced by the group's encouragement of ethical behavior in everyday life and its concern with alleviating the misfortunes of others.

Kollwitz took her first drawing lessons when she was in her teens and early on her family recognized and encouraged her talent. Although she became engaged to Karl Kollwitz at seventeen, her marriage was delayed while she studied art, first at the Women's School of the Berlin Academy of Art with Karl Stauffer-Bern, and then with Ludwig Herterich at the Women's School for Art in Munich. The freedom and exhilaration of these student days stayed with her throughout her life, as did a respect for the concentration and persistence that are necessary for artistic achievement. During these years, too, she began to understand that the graphic arts, with their dependence on tonality, suited her better than painting. Stauffer-Bern had recognized her extraordinary talent in graphic media and introduced her to the work of Max Klinger. While in Munich, Kollwitz encountered a pamphlet written by Klinger in which he asserted that some subjects, particularly those embodying the darker sides of life, were expressed more appropriately through drawing than through painting. Although she did not abandon her painting studies until several years later, she was deeply influenced by Klinger's defense of the primacy of drawing.

Käthe Schmidt married Karl Kollwitz when she was twenty-four. Shortly before their wedding her father expressed his disappointment at what he expected was the end of her artistic career, saying that since she would be unable to be effective as both a wife and an artist, she might as well concentrate on being a good wife. In fact, her marriage turned out to be conducive to the success of Kollwitz's working life. Karl, an intellectual and a socialist, had been a medical student in Berlin during the years Käthe had studied art. In 1891, when he found a job as the physician for a tailor's *Krankenkass*, the equivalent of a medical clinic for working people, in Berlin, they decided to marry. During the 1890s their sons, Hans and Peter, were born. The Kollwitzes lived a sober life devoted to work; their living space and her studio were in the same building as his clinic. Her husband's patients became Kollwitz's models, contributing to her realization of what became her primary artistic subject. Kollwitz later said that she had been drawn to the life of the workers because they seemed "beautiful," while bourgeois life was "pedantic."

Kollwitz's artistic career can be divided into three phases. The first, beginning in the 1890s when she moved to Berlin with her husband and extending until 1911–12, was characterized by etchings that have revolutionary, socialist messages. Although one sees these works now as early pieces of a not-yet-mature artist, they are still remarkable, distinguished by their intensity of line and emotional contrast of light and dark. Kollwitz's first big success came with her *Revolt of the Weavers* series (1898), six intense images illustrating Gerhart Hauptmann's play of the same title, about the revolt of Silesian weavers fifty years earlier. For the next ten years, she continued to work in this vein, executing a series of etchings entitled *The Peasants War* (1908) and numerous images of working women. During this period, Kollwitz made two noteworthy trips out of Germany. In 1904 she traveled to Paris, where she briefly studied sculpture at the Académie Julian and made several visits to Rodin's studio. In 1907, she was awarded the Villa Romana Prize, which enabled her to spend a year in Italy with all her expenses paid. (In her autobiographical statement, Kollwitz admits that she did not work much during this period.)

Kollwitz then went through a period of artistic searching, during which time she tired of etching, feeling that she had taken it as far as she could. She experimented with other graphic media, notably lithography and woodcuts, and also began to concentrate on studying sculpture, which she had first attempted in Paris. Around this time, she first encountered both the woodcuts and sculpture of Ernst Barlach, an artist who became a friend. This period of uncertainty in her career was brutally punctuated by the most crushing event in her life, the death of her second son, Peter, in 1914 at the start of the First World War. Although his death left her psychically wounded for the rest of her life, it also (after a time) galvanized her creative energies. By 1920, Kollwitz felt that her mission as an artist required her to speak out against the lunacy and destructiveness of society, against the ways in which human life was devalued — through war, starvation, exploitation. Through her art she wanted "to be effective in this time when people are so helpless and in need of aid."

Her "mature" style is represented by the resulting drawings, lithographs, and some woodcuts in which she concentrated on showing the suffering of ordinary people, in the hope of achieving social change. Works such as *Bread, Vienna is Dying . . . Save Her Children* and *Never Again War*, come from this period. During these years, too, she devoted much time and emotion to making a sculpted memorial to her son. *The Parents*, the image of Karl and Käthe Kollwitz, was installed in 1927 in the Roggevelde Cemetery near where Peter had fallen in Belgium. Ironically, it was through the making of this piece that she overcame her feelings of inadequacy as a sculptor.

During the 1930s Kollwitz's style entered its last phase. She continued to produce drawings and lithographs, and made some of her most dynamic sculptures. These years were punctuated by increasing depression, on a personal level, as both Kollwitzes began to feel the effects of old age, and politically as Hitler rose to power and began to have an increasingly repressive impact on everyday life in Germany. Early in the 1930s Kollwitz was fired from her position at the Prussian Academy, her work reviled, with that of other artists, as "degenerate" by the Nazis. Karl died in 1940; her grandson Peter, namesake of her own son, was killed during the Second World War, and she herself became homeless as she was forced to escape the bombings of Berlin. Nonetheless, she produced some of her strongest, most effective works during these years. Such pieces as the sculpture *Tower of Mothers* (1937–38) and the lithograph *Seed Corn Shall Not Be Ground Up* (1942) show a simplification of both line and form that communicate her increasingly intense repulsion at the destructive forces of the world. During these years Kollwitz also worked on her last series of prints, eight lithographs on the theme of death.

Kollwitz is often characterized as an Expressionist because the intensity of her images, as well as her time and place, are similar to those of the artists who accepted that title. The artist, however, would not have accepted this assessment. Kollwitz referred to the Expressionists as "studio painters," objecting to their dissociation from the life of the people, and to the frivolously decorative quality of their art. (Marianne Werefkin's meditations on her "self" would have been anathema to Kollwitz.) Kollwitz's belief that art is a viable social force that can express the pent-up emotions of silenced groups is paralleled in the work of Elizabeth Catlett, also a graphic artist and sculptor discussed in this book. In some ways Kollwitz's rejection of Expressionism is similar to Catlett's rejection of artistic abstraction several decades later.

Whereas most Expressionists concerned themselves primarily with aesthetic issues, Kollwitz strove to create an art that had social impact. This approach, opposing as it did the critical dictum that art not be tainted by political propaganda, may provide a partial explanation for Kollwitz's never having been fully integrated into the mainstream of the art historical canon, despite general acknowledgment of her remarkable vision and oeuvre. Notwithstanding her opposition to the Expressionists' theoretical stance, some stylistic similarities between their work and her own exist: like the Expressionists, Kollwitz deliberately manipulated her artistic media to evoke strong emotional responses from her viewers. Seen in works that do not have overt political content — such as the jagged line that communicates the tension in her drawing arm in *Self-Portrait with a Pencil* (1935) — it was also used to intensify the drama of social protest, as in *Seed Corn Shall Not Be Ground Up*, in which the mother's fierce expression and jutting arm emphasize her opposition to war. Kollwitz was able to wed social message with aesthetic form, so that the two became one.

Throughout her working life Kollwitz explored the relationship between mothers and children. She placed this private relationship in its social setting, making her conception of this theme different from its usual treatment in Western art and from its restatement by other women artists at the turn of the century. Although images from the middle of her career, such as *Municipal Shelter* (1926), show the vulnerability of mothers in their attempts to protect their children from the brutality of the world, her later images of mothers became more fierce. In such works as *Seed Corn Shall Not Be Ground Up* and *Towers of Mothers*, the mothers are heroes rather than victims, actively resolute in defense of the life they have brought forth. Their concern transcends the personal protection of their own biological children to a desire to protect the entire human species, not through passive individual fertility but through communal social action. The philosophy expressed in her works anticipated that of some contemporary activist groups, such as the women's peace movement, and departed radically from traditional conceptions and representations of motherhood.

Kollwitz also transcended conventional and stereotypical views in her explorations of old age and death. One of the major endeavors of her last decade was a series of lithographs on the subject of death. Earlier depictions of death were not uncommon in her work, but now death came as a maternal lap or a dear friend, rather than the malevolent or hostile force it had previously been. Perhaps this change resulted from Kollwitz's own resignation and weariness. She often showed her own androgynous image responding to death's call, and even made her own grave marker, inscribed "Rest in the peace of thine hands," in which her face is protectively enfolded. That she did not prettify her face in these works or seek to make it more "feminine" is also significant; instead, Kollwitz's face is poignantly human in its ragged dignity, suggesting the special knowledge held by the older woman's passage to a wise matriarch who looks at the whole cycle of life. In this, Kollwitz departed from Western art's stereotypical expression of the fear of death and dying through caricatured, unsympathetic images of withered old women.

Kollwitz used her journal — a vivid, moving document — to help reconcile herself to personal and professional changes in her life. Like Marianne Werefkin, she began it at midlife, in 1909 shortly after she turned forty, and continued to write regularly for the next thirty-five years, stopping shortly before she was evacuated from Berlin in 1943. When she began writing, she realized that her childbearing years had passed and that she was "gradually approaching the period in [her] life where work comes first." She concludes her final entry, written the day after her son's fifty-first birthday, by quoting Goethe: "I have gone beyond purely sensual truth." Like so many women artists, Kollwitz used her journal to explore her aesthetic aims, social beliefs, family relationships, and working rhythms. (For example, she wrote that she noticed a rhythm in her ability to work, that at times for no external reason she felt creatively barren, but then the images would start to flow once more.) Her voice is articulate and captivating, and the issues she explores have immediate and continuing relevance. As Elizabeth Curry points out, the correspondences between Kollwitz's verbal and visual self-portraits are also remarkable.

Her diaries and letters, edited by her son Hans, were published in English in 1955 (based on eleven volumes of handwritten material deposited in the Akademie der Kunst, Berlin) and include two autobiographical pieces, one concerning her early years that she wrote at Hans's insistence when he was about thirty, the other — In Retrospect — written in 1941 and discussing her professional life before she started to keep a journal. Most current biographical writing about Kollwitz has relied on these two works. Her comments about the intensity of her early sexuality and her belief in the "necessity" of bisexuality for artistic production are particularly intriguing.

In her art, Kollwitz expressed her deep commitment to humanity in an accessible visual language. What mattered was that, through her art, she could be an advocate for the suffering and downtrodden of humanity. "I have never done any work cold," she wrote to Hans. "I have always worked with my blood."

SOURCES

Curry, Elizabeth. "Käthe Kollwitz as Role Model for the Older Woman." *Chrysalis* 7: 55-69.

Kollwitz, Käthe. *The Diary and Letters of Käthe Kollwitz.* Edited by Hans Kollwitz. Translated by Richard Winston and Clara Winston. Evanston, Ill.: Northwestern University Press, 1989.

Kearns, Martha. *Käthe Kollwitz: Woman and Artist.* Old Westbury, N.Y.: Feminist Press, 1976.

Klein, Mina C., and Arthur Klein. *Käthe Kollwitz: Life in Art.* New York: Schocken Books, 1975.

Lauter, Estella. *Women as Mythmakers.* Bloomington: Indiana University Press, 1984.

Harris, Ann Sutherland, and Linda Nochlin. *Women Artists 1550-1950.* New York: Alfred A. Knopf, 1977.

FROM KÄTHE KOLLWITZ
AUTOBIOGRAPHICAL STATEMENT FOR HER SON HANS, CA. 1922

. . . On the upper floor of our house lived a boy named Otto Kunzemueller who was my first love. We played out in the yard and garden with the other children of the house and were allowed a fair degree of freedom. . . .

. . . Otto and I sometimes went down into the cellar to exchange kisses. . . . Our kisses were childish and highly solemn. Each time, we gave one another only one kiss, which we called "a refreshment." . . . I don't think anyone found us out, for we used to clamber over the fence into the abandoned next-door garden, or go down into the cellar, for our kisses.

I know that it was a wonderful feeling. I literally loved Otto so deeply that my whole being was filled to the brim. But since I was wholly ignorant in matters of love and he, I imagine, no less so, the refreshment kiss was as far as we went. . . .

After this first crush of mine I was always in love. It was a chronic condition; sometimes it was only a gentle undertone to my ordinary life, and sometimes it took stronger hold of me. I was not particularly discriminating about my love-objects. Sometimes I fell in love with women. Rarely did the person I was in love with have the slightest suspicion of my feelings. At the same time I was plunged into those states of longing for I knew not what which torment the child at puberty. . . .

As I look back upon my life I must make one more remark upon this subject: although my leaning toward the male sex was dominant, I also felt frequently drawn toward my own sex — an inclination which I could not correctly interpret until much later on. As a matter of fact I believe that bisexuality is almost a necessary factor in artistic production; at any rate, the tinge of masculinity within me helped me in my work.

I turn now from discussion of my physical development to my nonphysical development. By now my father had long since realized that I was gifted at drawing. The fact gave him great pleasure and he wanted me to have all the training I needed to become an artist. Unfortunately I was a girl, but nevertheless he was ready to risk it. He assumed that I would not be much distracted by love affairs, since I was not a pretty girl; and he was all the more disappointed and angry later on when at the age of only seventeen I became engaged to Karl Kollwitz. . . .

I was hard-working and conscientious, and my parents took pleasure in each drawing I turned out. That was a particularly happy time for my father, in respect to us. . . . He had been astonished by one of Lise's drawings, and said to Mother: "Lise will soon be catching up to Käthe." . . .

Now when I ask myself why Lise, for all her talent, did not become a real artist, but only a highly gifted dilettante, the reason is clear to me. I was keenly ambitious and Lise was not. I wanted to and Lise did not. I had a clear aim and direction. . . .

. . . I wanted my education to be in art alone. If I could, I would have saved all my intellectual powers and turned them exclusively to use in my art, so that this flame alone would burn brightly. . . .

One thing for which I shall always be very grateful to my parents is the fact that they allowed Lise and me to wander about the town for hours in the afternoons. In this, too, they exhibited an attitude of generous confidence and never checked up on us afterwards. . . .

All this apparently aimless loafing undoubtedly contributed to my artistic growth. For a long period my later work dealt with the world of the workers, and it can all be traced back to these casual expeditions through the busy commercial city teeming with work. From the first I was strongly attracted to the workman type — and this bent became even more marked later on. I was about sixteen when I made my first drawing of characteristic workman types; the drawing was based on the poem by Freiligrath, "The Emigrants." A year later, at my father's request, I showed this drawing to my teacher in Berlin, Stauffer-Bern, who recognized it as altogether typical — both of me and of the environment from which I came. . . .

❖

FROM KÄTHE KOLLWITZ, *IN RETROSPECT* (1941)

From my childhood on my father had expressly wished me to be trained for a career as an artist, and he was sure that there would be no great obstacles to my becoming one. . . .

In my seventeenth year I became engaged to Karl Kollwitz, who was then studying medicine. My father, who saw his plans for me endangered by this engagement, decided to send me away once more, this time to Munich instead of Berlin. That was in 1889.

In Munich I lived in Georgenstrasse, near the Academy, and attended the girls' art school. Once more I had good luck in my teacher, Ludwig Herterich. He did not put so great a stress upon my drawing and took me into his painting class. The life I plunged into in Munich was exciting and made me very happy. Among the girls who were studying there were some who were very gifted. . . .

I so liked the free life in Munich that I began to wonder whether I had not made a mistake in binding myself by so early an engagement. The free life of the artist allured me. . . .

My father no longer watched my work with the serene confidence that I was making progress. He had expected a much faster completion of my studies, and then exhibitions and success. Moreover, as I have mentioned, he was very skeptical about my intention to follow two careers, that of artist and wife. My fiancé had been put in charge of the tailors' *Krankenkasse*, and with this prospect for earning a livelihood we decided to take the leap. Shortly before our marriage my father said to me, "You have made your choice now. You will scarcely be able to do both things. So be wholly what you have chosen to be."

In the spring of 1891 we moved into the home in North Berlin where we were to live for fifty years. My husband devoted most of his time to his clinic and was soon burdened with a great deal of work. In 1892 I had my first child, Hans, and in 1896 my second, Peter. The quiet, hardworking life we led was unquestionably very good for my further development. My husband did everything possible so that I would have time to work. My occasional efforts to exhibit failed. But in connection with one of these exhibitions, a show of the rejected applicants was arranged, and I took part in this. . . .

A great event took place during this time: the Freie Buehne's première of Hauptmann's *The Weavers*. . . .

That performance was a milestone in my work. I dropped the series on *Germinal* and set to work on *The Weavers*. At the time I had so little technique that my first attempts were failures. For this reason the first three plates of the series were lithographed, and only the last three successfully etched: the *March of the Weavers*, *Storming the Owner's House*, and *The End*. My work on this series was slow and painful. But it gradually came, and I wanted to dedicate the series to my father. I intended to preface it with Heine's poem, "The Weavers." But meanwhile my father fell critically ill, and he did not live to see the success I had when this work was exhibited. On the other hand, I had the pleasure of laying before him the complete *Weavers* cycle on his seventieth birthday in our peasant cottage at Rauschen. He was overjoyed. I can still remember how he ran through the house calling again and again to Mother to come and see what little Käthe had done. . . .

I should like to say something about my reputation for being a "socialist" artist, which clung to me from then on. Unquestionably my work at this time, as a result of the attitudes of my father and brother and of the whole literature of the period, was in the direction of socialism. But my real motive for choosing my subjects almost exclusively from the life of the workers was that only such subjects gave me in a simple and unqualified way what I felt to be beautiful. For me the Koenigsberg longshoremen had beauty; the Polish *jimkes* on their grain ships had beauty; the broad freedom of movement in the gestures of the common people had beauty. Middle-class people held no appeal for me at all. Bourgeois life as a whole seemed to me pedantic. The proletariat, on the other hand, had a grandness of manner, a breadth to their lives. Much later on, when I became acquainted with the difficulties and tragedies underlying proletarian life, when I met the women who came to my husband for help and so, incidentally, came to me, I was gripped by the full force of the proletarian's fate. . . .

My longest absence from home came about through my winning the Villa Romana prize, which was given by Klinger. The prize was a grant for a year's living abroad; the purpose of the foundation was to acquaint artists with Florence and its art treasures. Supposedly, the artists would also carry on their own work. I did not work at all, although I was given a handsome studio in the Villa Romana. . . .

My impression of Rome was that it was scarcely worthwhile to begin studying its art treasures. The superabundance of classical and medieval art was almost frightening. After spending much too short a time there, I went back to Florence with Hans, and from there to Spezia. The same minute our train from Florence arrived in Spezia, another train pulled in from the north bringing my husband and little Peter. We hired a boat and were rowed across to Fiascherino, a tiny fishing village. There we lived among the fishermen. After a while Stan and her husband followed us out there and we spent a glorious vacation together. A rather battered fishing boat was placed at our disposal. We spent whole afternoons on the water and in the cool grottoes. Once we rowed over to

Carrara at dawn, climbed up to the marble quarries and rowed back at night. The night was so quiet that the stars were reflected in the sea and the drops of water fell like glittering stars from the oars. That summer I reached my fortieth year. Thin and brown from the sun and the Ligurian Sea, we finally returned home. . . .

❖

FROM KÄTHE KOLLWITZ,
SELECTIONS FROM THE DIARIES, 1909–1943

December 30, 1909

On Saturday the Secession show was opened. I went there with Hans. My things were hung well, although the etchings were separate. Nevertheless I am no longer so satisfied. There are too many good things there that seem fresher than mine. . . .

In my own work I find that I must try to keep everything to a more and more abbreviated form. The execution seems to be too complete. I should like to do the new etching so that all the essentials are strongly stressed and the inessentials almost omitted.

❖

April 1910

I am gradually approaching the period in my life when work comes first. When both the boys went away for Easter, I hardly did anything but work. Worked, slept, ate and went for short walks. But above all I worked. And yet I wonder whether the "blessing" is not missing from such work. No longer diverted by other emotions, I work the way a cow grazes; but Heller once said that such calm is death. Perhaps in reality I "accomplish" little more. The hands work and work, and the head imagines it is producing God knows what; and yet formerly, in my so wretchedly limited working time, I was more productive because I was more sensual; I lived as a human being must live, passionately interested in everything. Now I am working on the second plate of *Death*. Sometimes, infatuated with my work, I think I am far surpassing myself. But after a two-hour pause — where is the stroke of genius? Then there seems to me nothing special about what I have done. That torments me. Potency, potency is diminishing.

❖

September 1, 1911

I imagine the following sculpture as utterly beautiful: a pregnant woman chiseled out of stone. Carved only down to the knees so that she looks the way Lise said she did the time she was pregnant with Maria: "As if I am rooted to the ground." The immobility, restraint, introspection. The arms and hands dangling heavily, the head lowered, all attention directed inward. And the whole thing in heavy, heavy stone. Title: *Pregnancy*.

❖

New Year's Day, 1912

. . . What about myself? Summing up of 1911? Progress? No progress in my relationship with Karl. What he always speaks of, what seems to him still the sole worthwhile goal of our long living together — that we should grow together in the deepest intimacy — I still do not feel and probably never will learn to feel.

Are not the ties with the boys also growing slacker? I almost think so. For the last third of life there remains only work. It alone is always stimulating, rejuvenating, exciting and satisfying. This year I have made excellent progress in sculpture. I can see an advance between the first group of mother with child and the last finished group. This group, in which the child sits between the mother's legs and she holds his feet with her left hand, is about done as far as working from the model goes. Now I have taken it up again; but it still has a dead side that I do not know how to attack.

❖

New Year's 1912–13

... Sometimes I stop believing in the value of my working, and that is bad. Formerly I did not look to either side. Now I feel myself vulnerable; sometimes I am a prey to despair. And I am too much upset by the young people with their different point of view. If I had great strength within myself they would hardly trouble me, but now I feel that my work has no echo, feel as if I have been tossed into the scrapheap. And so I have. All that one can do is put on blinkers and plod along by oneself, paying no attention to anything else. I've worked almost exclusively in sculpture this year. I don't know whether I will get anywhere. If not, what then? Can I possibly go back to etching?

❖

August 27, 1914

... A piece by Gabriele Reuter in the *Tag* on the tasks of women today. She spoke of the joy of sacrificing — a phrase that struck me hard. Where do all the women who have watched so carefully over the lives of their beloved ones get the heroism to send them to face the cannon? I am afraid that this soaring of the spirit will be followed by the blackest despair and dejection. The task is to bear it not only during these few weeks, but for a long time — in dreary November as well, and also when spring comes again, in March, the month of young men who wanted to live and are dead. That will be much harder.

Those who now have only small children, like Lise her Maria, seem to me so fortunate. For us, whose sons are going, the vital thread is snapped.

[Peter Kollwitz was killed on October 22, 1914.]

❖

February 15, 1915

In the studio I looked at my former sketches. Saw that I have gone along by roundabout ways — which were perhaps necessary — and yet am making progress. I do not want to die, even if Hans and Karl should die. I do not want to go until I have faithfully made the most of my talent and cultivated the seed that was placed in me until the last small twig has grown. This does not contradict the fact that I would have died — smilingly — for Peter, and for Hans too, were the choice offered me. Oh how gladly, how gladly. Peter was seed for the planting which should not have been ground. He was the sowing. I am the bearer and cultivator of a grain of seed-corn. What Hans will become, the future will show. But since I am to be the cultivator, I want to serve faithfully. Since recognizing that, I am almost serene and much firmer in spirit. It is not only that I am permitted to finish my work — I am obliged to finish it. This seems to me to be the meaning of all the gabble about culture. Culture arises only when the individual fulfils his cycle of obligations. If everyone recognizes and fulfils his cycle of obligations, genuineness emerges. The culture of a whole nation can in the final analysis be built upon nothing else but this.

❖

February 21, 1916

Read an article by E. von Keyserling on the future of art. He opposes expressionism and says that after the war the German people will need eccentric studio art less than ever before. What they need is realistic art.

I quite agree — if by realistic art Keyserling means the same thing I do. Which refers back to a talk I had recently with Karl about my small sculptures.

It is true that my sculptural work is rejected by the public. Why? It is not at all popular. The average spectator does not understand it. Art for the average spectator need not be shallow. Of course he has no objection to the trite — but it is also true that he would accept true art if it were simple enough. I thoroughly agree that there must be understanding between the artist and the people. In the best ages of art that has always been the case.

Genius can probably run on ahead and seek out new ways. But the good artists who follow after genius — and I count myself among these — have to restore the lost connection once more. A pure studio art is unfruitful and frail, for anything that does not form living roots — why should it exist at all? . . .

❖

March 31, 1916

I am overcome by a terrible depression. Gradually I am realizing the extent to which I already belong among the old fogies, and my future lies behind me. Now I am looked upon more or less kindly as a dignitary. If I had less of a name . . . I would be rejected.

What can be done? Return, without illusions, to what there is in me and go on working very quietly. Go on with my work to its end. Show seasons are naturally always disturbing because I see all the strange, youthful and new things passing before me, and they excite me. I compare them with myself and see with disgusting clarity what is feeble and reactionary in my own work. When I am at the Secession, in the midst of artists who are all thinking about their own art, I also think of mine. Once I am back home this horrible and difficult life weighs down upon me again with all its might. Then only one thing matters: the war.

❖

April 8, 1916

Last night I dreamed once more that I had a baby. There was much in the dream that was painful, but I recall one sensation distinctly. I was holding the tiny infant in my arms and I had a feeling of great bliss as I thought that I could go on always holding it in my arms. It would be one year old and then only two, and I would not have to give it away.

❖

September 1916

My work seems so hopeless that I have decided to stop for the time being. My inward feeling is one of emptiness. How shall I find joy outside of the work?

Talking to people means nothing at all. Nothing and no one can help me. I see Peter far, far in the distance. Naturally I will not give it up — possibly I cannot — but I shall make a pause. Now I have no joy in it. All day yesterday I took care of a host of things. But what for?

❖

March 1917

Looking through my drawings for the show I found some of my very old ones, done between the ages of fourteen and seventeen. It is the same as it always is with me — I can hardly endure my old things. Not hard to understand. At one glance you see your shortcomings, and usually they are shortcomings which have been somewhat repressed later on, but which still represent a danger. In my work it is the story-telling aspect. Almost all my early drawings are anecdotes. I drew almost everything imaginable that I saw or thought of or that happened. One way to put it, I suppose, is that then too I was "contending with life." It is quite clear where this impulse comes from. At the time I knew only narrative art and was interested in nothing else, and that was the case for a long time. Actually it was only after Munich that my things stopped being so painfully anecdotic. . . .

Goethe speaks of the complacent conceit which makes the production of a period just past seem so odious to one. That does not really apply here. I still say that one has every reason to writhe inwardly over one's youthful works. The shortcomings are not even compensated for by technique; they lie smugly exposed in all their naïveté.

❖

October 30, 1918

Article from *Vorwaerts* (newspaper)

Reply from Käthe Kollwitz to Richard Dehmel

In the *Vorwaerts* of October 22 Richard Dehmel published a manifesto entitled *Sole Salvation*. He appeals to all fit men to volunteer. If the highest defense authorities issued a call, he thinks, after the elimination of the "poltroons" a small and therefore more select band of men ready for death would volunteer, and this band could save Germany's honor.

I herewith wish to take issue with Richard Dehmel's statement. . . . The result would most probably be that these young men who are ready for sacrifice would in fact be sacrificed. We have had four years of daily bloodletting — all that is needed is for one more group to offer itself up, and Germany will be bled to death. . . .

I respect the act of Richard Dehmel in once more volunteering for the front, just as I respect his having volunteered in the fall of 1914. . . .

But what about the countless thousands who also had much to give — other things beside their bare young lives. That these young men whose lives were just beginning should be thrown into the war to die by legions — can this really be justified?

There has been enough of dying! Let not another man fall! Against Richard Dehmel I ask that the words of an even greater poet be remembered: "Seed for the planting must not be ground."

❖

January 4, 1920

I have again agreed to make a poster for a large-scale aid program for Vienna. I hope I can make it, but I do not know whether I can carry it out because it has to be done quickly and I feel an attack of grippe coming on.

I want to show Death. Death swings the lash of famine — people, men, women and children, bowed low, screaming and groaning, file past him.

While I drew, and wept along with the terrified children I was drawing, I really felt the burden I am bearing. I felt that I have no right to withdraw from the responsibility of being an advocate. It is my duty to voice the sufferings of men, the never-ending sufferings heaped mountain-high. This is my task, but it is not an easy one to fulfil. Work is supposed to relieve you. But is it any relief when in spite of my poster people in Vienna die of hunger every day? And when I know that? Did I feel relieved when I made the prints on war and knew that the war would go on raging? Certainly not. Tranquillity and relief have come to me only when I was engaged on one thing: the big memorial for Peter. Then I had peace and was with him.

❖

April 1921

Low. Low. Touching bottom.

I hope to get through it anyhow. Finish the woodcuts by the time of the Jury. Then the Jury; then a week's rest in Neuruppin, and then it may go better. But no. Poor work right along recently and no longer able to see things right. Then I was ripe for illness and fell ill, and at the same time everything slid and dropped and collapsed with a thoroughness I have not experienced for a long time. Now my work disgusts me so that I cannot look at it. At the same time total failure as a human being. I no longer love Karl, nor Mother, scarcely even the children. I am stupid and without any thoughts. I see only unpleasant things. The spring days pass and I do not respond. A weariness in my whole body, a churlishness that paralyzes all the others. You don't notice how bad you get when in such a state until you are beginning to rise out of it. One horrid symptom is this: not only do you not think a single matter through to the end, but you don't even feel a feeling to the end. As soon as one arises, it is as though you threw a handful of ashes on it and it promptly goes out. Feelings which once touched you closely seem to be behind thick, opaque window panes; the weary soul does not even try to feel because feeling is too strenuous. So that there is *nothingness* in me, neither thoughts nor feelings, no challenge to action, no participation. Karl feels that I am strange — and nothing matters at all to me. . .

❖

April 30, 1922

Plans for woodcuts which are going along with the series on war. Reworked the Vienna poster of Death reaching into the band of children. The more I work, the more there dawns upon me how much there is still to be done. It is like a photographic plate which lies in the developer: the picture gradually becomes recognizable and emerges more and more from the mist. So these days I no longer think that I shall soon be able to return to sculpture. Since I have been doing woodcuts I find the technique full of temptations. But above all I am afraid of sculpture. I suppose it is an insuperable problem for me; I am too old ever really to conquer it. It is not impossible that I shall gradually move from woodcut technique to woodcarving. But that is still very nebulous. I toy with the thought of doing the mothers standing in a circle, defending their children, as sculpture in the round.

❖

June 1924
The first day of Whitsun, a joyous and happy day for me. I went out to spend it with the children. Magnificent weather. . . .

. . . The twins are precious. Sturdy, droll, innocent little white heads. Babbling their own language. When Ottilie sits between them to feed them and gives each in turn a spoonful of pap, the one who doesn't have her turn clenches her fists and her face turns red at having to wait, while the other opens her mouth for the spoon with the smuggest air of contentment. It is wonderful to see. Happy Ottilie, who is so thoroughly maternal. Whatever comes later on, these three years of work with the babies will always give her a kind of satiated feeling. She is a mother through and through, much as she sometimes rants against being one. . . .

❖

October 13, 1925
I am with Peter only when my plans for the soldiers' cemetery in Roggevelde are stirring again. Recently I once more set to work on the big sculpture with relatively fresh vigor, with the thought that I should have it ready by spring and to be able to show it in the Academy. Once I have done that, I can go back to the Roggevelde figures. This time I want to make them half life-size at most, and then have them enlarged.

The mother is to kneel and look out over the multitude of graves. The unhappy woman spreads out her arms over all her sons. The father kneeling too. He has his hands clasped in his lips.

When I am making such progress in sculpture I do not care that our planned trip to India is falling through.

❖

New Year's Eve, 1925–6
Recently I began reading my old diaries. Back to before the war. Gradually I became very depressed. The reason for that is probably that I wrote only when there were obstacles and halts to the flow of life, seldom when everything was smooth and even. So there were at most brief notes when things went well with Hans, but long pages when he lost his balance. And I wrote nothing when Karl and I felt that we belonged intimately to one another and made each other happy; but long pages when we did not harmonize. As I read I distinctly felt what a half-truth a diary presents. Certainly there was truth behind what I wrote; but I set down only one side of life, its hitches and harassments. I put the diaries away with a feeling of relief that I am safely out of those times. Yet they were times which I always think of as the best in my life, the decade from my mid-thirties to my mid-forties. . . . I have fully realized only in these last years — that he and I are together. Now we are wonderfully fond of

one another. He is no longer the same man he once was, as I am no longer the same woman. . . .

❖

December 21, 1926

A long time since I last made an entry. A sweetish-sour condition, physically and mentally. In the work, which I began naively, so to speak, I have reached the first stumbling-block. I do not know what to do about it. I keep my hands timidly in my lap and evade the issue. The obstacle is the clothing. Once again I confront the great difficulty of having to do something that isn't in me, for which I have no talent. And yet it must be done. The naturalistic folds disgust me and the stylized folds disgust me, and if I try to do it in Barlach's manner, that too disgusts me. To get across what I want — so that only the silhouette matters — takes a great deal of technique. More than I possess, working in this material. — I am not afraid of the head, but the big, clothed mass worries me.

On top of all that, for some time now I have been haunted by the thought: Sixty years old — how can I manage to do anything important any more? In addition I am physically dragged down. Christmas coming, with its multitude of trivial, wearisome concerns.

❖

April 1928

I had asked Lise to sit for me a while, for the head of the mother. I thought I now knew exactly what was needed. But nevertheless I did not make any progress. Suddenly I recalled my self-portrait in plaster, which had been standing in the studio for three-quarters of a year, and which I had not even unpacked. I unwrapped it, and it was as if scales fell from my eyes. I saw that my own head could well be used after all, and that I can work from this over-size study.

❖

Easter 1932

For a short time I have once more had that glorious feeling of happiness, that happiness which cannot be compared with anything else, which springs from being able to cope with one's work. What I've had in my best periods — and how short-lived these were. How long were the stretches of toilsome tacking back and forth, of being blocked, of being thrown back again and again. But all that was annulled by the periods when I had my technique in hand and succeeded in doing what I wanted. Now only a faint reflection of all that is left.

And then the unspeakably difficult general predicament. The misery. People sinking into dark wretchedness. The repulsive political hate-campaigns.

❖

August 14, 1932

Looking back upon the time in Belgium, my loveliest memory is of the last afternoon when van Hauten drove us out there once more. He left us alone and we went from the figures to Peter's grave, and everything was alive and *wholly* felt. I stood before the woman, looked at her — my own face — and I wept and stroked her cheeks. Karl stood close behind me — I did not even realize it. I heard him whisper, "Yes, yes." How close we were to one another then!

❖

August 1934

It is curious the way I am working during these summer months. As with the spring procession, I always keep making a few steps forward — and a few back. I had intended during this period when I cannot work in sculpture to carry out my old plan of doing a series of prints on the theme of death. . . .

I thought that now that I am really old I might be able to handle this theme in a way that would plumb depths. As old Goethe said, "Thoughts hitherto inconceivable. . . ." But that is not the case. The period of aging is, to be sure, more difficult than old age itself, but it is also more productive. At the very point when death becomes visible behind everything, it disrupts the imaginative process. The menace is more stimulating when you are not confronting it from close up. When it is upon you, you do not see its full extent; in fact you no longer have such respect for it.

In any case, so far I have done nothing *essential* in that direction. At the same time I have a curious doubt about the technical aspects. Decided on lithography, but when I started the work itself I no longer felt sure. Continually vacillating between stone and transfer. Formerly I could properly say, I carry a job to completion. Now it is no longer *I* who carry out *my* idea, *my* plan. I start off indecisively, soon tire, need frequent pauses and must turn for counsel to my own earlier works.

That is not a pretty state of affairs. But strangely enough it does not sadden me as much as it might. The simple fact is that nothing is terribly important to me any more.

❖

November 1936

I am gradually realizing now that I have come to the end of my working life. Now that I have had the group cast in cement, I do not know how to go on. There is really nothing more to say. I thought of doing another small scultpure, *Age*, and I had some vague ideas about a relief. But whether I do them or not is no longer important. Not for the others and not for myself. Also there is this curious silence surrounding the expulsion of my work from the Academy show, and in connnection with the Kronprinzenpalais. Scarcely anyone had anything to say to me about it. I thought people would come, or at least write — but no. Such a silence all around us. — That too has to be experienced. Well, Karl is still here. I see him every day and we talk and show one another our love. But how will it be when he too is gone?

One turns more and more to silence. All is still. I sit in Mother's chair by the stove, evenings, when I am alone.

❖

December 1941

My days pass, and if anyone asks me how things are I usually answer, "Not so good," or something of the sort. . . .

The fact is that I am still pretty well off. I do not yet have any constant pain; my eyes are holding out; I am living with Klara and Lina, who are so sweet about taking care of my food; at least once a week my dear Hans comes; pleasant people visit me. I have not been able to work for months, but this too I do not take too hard as I formerly thought I would. Yes, at intervals this weighs on my mind and makes me very sad. But on the other hand, it is an adjustment to the order of things. It is in the order of things that man reaches his peak and descends again. No sense grumbling about it.

It is of course bitter to experience it. The old Michelangelo drew a picture of himself in a kiddie car, and Grillparzer says: "Once I was a poet, now I am none; the head on my shoulders is no longer mine." But that is simply the way things are.

Yes, I must still say as I always have, that when a certain measure of suffering has been reached, man has the right to cut his life short. I am still far from that measure of suffering, in a physical or spiritual sense. And I also feel a timidity and fear of bringing death upon myself. I am afraid of dying — but being dead, oh yes, that to me is often an appealing prospect. If it were only not for the necessity of parting from the few who are dear to me here.

❖

May 1943, the last diary entry

Hans has reached the age of 51. Air-raid alarm the night of May 14. It was the loveliest of May nights. Hans and Ottilie did not go to sleep until very late. They sat in the garden and listened to a nightingale.

After work Hans came, then Ottilie and finally Lise. The four of us sat together. On his birthday table, below the grave relief, I had placed the lithograph *Death Calls*, the print of which I worked over. Then there was a drawing I had made of Karl one time when he was reading aloud to me. We were sitting around the living room table at the time. This drawing is a favorite of Hans'. And there was also the small etching, *Greeting*, which is closely connected with his birthday.

We lit Josef Faasen's large candle.

Early next morning, Hans came again and brought a great bouquet of lilies from the garden. What happiness it is for me that I still have my boy whom I love so deeply and who is so fond of me.

Goethe to Lavater, 1779: "But let us stop worrying our particular religions like a dog its bone. *I have gone beyond purely sensual truth.*"

❖

KÄTHE KOLLWITZ, SELECTIONS FROM LETTERS, 1915–1945

KÄTHE KOLLWITZ TO HANS KOLLWITZ (SON OF KOLLWITZ)
February 21, 1915

Very slowly and gradually I have been getting to the work for Peter. During these past weeks of working I have again realized what I spoke of to you months ago, but what in the intervening time became so obscured that I almost ceased to believe in it. . . .

Why does work help me in these times? It is not enough to say that it relaxes me very much. It is simply that it is a task I may not shirk. As you, the children of my body, have been my tasks, so too are my other works. Perhaps that sounds as though I meant that I would be depriving humanity of something if I stopped working. In a certain sense — yes. Because this is my post and I may not leave it until I have made my talent bear interest. Everyone who is vouchsafed life has the obligation of carrying out to the last item the plan laid down in him. Then he may go. Probably that's the point at which most people die. Peter was "seed for the planting which must not be ground."

If it had been possible for Father or me to die for him so that he might live, oh how gladly we would have gone. For you as well as for him. But that was not to be.

I am not seed for planting. I have only the task of nurturing the seed placed in me. And you, my Hans? May you have been born for life after all! You must have been, and you must believe it.

KÄTHE KOLLWITZ TO HANS KOLLWITZ (SON OF KOLLWITZ)
April 16, 1917

The show is open. There was a preview from three until five. Two minutes before three I pasted labels on the pictures in insane haste. Then I fled. I have already heard some reactions from those who were there. This show *must* mean something, for all these prints are the distillation of my life. I have never done any work cold (except for a few trivial things which I am not showing here). I have always worked with my blood, so to speak. Those who see the things must feel that.

KÄTHE KOLLWITZ TO FRAU HASSE (FRIEND OF KOLLWITZ)
July 20, 1917

Of all the letters I received for my fiftieth birthday, your letter stands out. My heartfelt thanks. When you wish that all the good spirits of creative joy, love and peace of mind may be at my side, I must say a hearty Amen to that. Such wishes bring new strength, and I need strength. Everyone needs it. And people can help one another a great deal through their sympathy, through their thinking of one another.

I dearly wish that my health may stand up for a long time to come. Primarily in order to finish the work — to finish it well — which I am doing for my boy who fell in battle. But beyond that I have in mind many other things still to be done. Growing old is fine if one keeps strong and well. Today we celebrated Liebermann's birthday. At seventy he is wholly unbent; his last works are perhaps his best. May the same be granted to me.

But not to grow old and be an invalid. . . .

KÄTHE KOLLWITZ TO FRAU HASSE (FRIEND OF KOLLWITZ)
March 20, 1925

Yes, you are right, it is a glory and a privilege just to live. And if your work goes badly, you need only remind yourself of Goethe's: "In times of slack do not drive yourself, for fullness and strength are never far off. If you have rested during the bad day, the good one will prove doubly good." I am used to long involuntary halts which drag on so wretchedly that I often think fullness and strength will never come again. And yet they do come, although in the measure that is the due of age. And *when they come*, I say as you do: how glorious, what a privilege!

With the warmest regards.

❖

KÄTHE KOLLWITZ TO BEATE BONUS-JEEP
(FRIEND OF KOLLWITZ FROM ART SCHOOL)

February 1933

Has the Academy affair reached your ears yet? That Heinrich Mann and I, because we signed the manifesto calling for unity of the parties of the left, must leave the Academy. It was all terribly unpleasant for the Academy directors. For fourteen years (the same fourteen that Hitler has branded the "evil years") I have worked together peacefully with these people. Now the Academy directors have had to ask me to resign. Otherwise the Nazis had threatened to break up the Academy. Naturally I complied. So did Heinrich Mann. Municipal Architect Wagner also resigned, in sympathy with us. — But they are allowing me to keep my position until October 1, along with my full salary and the rooms I use. I am greatly relieved about this, because I have a largish group in clay over there and would have had no place to put it if they had evicted me straight off. . . .

❖

KÄTHE KOLLWITZ TO OTTILIE KOLLWITZ
(NÉE EHLERS, DAUGHTER-IN-LAW OF KOLLWITZ)

Reinerz, July 15, 1937

Our practical presents, the two handbags, are lying on your birthday table. This post-birthday present that I am sending now, the cast of the group, unfortunately has not turned out well. For some time I have had the idea of giving you a very good reproduction of the group, and inscribing it: "The Mother — to the Mother — from the Mother." For there is a close tie between you and me and the work itself. I was working on this theme even before the war. Then everything else intervened. When I transferred from Siegmundshof to the Academy, I had a mold made and the piece cast along with the work for the soldiers' cemetery. But the piece had to be totally changed. For in the mean time the twins had come into the world, and ever since seeing you with a child in each arm I knew that I had to extend the work and have a child in it. And so the whole grew slowly until now, when it is finished at last. Now you know how intimately you are a part of it. — You Mother! I thank you from the bottom of my heart for all that you have given Hans and us. Not to speak of the children. . . .

KÄTHE KOLLWITZ TO FRAU HASSE (FRIEND OF KOLLWITZ)

May 10, 1941

. . . I am living along on the fringe of life. Since the fall I have moved my studio from Klosterstrasse back to my apartment. That more befits my present situation. Since my strength is greatly reduced — I can walk along the street only with the aid of a cane, and so on — I was able to go out to the studio only now and then. But here at home, where my working room is also my sleeping room and where I have everything I need all crowded together and handy, I can work whenever I feel strong enough to do so for an odd half hour. There are still so many things to be completed. — My sister visits frequently. About twice a week my son Hans comes, talks everything over with me and helps me in all business affairs. . . .

... Sometimes these days seem intolerably dreary. I miss my husband and at night often feel utterly miserable, as if I were about to follow him immediately. But there is nothing surprising about that. — Yet think of me as sheltered, more or less. My life has been long and rich enough, so that I am thankful to have been granted it.

Thank you again for what you have written me. Whether or not we see one another again — my heartfelt greetings.

❖

KÄTHE KOLLWITZ TO BEATE BONUS-JEEP (FRIEND OF KOLLWITZ FROM ART SCHOOL)

January 1942

Yesterday I had a joyful day. First, early in the morning came a note from Peter in Russia. He is well. Unfortunately we must reckon with his probable discharge from the hospital this week. There is no way of knowing whether he will be sent homeward first, or right back to the front. I still keep hoping it will be home. Then I have given the plaster relief to the stone sculptor and he can now begin his work. And today I have finished my lithograph, "Seed for the planting must not be ground." This time the seed for the planting — sixteen-year-old boys — are all around the mother, looking out from under her coat and wanting to break loose. But the old mother who is holding them together says, No! You stay here! For the time being you may play rough-and-tumble with one another. But when you are grown up you must get ready for life, not for war again. — The stone will be sent to the printer tomorrow, and if it turns out well, that will be one more thing off my chest.

❖

KÄTHE KOLLWITZ TO OTTILIE KOLLWITZ (NÉE EHLERS, DAUGHTER-IN-LAW OF KOLLWITZ)

Nordhausen, February 21, 1944

... It is almost incomprehensible to me, what degrees of endurance people can manifest. In days to come people will hardly understand this age. It must have been like this after the Thirty Years' War. . . . the worst of all is that every war already carries within it the war which will answer it. Every war is answered by a new war, until everything, everything is smashed. The devil only knows what the world, what Germany will look like then. That is why I am wholeheartedly for a radical end to this madness, and why my only hope is in a world socialism. You know what my conception of that is and what I consider the only possible prerequisites for it. Pacifism simply is not a matter of calm looking on; it is work, hard work. . . .

❖

KÄTHE KOLLWITZ TO HANS AND OTTILIE KOLLWITZ (SON AND DAUGHTER-IN-LAW OF KOLLWITZ)

Nordhausen, June 13, 1944

... Do not misunderstand what I am writing today and do not think me ungrateful; but I must say this to you: My deepest desire is no longer to live. I know that many people grow older than I, but everyone knows when the desire to lay aside his life has come to him. For me it has come. The fact that I may or may not be able to stay here a while does not change that. Leaving you two, you and your children, will be terribly hard for me. But the unquenchable longing for death remains. If only you could make up your minds to take me in your arms once more, and then let me go. How grateful I would be. Do not be frightened and do not try to talk me out of it. I bless my life, which has given me such an infinitude of good along with all its hardships. Nor have I wasted it; I have used what strength I had to the best of my ability. All I ask of you now is to let me go — my time is up. I could add much more to this, and no doubt you will say that I am not yet done for, that I can write quite well and my memory is still clear. Nevertheless, the longing for death remains. . . . The desire, the unquenchable longing for death remains. — I shall close now, dear children. I thank you with all my heart.

❖

KÄTHE KOLLWITZ TO LISE STERN (NÉE SCHMIDT, SISTER OF KOLLWITZ)
February 1945
. . . You say that all my life I have had a dialogue with Death. — Oh, Lise, being dead must be good, but I am too much afraid of dying, of being terribly afraid at the moment of death. Jutta is so marvelously kind; it is so awful of me to be such a burden on her, and yet I have no choice. Good-bye, my Lise; give my love to dear Katta. — Your old, old Käthe.

❖

KÄTHE KOLLWITZ TO HANS KOLLWITZ (SON OF KOLLWITZ)
March 1945
I am very old now; am I to add still another year to my age? Every night I dream about you. I must see you once more. If it is really so that you cannot come under any circumstances, I do believe you.

But I must hear that from you yourself. Then give me the freedom to make an end of it. Then write to me: Dearest Mother, I cannot see you any more. For without having seen you one more time, I cannot go. My darling boy, if only I could see you just one more time.

❖

KÄTHE KOLLWITZ TO HANS AND OTTILIE KOLLWITZ
(SON AND DAUGHTER-IN-LAW OF KOLLWITZ)
April 16, 1945
Sometimes the notion strikes me that someone is coming, and then I think it might be you.

It cannot be, I know, but again and again the thought comes that I might be able to hold you in my arms, and then I would clasp you with such rejoicing.

I am told it is cold outside. Juttel has postponed her trip for the time being; perhaps she will plan it again for later.

The war accompanies me to the end. . . .

Beloveds, take only this greeting. — Your very old Käthe.

Käthe Kollwitz, *The Diaries and Letters of Käthe Kollwitz*, edited by Hans Kollwitz, translated by Richard and Clara Winston. Copyright © 1988, Northwestern University Press, Evanston, Illinois. First published 1955 by the Henry Regnery Co. Reprinted by permission of Northwestern University Press.

Forest Landscape No. 1, c.1938. Oil on wove paper, mounted on plywood. 36½" x 24".
National Gallery of Canada, Ottawa

EMILY CARR

1871–1945

NOW SOMETHING OF a Canadian heroine, Emily Carr worked most of her life in isolation, capturing in paint the vitality of the Northwest woods. Although she embarked on an artistic career early in life, she followed a somewhat erratic path and did not come into her own until she was fifty-six, when she took on nature's "roar" as her main subject. Like Rosa Bonheur, Carr expressed her empathy for the natural world by living among a large menagerie of creatures; quite unlike Bonheur, she lived a solitary life and seemed to hold herself back from intimate involvements with other people. Carr was a prolific writer who used a variety of genres to develop and communicate her perception of reality. Many of Carr's published works are autobiographical sketches, embellished and restructured for the purpose of creating a better story. Her conscious self-representation in these works is quite deliberate; they challenge the reader to see beyond the persona that she chose to reveal to Carr's internal motivations, and to reconcile the feisty, good-natured protagonist of her anecdotal adventures with the intense creator of her moving visual images.

In her writings, Carr presents her family background as an impediment to her artistic development, and her ability to break from its repressive atmosphere as indicative of her independence of spirit and creative drive. She was the youngest daughter of conservative and religious English immigrants who settled in Victoria, British Columbia, when the city was still farmland in the late nineteenth century. Carr liked to characterize herself as the black sheep of this bourgeois family, in continual conflict with its strict Victorian values. Even after her parents' deaths within a few years of each other while she was still a teenager, Carr enthusiastically rebelled against their conservatism, now embodied in her elder sisters.

One way in which Carr was able to escape their world was through immersion in artistic pursuit. She left Canada several times between the ages of twenty and forty in order to study art. Her decision in 1891 to attend the California School of Design in San Francisco, the closest cosmopolitan center to Victoria, was her first independent action toward self-definition as an artist. She stayed in San Francisco for three years, maintaining her independence on her return to Victoria by setting up her own studio and offering art classes. In 1899, she left again, to study at the Westminster School of Art in London. Although she remained in England for five years, she never felt comfortable there: "Englishness" seemed to embody all those stuffy qualities against which she had rebelled in Canada. She left London after two years to explore the landscapes of Cornwall and Suffolk, but her deteriorating physical and mental health caused a breakdown that resulted in her confinement in an East Anglia sanatorium for sixteen months. (Her ailment was diagnosed as "hysteria," an illness commonly ascribed to Victorian women who could not, or would not, conform to their roles as "ladies.")

Despite her less than triumphant return to North America, Carr continued her artistic autonomy from her family by moving from Victoria to Vancouver, where she established a studio and remained for six years. Like many earlier women artists, Carr never married and was said to be reticent with men, a restraint that one recent biographer suggests might have been an unconscious protection of her vocation. During 1910 and 1911, Carr left North America for the last time in her life, on a study trip to France. This trip was significant in her artistic development because it introduced her to the modernist idiom of the Fauves that formed the basis of her later style. Although she based herself in Paris, studying privately and at Colarossi's, she also made several trips to Brittany where she found the peasants particularly interesting as painting subjects. In 1911, two of her works were accepted at the Salon d'Automne.

Both before and after her trips to England and France, Carr also frequently traveled to the northern wilderness to study the Indians, whose art and way of living with nature evoked in her a deep response. The first such trip, probably in 1899, was a visit to the village of Ucluelet, perhaps in the company of her sister, Lizzie, whose missionary friend was working there. While living in Vancouver, she made yearly trips north to paint and record the Indians' vanishing life style, most of the time traveling alone (except for a visit to Alaska with her sister, Alice). These trips represented Carr's introduction to the themes that inspired her throughout her life. The summer after her return to Canada from France found Carr traveling to the northern villages once more. By 1913, she had achieved her first public recognition as a painter of Indians and their lore.

The enigma concerning Carr's artistic career is why, despite these auspicious beginnings, it became stagnant, her "creativity submerged" (to use her words) for over ten years. Shortly after her return from France in 1911, Carr moved back to her native Victoria where she built a rooming house on her inherited portion of her father's property on Simcoe Street; she planned through this to support herself while continuing to work at her art. The task of maintaining such a venture proved more strenuous than she had expected, and the daily operation of the household distracted her from full-time pursuit of her career. It is ironic that, even though Carr did not marry and have children, her ability to create art was still deflected by mundane responsibilities, a fate more typically suffered by women artists with families to care for.

In several writings, including "Rejected" in *Growing Pains*, her autobiography, Carr explained the negative impact on her ability to continue painting of the provincial attitudes of those around her. Her new modernist pictorial style was rejected by the public and even her sisters were unenthusiastic about her new work. While it is possible that Carr exaggerated the length of time during which she abandoned painting (it may have been ten, rather than the fifteen years that she claimed), she clearly experienced a long fallow period.

By the early 1920s Carr was in contact with a group of Seattle painters, including the young Mark Tobey. The most fortuitous event in Carr's professional life occurred in 1927, when Eric Brown, director of Canada's National Gallery in Ottawa, literally showed up at her doorstep and selected fifty of her earlier pieces depicting Indian life and culture for inclusion in an exhibition of western Canadian art. This event was the catalyst that enabled Carr to refocus her energies, and that year marks the turning point in her creative life. When Carr traveled east to see the installation, she encountered the Group of Seven, a circle of serious artists working in a modern idiom who identified with the landscape and spirit of Canada as strongly as she did. Seeing their work was a revelation to Carr that fired her imagination and sparked her artistic drive. She returned to western Canada inspired, energized, and, at fifty-six, finally ready to concentrate on creating art that expressed her internal vision. Her commitment to the production of a significant body of work did not flag until old age and ill health forced her to curtail her activities during the last few years of her life.

Prior to Carr's meeting with the Group of Seven, the most profound inspiration of her career had been her deep affinity with the northwest Indians; she was affected both by their harmonious relationship with nature and the aesthetic structure of their art. Until 1913, she had considered it her artistic mission to record their vanishing life-style. Carr was impressed by the expressive potential of the Indians' aesthetics in her search for a visual language that could express "fresh seeing." Her fascination with the abstract structure of their art was similar to Picasso's response to the bold arrangement of formal elements in African sculpture; Picasso was primarily interested in form, however, while Carr was also influenced by the Indians' connection with the earth, which ultimately led her to explore and express in her work the dynamism embodied in nature. The additional lessons of French modernisn provided her with a pictorial structure that enabled her to give form to her intense original responses to the material world.

After Carr's return to British Columbia from Ottawa in 1927, her mature style evolved quickly. She was no longer quite so isolated, having established dialogues with several members of the Group of Seven, most notably Lawren Harris, at whose suggestion she immersed herself in theosophical writings. Perhaps as a result, Carr's works became more monumental in conception, as in *Totem Mother, Kitwancool*, in which the shapes of the totem loom in the foreground rather than remaining passive and picturesque details of the scene. In 1929, Harris suggested that Carr abandon Indian subject matter completely, and concentrate on the woods themselves. By the early 1930s, her major theme had become the activation of the painted surface for the purpose of expressing nature's unity. In the thirties, she took many trips into the wilderness, in a specially outfitted caravan she called "the Elephant," accompanied by her favorite animals.

To better achieve in her painting a sense of immediacy, she developed a technique in which she used highly thinned oil paint on paper. Her mature style now integrated a cosmic spiritualism and modernist picture structure. All the pictorial elements of her paintings — usually landscapes — are united by a restless rhythm that reflects the force of nature, illuminated and energized by intense rays of light. Even the titles of these works — *A Rushing Sea of Undergrowth* or *Scorned as Timber, Beloved by the Sky* — reveal a cosmic consciousness, an awareness expressed also in "Green," an essay in *Growing Pains*.

Despite her geographical isolation, Carr's aesthetic concerns reflected the major artistic issues of her day. Carr's work is most similar to that of artists associated with the various early twentieth-century expresssionist movements. Like them, she abandoned literal depiction of local color and illusionistic form to achieve a more emotive, abstract reality. The surfaces of her works express the spiritual life force of nature and attempt to achieve communion with it. Stylistically, Carr's work forms a bridge between early expressionists, such as the Fauves, and the mid-century Abstract Expressionists. Like many artists identified with those movements, Carr understood the dynamic potential of the activated picture surface and used her art to express a mystical identification with larger aspects of the universe.

Carr's intense identification with the cosmos, as expressed in her emotive landscape paintings, can also be seen in the context of works by other contemporary women artists who respond to nature's "roar." Although there are few well-known nineteenth-century women landscapists, perhaps because of the restrictions on women's freedom of movement, connection with the land has assumed mythic proportions for many women painters and writers in the twentieth century. The writer Margaret Atwood, for example, seems to echo Carr's feelings about the Canadian landscape. The conception of landscape and nature used by these women differs from the traditional in that they do not perceive nature as a female principle waiting to be dominated by man. Rather, they seek to create an art based on human bonding with the earth, with the stuff of which we are made, which (as Susan Griffin wrote) we "don't walk on but in." Carr understood the existence of a mystical relationship with the organic processes of the eternally growing universe, and her affinity for Indian culture and its comprehension of life's essentials is an important aspect of her connected consciousness. Carr's attraction to the indigenous culture of the Canadian Northwest was similar to that of other women writers and artists, such as Mary Austin and Georgia O'Keeffe for the United States's Southwest — all of them moved by the land as well as the people.

Carr was also notable as a prolific writer who used several genres as vehicles for self-expression. Like many other women artists, she kept a journal partly as a means of validating her commitment to her artistic vocation. She began the journal in 1927, just as she was redefining her creative direction. As Paula Blanchard points out, Carr achieved simultaneously a new fluency with words and new mastery as a painter. The journal entries reveal an internal dialogue about herself and its relationship to the production of art and her ideas about aesthetic issues, for instance, her belief that "a picture is a movement in space." In these passages, the reader hears Carr's most intimate written voice. (Parts of the journal have been published as *Hundreds and Thousands*; the manuscript is in the National Library in Ottawa.)

On the other hand, the voice in most of her published stories is that of a good-natured, feisty, often maligned and misunderstood heroine. Although she flirted with story-writing for most of her adult life, Carr did not begin to write prolifically until after a stroke in 1937. Her first volume of autobiographical anecdotes was entitled *Klee Wyck*, "laughing one," the name given her by the Indians, in which she recounted her first trip to the village of Ucluelet. When this was published in 1941, it became an immediate success in Canada; Carr followed with two other collections of stories and sketches, both published during her lifetime. After her death in 1945, her literary executors arranged for publication of several other such works. Like Élisabeth Vigée-Lebrun and Cecilia Beaux, Carr took to writing about her past at a time when old age and infirmity precluded painting. The voice in these sketches, Carr's public persona, contrasts markedly with the raw, emotive quality of her landscapes, and also with the voice she used to talk to herself in her journal.

Carr, like Marianne Werefkin, constructed an alter ego in her writings. Carr's was "Small," the protagonist of the *Book of Small*, her indomitable, child-self who rebelled against restrictions and ultimately enabled her to make her art. Carr's biographers have established that she took numerous liberties in shaping the facts of her stories; as Blanchard points out, however, they are accurate as "records of feelings," if not of facts. Carr was also quite articulate about her aesthetic inclinations, (although she was totally antipathetic to stuffy academicism) and, in the text of a 1930 address sometimes referred to as "Fresh Seeing," Carr emphasizes her dual commitment to modernism and the Canadian landscape. Her essay "Indian Bird Carving" contains Carr's theory of the dynamic aesthetic of abstraction in Indian carving.

Rather than being an isolated, idiosyncratic departure from the mainstream, as might be expected from her geographic isolation, Carr's work provides a vital contribution to twentieth-century landscape painting. In its erratic, non-linear path, her career typifies the circuitous route that many women have followed, notwithstanding the premium placed by our culture on precocious achievement. Carr was noteworthy also as a writer, piecing together the fragments of her daily life into a significant oeuvre with an articulate voice. Although her work has been rightfully claimed as distinctively Canadian, Carr's powerful images transcend regional limitations, and she deserves a far wider audience than she has yet received.

SOURCES

Blanchard, Paula. *The Life of Emily Carr*. Seattle: University of Washington Press, 1987.

Carr, Emily. *An Address*. Toronto: Oxford University Press, 1955.

_____. *Growing Pains: The Autobiography of Emily Carr*. Toronto: Oxford University Press, 1946.

_____. *The Heart of a Peacock*. Toronto: Oxford University Press, 1953.

_____. *Hundreds and Thousands: The Journals of Emily Carr.*, 2d ed. Toronto: Clark, Irwin and Co., 1966.

Griffin, Susan. *Woman and Nature: The Roaring Inside Her.* Boston: Beacon Press, 1978.

Lauter, Estella. *Women as Mythmakers: Poetry and Visual Art by Twentieth- Century Women.* Bloomington: Indiana University Press, 1984.

Shadbolt, Doris. *The Art of Emily Carr.* Seattle and Toronto: University of Washington Press and Clarke, Irwin and Co., 1979.

Tippett, Maria. *Emily Carr: A Biography.* Toronto: Oxford University Press, 1979.

FROM EMILY CARR, "REJECTED"
GROWING PAINS: THE AUTOBIOGRAPHY OF EMILY CARR
(TORONTO: OXFORD UNIVERSITY PRESS, 1946)

I came home from France stronger in body, in thinking, and in work than I had returned from England. My seeing had broadened. I was better equipped both for teaching and study because of my year and a half in France, but still mystified, baffled as to how to tackle our big West.

I visited in Victoria, saw that it was an impossible field for work; then I went to Vancouver and opened a studio, first giving an exhibition of the work I had done in France.

People came, lifted their eyes to the walls — laughed!

"You always were one for joking — this is small children's work! Where is your own?" they said.

"This is my own work — the new way."

Perplexed, angry, they turned away, missing the old detail by which they had been able to find their way in painting. They couldn't see the forest for looking at the trees.

"The good old camera cannot lie. That's what we like, it shows everything," said the critics. This bigger, freer seeing now seemed so ordinary and sensible to me, so entirely sane! It could not have hurt me more had they thrown stones. My painting was not outlandish. It was not even ultra.

The Vancouver schools in which I had taught refused to employ me again. A few of my old pupils came to my classes out of pity, — their money burnt me. Friends I had thought sincere floated into my studio for idle chatter; they did not mention painting, kept their eyes averted from the walls, while talking to me.

In spite of all the insult and scorn shown to my new work I was not ashamed of it. It was neither monstrous, disgusting nor indecent; it had brighter, cleaner colour, simpler form, more intensity. What would Westerners have said of some of the things exhibited in Paris — nudes, monstrosities, a striving after the extraordinary, the bizarre, to arrest attention. Why should simplification to express depth, breadth and volume appear to the West as indecent, as nakedness? People did not want to see beneath surfaces. The West was ultraconservative. They had transported their ideas at the time of their migration, a generation or two back. They forgot that England, even conservative England, had crept forward since then; but these Western settlers had firmly adhered to their old, old, outworn methods and, seeing beloved England as it had been, they held to their old ideals.

. . . I was glad I had been to France. More than ever was I convinced that the old way of seeing was inadequate to express this big country of ours, her depth, her height, her unbounded wideness, silences too strong to be broken — nor could ten million cameras, through their mechanical boxes, ever show real Canada. It had to be sensed, passed through live minds, sensed and loved. . . .

Having so few pupils, I had much time for study. When I got out my Northern sketches and worked on them I found that I had grown. Many of these old Indian sketches I made into large canvases. Nobody bought my pictures; I had no pupils; therefore I could not afford to keep on the studio. I decided to give it up and to go back to Victoria. My sisters disliked my new work intensely. One was noisy in her condemnation, one sulkily silent, one indifferent to every kind of Art.

The noisy sister said, "It is crazy to persist in this way, — no pupils, no sales, you'll starve! Go back to the old painting."

"I'd rather starve! I could not paint in the old way — it is dead — meaningless — empty."

One sister painted china. Beyond mention of that, Art was taboo in the family. My kind was considered a family disgrace. . . .

I ornamented my pottery with Indian designs — that was why the tourists bought it. I hated myself for prostituting Indian Art; our Indians did not "pot," their designs were not intended to ornament clay — but I did keep the Indian design pure.

Because my stuff sold, other potters followed my lead and, knowing nothing of Indian Art, falsified it. This made me very angry. I loved handling the smooth cool clay. I loved the beautiful Indian designs, but I was not happy about using Indian design on material for which it was not intended and I hated seeing them distorted, cheapened by those who did not understand or care as long as their pots sold.

I never painted now — had neither time nor wanting. For about fifteen years I did not paint. . . .

❖

FROM EMILY CARR, "GREEN"
GROWING PAINS: THE AUTOBIOGRAPHY OF EMILY CARR
(TORONTO: OXFORD UNIVERSITY PRESS, 1946)

Woods you are very sly, picking those moments when you are quiet and off guard to reveal yourselves to us, folding us into your calm, accepting us to the sway, the rhythm of your spaces, space interwoven with the calm that rests forever in you.

For all that you stand so firmly rooted, so still, you quiver, there is movement in every leaf.

Woods you are not only a group of trees. Rather you are low space intertwined with growth.

Bless John Whiteley! Bless Algernon Talmage! the two painting masters who first pointed out to me (raw young pupil that I was) that there was coming and going among trees, that there was sunlight in shadows. . . .

On the whitewashed underside of the roof shingles of my attic room I painted two immense totemic Indian Eagles. Their outstretched wings covered the entire ceiling. They were brave birds, powerful of beak and talon. Their plumage was indicated in the Indian way — a few carefully studied feathers painted on wing, breast, and tail gave the impression that the bird was fully plumed.

Sleeping beneath these two strong birds, the stout Western maple tree beneath my window, is it wonder that I should have strong dreams, dreams that folded me very close!

One night I had a dream of greenery. I never attacked the painting of growing foliage quite the same after that dream I think; growing green had become something different to me.

In my dream I saw a wooded hillside, an ordinary slope such as one might see along any Western roadside, tree-covered, normal. No particular pattern or design to catch an artist's eye were he seeking subject-matter. But, in my dream that hillside suddenly lived — weighted with sap, burning green in every leaf, every scrap of it vital!

Woods, that had always meant so much to me, from that moment meant just so much more.

❖

FROM EMILY CARR, "INDIAN BIRD CARVING"
THE HEART OF A PEACOCK
(TORONTO: OXFORD UNIVERSITY PRESS, 1953)

All kinds of nationalities have carved all kinds of birds in all kinds of ways, and from all kinds of material. I think the Indian has used deeper insight, carved with greater sincerity than most. The totemic carvings of his crest emblem, animals and very frequently birds, lived with all their attributes in his work. An Indian believed himself actually related to his totem. This relationship was considered closer even than a blood tie.

Unlike the designers of our heraldry, an Indian might use the creature that was his crest in any pose that suited his fancy; but it must be endowed with the characteristics of the bird or animal represented — never must he waver from the concrete actuality which represented the living creature. From bones to feathers the Indian *knew* his bird — every characteristic, every minutest detail of its true self. He need not arrange its parts in the way nature had sequenced them. For the purpose of decoration, space filling, and symmetry, he might distort, separate, re-colour, but he *must* show the creature as complete in being, though he might conventionalize it. The carver must make it express weight, power, being. Let wings, tail, talons be unconnected: they must be told. Three or four conventionalized feathers on a bird's wing or breast suggested through the carver's art a bird fully feathered. . . .

Some of the eagles and ravens which topped the totem poles were really magnificent. Certain carvers projected the upper part of the great black eye–pupil of their birds to give the impression that the creature was looking earthward. Bird eyes were humanly shaped and deep–set. They were frequently overhung by a heavy eyebrow painted black. The eyeball was shown in an oblong of white such as the human eye has. These crest birds, endowed with supernatural powers, were supposed to see more, hear more, know more than ordinary birds. Ravens and eagles were provided with huge square ears, one on either side of the top of the head. Birds that had wings wide spread were crudely braced from the back to prevent the wind from tearing the wings away. Cumbersome, heavy as was the build of these wooden birds, you felt the lift and sweep of the carved wings amazingly.

How well I remember one old eagle sitting her pole in Skidigate village. She was uncoloured except where wind and rain had stained and mossed her. The rest of the pole was plain but for the figure of a beaver carved at its base. This eagle had folded wings. Her head was slightly raised, slightly twisted. I called her Old Benevolence. Maternal, brooding, serene, she seemed to dominate Skidigate.

❖

AN ADDRESS BY EMILY CARR TO THE VICTORIA WOMEN'S CANADIAN CLUB ON MARCH 1930
(TORONTO: OXFORD UNIVERSITY PRESS, 1955)

I hate like poison to talk. Artists talk in paint — words do not come easily. But I have put my hate in my pocket because I know many of you cordially detest "Modern Art." There are some kinds that need detesting, done for the sake of being bizarre, outrageous, shocking, and making ashamed. This kind we need not discuss but will busy ourselves with what is more correctly termed "Creative Art." I am not going to tell you about the 'ists and 'isms and their leaders, and when they lived and when they died. You can get that out of books. They all probably contributed something to the movement, even the wild ones. The art world was fed up, saturated, with lifeless stodge — something had to happen. And it did. . . .

To return to the term "Creative Art." This is the definition a child once gave it: "I think and then I draw a line round my think." Children grasp these things more quickly than we do. They are more creative than grown-ups. It has not been knocked out of them. When a child draws he does so because he wants to express something. If he draws a house he never fails to make the smoke pour out of the chimney. That moves, it is alive. He feels it. The child's mind goes all round his idea. He may show both sides of his house at once. He feels the house as a whole, why shouldn't he show it? By and by he goes to school and they train all the feeling out of him. He is told to draw only what he sees, he is turned into a little camera, to be a mechanical thing, to forget that he has feelings or that he has anything to express; he only knows that he is to copy what is before him. The art part of him dies. . . .

We may copy some thing as faithfully as the camera, but unless we bring to our picture something additional — something creative — something of ourselves — our picture does not live. It is but a poor copy of unfelt nature. We look at it and straightway we forget it because we have brought nothing to it. We have had no new experience.

Creative Art is "fresh seeing." Why, there is all the difference between copying and creating that there is between walking down a hard straight cement pavement and walking down a winding grassy lane with flowers peeping everywhere and the excitement of never knowing what is just round the next bend!

Great art of all ages remains stable because the feelings it awakens are independent of time and space. The Old Masters did the very things that the serious moderns of today are struggling for, namely, trying to grasp the spirit of the thing itself rather than its surface appearance; the reality, the "I am" of the thing, the thing that means "you," whether you are in your Sunday best or your workday worst; or the bulk, weight, and impenetrability of the mountain, no matter if its sides are bare or covered with pine; the bigger actuality of the thing, the part that is the same no matter what the conditions of light or seasons are upon it — the form, force, and volume of the thing, not the surface impression. It is hard to get at this. You must dig way down into your subject, and into yourself. And in your struggle to accomplish it, the usual aspect of the thing may have to be cast aside. This leads to distortion, which is often confused with caricature, but which is really the emotional struggle of the artist to express intensely what he feels. This very exaggeration or distortion raises the thing out of the ordinary seeing into a more spiritual sphere, the spirit dominating over the subject matter. From distortion we take another step on to abstraction where the forms of representation are forgotten and created forms expressing emotions in space rather than objects take their place; where form is so simplified and abstracted that the material side, or objects, are forgotten — only the spiritual remains. . . .

People complain that modern art is ugly. That depends on what they are looking for and what their standard of beauty is. In descriptive or romantic art they are looking for a story or a memory that is brought back to them. It is not the beauty of the picture in itself that they observe. What they want is the re–living of some scene or the re–visiting of some place — a memory. The beauty concealed in modern art consists more in the building up of a structural, unified, beautiful whole — an enveloped idea — a spiritual unity — a forgetting of the individual objects in the building up of the whole.

By the right disposition of lines and spaces the eyes may be led hither and thither through the picture, so that our eyes and our consciousness rest comfortably within it and are satisfied. Also, by the use of the third dimension, that is, by retrogression and projection, or, to be plainer, by the going back and the coming forward in the picture — by the creation of volume — we do not remain on the flat surface having only height and breadth but are enabled to move backward and forward within the picture. Then we begin to feel space. We begin to feel that our objects are set in space, that they are surrounded by air. We may see before us a dense forest, but we feel the breathing space among the trees. We know that, dense as they may appear, there is air among them, that they can move a little and breathe. It is not like a brick wall, dead, with no space for light and air between the bricks. It is full of moving light playing over the different planes of the interlocked branches. There are great sweeping directions of line. Its feelings, its colour, its depth, its smell, its sounds and silences are bound together into one great thing and its unfathomable centre is its soul. That is what we are trying to get at, to express; that is the thing that matters, the very essence of it.

. . . When a picture is looked at, the relation of its forms and spaces should be felt emotionally rather than thought about intellectually. Today we have almost lost the ability to respond to pictures emotionally — that is, with aesthetic emotion. Modern art endeavours to bring this ability to consciousness again. . . .

What about our side of Canada — the Great West, standing before us big and strong and beautiful? What art do we want for her art? Ancient or modern? She's young but she's very big. If we dressed her in the art dresses of the older countries she would burst them. So we will have to make her a dress of her own. . . . Her great forests, wide spaces, and mighty mountains and the great feel of it all should produce courageous artists, seeing and feeling things in a fresh, creative way. "Modern" we may call it, but remember, all modern art is not jazz. Canada wants something strong, big, dignified, and spiritual that shall make her artists better for doing it and her people better for seeing it. And we artists need the people at our back, not to throw cold water over us or to starve us with their cold, clammy silence, but to give us their sympathy and support. I do not mean money support. I mean moral support, whether the artists are doing it in the old way or in the new way, it does not matter, so long as it is in the big way with the feel and spirit of Canada behind it. . .

Some say the West is unpaintable and our forests monotonous. Oh, just let them open their eyes and look! It isn't pretty. It's only just magnificent, tremendous. The oldest art of our West, the art of the Indians, is in spirit very modern, full of liveness and vitality. They went for and got so many of the very things that we modern artists are striving for today. One frequently hears the Indians' carvings and designs called grotesque and hideous. That depends on the vision of the onlooker. The Indian used distortion or exaggeration to gain his ends. All nature to him seethed with the supernatural. Everything, even the commonest inanimate objects — mats, dishes, etc. — possessed a spirit. The foundation that the Indian built his art upon was his Totem. He did not worship it, but he did reverence it tremendously. Most of the totems were animal representations, thus animal life played a great part in the life of the Indian and his art. They endowed their totem with magic powers. In the totem image the aspect or part of the animal that was to work magic was distorted by exaggeration. It was made as the totem–maker saw it — only more so. The Indians were supposed to partake of the nature of their totems. . . .

It is not my own pictures I am pleading for. They are before you to like or to dislike as you please. That is immaterial. For the joy of the artist is in the creating, the making of his picture. When he has gone as far as he understands, pushed it to the limits of his knowledge and experience, then for him that picture is a thing of the past, over and done with. It then passes on to the onlooker to get out of it what there is for him in it, for what appeals to him, what speaks to him; but the struggles, hopes, desires of the artist are all centred on his next problem: how to make his next picture a little better, profiting by his failures and experiences in the last, determined to carry the next one a little further along, to look higher and to search deeper, to try to get a little nearer to the reality of the thing. . . .

❖

EXCERPTS FROM EMILY CARR, *HUNDREDS AND THOUSANDS*
(TORONTO: CLARK, IRWIN & CO., 1966)

December 2, 1932

. . . Half of painting is listening for the "eloquent dumb great Mother" (nature) to speak. The other half is having clear enough consciousness to see God in all.

Do not try to do extraordinary things but do ordinary things with intensity. Push your idea to the limit, distorting if necessary to drive the point home and intensify it, but stick to the one central idea, getting it across at all costs. Have a central idea in any picture and let all else in the picture lead up to that one thought or idea. Find the leading rhythm and the dominant style or predominating form. Watch negative and positive colour.

❖

September 7, 1933

. . . I got to work, with my things for the first time all comfortably placed about, everything to hand. I made a small sketch and then worked a larger paper sketch from it. The woods were in quiet mood, dreamy and sweet. No great contrasts of light and dark but full of quiet glowing light and fresh from the recent rain, and the growth full, steady and ascending. Whitman's "Still Midnight" — "This is thine hour, O soul, thy free flight into the wordless" — sang in my heart. I've a notion, imagination perhaps, that if you are slightly off focus, you vision the spiritual a little clearer. Perhaps it is that one is striving for something a bit beyond one's reach, an illusive something that can scarcely bear human handling, that the "material we" scarcely dare touch. It is too bright and vague to look straight at; the brutality of a direct look drives it away half imagined, half seen. It is something that lies, as Whitman says, in that far off inaccessible region, where neither ground is for the feet nor path to follow.

I do not say to myself, I will do thus or so. I leave myself open to leads, doing just what I see to do at the moment, neither planning nor knowing but quietly waiting for God and my soul.

❖

September 8, 1933

Oh, what a joy morning! Sun blazing, whole woods laughing, dogs hilarious. Camp all in order, calm radiance everywhere. . . .

I had thought this place somehow incongruous, the immensity of the old trees here and there not holding with the rest but belonging to a different era, to the forest primeval. . . . Today I see that I am what Whitman would call "making pictures with reference to parts" not with reference to "ensemble." The individual mighty trees stagger me. I become engaged with the figures and not the sum and so I get no further with my reckoning up of the total. Nothing stands alone; each is only a part. A picture must be a portrayal of relationships.

❖

September 8, 1933 (later)

Such a terrible loneliness and depression is on me tonight! My heart has gone heavier and heavier all day. I don't know any reason for it so I've mixed a large dose of Epsom Salts, put my sulky fire, which simply would not be cheerful, out, smacked the dogs all round for yapping and shut myself in the Elephant, although by clocks I should not be thinking of bed for three hours yet. This is the dampest spot I was ever in in my life. The bed, my clothes, the food, everything gets clammy. I burst two hot bottles two nights running. I took a brick to bed the next night; too hot, set fire to the cover. Tonight I invented a regular safety furnace. I put the hot brick into an empty granite saucepan with a lid on. It is safe and airing the bed out magnificently. (One thing that *did* go right.)

I made two poor sketches today. Every single condition was good for work, but there you are — cussedness! What a lot I'd give tonight for a real companionable pal, male or female, a soul pal one wasn't afraid to speak to or to listen to. I've never had one like that. I expect it is my own fault. If I was nice right through I'd attract that kind to me. I do not give confidences. . . .

❖

April 4, 1934

I woke this morning with "unity of movement" in a picture strong in my mind. I believe Van Gogh had that idea. I did not realize he had striven for that till quite recently so I did not come by the idea through him. It seems to me that clears up a lot. I see it very strongly out on the beach and cliffs. I felt it in the woods but did not quite realize what I was feeling. Now it seems to me the first thing to seize on in your layout is the direction of your main movement, the sweep of the whole thing as a unit. One must be very careful about the transition of one curve of direction into the next, vary the length of the wave of space but *keep it going*, a pathway for the eye and the mind to travel through and into the thought. For long I have been trying to get these movements of the parts. Now I see there is only *one* movement. It sways and ripples. It may be slow or fast but it is only one movement sweeping out into space but always keeping going — rocks, sea, sky, one continuous movement.

❖

April 12, 1934

. . . Be careful that you do not write or paint anything that is not your own, that you don't know in your own soul. You will have to experiment and try things out for yourself, and you will not be sure of what you are doing. That's all right; you are feeling your way into the thing. But don't take what someone else has made sure of and pretend it's you yourself that have made sure of it till it's yours absolutely by conviction. It's stealing to take it and hypocrisy and you'll fall in a hole. . . .

❖

April 15, 1934

Am eating today after a fast of seven days and it feels very good inside. I wish I had been brought up to think nothing of food, instead of encouraged to have a palate sensitive to and demanding good eats. I believe those who are reared on short–comings are best off spiritually and bodily. I was reared an earthy child. I remember the spirit in me used to try and look up but the fat earth body sat on it. Now it fights to lift but sixty years of being sat on has flattened it. . . .

❖

In the caravan at Albert Head, June 12, 1934

Many things need clearing up in my mind so I'd better try to write them out. I figure that a picture equals a movement in space. Pictures have swerved too much towards design and decoration. These have their place, too, in a picture but there must be more. The idea must run through the whole, the story that arrested you and urged the desire to express it, the story that God told you through that combination of growth. The picture side of the thing is the relationship of the objects to each other in one concerted movement, so that the whole gets up and goes, lifting the looker with it, sky, sea, trees, affecting each other. Lines at right angles hold the eye fixed. Great care should be taken in the articulation of one movement into another so that the eye swings through the whole canvas with a continuous movement and does not find jerky stops, though it may be bucked occasionally with quick little turns to accelerate the motion of certain places. One must ascertain first whether your subject is a slow lolling one, or smooth flowing and serene, or quick and jerky, or heavy and ponderous. . . .

Selections from *Growing Pains*, *Hundreds and Thousands*, and *Heart of a Peacock* reproduced with the permission of Stoddart Publishing Co. Limited, 34 Lesmill Rd., Don Mills, Ontario, Canada.

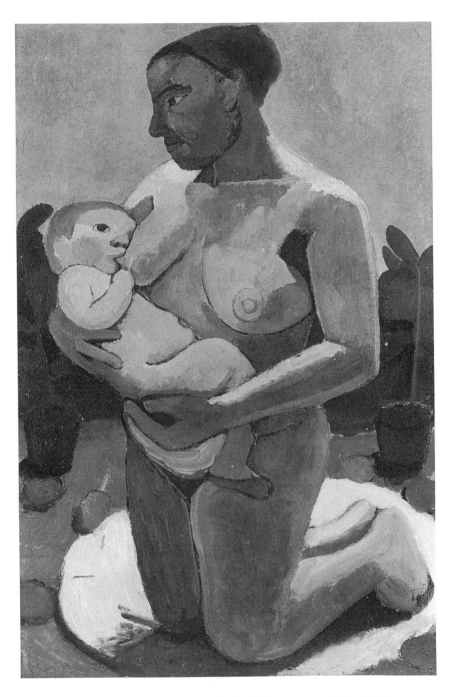

Kneeling Mother with Child, 1907. Oil on canvas. 45" x 29½".
Staatliche Museen Preussischer Kulturbesitz, Nationalgalerie, Berlin (West)

PAULA MODERSOHN-BECKER

1876–1907

DURING HER LIFETIME, Paula Modersohn-Becker sold only two of her works, and one might expect her impact on the course of Western art history to be negligible. In retrospect, however, we can see a strong relationship between her body of work and many significant issues in early-twentieth-century modernism. Although she aligned herself with neither the Symbolist nor Expressionist movements, her painting embodies significant aspects of both; at the time of her death at thirty-one, a recent breakthrough in her own artistic quest defined a new personal style based on monumental simplification of form and color. Like many other artists included in this volume, Modersohn-Becker's journal provided her with protected space in which to mediate between the conflicting demands of her roles as "woman" and "artist." She explored these issues also in her prolific and discursive letters, particularly those to family members. Shortly after her death, her family encouraged the publication (and several reprintings) of excerpts from her letters and journals, and at the time Modersohn-Becker achieved wider fame for her life story than for her art. Several years before her death, her husband had remarked in his own journal that nobody really knew her artistic distinctiveness; in fact, her work has only recently been given due attention.

Paula Becker was the third child of seven in a middle-class German family that most biographers describe as having encouraged the development of cultural values. When she was still young, the family — including her mother, a homemaker, and her father, an official with the German railway — moved the family from Dresden to Bremen. She began to study drawing in Bremen with a local painter, and at sixteen convinced her parents to allow her to study art in London, where she could live with an aunt. Despite their espousal of cultural values, for many years Modersohn-Becker and her parents were locked in a struggle of wills over her future career. Like many bourgeois parents, they argued that she would have more financial security as a teacher than as an artist. During her late teens and early twenties Modersohn-Becker alternated between following her parents' directives and her own will. In 1893, she agreed to attend a two-year course at the Bremen teachers' college, provided they would allow her to continue her art studies once she received her degree. Upon receiving her teaching certificate in 1895, she began studies at the Berlin School of Art for Women, where Käthe Kollwitz was later to become established, continuing there until the summer of 1898, although during late1897 her father again tried to convince her to pursue the financial security of a teaching career, urging her to assume a position as a governess.

Modersohn-Becker was by that time more resistant to her parents' pressure and committed herself to the study of art. A decisive factor in this respect was her first trip, during the summer of 1897, to the artists' colony in Worpswede, a place that ultimately played major roles in both the personal and professional aspects of her life. After another year of study in Berlin and a trip to Scandinavia, she returned there to settle permanently. Worpswede was a peasant community not far from Bremen that attracted numerous artists who wanted to escape the ills of modern life and to retrieve something "basic" that they found missing in modern civilization. The desire of the Worpswede group to return to nature stemmed from a broader cultural movement that was then popular in Germany and reflected also the thinking of many artists in the late nineteenth and early twentieth centuries. Paul Gauguin, for example, lived among the peasants in Pont-Aven (France), as did Vincent Van Gogh in Nuenen (the Netherlands), and Wassily Kandinsky in Murnau (Germany), each of these painters seeking a greater simplicity than that they found in the dominant urban culture. When Paula Becker arrived in Worpswede, she felt that she had found her spiritual home and all her early communications show that she was enamored of the life-style it represented. Initially her reactions were shrouded in a romanticism that she referred to as her *"versunkene glock* (sunken bell) feeling," through which she saw a hidden "wonderland." Many of the other artists in the community responded similarly to the landscape's remote lyricism, expressed in their art through a conservative, descriptive style. Gradually Modersohn-Becker distilled the essentials from their romantic trappings and ultimately (to an extent that no other Worpswede artist did) succeeded in using the Worpswede milieu to express herself in an artistically modernist idiom.

Modersohn-Becker arrived in Worpswede still a student; by the time of her death ten years later, she had developed a sophisticated artistic vision. Precisely when she crossed the line from apprentice to mature artist is difficult to determine; it is clear, however, that her four trips to Paris, at that time the world capital of artistic modernism, exerted an important influence on her development. The first of these visits occurred from January through June 1900 during which time she studied at Colarossi's atelier (where Cecilia Beaux had taken courses little more than a decade earlier). In June, she was joined by several artists from Worpswede, including Otto Modersohn, one of the group's leaders. While in Paris, Modersohn's wife, Helene, died and the contingent returned to Worpswede. By that fall Becker and Modersohn, eleven years her senior and the father of a small daughter, had become secretly engaged; by the following spring they were married. At the time of her marriage, Modersohn-Becker's artistic maturity was not considered equal to that of either her new husband or her former teacher, Fritz Mackensen, another Worpswede luminary. Her new husband respected her talent and she was determined to pursue her vocation as an artist; nonetheless, her parents persuaded her to interrupt her artistic career once more, this time to study cooking in Berlin, in order to prepare herself for her role as a wife.

By the time of Modersohn-Becker's second trip to Paris, during February and March 1903, she had entered the first phase of her mature style. Two diary entries corroborate the visual evidence of her works of this period. In one, from late 1902, she speaks of wanting to obtain a "broad runic" quality in her work, something she found missing from Mackensen's drawings. Two months later, in Paris, she wrote that she wanted to "learn to express the gentle vibration of things; their intrinsically rough texture." The surfaces of her paintings at this time are characterized by a thick impasto, a certain roughness. Studying life-drawing at Colarossi's, observing antiquities at the Louvre, and coming into contact with the works of Auguste Rodin enabled her to begin to surpass the pictorial descriptiveness of the other Worpswede painters and to reach toward the more symbolic and universal abstraction she desired. Over the next four years of her life, this tendency became increasingly sharply focused. It is ironic that during this trip her friend, the poet Rainer Maria Rilke, wrote for her a letter of introduction to Rodin, in which Rilke described her as "the wife of a very famous painter." (In fact, Rilke later omitted both Modersohn-Becker and her friend and his future wife, the sculptor Clara Westhof, from his published discussion of Worpswede artists.)

Although Modersohn-Becker's subsequent two trips to Paris were carried out under personally trying circumstances, they contributed substantially to her stylistic development. Her work became increasingly more related to work she observed in Paris, particularly that of Gauguin, and less similar, except in subject matter, to that of other Worpswede artists. She began to find Worpswede an oppressive environment from which she needed to escape. Interestingly, all her trips to Paris and the one to Berlin for cooking courses occurred in January and February, the dead of winter and a low-energy period after the excitement of the Christmas season. This time of year is characterized by intense cabin fever and an increase in suicides in isolated northern communities worldwide. In addition to providing an escape, Paris may have fulfilled for Modersohn-Becker what New Mexico later did for Georgia O'Keeffe, a need for sufficient distance from her marriage to develop her independent artistic identity.

Modersohn-Becker went to Paris for the third time in 1905, although Otto opposed it; he met her there at the end of March, a time he described in his own journal as "not pleasant" and the couple returned home together at Easter. The following February, to avoid confrontation, Modersohn-Becker planned her departure from Worpswede in secret, defining it in her journal as a break in her marriage. She remained in Paris for over a year, urging her husband to understand her need for freedom. He did not. Instead, he visited twice, in June and then for a long stint, from September 1906 until April 1907. They again returned to Worpswede together, Modersohn-Becker pregnant and, according to her mother, "wondrously reconciled to her domestic situation." (Given the overwhelming familial and social pressure, it seems that she had little choice; even today it is difficult for a woman artist to satisfactorily resolve the internal war between her artistic vocation and her maternal instinct.) For Modersohn-Becker, her reconciliation with Otto Modersohn proved to be fatal; she died only three weeks after childbirth. Although she described the summer during her pregnancy as "not especially productive," during that time her ability to express her vision appeared to rise to a new level.

Despite her relative youth, Modersohn-Becker had achieved the formal vocabulary that she had sought: broad, monumental forms and flat areas of color that expressed universal states of human being. Her forms did become more "runic" and her use of the painting medium more detached from three-dimensional illusion. People, the things that surrounded them, and the landscape they inhabited became important too for the way in which they expressed basic inner truths about being. Comparing her 1903 image of a nursing mother with *Kneeling Mother and Child* (1907) clearly demonstrates her development. In the later work, she eschews descriptive detail in favor of abstract form so that, rather than being a painting "about" an intimate encounter, the work communicates a primal and mystical sensibility, a vision that is congruous with that of the Symbolists and Expressionists.

Like many women artists of the late nineteenth and early twentieth centuries, Modersohn-Becker explored the mother-child theme from a non-traditional perspective. She emphasized the strong, physical ties between mothers and their children and showed the primal strength of that bond in works like *Kneeling Mother and Child* and the image of a reclining mother and child painted in 1906. The former is an effective visualization of a diary entry in which she described a nursing mother as "a heroic figure." Critics have questioned the extent to which Modersohn-Becker unquestioningly accepted J. J. Bachhofen's ultraconservative concept of "mother-right," popular at the turn of the century. In contrast to Bachhofen's views, however, her work is not sentimental and does not show a patriarchial vision of motherhood. Rather, she celebrates women as strong and powerful, connected to their children with a physical bond that does not necessarily imply the identification of one's life goal with the power of fertility, but instead communicates the "understanding that our bodies are to be owned as good," a point of view antithetical to patriarchal attitudes about women.

Similarly, Modersohn-Becker's images of adolescent sexual awakening, such as *Young Girl With Stork* (1906) or *Young Girl Seated on Bed* (1907), break the conventions of stereotypical representation. Although the latter work is similar in subject and format to Edvard Munch's *Puberty*, Munch presents female sexualization as an encounter with evil, while Modersohn-Becker conceives the passage from childhood to womanhood as a solemn event, a rite of passage that should be marked. Modersohn-Becker was able to express the internal drama of "becoming woman," a motif rarely used by male artists and then only to be exploited for its prurient potential. Modersohn-Becker did not see children as cute, or women as sexual objects; she captured their essentially human, vulnerable yet life-affirming qualities, as can be seen in works such as her paintings of a little girl with a goose and an old woman at prayer.

Finally, Modersohn-Becker's use of her own self as an artistic subject is also distinctive. As for many women artists, self-portraiture formed a major part of her oeuvre. The argument that self-portraits saved model fees and were produced for that reason, or for the sake of convenience, may be true in some instances, but seems inappropriate in Modersohn-Becker's case. Her treatment of her own image was sufficiently rich, evocative, and diverse to suggest that she engaged in a profound process of psychic exploration in her self-representations, much as Frida Kahlo was to do later in the century. A work such as her *Self-Portrait On Her Sixth Wedding Day* (1906), in which she depicts herself as if pregnant, is laden with symbolic meaning about her fruitfulness and creativity, in both physical and spiritual senses. Her self-portraits are provocative (not "failed" as some critics have suggested), explorations in imaging the creative self of the woman artist.

Modersohn-Becker was important as a writer of letters and journals, especially so since she used the written word to mediate many personal and artistic issues. She based her own diary on that of the late nineteenth-century Russian painter Marie Bashkirtseff, using it as a model in the process of constructing her own artistic persona. She often used the written word as a means of exploring the aesthetic issues with which she was concerned, such as, for example, her search for monumental form, or her interest in the art of Cézanne, or the meaning she ascribed to images of nursing mothers. After 1903, her journal entries decreased in frequency, perhaps because she began to resolve some of the artistic problems in her work. The importance and persistence of work in her life is clearly communicated in both her journals and letters, in one of which she wrote to Modersohn that she was thinking about her work "night and day." Modersohn-Becker's connection with Symbolist thought is also evident, in several short sketches and poems in which she invokes a sense of her soul in relation to the cosmos.

Unfortunately, most of the original manuscript of Modersohn-Becker's written work was apparently lost at the end of the Second World War. Thus, readers today must depend on texts published with the approval of her family (such works often prove inaccurate when compared with the original). Several editions of her diaries and letters were published just after her death, but only became available in English in the early 1980s, in Diane Radycki's translation. A more recent, annotated edition has been published in an English version, corrrecting many gaps and inconsistencies in the earlier edition. The newer edition includes supplementary material not previously available, as well.

Modersohn-Becker's last words were alleged to have been "What a pity!" It is indeed a pity that she died so young, at a point when she had just achieved a breakthrough in her work. One wonders what impact her motherhood would have had on her conceptualization of maternal themes. In its directness and lack of pretension, her voice has an immediacy that speaks without need of translation, even to an audience hearing it almost a century later, and her vision resonates with a contemporary relevance.

SOURCES

Modersohn-Becker, Paula. *Paula Modersohn-Becker: The Letters and Journals.* German edition edited by Gunter Busch and Liselotte von Reinken. English edition edited and translated by Arthur S. Wensinger and Carole Clew Hoey. Evanston, Ill.: Northwestern University Press, 1990.

_____. *The Letters and Journals of Paula Modersohn-Becker*. Translated and annotated by J. Diane Radycki. Metuchen, N.J.: Scarecrow Press, 1980.

Harris, Ann Sutherland, and Linda Nochlin. *Women Artists: 1550-1950*. New York: Alfred A. Knopf, 1977.

Perry, Gillian. *Paula Modersohn-Becker: Her Life and Work*. London: Women's Press, 1979.

Pollock, Griselda. "What's Wrong With 'Images of Women'?" In *Framing Feminism*, edited by Rozsika Parker and Griselda Pollock. London and New York: Pandora Press, 1987.

Washbourne, Penelope. *Becoming Woman: The Quest for Wholeness in Female Experience*. New York: Harper and Row, 1977.

Witzling, Mara. "With Reluctant Feet: The Meeting of Childhood and Woman-hood in Works by Women Artists." In *Politics, Gender and the Arts*, edited by Susan Bowers and Ronald L. Doetterer. Susquehanna University Studies, Selinsgrove, Pa.: Susquehanna University Press, 1991.

FROM PAULA MODERSON–BECKER
JOURNAL EXCERPTS, 1897–1907

Worpswede, July 24, 1897

Worpswede, Worpswede, Worpswede! My Sunken Bell mood! Birches, birches, pine trees, and old willows. Beautiful brown moors — exquisite brown! The canals with their black reflections, black as asphalt. . . .

❖

Worpswede (Summer 1897?)

Worpswede, Worpswede, I cannot get you out of my mind. There was such atmosphere there — right down to the tips of your toes. Your magnificent pine trees! I call them my men — thick, gnarled, powerful, and tall — and yet with the most delicate nerves and fibers in them. That is my image of the ideal artist. And your birch trees — delicate, slender young virgins who delight the eye. With that relaxed and dreamy grace, as if life had not really begun for them yet. They are so ingratiating — one must give oneself to them, they cannot be resisted. But then there are some already masculine and bold, with strong and straight trunks. Those are my "Modern Women." . . . And you willows, with your knotty trunks, with your little silvery leaves. The wind blows so mysteriously through your branches, speaking of days long gone by. You are my old men with silver beards. I have company enough, indeed I do, and it's my own private company. We understand each other well and nod friendly answers back and forth.

Life, life, life!

❖

October 4, 1898

I walked through the darkened village. The world lay black around me, deep black. It seemed as if the darkness were touching me, kissing, caressing me. I was in another world and felt blessed where I was. For it was beautiful. Then I came back to myself and was still happy, for everything here was also beautiful and dark and soft like a kind and grown-up person. And the little lights shone in the houses and laughed from the windows out onto the street and at me. And I laughed back, bright and joyful and grateful. I am *alive*. . . .

❖

October 25, 1898

I sketched a young mother with her child at her breast, sitting in a smoky hut. If only I could someday paint what I felt then! A sweet woman, an image of charity. She was nursing her big, year-old bambino, when with defiant eyes her four-year-old daughter snatched for her breast until she was given it. And the woman gave her life and her youth and her power to the child in utter simplicity, unaware that she was a heroine.

❖

undated (1898)

I feel as if I were seated in eternity
And my soul scarcely dares to breathe.
It sits with tightly folded wings
And wide-eyed it eavesdrops on the Universe.
And gentle mildness comes over me
And over me comes a feeling of great strength,
As if I wanted to kiss white petals
And to battle mightily beside great warriors.
And I awaken trembling, full of wonder . . .
So small, Child of Man! And yet so very huge,
The waves that kiss your soul.

❖

November 15, 1898

The journal of Marie Bashkirtseff. Her thoughts enter my bloodstream and make me very sad. I say as she does: if only I could accomplish something! My existence seems humiliating to me. We don't have the right to strut around, not until we've made something of ourselves. I am exhausted. I want to accomplish everything and am doing nothing. Today Mackensen was confused and dissatisfied during his critique. If the little woman from Bergedorf hadn't been there, I would have cried afterward. And so I simply tormented myself for two long hours — and did the same thing again this afternoon. The result: less than nothing. And now I am placing all my hope in my little nude model this evening. . . .

I am wrapped in the riddle of the universe. And I sit down and say nothing. The water rushes along, the sound making my soul ill at ease. I tremble. Brilliant drops of water hang in the pine tree. Are they tears?

❖

December 16, 1898

My blonde was here again today. This time with her little boy at her breast. I had to draw her as a mother, had to. That is her single true purpose. Marvelous, these gleaming white breasts in her fiery red blouse. The whole thing is so grand in its shape and color. . . .

I think I'm getting into the real mood and atmosphere of Worpswede now. What I used to call my Sunken Bell mood, the spell I was under when I first got here, was sweet, very sweet — but it was really only a dream, and one that couldn't last long in any sort of active life. Then came the reaction to it, and after that something truer — serious work and serious living for my art, a battle I must fight with all my strength.

I am filled with the sun, every part of me, and with the breezy air, intoxicated with the moonlight on the bright snow. It lay heavy on all the twigs and branches, and a deep silence surrounded me. And into this silence the snow fell from the trees with a gentle and crisp sound, and then there was peace again. An indescribably sweet web of moonlight and soft snow air enveloped me. Nature was speaking with me and I listened to her, happy and vibrant. Life.

❖

undated (January 1899?)
Nature is supposed to become greater to me than people. It ought to speak louder from me. I should feel small in the face of nature's enormity. That is the way Mackensen thinks it should be. That is the alpha and omega of all critique. What I should learn, he says, is a more devout representation of nature. It seems that I let my own insignificant person step to the forefront too much.

I became aware of something today when I was with Fräulein Weshoff.*
She had just finished sculpting a bust of an old woman, intimate and heartfelt. I admired the girl, the way she stood next to her sculpture and added little touches to it. I should like to have her as a friend. She is grand and splendid to look at — and that's the way she is as a person and as an artist. Today we raced down the hill on our little sleds. It was such fun. My heart laughed and my soul had wings. Life —

*Clara Westhoff, later the wife of Rainer Maria Rilke, Modersohn-Becker's close friend.

❖

March 23, 1899
Snow and a shimmering moon. . .
Slender trees inscribing
the image of their
soul, lying on winter's white shroud,
searching, trembling.
In piety they lay their lovely essence
down upon the simple ground. . .
When will my day come
that I in all humility
can cast upon that pure
and chaste same ground
a shadow of myself . . .
A shadow of my soul.

❖

October 22, 1899
When I awaken in the middle of the night, and when I get up in the morning, I feel as if something beautiful and dreamlike hovers over me. And then it simply turns out to be life standing before me with its beautiful arms outstretched for me to fly into.

❖

Paris, undated (January 1900)

I am in Paris. I departed on New Year's Eve. I listened to the New Year's bells from our dear old rooftop overlooking the Weser in Bremen. Then my family accompanied me in a great procession to the station. My trip lasted seventeen hours. And now I am living here in the bustle of this great city. Everything rushes and swirls around me in a damp and foggy atmosphere. It's filthy here, very filthy — an inward filth, way down deep inside. Sometimes it makes me shudder. It seems to me as if I needed more strength than I have to live here, a brutal strength. But I feel that only sometimes. At other times, I feel blissfully clear, and serene. I can feel a new world arising in me.

❖

Ca. April 13, 1900

If I could really paint! A month ago I was so sure of what I wanted. Inside me I saw it out there, walked around with it like a queen, and was blissful. Now the veils have fallen again, gray veils, hiding the whole idea from me. I stand like a beggar at the door, shivering in the cold, pleading to be let in. It is hard to move patiently, step by step, when one is young and demanding. Now I'm beginning to awaken as a human being. I'm becoming a woman. The child in me is beginning to recognize life, the purpose of a woman; and it awaits fulfillment. It will be beautiful, full of wonder. I walk along the boulevards and crowds of people pass by and something inside me cries out, "I still have such beautiful things before me. None of you, not one, has such things." And then it cries, "When will it come? Soon?" And then up speaks art, insisting on two more serious, undivided years of work.

Life is serious, and full, and beautiful.

❖

End of April 1900

I have been depressed for days. Profoundly sad and solemn. I think the time is coming for struggle and uncertainty. It comes into every serious and beautiful life. I knew all along that it had to come. I've been expecting it. I am not afraid of it. I know it will mature and help me develop. But everything seems so serious and hard, serious and sad to me. I walk through this huge city, I look into a thousand thousand eyes. But I almost never find a soul there. We acknowledge each other with a glance, greet each other, and then continue on our lonely way. But we have understood each other. Kindred souls embrace for an instant. Then there are others. With them one speaks many many words and lets the little brook of their talk flow over oneself and hears the wellspring of their laughter, and one laughs along. And beneath it all flows the Styx, deep and slow, knowing nothing of these brooks and wells of ours. I am sad. And all around me are the heavy, pregnant, perfumed breezes of spring.

❖

July 5, 1900

Father wrote today and told me that I should look around for a job as a governess. All afternoon I had been lying in the dry sand on the heath reading Knut Hamsun's *Pan*.

❖

Worpswede, July 26, 1900

As I was painting today, some thoughts came to me and I want to write them down for the people I love. I know that I shall not live very long. But I wonder, is that sad? Is a celebration more beautiful because it lasts longer? And my life is a celebration, a short, intense celebration. My powers of perception are becoming finer, as if I were supposed to absorb everything in the few years that are still to be offered me, everything. My sense of smell is unbelievably keen at present. With almost every breath I take, I get a new sense and understanding of the linden tree, of ripened wheat, of hay, and of mignonette. I suck everything up into me. And if only now love would blossom for me, before I depart; and if I can paint three good pictures, then I shall go gladly, with flowers in my hair. . . .

❖

Easter Week, March 1902

In this first year of my marriage I have cried a great deal and my tears often come like the great tears of childhood. They come when I hear music and when I am moved by beauty. When all is said and done, I'm probably just as lonely as I was when I was a child. . . .

❖

Easter Sunday, March 30, 1902

My experience tells me that marriage does not make one happier. It takes away the illusion that had sustained a deep belief in the possibility of a kindred soul.

In marriage one feels doubly misunderstood. For one's whole life up to one's marriage has been devoted to finding another understanding being. And is it perhaps not better without this illusion, better to be eye to eye with one great and lonely truth?

I am writing this in my housekeeping book on Easter Sunday, 1902, sitting in my kitchen, cooking a roast of veal.

❖

June 3, 1902

Someday I must be able to paint truly remarkable colors. Yesterday I held in my lap a wide, silver-gray satin ribbon which I edged with two narrower black, patterned silk ribbons. And I placed on top of these a plump, bottle-green velvet bow. I'd like to be able to paint something one day in those colors. . . .

❖

August 7, 1902
Warmly the evening
Lets down its arms
And at the edges of the world
There its hands rest. . . .
The little gnats hum
Gently in their brilliant way,
And all creatures quiver
And sing quietly of life. . . .
It is not great
It is not broad
It is a little space of time

Eternity is forever. . . .
(Written at my clay pit)

❖

October 1, 1902

I believe that one should not think about nature too much in painting pictures. At least not during the process of conceiving the image. An oil sketch should be made just according to the way one once felt something in nature. But my own personal feeling, that is the main thing. Once I have got that pinned down, clear in its form and color, only then do I introduce things from nature which will make my picture have a natural effect, so that a layman will be totally convinced that I painted my picture from nature.

Recently I have felt just what the mood of colors means to me: it means that everything in this picture changes its local color according to the same principle and that thereby all muted tones blend in a unified relationship, one to the other.

❖

December 1, 1902

I was reading about and looking at Mantegna. I can sense how good he is for me. His enormous plasticity — it has such powerful substance. That is just what is lacking in my things. I could do something about that if I could add his substantiality to the greatness of form I'm struggling for. At present I see before my eyes very simple and barely articulated things.

My second major stumbling block is my lack of intimacy.

Mackensen's way of portraying the people here is not great enough for me, too genrelike. Whoever could, ought to capture them in runic script. . . .

Strange. It seems to me as if my voice had completely new tones to it, and as if my being had new registers. I can feel things growing greater in me, expanding. God willing, I will become something.

❖

February 15, 1903

Today I saw an exhibition of old Japanese paintings and sculpture.

I was seized by the great strangeness of these things. It makes our own art seem all the more conventional to me. Our art is very meager in expressing the emotions we have inside. Old Japanese art seems to have a better solution for that. The expression of nocturnal things, of horrors, of sweetness, of the feminine, of coquetry, all these things seem to be solved in a more childlike and concise way than we would do it. We must put more weight on the fundamentals!! When I took my eyes from these pictures and began looking at the people around me, I suddenly saw that human beings are more remarkable, much more striking and surprising than they have been painted. A sudden realization like that comes only at moments. Our routine way of life tends to blur such realizations. But it's from moments like these that art must arise. . . .

I didn't feel at home during my first few days in Paris and felt that it wasn't going to help me get anywhere. But now I think it will. . . .

❖

February 20, 1903

I must learn how to express the gentle vibration of things, their roughened textures, their intricacies. I have to find an expression for that in my drawing, too, in the way I sketched my nudes here in Paris, only more original, more subtly observed. The strange quality of expectation that hovers over muted things (skin, Otto's forehead, fabrics, flowers); I must try to get hold of the great and simple beauty of all that. In general, I must strive for the utmost simplicity united with the most intimate power of observation. That's where greatness lies. In looking at the life-size nude of Frau M., the simplicity of the body called my attention to the simplicity of the head. It made me feel how much it's in my blood to want to overdo things.

To get back again to that "roughened intricacy of things": that's the quality that I find so pleasing in old marble or sandstone sculptures that have been out in the open, exposed to the weather. I like it, this roughened alive surface. . . .

❖

February 25, 1903

I am constantly observing things and believe that I am coming closer to beauty. In the last few days I have discovered form and have been thinking much about it. Until now I've had no real feeling for the antique. I could find it very beautiful by itself. But I could never find any thread leading from it to modern art. Now I've found it, and that is what I believe is called progress. I feel an inner relationship which leads from the antique to the Gothic, especially from the early ancient art, and from the Gothic to my own feeling for form.

A great simplicity of form is something marvelous. As far back as I can remember, I have tried to put the simplicity of nature into the heads that I was painting or drawing. Now I have a real sense of being able to learn from the heads of ancient sculpture. . . .

❖

Paris, ca. March 1905

The intensity with which a subject is grasped (still lifes, portraits, or creations of the imagination) — that is what makes for beauty in art.

❖

Paris, February 24, 1906

Now I have left Otto Modersohn and am standing between my old life and my new life. I wonder what the new one will be like. And I wonder what will become of me in my new life? Now whatever must be, will be.

❖

March 8, 1906

Last year I wrote: the intensity with which a subject is grasped, that is what makes for beauty in art. Isn't it also true for love?

❖

FROM PAULA MODERSOHN-BECKER, EXCERPTS FROM LETTERS, 1897–1907

PAULA MODERSOHN-BECKER TO HER FAMILY

Worpswede, August 1897

I am happy, happy, happy. . . .

All of Worpswede is asleep, except for a few restless spirits still making a racket at the bowling lane across the way. It is a beautiful, clear night, filled with stars.

Today I painted my first plein air portrait at the clay pit, a little blond and blue-eyed girl. The way the little thing stood in the yellow sand was simply beautiful — a bright and shimmering thing to see. It made my heart leap. Painting people is indeed more beautiful than painting a landscape. I suppose you can notice that I am dead tired, after this long day of hard work, can't you? But inside I am so peaceful and happy. . . .

PAULA MODERSOHN-BECKER TO HER PARENTS
Worpswede, September 10, 1899
. . . I really see nothing of other people. I'm trying to dig my way back again into my work. One absolutely has to dedicate oneself, every bit of oneself, to the *one* inescapable thing. That's the only way to get somewhere and to become something. I've made use of the beautiful weather to sketch and paint outside. I had been staying away from color for such a long time that it had become something quite foreign to me. Working in color was always a great joy to me. And now it *is* a great joy again. Still, I have to battle with it, wrestle with it, with all my strength. And one must be victorious. But if it weren't for the fight, all the beauty of it wouldn't exist at all, would it?

I'm writing this mostly for Mother who, I believe, thinks my whole life is one constant act of egotistic ecstasy.

But devotion to art also involves something unselfish. Some people give their lives to others, and some give their lives to an idea. Does that mean that the former are to be praised and the latter blamed? People must do what nature demands of them. Excuse this defensive letter of mine. It comes from an instinct for self-preservation. . . .

PAULA MODERSOHN-BECKER TO MILLY BECKER
(SISTER OF MODERSOHN-BECKER)
Worpswede, September 21, 1899
A word before I go to sleep. I've just come back from a walk in the moonlight. It was very beautiful. Is the fall just as beautiful for you on the Weser?

I'm going through a strange period now. Maybe the most serious of all my short life. I can see that my goals are becoming more and more remote from those of the family, and that you and they will be less and less inclined to approve of them. And in spite of it all, I must pursue them. I feel that everybody is going to be shocked by me. And still I must go on. I must not retreat. I struggle forward, just as all of you do, but I'm doing it within my own mind, my own skin, and in the way I think is right.

I'm a little frightened by my loneliness in my unguarded hours. But perhaps those are the very hours that help me along toward my goal. You needn't show this letter to our parents. It's an attack of despondency which is really best left undiscussed. . . .

PAULA MODERSOHN-BECKER TO HER MOTHER
Worpswede, November 10, 1899
I want to repeat what I could only shout to you from the omnibus: please don't worry about me, dear! There is really no need to, none at all, dear Mother. I have

such a firm desire and determination to make something of myself, something that won't have to be afraid of the sunshine and something that will shed a little light itself. I am tremendously determined and this determination will amount to something. Please, please let it struggle where it must go; it cannot do otherwise. Don't try to change it because that only makes it sad and gives my heart and tongue a harshness which is painful. Be patient, wait for yet a while. . . .

Just wait a little while. Everything must turn out all right.

❖

PAULA MODERSOHN-BECKER TO MILLY BECKER
(SISTER OF MODERSOHN-BECKER)

Paris, February 29, 1900

Today you get the first family letter, so kisses for everyone at the round table, members of the inner circle only, naturally. . . .

My art is going well. I have a feeling of satisfaction about it. Afternoons I stroll around the city, taking a good look at everything and trying to absorb it all. Or else I work here in my little atelier. On my last stroll I saw many pictures but most of them seemed terribly sweet and poorly done. The best things are being kept aside for the Salon.

I went back to Notre Dame again. Such wonderful Gothic detailing, those monstrous gargoyles, each one with its own character and face. . . . Directly behind Notre Dame, almost encircled by the Seine, lies the morgue. Day after day they fish corpses from the river there, people who didn't want to go on living, or sometimes someone who was robbed and thrown into the water. Under the colorful surface of this laughing city there lies a great deal that is black and horrible. I sometimes fear it will tear my heart to pieces.

❖

PAULA MODERSOHN-BECKER TO OTTO MODERSOHN
(HUSBAND OF MODERSOHN-BECKER)

after September 12, 1900

I was thinking about the two of us, and then I slept on it, and now I am clearer about everything. We are not on the right path, dear. You see, we must first look very, very deeply into each other before we give each other the final things, or before we even awaken the demand for them. It is not good, dear. First we must pick the thousand other flowers in our garden of love before we pick, at a beautiful moment, the wonderful deep red rose. And to do that, we must submerge ourselves even more deeply in one another. Please let your "hot-blooded iconoclasm" slumber a bit longer, and for a while permit me simply to be your Madonna. It's meant to be for your own good, do you believe that? Keep your mind on art, our gracious muse, dear. Let us both plan to paint all this week. And then early Saturday I shall come to you. And then we will be good and gentle with each other. . . .

❖

PAULA MODERSOHN-BECKER TO OTTO MODERSOHN
(HUSBAND OF MODERSOHN-BECKER)

Berlin, January 13, 1901

Well, now I'm in Berlin and feel very tamed and very confined and would like to blow up these walls so that I could see a little bit of the sky. I think I'm going to have a very hard time of it for the next two months. I don't fit into a city like this, and particularly not into this elegant district. I fall right out of the frame. It was quite a different thing being in Paris, in the Latin Quarter. . . .

PAULA MODERSOHN-BECKER TO OTTO MODERSOHN
(HUSBAND OF MODERSOHN-BECKER)

Berlin, February 4, 1901

Is it true that all I ever write you about is painting and nothing else? Isn't there love in my lines to you and between the lines, shining and glowing and quiet and loving, the way a woman should love and the way your woman loves you? . . .

PAULA MODERSOHN-BECKER TO HER MOTHER

Berlin, March 8, 1901

It makes me very sad that my return will be so unwelcome and upsetting for the family. I am very sorry to disturb Father, especially knowing as I do that he is more nervous these days than ever. My dears, how can I explain in words to you that there is no other course for me than to come home now? I so wish our reunion not to be a gloomy one. That is hardly an occasion to be sad and gloomy. From the beginning I firmly set my stay in Berlin at two months. I have used my time well, Mother. But now that cannot continue. Something in me cries out for air. And that cannot be silenced. I have already written that to you in a letter which you evidently thought I meant to be a joke. . . .

It is not only my longing for Otto Modersohn that compels me. It also happens that I can no longer endure this rug-beating environment and all these tall buildings. And why? I have learned a great many things here that I shall need for my domestic life. And I know without being told that I am not perfect. But that I can learn only when I am back in my own element. . . .

PAULA MODERSOHN-BECKER TO CLARA RILKE-WESTHOFF
(FRIEND OF MODERSOHN-BECKER)

Worpswede, May 13, 1901

. . . In the last few days I have been thinking very intensively about my art and I believe that things are progressing for me. I even think that I'm beginning to have a liaison with the sun. Not with the sun that divides everything up and puts shadows in everywhere and plucks the image into a thousand pieces, but with the sun that broods and makes things gray and heavy and combines them all in this gray heaviness so that they become one. I'm thinking about all of that very much and it lives within me beside my great love. A time has come when I think that I shall again be able to say something [in my painting] one day; I am again devout and full of expectation. . . . *Dear* Clara Westhoff, I'm almost beginning to get used to not seeing you and being able to talk about all these things with you. But not yet completely, and I feel how much remains unspoken within me because you are not here. Your letter was a big part of you. It was lovely to read. . . .

PAULA MODERSOH-BECKER TO CLARA RILKE-WESTHOFF
(FRIEND OF MODERSOHN-BECKER)

Worpswede, February 10, 1902

Ever since that afternoon when I brought the money to your little room in the hotel behind the castle you have been very selfish with me. And I, who approach life very differently from you, I felt a great hunger. Isn't love thousandfold? Isn't it like the sun that shines on everything? Must love be stingy? Must love give *everything* to *one* person and take from the others? Is love permitted to take? Isn't it much too precious, too great, too all-embracing? Clara Westhoff, live the way nature does. The deer gather in herds, and even the little titmice at our window have their own community, too, not merely that of the family. I follow after you, a little melancholy. Rilke's voice speaks too strongly and too ardently from your words. Do you think that love demands that one person become just like the other? No, it doesn't, a thousand times no. Isn't it true that the union of two strong people becomes rich and rewarding by virtue of the fact that both are ruling and both are serving in simplicity and peace and joy and quiet contentment? I don't know much about the two of you; but it seems to me that you have shed too much of your old self and spread it out like a cloak so that your king can walk on it. I wish for your sake and for the world and for art and also for my sake that you would wear your own golden cape again. . . . Don't put your soul in chains, even if they are golden chains and no matter how gorgeously they might resound and sing. . . .

❖

PAULA MODERSOHN-BECKER TO HER MOTHER
July 6, 1902
. . . Mother, the dawn has broken in me and I can feel the day approaching. I am going to become somebody. If only I had been able to show Father that my life has not been fishing in troubled waters, pointless; if only I had been able to repay him for the part of himself that he planted in me! I feel that the time is soon coming when I no longer have to be ashamed and remain silent, but when I feel with pride that I am a painter. . . .

❖

PAULA MODERSOHN-BECKER TO OTTO MODERSOHN
(HUSBAND OF MODERSOHN-BECKER)
February 26, 1903
. . . I get up at eight o'clock in the morning, open my windows and look out into my garden where the lilacs already have big green buds, and I take a look at the weather. Then I make my cocoa. My bread is delivered to my door and I still have milk left over from the previous evening. And then my adventures begin. First of all, the Louvre. My midday meal I eat either at a Duval or I make a couple of fried eggs here; then I nap and read, and then at four thirty I make my pilgrimage through the Luxembourg Gardens to my *croquis*. The gardens are swarming at that time with the little children of Paris who are supposed to be breathing in the so-called fresh air. After *croquis* I make my way home and brew myself another cup of cocoa and spend the evening very pleasantly with writing and reading and thinking by an open window, all the while keeping an eye on the Carmelite convent whose little eternal lamp glows at the other end of my garden. I also frequently spend evenings with the Rilkes. In general though, I'm not much interested in company right now. I'm so full of thoughts and impressions that I want to work out alone. When I do this, time doesn't lie heavy on my hands. Those are my days. . . .

❖

PAULA MODERSOHN-BECKER TO OTTO MODERSOHN
(HUSBAND OF MODERSOHN-BECKER)

Paris, March 2, 1903

Just listen, I'm getting the feeling more and more that you must come here, too. There are so many reasons why you should. But I'll tell you only one, a great reason, the greatest: Rodin. You must get an impression of this man and of his life's work, which he has gathered together in castings all around him. I have the feeling that we shall probably never experience anything like this again in our lifetime. This great art came into full blossom with incredible determination, silently, and almost hidden from view. . . .

Armed with a little calling card from Rilke, which referred to me as "femme d'un peintre très distingué" [wife of a very distinguished painter], I went to Rodin's studio last Saturday afternoon, his usual day for receiving people. There were all sorts of people there already. He didn't even look at the card, just nodded and let me wander freely among his marble sculpture. So many wonderful things there. But some I cannot understand. Nevertheless, I don't dare judge those too quickly. As I was leaving, I asked him if it would be possible to visit his *pavillon* in Meudon, and he said that it would be at my disposal on Sunday. And so I was permitted to wander about the *pavillon* undisturbed. What a wealth of work is there and such worship of nature; that's really beautiful. He always starts from nature. And all his drawings, all his compositions, he does from life. The remarkable dreams of form which he quickly tosses onto paper are to me the most original aspects of all his art. He uses the most simple and sparse means. He draws with pencil and then shades in with strange, almost passionate, watercolors. It is a passion and a genius which dominate in these drawings, and a total lack of concern for convention. The first thing that comes into my mind to compare them with are those old Japanese works which I saw during my first week here, and perhaps also ancient frescoes or those figures on antique vases. *You simply must see them.* Their colors are a remarkable inspiration, especially for a painter. He showed them to me himself and was so charming and friendly to me. Yes, whatever it is that makes art extraordinary is what he has. In addition there is his piercing conviction that all beauty is in nature. He used to make up these compositions in his head but found that he was still being too conventional. Now he draws only from models. When he is in fresh form he does twenty of them in an hour and a half. His *pavillon* and his two other ateliers lie in the midst of strangely intersecting hills which are covered with a growth of stubbly grass. There is a wonderful view down to the Seine and the villages along it, and even as far as the domes of Paris. The building where he lives is small and confined and gives one the feeling that the act of living itself plays hardly any role for him. "La travaille [*sic*], c'est mon bonheur," he says. . . .

❖

PAULA MODERSOHN-BECKER TO OTTO MODERSOHN
(HUSBAND OF MODERSOHN-BECKER)

March 10, 1903

. . . I look at little children with love, and when I'm reading I look up words like swaddling and nursing and so on with great understanding. I have been very aware how these two years at your side have gently turned me into a woman. When I was a girl I was always full of jubilant expectation. Now, as a woman, I am also full of expectations, but they are quieter and more serious. And they have also rid me of the vagueness of my girlhood. I believe that there are only two very definite expectations left in me now: my art and my family — My dear husband. With all the things that are going on inside me here, I'm having an odd and wonderful time. It often seems to me incredible that I really have you and Elsbeth and our little house. And then when I think about it all, I know that it is the wonder of these secure possessions that gives me peace of mind to approach things here with composure and happiness. You know, I don't feel erotic in the least right now. No doubt that comes from all the mental concentration inside me. But if such a thing is possible, I love you more recklessly with each passing day. I love every fiber of your being. I am so very proud of you, my dear Red. . . .

❖

PAULA MODERSOHN-BECKER TO OTTO MODERSOHN
(HUSBAND OF MODERSOHN-BECKER)
Paris, February 16, 1905
You know, I am always unhappy when I first get here — and that's the way I feel now. This big city still gets on my nerves, but most of all, things aren't in order yet in the rue Cassette, my quiet haven. Sad to say, my pretty room with the view of the garden and the tree is occupied. I have a little, uncomfortable room, and I haven't quite made up my mind yet whether to move out or not. This morning I'll visit Herma. Her job seems to be a really nice one. She has great freedom, can take long walks with her girls, etc., so that we will probably be able to see each other frequently. . . .

Greetings to the three of you. I'm writing this letter just so you can read my mood, which is still somewhat below the freezing point, even though it's so warm outside that the pussy willows are in blossom.

❖

PAULA MODERSOHN-BECKER TO RAINER MARIA RILKE
Worpswede, February 17, 1906
. . . I look forward to seeing you again soon, either during or after your tour. I look forward to seeing Rodin and a hundred thousand other things.

And now, I don't even know how I should sign my name. I'm not Modersohn and I'm not Paula Becker anymore either.

I am
Me,
and I hope to become Me more and more. That is surely the goal of all our struggles.

❖

PAULA MODERSOHN-BECKER TO OTTO MODERSOHN
(HUSBAND OF MODERSOHN-BECKER)
Paris, April 9, 1906
I have just finished your letter. It moved me deeply. I was also moved by the words from my own letters which you quoted. *How* I loved you. Dear Red, if

you can do it, please hold your hands over me for just a little while longer, without condemning me. I *cannot* come to you *now*. I *cannot* do it. And I do not want to meet you in any other place, either. And I do not want any child from you at all; not *now*.

Much of you was once a part of me but has now disappeared. All I can do is wait to see whether it will return or whether something else will come in its place. I have been considering over and over what the best thing to do might be. I feel so insecure about myself since I have abandoned everything that was secure in me and around me. I must stay for a while longer out here in the world where I can be tested by others and can test myself. Will you send me, at least for the immediate future, one hundred and twenty marks each month so that I can live? In fact, for this month I even ask you for two hundred marks because I have to pay my quarterly rent on the fifteenth. . . .

❖

PAULA MODERSOHN-BECKER TO HER MOTHER
Paris, May 10, 1906

You are not angry with me! I was so afraid you would be. And that would have made me sad and hard. And now you are so good to me. Yes, Mother, I was not able to endure it any longer. And I shall probably never be able to endure it again. Everything was so confining and becoming less and less of what I needed.

I am beginning a new life now. Don't interfere with me; just let me be. It is so wonderfully beautiful. I lived the past week in such a state of excitement. I believe I have accomplished something good.

And don't be sad for me. Even if my life might not lead me back to Worpswede again, the eight years that I spent there were very beautiful.

I, too, find Otto touching. That, and the thought of all of you, were what made my decision especially difficult. . . .

. . . And you, dear Mother, stay close to me and give your blessing to what I am doing.

I am your Child

❖

PAULA MODERSOHN-BECKER TO OTTO MODERSOHN
(HUSBAND OF MODERSOHN-BECKER)
Paris, May 15, 1906

I have been so hard at work that I've neglected writing you for what I'm afraid has been a long time. These two weeks have gone very well for me. Night and day I've been most intensely thinking about my painting, and I have been more or less satisfied with everything I've done. I am slacking a little now, not working as much, and no longer so satisfied. But all in all, I still have a loftier and happier perspective on my art than I did in Worpswede. But it does demand a very, very great deal from me — working and sleeping in the same room with my paintings is a delight. Even in the moonlight the atelier is very bright. When I wake up in the middle of the night, I jump out of bed and look at my work. And in the morning it's the first thing I see — . . .

PAULA MODERSOHN-BECKER TO OTTO MODERSOHN
(HUSBAND OF MODERSOHN-BECKER)

Paris, September 3, 1906

The time is getting closer for you to be coming. Now I must ask you for your sake and mine, please spare both of us this time of trial. Let me go, Otto. I do not want you as my husband. I do not want it. Accept this fact. Don't torture yourself any longer. Try to let go of the past — I ask you to arrange all other things according to your wishes and desires. If you still enjoy having my paintings, then pick out those you wish to keep. Please do not take any further steps to bring us back together. It would only prolong the torment.

I must still ask you to send money, one final time. I ask you for the sum of five hundred marks. I am going to the country for a while now, so please send it to B. Hoetger, 108, rue Vaugirard. During this time I intend to take steps to secure my livelihood.

I thank you for all the goodness that I have had from you. There is nothing else I can do.

PAULA MODERSOHN-BECKER TO OTTO MODERSOHN
(HUSBAND OF MODERSOHN-BECKER)

Paris, September 9, 1906

My harsh letter was written during a time when I was terribly upset. . . . Also my wish not to have a child by you was only for the moment, and stood on weak legs. . . I am sorry now for having written it. If you have not completely given up on me, then come here soon so that we can try to find one another again.

The sudden shift in the way I feel will seem strange to you.

Poor little creature that I am, I can't tell which path is the right one for me.

All these things have overtaken me, and yet I still do not feel guilty.

I don't want to cause pain to any of you.

PAULA MODERSOHN-BECKER TO CLARA RILKE -WESTHOFF
(FRIEND OF MODERSOHN-BECKER)

Paris, November 17, 1906

I shall be returning to my former life but with a few differences. I, too, am different now, somewhat more independent, no longer so full of illusions. This past summer I realized that I am not the sort of woman to stand alone in life. Apart from the eternal worries about money, it is precisely the freedom I have had which was able to lure me away from myself. I would so much like to get to the point where I can create something that is me.

It is up to the future to determine for us whether I'm acting bravely or not. The main thing now is peace and quiet for my work, and I have that most of all when I am at Otto Modersohn's side.

I thank you for your friendly help. My birthday wish for you is that the two of us will become fine women. . . .

PAULA MODERSOHN-BECKER TO MILLY ROHLAND-BECKER
(SISTER OF MODERSOHN-BECKER)

Paris, November 18, 1906

You really seem to love me as a sister, and I thank you for it. I love you in
my own way, with much reserve, but very deeply. If you feel a little cheated by
me, heaven will see to it that you are compensated for that in some other way.
I'm convinced that we are rewarded or punished one way or another for everything we do while we are still on this earth. The review was more a satisfaction
to me than a joy. Joy, overpoweringly beautiful moments, comes to an artist
without others noticing. The same is true for moments of sadness. That is why
it's true that artists live mostly in solitude. But for all of that, the review will be
good for my reappearance in Bremen. And it will perhaps also cast a different
light on my reasons for leaving Worpswede.

Otto and I shall be coming home again in the spring. That man is touching in his love. We are going to try to buy the Brünjes place in order to make
our lives together freer and more open. We will also have all kinds of animals
around us. My thoughts run like this just now: if the dear Lord will allow me
once again to create something beautiful, then I shall be happy and satisfied;
if only I have a place where I can work in peace. I will be grateful for the portion of love I've received. If one can only remain healthy and not die too
young. . . .

❖

PAULA MODERSOHN-BECKER TO BERNHARD HOETGER

Summer 1907

I have not done much work this summer, and I have no idea if you will like
any of the little that I have accomplished. In conception, all the work has probably remained much the same. But the execution, I think, is quite another matter. What I want to produce is something compelling, something full, an
excitement and intoxication of color — something powerful. The paintings I did
in Paris are too cool, too solitary and empty. They are the reaction to a restless
and superficial period in my life and seem to strain for a simple, grand effect.

I wanted to conquer Impressionism by trying to forget it. What happened
was that it conquered me. We must work with digested and assimilated
Impressionism. . . .

❖

PAULA MODERSOHN-BECKER TO MILLY ROHLAND-BECKER
(SISTER OF MODERSOHN-BECKER)

Worpswede, October 1907

As Anna Dreebeen's relative said when everything was churning and
growing inside of her, "Why, the kid knocked me right off the chair!" I'm feeling the same way. All of you must be nice and patient with me; otherwise he, or
she, is going to get all frantic, too. And don't ever write me another postcard
with words like "diapers," or "blessed event." You know me well enough to
realize that I'm the type who prefers to keep the fact that I'm about to be concerned with diapers away from other people. . . .

PAULA MODERSOHN-BECKER TO CLARA RILKE -WESTHOFF
(FRIEND OF MODERSOHN-BECKER)

Worpswede, October 21, 1907

My mind has been so much occupied these days by the thought of Cézanne, of how he has been one of the three or four powerful artists who have affected me like a thunderstorm, like some great event. Do you still remember what we saw at Vollard in 1900? And then, during the final days of my last stay in Paris, those truly astonishing early paintings of his at the Galerie Pellerin. Tell your husband he should try to see the things there. Pellerin has a hundred and fifty Cézannes. I saw only a small part of them, but they are magnificent — My urge to know everything about the Salon d'Automne was so great that a few days ago I asked him to send me at least the catalogue. Please come soon and bring the letters [about Cézanne]. Come right away, Monday if you can possibly make it, for I hope soon, finally, to be otherwise occupied. If it were not absolutely necessary for me to be here right now, nothing could keep me away from Paris.

I look forward to seeing you and to your news.

I also send two lovely greetings to Ruth.

Paula Modersohn-Becker: The Letters and Journals. Edited by Günter Busch and Liselotte S. Wensinger and Carole Clew Hoey. English translation © 1983, Taplinger Publishing Co. Republished in 1990 by Northwestern University Press in arrangement with S. Fischer Verlag. Reprinted by permission of Northwestern University Press.

Wave, Night, 1928. Oil on canvas. 30" x 36".
Gift of Charles L. Stillman. ©Addison Gallery of American Art, Phillips Academy,
Andover, Massachusetts. All Rights Reserved.

GEORGIA O'KEEFFE

1887–1986

LONG ACCEPTED AS a major artist with an organic vision of nature and the landscape, Georgia O'Keeffe had become something of a cultural icon by the time of her death at ninety-eight, her mythic stature enhanced by her way of living, alone in the desert in a pristine environment that seemed to be reflected in her art. In her identification with the land, her exclusively American training, and her merging of abstract with concrete in her work, she was a quintessentially American artist. O'Keeffe gained public exhibition of her paintings at an early point in her career; in that respect, her career pattern differed from that of many women artists. Yet O'Keeffe, too, felt the negative impact of her gender, particularly in critical interpretation of her works according to stereotypical views of femininity.

O'Keeffe's relationship to the written word was filled with conflict. She never considered herself a writer and often said that painting enabled her to express that which she could not otherwise communicate. She was scornful of intellectual analysis, and her stated reason for writing her own book in 1976 was to correct the "lies" that she said had been written about her by others. That autobiography, statements that accompanied her exhibitions, and private letters from various collections comprise her written record. Together they offer significant insights into her personal iconography, her working method, and her way of seeing.

O'Keeffe was "from the plains," the vast, big sky country that was both her spiritual home and her artistic muse. The second of seven children, she was born near Sun Prairie, Wisconsin, where she lived until her parents sold their farm and moved to Williamsburg, Virginia, while she was a teenager. She spent her last two high-school years at Chatham Episcopal Institute in Virginia, where her artistic talent was first validated by her teacher, Elizabeth May Willis,who encouraged her to attend art school after graduation.

The decade that followed O'Keeffe's high-school graduation was marked by restless searching; her art education was uneven and she did not yet consider herself an artist. In 1905, while living with an aunt, she studied at the Art Institute of Chicago with John Vanderpoel. Weakened by typhoid fever during the summer, she spent the following year in Williamsburg with her family. She moved to New York in 1907 to study at the Art Students League; while there, she took an influential painting class with William Merritt Chase. During that year she first met Anita Pollitzer, who later became a feminist activist and with whom she remained friends until an argument late in their lives. Because of setbacks in her family's finances, she spent only one year in New York, moving back to Chicago the next,where she worked as a commercial artist. Her eyes weakened by a case of measles during that time, she returned to Virginia to live with her family. Except for a few weeks in 1911 when she filled in for her former teacher at the Chatham Episcopal Institute, O'Keeffe appeared to have abandoned her artistic pursuits.

Persuaded by her sister, O'Keeffe enrolled in the advanced drawing class at the University of Virginia during the summer of 1912. Her encounter with the teacher Alon Bement helped catalyze her commitment to an artistic career. She immediately responded to his teaching method, developed with his Columbia University colleague Arthur Wesley Dow, that stressed exploration of abstract design principles as a means of unlocking the artist's internal sentiments. Returning to the university for the next four summers to be Bement's teaching assistant, O'Keeffe pursued various activities during the academic years. After two years of teaching in Amarillo, Texas, she enrolled at Columbia University's Teachers College in 1914 to study with Dow himself. Here she became part of a vibrant group of art students and reestablished her friendship with Anita Pollitzer. Together, they often visited Alfred Stieglitz's 291 Gallery to keep up with contemporary art trends; their letters reveal that exhibitions there were a frequent topic of discussion. In the fall of 1915, O'Keeffe returned to teaching, this time at Columbia College in South Carolina, according to her description, "a place of little consequence."

It was in South Carolina, however, that she had the epiphany that enabled her to find the form that expressed her internal vision. She realized that since she had to live every other aspect of her life according to other people's precepts, she was "a fool if she didn't at least paint the way [she] wanted to." To tap the hidden source of her creativity by unlearning what she had been taught, "to accept as true [her] own thinking," she began by making a series of charcoal drawings late in 1915, and progressed to using only blue watercolor early in 1916. O'Keeffe's art was always a give-and-take between the abstract and what she called the "objective." Initially abstractions predominated, but by 1917 she had added more colors and was working in response to direct environmental stimuli in several series of paintings, such as *Evening Star* and *Light Coming on the Plains*. Music inspired some paintings from that early period, including *Music — Pink and Blue*. All O'Keeffe's work from that time revealed the influence of her studies of abstract form with Dow and Bement. Some of those early pieces bear an uncanny resemblance to works executed much later, as the grid of white rectangles she established in both *Starlight Night* (1917) and *Sky Above the Clouds* (1963). Many show her characteristic interest in transparent layers of overlapping forms echoing around a vibrating core.

O'Keeffe's decision to follow her own vision received immediate positive reinforcement from Alfred Stieglitz, which soon altered the course of her career and her personal life. O'Keeffe had sent her first new drawings to Anita Pollitzer with the admonishment not to show them to anyone. In a much recounted incident, Pollitzer brought them on impulse to Stieglitz, of whom O'Keeffe had written that she "would rather have [him] like anything I had done than anyone else I know of." Whether or not he actually made the legendary remark, "At last, a woman on paper," Stieglitz thought O'Keeffe's drawings very impressive and offered to exhibit them. This encouragement came at a critical juncture in her career, as her letters reveal that she felt uncertain about the new direction she was taking. She was plagued by doubts that "there wasn't any use ruining good paper," that she "wasn't even sure that [she] had anything worth expressing," and that she "had almost decided never to try any more."

In February 1915, O'Keeffe began corresponding directly with Stieglitz, marking the start of their complex personal relationship. While there is no question that O'Keeffe's work was worthy of the attention it received, Stieglitz's support at that particular time was an extraordinary gift, one that far too few artists, male or female, ever receive. Although O'Keeffe initially took another teaching position, as head of the art department at West Texas Normal School, by the summer of 1918 she had made art the center of her life. She moved to New York and soon began living with Stieglitz, whom she married in 1924 after his divorce. She had entered the ranks of influential, avant-garde American artists and gained a continuing public forum. Her first one-person show was the 291 Gallery's final exhibition, held in 1917 while she still taught in Texas. From 1923 on, she exhibited regularly until Stieglitz's death in 1946.

During the early twenties, O'Keeffe conceptualized the major theme on which she continued to work during the following decade. Her close-up paintings of flowers, begun about 1923, received overwhelming critical response, although perhaps never any that the artist found satisfactory. Practically all critics, both denigrating and complimentary, spoke of them in sexual terms, as the expression of O'Keeffe's innate and inescapable femaleness, an association that O'Keeffe always denied in her public statements. This issue of her gender in reference to the flower paintings is problematic. On the one hand, many early critics did not see her as an artist, but as a sex object, the subject of Stieglitz's photographs, which were often exhibited with her paintings. Furthermore, the critics' description of her art as "feminine" and allusions to her as a kind of goddess, seemed rooted in a condescending belittlement of her skill and perspicacity as an artist, perpetuating a stereotypical assumption that creations emerge from women's bodies without intellectual effort . On the other hand, her letters reveal that O'Keeffe herself grappled with the ways in which these images of sensuously layered folds expressed a "woman's consciousness." For that reason she asked Mabel Dodge Luhan to write about them, with results that were not particularly effective. It must also be pointed out that flowers are the sex organs of plants, giving them, almost by definition, sensual associations. O'Keeffe's images of flowers do embody a new visual language, one that the critical language is only beginning to describe, just as it took decades to find the appropriate words with which to discuss Cézanne's works. In the late twenties, O'Keeffe began to use New York City's buildings as her subject, despite or perhaps because of the fact that she had been told that "even the men hadn't done well at it." Some critics chose to see these as her "real" paintings as opposed to the flowers that they thought showed "an unhealthy preoccupation with sex."

By the early1930s, O'Keeffe entered her most developed phase, in which the desert became her major theme. She also evolved a life-style that enabled her to live more according to her own rhythm. Until 1929, O'Keeffe and Stieglitz spent their summers together at his family home on Lake George in New York. O'Keeffe became increasingly dissatisfied with this arrangement, partly because of the domestic obligations it imposed on her (as described in a letter to Ettie Stettheimer) and partly because she found the landscape claustrophobic, as can be seen in her painting *Lake George With Crows*. She accepted an invitation from Mabel Dodge Luhan to spend the summer of 1929 at Luhan's ranch in New Mexico; her letters reveal how deeply and immediately she was moved by the landscape. Subsequently she divided her time between New York and New Mexico, although taking the step to leave Stieglitz each year never became routine. During her most emotionally vulnerable periods, as in the years between 1932 and 1934 when she suffered something of a breakdown, she could not bring herself to go. O'Keeffe did not take up permanent, year-round residence in New Mexico until 1949, after she had settled Stieglitz's estate.

In her personal iconography the desert became at least as important as the flowers. Her way of looking from an unusual perspective, intended to find the organic rhythm of things, is evident in both desert and flower images (and also in her few images of the ocean, such as *Wave Night*). Initially, critics offered simplistic interpretations of the desert paintings, erroneously associating the bones that figured so prominently in these works with death. O'Keeffe recounts that she took a barrel of bones home at the end of her first New Mexican summer because she wanted to bring part of the desert back east with her. For her these bones were not representative of death, but of life and process; she wrote that "the bones cut sharply to the center of something that is keenly alive on the desert." She expressed this awareness in such works as *The Bones and the Blue* and *From the Faraway Nearby*, looking at the sky and the hills through blanched pelvis bones and establishing a connective rhythm, an organic flow, between them. For O'Keeffe, the "faraway" was "a beautiful, untouched, lonely-feeling place." In her search for inner truth through identification with the desert landscape, O'Keeffe was not the first woman artist or writer for whom the desert embodied the internal wilderness. Like Mary Austin's "walking woman" from the story of that title who walked off society's expectations and values, in the desert O'Keeffe purified her life and art of extraneous distractions. Like the artist Emily Carr, nature's rhythm and flow was O'Keeffe's most important subject.

O'Keeffe would have bristled at the suggestion that she was a writer, yet she expressed herself quite eloquently in words. The book she wrote in 1976 follows the conventions of many artists' autobiographies, including her reason for writing it, that is, in order to set the record straight. She began by showing her precocious visual sensitivity, a memory of bright light, a quilt, an image of her mother from before she could talk; in a later section she discussed the epiphany that led to her finding her vision. The book is characterized by a polemical tone: she complains about how other people were wrong — in their understanding of the flowers, in wanting her not to progress and to always paint flowers, in thinking she was ungrateful. Throughout, though, her voice is wry, even funny, as in her description of how she came to paint a red, white, and blue cow skull in response to the "city men's" desire for the "Great American" something.

Her letters are breezy, enthusiastic, written in a stream-of-consciousness style in which phrases are separated by dashes. Their concrete voice is much like her way of seeing. O'Keeffe professed mistrust of the written word; however, it is clear that she was capable of recording her responses to the world spontaneously and skillfully. She sustained several significant correspondences throughout her life, particularly the one with Anita Pollitzer, which lasted from 1915 until their falling-out in the 1950s, when O'Keeffe would not grant Pollitzer permission to publish a monograph about her life. The first two years of this correspondence are especially important because they document the turning point in O'Keeffe's artistic development.

During the latter part of her life, O'Keeffe reaped the rewards of her career, a grande dame of American arts and letters. She remained productive, working on several new themes until she was forced to give up painting because of her failing eyesight (something she hid from the public as long as she could). Some of her most effective images, painted when she was in her seventies, are based on her experience of air travel, including a series of rivers seen from the air and of the sky seen from above the clouds, the last of which was a huge panoramic canvas, a physical ordeal to produce. For the last fourteen years of her life her companion was Juan Hamilton, a potter some fifty years her junior. As her eyesight failed, he taught her how to play with clay. Their relationship provides an interesting reflection of the relationship between the young O'Keeffe and the much older Stieglitz. O'Keeffe almost made her goal of living to be one hundred years old in an environment that seemed to be cut from the same cloth as her art. Many contemporary women artists look to her as a foremother and an inspiration. While her biography followed a pattern more common for men, in that she was able to gain a significant place in the public realm during her working life, she did not compromise her own vision to conform to external expectations. She told her own truth in direct terms, not finding it necessary to resort to the "slant vocabulary" that many women artists and writers have used to reconcile the expression of their personal experiences with the language of the dominant discourse.

SOURCES
Castro, Jan Garden. *The Art and Life of Georgia O'Keeffe*. New York: Crown Publishers, 1985.

Cowart, Jack, Juan Hamilton, and Sarah Greenough. *Georgia O'Keeffe: Art and Letters*. Washington, D.C. and Boston: National Gallery of Art with New York Graphic Society Books, and Little, Brown and Co., 1987.

Hoffman, Katherine. *An Enduring Spirit, The Art of Georgia O'Keeffe*. Metuchen, N.J.: Scarecrow Press, 1984.

O'Keeffe, Georgia. *Georgia O'Keeffe*. New York: Viking Press, 1976.

Pollitzer, Anita. *A Woman on Paper: Georgia O'Keeffe*. New York: Simon and Schuster, 1988.

Robinson, Roxana. *Georgia O'Keeffe, A Life*. New York: Harper & Row, 1989.

SELECTIONS FROM GEORGIA O'KEEFFE, *GEORGIA O'KEEFFE*
(NEW YORK: THE VIKING PRESS, 1976)

The meaning of a word — to me — is not as exact as the meaning of a color. Colors and shapes make a more definite statement than words. I write this because such odd things have been done about me with words. I have often been told what to paint. I am often amazed at the spoken and written word telling me what I have painted. I make this effort because no one else can know how my paintings happen.

Where I was born and where and how I have lived is unimportant. It is what I have done with where I have been that should be of interest.

My first memory is of the brightness of light — light all around. I was sitting among pillows on a quilt on the ground — very large white pillows. The quilt was a cotton patchwork of two different kinds of material — white with very small red stars spotted over it quite close together, and black with a red and white flower on it. I was probably eight or nine months old. The quilt is partially a later memory, but I know it is the quilt I sat on that day.

This was all new to me — the brightness of light and pillows and a quilt and ground out beyond. . . .

My next memory must be of the following summer — the first memory of pleasure in something seen with my eye and touched with my hand. There was a good-sized lawn all around our house. There was a long entrance drive with a high arborvitae hedge. I don't remember walking across the grass but I remember arriving at the road with great pleasure. The color of the dust was bright in the sunlight. It looked so soft I wanted to get down into it quickly. It was warm, full of smooth little ridges made by buggy wheels. I was sitting in it, enjoying it very much — probably eating it. It was the same feeling I have had later when I've wanted to eat a fine pile of paint just squeezed out of the tube. . . .

The year I was finishing the eighth grade, I asked our washwoman's daughter what she was going to do when she grew up. She said she didn't know. I said very definitely — as if I had thought it all out and my mind was made up — "I am going to be an artist."

I don't really know where I got my artist idea. The scraps of what I remember do not explain to me where it came from. I only know that by that time it was definitely settled in my mind. I hadn't seen many pictures and I hadn't a desire to make anything like the pictures I had seen. But in one of my mother's books I had found a drawing of a girl that I thought very beautiful. The title under it was "Maid of Athens." It was a very ordinary pen-and-ink drawing about two inches high. For me, it just happened to be something special — so beautiful. Maybe I could make something beautiful . . . I think my feeling wasn't as articulate as that, but I believe that picture started something moving in me that kept on going and has had to do with the everlasting urge that makes me keep on painting. . . .

It was in the fall of 1915 that I first had the idea that what I had been taught was of little value to me except for the use of my materials as a language — charcoal, pencil, pen and ink, watercolor, pastel, and oil. I had become fluent with them when I was so young that they were simply another language that I handled easily. But what to say with them? I had been taught to work like others and after careful thinking I decided that I wasn't going to spend my life doing what had already been done.

I hung on the wall the work I had been doing for several months. Then I sat down and looked at it. I could see how each painting or drawing had been done according to one teacher or another, and I said to myself, "I have things in my head that are not like what anyone has taught me — shapes and ideas so near to me — so natural to my way of being and thinking that it hasn't occurred to me to put them down." I decided to start anew — to strip away what I had been taught — to accept as true my own thinking. This was one of the best times of my life. There was no one around to look at what I was doing — no one interested — no one to say anything about it one way or another. I was alone and singularly free, working into my own, unknown — no one to satisfy but myself. I began with charcoal and paper and decided not to use any color until it was impossible to do what I wanted to do in black and white. I believe it was June before I needed blue.

"Blue Lines" was first done with charcoal. Then there were probably five or six paintings of it with black watercolor before I got to this painting with blue watercolor that seemed right. . . .

We [O'Keeffe and her sister] often walked away from the town in the late afternoon sunset. There were no paved roads and no fences — no trees — it was like the ocean but it was wide, wide land.

The evening star would be high in the sunset sky when it was still broad daylight. That evening star fascinated me. It was in some way very exciting to me. My sister had a gun, and as we walked she would throw bottles into the air and shoot as many as she could before they hit the ground. I had nothing but to walk into nowhere and the wide sunset space with the star. Ten watercolors were made from that star. . . .

That first summer I spent in New Mexico I was a little surprised that there were so few flowers. There was no rain so the flowers didn't come. Bones were easy to find so I began collecting bones. When I was returning East I was bothered about my work — the country had been so wonderful that by comparison what I had done with it looked very poor to me — although I knew it had been one of my best painting years. I had to go home — what could I take with me of the country to keep me working on it? I had collected many bones and finally decided that the best thing I could do was to take with me a barrel of bones — so I took a barrel of bones.

When I arrived at Lake George I painted a horse's skull — then another horse's skull and then another horse's skull. After that came a cow's skull on blue. In my Amarillo days cows had been so much a part of the country I couldn't think of it without them. As I was working I thought of the city men I had been seeing in the East. They talked so often of writing the Great American Novel — the Great American Play — the Great American Poetry. I am not sure that they aspired to the Great American Painting. Cézanne was so much in the air that I think the Great American Painting didn't even seem a possible dream. I knew the middle of the country — knew quite a bit of the South — I knew the cattle country — and I knew that our country was lush and rich. I had driven across the country many times. I was quite excited over our country and I knew that at that time almost any one of those great minds would have been living in Europe if it had been possible for them. They didn't even want to live in New York — how was the Great American Thing going to happen? So as I painted along on my cow's skull on blue I thought to myself, "I'll make it an American painting. They will not think it great with the red stripes down the sides — Red, White and Blue — but they will notice it." . . .

I must have seen the Black Place first driving past on a trip into the Navajo country and, having seen it, I had to go back to paint — even in the heat of mid–summer. It became one of my favorite places to work. . . .

I don't remember what I painted on my first trip over there. I have gone so many times. I always went prepared to camp. There was a fine little spot quite far off the road with thick old cedar trees with handsome trunks — not very tall but making good spots of shade. . . .

Another time we went on a warm still night. We were very comfortable in a new tent. I was up before the sun and out early to work. Such a beautiful, untouched lonely–feeling place — part of what I call the Far Away. . . .

It is surprising to me to see how many people separate the objective from the abstract. Objective painting is not good painting unless it is good in the abstract sense. A hill or tree cannot make a good painting just because it is a hill or a tree. It is lines and colors put together so that they say something. For me that is the very basis of painting. The abstraction is often the most definite form for the intangible thing in myself that I can only clarify in paint. . . .

❖

FROM EXHIBITION CATALOGUE, ANDERSON GALLERIES, 1923

I grew up pretty much as everybody else grows up and one day seven years ago found myself saying to myself — I can't live where I want to — I can't do what I want to — I can't even say what I want to. School and things that painters have taught me even keep me from painting as I want to. I decided I was a very stupid fool not to at least paint as I wanted to and say what I wanted to when I painted as that seemed to be the only thing I could do that didn't concern anybody but myself — that was nobody's business but my own. So these paintings and drawings happened and many others that are not here. I found that I could say things with color and shapes that I couldn't say in any other way — things that I had no words for. Some of the wise men say it is not paint-ing, some of them say it is. Art or not Art — they disagree. Some of them do not care. Some of the first drawings done to please myself I sent to a girl friend requesting her not to show them to anyone. She took them to '291' and showed them to Alfred Stieglitz and he insisted on showing them to others. He is responsible for the present exhibition.

I say that I do not want to have this exhibition because, among other reasons, there are so many exhibitions that it seems ridiculous for me to add to the mess, but I guess I'm lying. I probably want to see my things hang on a wall as other things hang so as to be able to place them in my mind in relation to other things I have seen done. And I presume, if I must be honest, that I am also interested in what anybody else has to say about them and also in what they don't say because that means something to me, too. . . .

❖

FROM EXHIBITION CATALOGUE, "AN AMERICAN PLACE," 1939

A flower is relatively small. Everyone has many associations with a flower — the idea of flowers. You put out your hand to touch the flower — lean forward to smell it — maybe touch it with your lips almost without thinking — or give it to someone to please them. Still — in a way — nobody sees a flower — really — it is so small — we haven't time — and to see takes time, like to have a friend takes time. If I could paint the flower exactly as I see it no one would see what I see because I would paint it small like the flower is small.

So I said to myself — I'll paint what I see — what the flower is to me but I'll paint it big and they will be surprised into taking time to look at it — I will make even busy New Yorkers take time to see what I see of flowers.

Well — I made you take time to look at what I saw and when you took time to really notice my flower you hung all your own associations with flowers on my flower and you write about my flower as if I think and see what you think and see of the flower — and I don't.

Then when I paint a red hill, because a red hill has no particular association for you like the flower has, you say it is too bad that I don't always paint flowers. A flower touches almost everyone's heart. A red hill doesn't touch everyone's heart as it touches mine and I suppose there is no reason why it should. The red hill is a piece of the badlands where even the grass is gone. Badlands roll away outside my door — hill after hill — red hills of apparently the same sort of earth that you mix with oil to make paint. All the earth colors of the painter's palette are out there in the many miles of badlands. The light Naples yellow through the ochres — orange and red and purple earth — even the soft earth greens. You have no associations with those hills — our waste land — I think our most beautiful country. You must not have seen it, so you want me always to paint flowers. . . .

I have picked flowers where I found them — have picked up sea shells and rocks and pieces of wood where there were sea shells and rocks and pieces of wood that I liked. . . . When I found the beautiful white bones on the desert I picked them up and took them home too. . . . I have used these things to say what is to me the wideness and wonder of the world as I live in it. . . .

I was the sort of child that ate around the raisin on the cookie and ate around the hole in the doughnut saving either the raisin or the hole for the last and best.

So probably — not having changed much — when I started painting the pelvis bones I was most interested in the holes in the bones — what I saw through them — particularly the blue from holding them up in the sun against the sky as one is apt to do when one seems to have more sky than earth in one's world. . . . They were most wonderful against the Blue — that Blue that will always be there as it is now after all man's destruction is finished.

❖

EXCERPTS FROM GEORGIA O'KEEFFE, SELECTED LETTERS, 1915–1930

GEORGIA O'KEEFFE TO ANITA POLLITZER
    Columbia, SC, October 11, 1915
    . . . arent you funny to wonder if I like your letters. I was walking up from the little bandbox post office with the mail under my arm — reading your letter this afternoon — and when I came to the part telling what Stieglitz said about "its worth going to Hell to get there" — I laughed aloud — and dropped all the things under my arm. . . .
    I came back and read your letter again.
    Anita — do you know — I believe I would rather have Stieglitz like something — anything I had done — than anyone else I know of — I have always thought that — If I ever make anything that satisfies me even ever so little — I am going to show it to him to find out if its any good — Don't you often wish you could make something he might like?
    Still Anita — I dont see why we ever think of what others think of what we do — no matter who they are — isn't it enough just to express yourself — If it were to a particular person as music often is — of course we would like them to understand — at least a little — but why should we care about the rest of the crowd — If I make a picture to you why should I care if anyone else likes it or is interested in it or not I am getting a lot of fun out of slaving by myself — The disgusting part is that I so often find myself saying — what would you — or Dorothy — or Mr. Martin or Mr. Dow — Mr. Bement — or somebody — most anybody — say if they saw it — It is curious — how one works for flattery —
    Rather it is curious how hard it seems to be for me right now not to cater to someone when I work — rather than just to express myself
    During the summer — I didn't work for anyone — I just sort of went mad usually — I wanted to say "Let them all be damned — I'll do as I please" — It was vacation after the winter — but — now — remember Ive only been working a week — I find myself catering to opinion again — and I think I'll just stop it.
    Anita — I just want to tell you lots of things — we all stood still and listened to the wind way up in the tops of the pines this afternoon — and I wished you could hear it — I just imagined how your eyes would shine and how you would love it — I haven't found anyone yet who likes to live like we do —
❖
GEORGIA O'KEEFFE TO ANITA POLLITZER
    Columbia, SC, October 20(?), 1915
    . . . Anita? What is Art — anyway?
    When I think of how hopelessly unable I am to answer that question I cannot help feeling like a farce — pretending to teach anybody anything about it —

I won't be able to keep at it long Anita — or I'll lose what little self respect I have — unless I can in some way solve the problem a little — give myself some little answer to it — What are we trying to do — what is the excuse for it all — If you could sit down and do just exactly what you wanted to right now for a year — what in the dickens would you do — The things Ive done that satisfy me most are charcoal landscapes — and — things — the colors I seem to want to use absolutely nauseate me —

I don't mean to complain — I am really quite enjoying the muddle — and am wondering if I'll get anything out of it and if I do what it will be — I decided I wasn't going to cater to what anyone else might like — why should I — and when you leave that element out of your work there is nothing much left

Im floundering as usual

Tell me what you think Art is — if you can — ask a lot of people — and see if anybody knows — What do you suppose Mr. Dow would say —

You asked me about music — I like it better than anything in the world — Color gives me the same thrill once in a long long time — I can almost remember and count the times — it is usually just the outdoors or the flowers — or a person — sometimes a story — or something that will call a picture a mind — will affect me like music —

Do you think we can ever get much of it in Art — I don't know — anything about anything — and Anita Im afraid I never will. . . .

Anita Im feeling fine and feel as if Im just having time to get my breath and stand still and look at the world — It is great sport I am really enjoying it hugely — . . .

The sky is just dripping today and it seems I have never seen or felt anything more perfectly quiet.

❖

GEORGIA O'KEEFFE TO ANITA POLLITZER
Columbia, SC, December 13, 1915

Did you ever have something to say and feel as if the whole side of the wall wouldn't be big enough to say it on and then sit down on the floor and try to get it on a sheet of charcoal paper — and when you had put it down look at it and try to put into words what you have been trying to say with just marks — and then — wonder what it all is anyway — Ive been crawling around on the floor till I have cramps in my feet — one creation looks too much like T.C. [Teachers College, Columbia University] the other too much like soft soap — Maybe the fault is with what Im trying to say — I dont seem to be able to find words for it —

I always have a hard time finding words for anything —

Anita — I wonder if I am a raving lunatic for trying to make these things — You know — I don't care if I am — but I do wonder sometimes.

I wish I could see you — I cant tell you how much I wish it. Im going to try some more — I turned them to the wall while I wrote this — One I made this afternoon — the other tonight — they always seem different when you have been away a little while. I hope you love me a little tonight — I seem to want everybody in the world to — Anita.

❖

GEORGIA O'KEEFFE TO ANITA POLLITZER
Columbia, SC, January 4, 1916

There seems to be nothing for me to say except Thank you — very calmly and quietly. I could hardly believe my eyes when I read your letter this afternoon — I haven't been working — except one night — all during the holidays — that night I worked till nearly morning — The thing seems to express in a way what I want it to but — it also seems rather effeminate — it is essentially a womans feeling — satisfies me in a way — I dont know whether the fault is with the execution or with what I tried to say — Ive doubted over it — and wondered over it till I had just about decided it wasnt any use to keep on amusing myself ruining perfectly good paper trying to express myself — I wasn't even sure that I had anything worth expressing — There are things we want to say — but saying them is pretty nervy — What reason have I for getting the notion that I want to say something and must say it — Of course marks on paper are free — free speech — press — pictures — all go together I suppose — but I was just feeling rather downcast about it — and it is so nice to feel that I said something to you — and to Stieglitz.

I wonder what I said — I wonder if any of you got what I tried to say — Isn't it damnable that I cant talk to you If Stieglitz says any more about them — ask him why he liked them —

Anyway, Anita — it makes me want to keep on — and I had almost decided that it was a fool's game — Of course I would rather have something hang in 291 than anyplace in New York — but wanting things hung is simply wanting your vanity satisfied — of course it sounds good but what sounds best to me is that he liked them — I dont care so much about the rest of it — only I would be interested in knowing what people get out of them — if they get anything — Wouldn't it be a great experiment — I'll just not even imagine such luck — but I'll keep working — anyway —

You say I am *living* in Columbia — Anita — how could I help it — balancing on the edge of loving like I imagine we never love but once — . Columbia is a nightmare to me — everything out here is deliciously stupid — and Anita — I — am simply walking along through it while — something — that I dont want to hurry seems to be growing in my brain — heart — all of me — whatever it is that makes me — I dont know Anita — I can't explain it even to myself but Im terribly afraid the bubble will break — and all the time I feel so ridiculously secure that it makes me laugh

Anita, I cant begin to tell you how much I have enjoyed that Camera Work — It surprised me so much — and you know how much I love what is inside of it — That Picasso Drawing is wonderful music isn't it — Anita — I like it so much that I am almost jealous of other people even looking at it — and I love the Gertrude Stein portrait — the stuff simply fascinates me — I like it all — you know how much without my trying to tell you — The word — food — seems to express what it gives me more than anything else. . . .

Im feeling fine — never felt better in my life and am weighing the most I ever do — It's disgusting to be feeling so fine — so much like reaching to all creation — and to be sitting around spending so much time on nothing —
Im disgusted with myself —

I was made to work hard — and Im not working half hard enough —
Nobody else here has energy like I have — no one else can keep up
     I hate it
     Still — its wonderful and I like it too
     At any rate — as you said in the fall — it is an experience. I am glad you
showed the things to Stieglitz — but how on earth am I ever going to thank you
or get even with you — I love these Nadelman things too Anita — I just have too
many things to thank you for tonight — I'll just have to stop and not try
     Goodnight.

❖

GEORGIA O'KEEFFE TO ALFRED STIEGLITZ [the ellipses in this selection are
O'Keeffe's]
     Columbia, SC, February 1, 1916
     I like what you write me — Maybe I dont get exactly your meaning — but I
like mine — like you liked your interpretation of my drawings . . . It was such a
surprise to me that you saw them — and I am so glad they surprised you — that
they gave you joy. I am glad I could give you once what 291 has given me many
times . . . You cant imagine how it all astonishes me.
     I have been just trying to express myself — . . . I just have to say things you
know — Words and I are not good friends at all except with some people —
when Im close to them and can feel as well as hear their response — I have to
say it someway — Last year I went color mad — but Ive almost hated to think of
color since the fall went — Ive been slaving on the violin — trying to make that
talk — I wish I could tell you some of the things Ive wanted to say as I felt them.
. . . The drawings dont count — its the life — that really counts — To say things
that way may be a relief — . . . It may be interesting to see how different people
react to them. . . . — I am glad they said something to you. — I think so much
alone — work alone — am so much alone — but for letters — that I am not
always sure that Im thinking straight — Its great — I like it — The outdoors is
wonderful — and Im just now having time to think things I should have
thought long ago — the uncertain feeling that some of my ideas may be near
insanity — adds to the fun of it — and the prospect of really talking to live
human beings again — sometime in the future is great. . . .– Hibernating in
South Carolina is an experience that I would not advise anyone to miss — The
place is of so little consequence — except for the outdoors — that one has a
chance to give one's mind, time, and attention to anything one wishes.
     I cant tell you how sorry I am that I cant talk to you — what Ive been think-
ing surprises me so — has been such fun — at times has hurt too . . . that it
would be great to tell you . . . Some of the fields are green — very very green —
almost unbelievably green against the dark of the pine woods — and its warm
— the air feels warm and soft — and lovely. . . .
     I wonder if Marin's Woolworth has spring fever again this year . . . I hope it
has. . . .
     I put this in the envelope — stretched and laughed.
     Its so funny that I should write you because I want to. I wonder if many
people do . . You see — I would go in and talk to you if I could — and I hate to
be completely outdone by a little thing like distance.

❖

GEORGIA O'KEEFFE TO ALFRED STIEGLITZ

Canyon, Texas, September 4, 1916

Your letter this morning is the biggest letter I ever got — Some way or other it seems as if it is the biggest thing anyone ever said to me — and that it should come this morning when I am wondering — no I'm not exactly wondering but what I have been thinking in words — is — *I'll be damned* and I want to damn every other person in this little spot — like a nasty petty little sore of some kind — on the wonderful plains. The plains — the wonderful great big sky — makes me want to breathe so deep that I'll break — There is so much of it — I want to get outside of it all — I would if I could — even if it killed me –. . . .

After mailing my last letter to you I wanted to grab it out of the box and tell you more — I wanted to tell you of the way the outdoors just gets me —

Some way I felt as if I hadn't told you at all — how big and fine and wonderful it all was –. . . .

Your letter coming this morning made me think how great it would be to be near you and talk to you — you are more the size of the plains than most folks — and if I could go with my letter to you and the lake — I could tell you better — how fine they are — and more about all the things I've been liking so much but I seem to feel that you know without as much telling as other folks need.

❖

GEORGIA O'KEEFFE TO MABEL DODGE LUHAN

New York, 1925(?)

About the only thing I know about you — from meeting you — is that I know I dont know anything. — That I like — because everybody else knows — So when they say — "Dont you think so?" I dont think so — I dont think at all because I cant. — No clue to think from — except that I have never felt a more feminine person — and what that is I do not know — so I let it go at that till something else crystalizes

Last summer when I read what you wrote about Katherine Cornell I told Stieglitz I wished you had seen my work — that I thought you could write something about me that the men cant —

What I want written — I do not know — I have no definite idea of what it should be — but a woman who has lived many things and who sees lines and colors as an expression of living — might say something that a man cant — I feel there is something unexplored about woman that only a woman can explore — Men have done all they can do about it. — Does that mean anything to you — or doesn't it?

Do you think maybe that is just a notion I have picked up — or made up — or just like to imagine? Greetings from us both — And kiss the sky for me —

You laugh — But I loved the sky out there

❖

GEORGIA O'KEEFFE TO ETTIE STETTHEIMER

Lake George, August 6, 1925

That I haven't written you isn't because I havent thought of you — As a matter of fact I think I have thought of you every day. . . .

The reason I didn't write to you before is that I have been lame since we came up till about a week ago — I was vaccinated a few days before coming up and it affected the glands in my hip so that I couldnt walk — It was most annoying — so I just went dumb and dont think I had much of a thought or feeling of any kind — I just sat around — and wanted to throw anything handy at anyone who said I looked better — because I always felt the same — felt fine — but I couldn't walk

— So — the ground hog ate the transplanted sunflowers — the potato bugs ate the potato vines — the hail storm ruined the tomatoes, the beans and the corn — They used my circular saw to trim a tree — They cut the whole top off the only early appletree to improve the view for the other house — and now wonder why we dont have applesauce like last year — I caught Stieglitz cutting — or trying to cut wire with my pruning shears — The first person we got to cook went to visit her uncle on Sunday and sprained her ankle — Rosenfeld tried to cook and he fell down in the lake and sprained his so Stieglitz had to stew the peaches and bake the potatoes for a day or two — Then we got another woman — her husband didn't want her to come so she had to be driven home every afternoon to get his supper before she got ours. She put onions in the salad and no Stieglitz could risk that — The next one we got weighs near 200 and after the first day I found her sobbing into the potatoes and scrambled eggs because she had no one to talk to when she was through working — Since then we have had enough people to keep her busy all the time and she is all right — She is very clean so I could say my daily prayers of thanksgiving to her and not mind a bit —

We had two yowling brats here for six weeks who carefully kept anyone from tasting their food or having anything resembling peace or conversation at table — Except for breakfast — Stieglitz, Rosenfeld and I ate that alone with great pleasure and appreciation — till the toaster short circuited — shortly after that Kreymborg and his wife came to live in a room that we are not using usually — It opens on a sleeping porch so I guess they live with relative peace away from the rest of us — They only eat breakfast with us and it is still pleasant — Stieglitz's sister — Mrs. Schubart arrived yesterday — and I thank my stars that she eats her breakfast in her bed —

The closets are cleaned — the attic is cleaned — the wood room is cleaned, there is a new oil hotwater heater — The garbage is finally being buried where you dont have to walk past it if you walk most anywhere — The much needed shelf is put up in the back bathroom — that iron bed in the attic is painted — also the back porch of that little house across the way and the benches — The benches are not all the same color green because when we went to get a second can of it they didn't have a second can of that color —. . . .

You see why I didn't write — Someone had to attend to all these things — . . .

I have decided that next summer I am going to tent on that 366th island that they talk about here — The one that only comes up for leap year — with the hope that there wont be anything on it to attend to —

Where there wont have to be a new barrel for oil and I wont have to hunt for the keys to the reservoirs that someone misplaced while I wasnt around — and the carving knife isn't as apt to be in the barn as in the dining room

— And the worst of it all is that I am feeling so dumb that I dont seem to mind having such stupid things to do — . . .

. . . I have one painting and have yards of failures dropped around me in bunches — They are so stupid I dont even destroy them

Why bother about paintings — No one but myself gets a grouch over them. . . .

GEORGIA O'KEEFFE TO MABEL DODGE LUHAN

Taos, June 1929

. . . I dont know whether you know how important these days are for me or not — And I am not sure that I am *really* clear about it — but I feel it is so — They seem to be like the loud ring of a hammer striking something hard — All this is why I have not written — the surface doings of the days are only important in so far as they do some thing for an undercurrent that seems to be running very strong in me — As I cant tell where it is going — all I can say is that I am enjoying the way — and many things it brings me to —. . . .

GEORGIA O'KEEFFE TO MABEL DODGE LUHAN

Taos, August 1929

. . . I knew that if I stayed long enough the day would come when I would feel right about going — as I feel this morning — I knew I would have to go back to my Stieglitz — but I didn't want to go till I was ready and today I am ready — and want to go —

May I kiss you goodby — very tenderly — for I am thanking you for much — much more than hours in your house — and will you give Tony my kindest Greetings

If I can do anything for you as far away as Lake George — I would like to — I had wanted to talk with you about lots of things. . . .

I am anxious to get to work for the fall — it is always my best time I had one particular painting — that tree in Lawrences front yard as you see it when you lie under it on the table — with stars — it looks as tho it is standing on its head — I wanted you to see it — Will send you photographs of paintings if I get any of them worth sending. . . .

GEORGIA O'KEEFFE TO ETTIE STETTHEIMER

On a train from New Mexico to New York, August 24, 1929

A week ago today I took this paper at this funny little hotel to write you because it seemed amusing. I have carried it so long that it isn't amusing any more — However — the paper having lost its flavor isn't going to stop me.

I am on the train going back to Stieglitz — and in a hurry to get there — I have had four months west and it seems to be all that I needed — It has been like the wind and the sun — there doesnt seem to have been a crack of the waking day or night that wasnt full — I haven't gained an ounce in weight but I feel so alive that I am apt to crack at any moment —

I have frozen in the mountains in rain and hail — and slept out under the stars — and cooked and burned on the desert so that riding through Kansas on the train when everyone is wilting about me seems nothing at all for heat — my nose has peeled and all my bones have been sore from riding — I drove with friends through Arizona — Utah — Colorado — New Mexico till the thought of a wheel under me makes me want to hold my head

— I got a new Ford and learned to drive it — I even painted — and I laughed a great deal — I went every place that I had time to go — and Im ready to go back East as long as I have to go sometime — If it were not for the Stieglitz call I would probably never go — but that is strong — so I am on the way. He has had a bad summer but the summers at Lake George are always bad — that is why I had to spend one away — I had to have one more good one before I got too old and decrepit — Well — I have had it — and I feel like the top of the World about it — I hope a little of it stays with me till I see you — It is my old way of life — you wouldn't like it — it would seem impossible to you as it does to Stieglitz probably — but it is mine — and I like it — I would just go dead if I couldn't have it — When I saw my exhibition last year I knew I must get back to some of my own ways or quit — it was mostly all dead for me — Maybe painting will not come out of this — I dont know — but at any rate I feel alive — and that is something I enjoy.

Tell me what the summer has been for you — I hope it has been good for all of you —

I will be in Lake George by the time you get this

My greetings to Carrie and Florine

❖

GEORGIA O'KEEFFE TO WILLIAM M. MILLIKEN
(DIRECTOR, CLEVELAND ART MUSEUM)

New York, November 1, 1930

I have been hoping that you would forget that you asked me to write you of the White Flower [in Cleveland Art Museum] but I see that you do not.

It is easier for me to paint it than to write about it and I would so much rather people would look at it than read about it. I see no reason for painting anything that can be put into any other form as well — .

At the time I made this painting — outside my door that opened on a wide stretch of desert these flowers bloomed all summer in the daytime — .

The large White Flower with the golden heart is something I have to say about White — quite different from what White has been meaning to me. Whether the flower or the color is the focus I do not know. I do know that the flower is painted large to convey to you my experience of the flower — and what is my experience of the flower if it is not color.

I know I can not paint a flower. I can not paint the sun on the desert on a bright summer morning but maybe in terms of paint color I can convey to you my experience of the flower or the experience that makes the flower of significance to me at that particular time.

Color is one of the great things in the world that makes life worth living to me and as I have come to think of painting it is my effort to create an equivalent with paint color for the world — life as I see it

❖

GEORGIA O'KEEFFE TO MRS. ELEANOR ROOSEVELT

February 10, 1944

Having noticed in the N.Y. Times of Feb. 1st that you are against the Equal Rights Amendment may I say to you that it is the women who have studied the idea of Equal Rights and worked for Equal Rights that make it possible for you, today, to be the power that you are in our country, to work as you work and to have the kind of public life that you have.

The Equal Rights Amendment would write into the highest law of our country, legal equality for all. At present women do not have it and I believe we are considered — half the people.

Equal Rights and Responsibilities is a basic idea that would have very important psychological effects on women and men from the time they are born. It could very much change the girl child's idea of her place in the world. I would like each child to feel responsible for the country and that no door for any activity they may choose is closed on account of sex.

It seems to me very important to the idea of true democracy — to my country — and to the world eventually — that all men and women stand equal under the sky —

I wish that you could be with us in this fight — You could be a real help to this change that must come.

GEORGIA O'KEEFFE TO WILLIAM HOWARD SCHUBART
(ALFRED STIEGLITZ'S NEPHEW)

Abiquiu, July 28, 1950

I have your letter telling me of your fears about my having a show — that it may not be good etc.

Dont think I havent thought that over — and that I think I have material for a very good show — it may be even rather startling.

However — as you know — I have 2 houses and there are paintings in both of them — within a few days I will get the paintings all in one room in one house and see how I look — I was willing to have a show just on what I have here in Abiquiu — so I feel pretty secure about that — I have always been willing to bet on myself you know — and been willing to stand on what I am and can do even when the world isnt much with me — Alfred was always a little timid about my changes in my work — I always had to be willing to stand alone — I dont even mind if I dont win — but for some unaccountable reason I expect to win —

It is as if I feel that my world is a rock — When a very prominent catholic priest — he was head of the chemistry department at Fordham — tried to convert me to the catholic church — I was amazed that he could only make the catholic church seem like a mound of jelly compared to my rock —

— I dont even care much about the approbation of the Art world — its politics stink

I dont see that it matters too much — I'll be living out here in the sticks anyway — What is the difference whether I win or lose — I am a very small moment in time. . . .

GEORGIA O'KEEFFE TO WILLIAM HOWARD SCHUBART
(ALFRED STIEGLITZ'S NEPHEW)

Abiquiu, August 4, 1950

It seems odd to think of you at Lake George tonight — I can smell the outdoors — and hear it — and see the stars — So often before I went to bed at night I would walk out toward the barn and look at the sky in the open space.

There was no light little house — there were no people — there was only the night — I will never go back there — unless — maybe to stand just for a moment where I put the little bit that was left of Alfred after he was cremated — but I think not even for that.

I put him where he would hear the Lake —

That is finished.

About my work Howard — I always have two opinions — one is my way of seeing it for myself — and for myself I am never satisfied — never really — I almost always fail — always I think — now next time I can do it — Maybe that is part of what keeps one working — I can also look at myself — by that I mean my work from the point of view of the looking public — and that is the way I look at it when I think of showing. I have always first had a show for myself — and made up my mind — then after that it doesnt matter to me very much what anyone else says — good or bad

What I put down as the most ordinary things I see and know is different than what others see and know — I cant help it — it just is that way.

Good night to you at Lake George — . . . .

G.

I am glad I am not there.

Suspension Bridge for the Swallows, 1957. Oil on canvas. 36" x 28".
The Currier Gallery, Manchester, N.H.

KAY SAGE

1898–1963

KATHERINE LINN SAGE is one of the most prolific writers included in this volume, although she did not begin to publish her fatalistic, acerbic poems until the last decade of her life. The ironic voice of her poetry is strikingly similar to the harsh, arid terrain depicted in her imaginary landscapes. In their muffled expression of pain and unease the paintings and poems convey the same vision. Sage followed an indirect route to achieving her artistic goals. She did not find the vehicle that so effectively expressed her inner vision until she was in her forties, and she never received more than a modest degree of public recognition for her achievements. Concerned that people would find her style derivative of that of her husband, Yves Tanguy, she was reluctant to exhibit her work. After Tanguy's death in 1955, Sage became increasingly depressed, and her mounting sense of desperation led her to take her own life in 1963. She was claimed as a Surrealist by the poet André Breton, and in some ways her work is consistent with the Surrealist approach. However, the existential malaise expressed in both her writings and paintings departs significantly from the Surrealist rhetoric, which purports to find release in peeling back the curtain of consciousness. For Sage the landscape of the mind was a barren, endless plain, devoid of life-forms, yet littered with the detritus of unrealized human endeavors.

Sage's upbringing was decidedly erratic. Although both parents came from prominent, wealthy families, they were of diametrically opposed temperaments, a fact which ultimately led to their separation. Sage's father was a conservative Albany patrician, with strict rules for proper behavior; her mother was an unconventional and independent woman who took her daughter on yearly extended jaunts to Europe. By an early age, Sage had become a cosmopolite, fluent in both French and Italian and carrying as one of her richest childhood memories a trip down the Nile. As a teenager at the beginning of the First World War, she returned to America with her mother and enrolled in the Foxcroft School in Virginia. By the end of the war, she had graduated and moved to Washington, D.C., where she worked as a translator for the government's censorship bureau.

Like many artists, Sage claimed that since her childhood she had "wanted to do nothing else but draw." Her formal art education did not begin, however, until 1919 when her mother returned to Italy and Kay remained in Washington, taking drawing classes at the Corcoran Gallery Art School. By the fall of 1920, she had "learned all that the school had to offer" and, shortly thereafter, moved to Rome to study art. Here, too, her formal study was quite limited; although she enrolled in at least two academies' life-drawing classes, she took pride in absenting herself from the regular critiques. At this time she met the painter Onorato Carlandi and joined his weekly painting trips into the Roman countryside. Sage wrote that she was primarily interested in the fellowship of these expeditions, and acknowledged Carlandi not as a painting instructor but as a mentor who "taught her how to think." The academic roots of her style can be traced to the time she spent in Rome, and her experience of the expansive, sun-drenched Mediterranean landscape informed her later dreamscapes. The several months at the Corcoran school and these years in Rome were the only times Sage studied art; she later said that she was opposed to all formal education for an artist. The few paintings that survive from this period are student pieces, soft-focus landscapes and portraits that barely hint at her later vision.

In 1925, Sage married Prince Ranieri di San Faustino, whom she had met in Rome in 1922, and withdrew from serious pursuit of her career for approximately a decade, focusing her life around their social activities. In 1935, Sage left the marriage and moved to Milan alone. She later described the tensions that led to the marriage's demise in her autobiographical essay, "China Eggs." Although she had not abandoned painting completely while she was married, her most significant creative piece during this ten-year period was a children's book that she both wrote and illustrated, and had published shortly after she left Prince Ranieri. She must have resumed painting with intensity, for her first solo exhibition was held in Milan within about a year, at the end of 1936. The hiatus in her career precipitated a change in the direction of her stylistic development, as it had for Marianne Werefkin, earlier in the century. The works Sage exhibited in Milan differed markedly from her earlier pieces: they were based on the modernist visual language of geometric abstraction to which she had probably been introduced through the poets Ezra Pound and T. S. Eliot (whom she met while summering in Rapallo, Italy, with her husband).

Like Emily Carr, who also resumed painting after a long hiatus, Sage reached an early phase of her mature style quite rapidly after she had begun to concentrate her energies on painting. During 1937 she moved to Paris, where she was exposed to Surrealist art and became acquainted with the group of Surrealists centered around André Breton, including her future husband, Yves Tanguy. Sage continued searching for a means of expressing her vision, and she began to experiment with looming shapes and evocative titles. A work such as *Danger, Construction Ahead* (1940), in which a sharp precipice juts out from jagged rocks, spanning a desolate plain, shows her early use of landscape as a means of communicating an interior state of being. With the outbreak of the Second World War, Sage returned to the United States, where she and Tanguy were married in 1940, an apparently successful marriage that lasted until his death in 1955. Sage used her family's money to help bring Breton and other members of the Surrealist group to the United States, and to purchase property in Woodbury, Connecticut. Sage and Tanguy were major figures in a social circle of artists in Connecticut that included such luminaries as Alexander Calder, André Masson, and Arshile Gorky.

Over the years Sage's technical skill became progressively refined and her personal iconography expanded. She continued to paint metaphorical dreamscapes depicting in her fully mature style expansive, barren landscapes, occupied by such human traces as scaffolding or drapery, but devoid of humans themselves. Such works as *The Instant* (1949) or *No Passing* (1954) typify her mature work. In 1954 Tanguy and Sage held a joint exhibition at the Wadsworth Atheneum in Hartford, Connecticut. When Tanguy died of a cerebral hemorrhage, Sage plunged into a state of deep depression which was exacerbated the next year when she began to exhibit symptoms of cataracts. Her failing eyesight forced her to abandon her poetic landscapes, and the titles of her last paintings, such as *The Answer is No* and *Watching the Clock* (both 1958), suggest that she felt she was running out of time to create. After a suicide attempt in 1959, it seemed in the years following as if she had overcome her despair: she had a one-artist gallery exhibition and she began to experiment with collage, using lenses, marbles, and sand to fabricate works that evoked a sense of landscape seen at close range. Her depression not conquered, however, Sage committed suicide in January 1963.

A vast, otherworldly landscape dominates most works by both Sage and Tanguy, as well as many by other Surrealists. Whereas Tanguy's canvases are inhabited by biomorphic, almost extraterrestrial, forms, Sage's contain abandoned geometric relics of human endeavor. Their tonalities also differ substantially; cooler tones predominate in Tanguy's works, while in Sage's paintings cool blues and grays are contrasted with parched ochres. Although these superficial similarities exist between Sage's and Tanguy's work, Sage was far more obviously influenced by the Italian metaphysical painter Giorgio de Chirico. That influence can be noted as early as 1938, most likely the same year she purchased one of his paintings, *The Torment of the Poet*, painted in 1914. Both Sage and de Chirico use expansive, disjunctive space, inhabited by oneiric, evocative objects. Although it is usually assumed that Sage was introduced to de Chirico's work after her move to Paris in 1937, it is possible that she encountered it earlier in Milan, where he worked during the 1930s.

Sage participated in the Surrealist scene in Paris, as a personal friend of many members of the group. André Breton, the self-appointed arbiter of the Surrealist canon, included her among the Surrealist artists and her style incorporated many significant characteristics of mainstream Surrealism. Specifically, Sage's approach to painting corresponded to that exemplified by Salvador Dali and René Magritte, as well as Tanguy. All these artists created visualizations of dream states through vast panoramic landscapes filled with forms and shapes that appear to be in a state of flux. As in the works of the better-known Surrealist painters, the meaning of Sage's pieces remains elusive, yet it is implied by the use of titles which suggest to the viewer the direction that his or her meditation might follow. Typical of the Surrealist approach, Sage developed a personal iconography to externalize her internal state through the repetition of significant images. Animated drapery, geometric forms, and, after 1946, abandoned scaffolding, recur in various and shifting relationships in her work. These images become imbued with a psychic resonance, particularly when viewed in the context of her complete oeuvre. Sage's resistance to explicating her work was also typical of the Surrealists: in response to a request to explain her painting *Suspension Bridge for the Swallows*, she said that she "know[s] nothing of [its] origin except that I painted it," suggesting that her imagery emerged automatically from a preconscious source.

Yet Sage's work departs from mainstream Surrealism in the relentless aridity of her landscapes and the raw pain that they express. In describing her mother's morphine addiction, Sage wrote of "taking pain out of yourself, setting it up as a monument and walking around it . . . as one would observe a piece of sculpture." This seems an apt description of some of her works. Stephen Miller compared Sage's usual arena to that described in T.S. Eliot's poem *The Waste Land*, consisting of "endless plains . . . cracked earth / ringed by the flat horizon." The intense negativity of the "omnipresent, psychological weight of impending doom" that characterizes these wasteland landscapes makes them far more nihilistic than the visions of most of Sage's male Surrealist colleagues. They are also markedly different from the works of other women Surrealists, most of whom tended to use more organic forms and descriptively autobiographical subject matter. Leonora Carrington and Remedios Varo, for example, celebrated the hidden power of the feminine and used their work as a forum in which female creativity was brought out from its source within the earth. Sage, on the other hand, conceived of the earth as parched and arid, strewn with abandoned building materials, the opposite of generative, organic, or "female" qualities. Her personal imagery was devoid of narrative, autobiographical details, here too differing from other women Surrealists, such as Frida Kahlo.

Sage's poetic voice, as expressed in four volumes published during the last six years of her life, is consistent with her artistic vision. Although she said that she began writing sonnets during her first marriage, none of her poems were published until after Tanguy's death. Whether it was the desolation she felt after his death or perhaps her failing eyesight and subsequent inability to paint that acted as a catalyst for Sage's writing, is not known: her verbal output during that period in any case was prolific. Sage wrote most of her poems in French — as she said in her autobiography, "English was not my native tongue. . . . I write much better in French." In addition, it is probable that French was the language that she and Tanguy spoke together. The poems, in both English and French, are characterized by an almost doggerel quality in their dependence on word play. "Where the cowslips / there slip I," she writes in English. Another, in French, "J'ai pas le vin gai / olé, olé." Translated from one language to the other, however, they lose their coy, playful quality, their tone becoming one of the utmost gravity, expressing a sense of the absurdity of life and the human drama, written from the point of view of an ironic observer. Occasionally one hears a muffled cry of pain, sometimes expressed in a tone of self-mockery.

Sage had an ambivalent relationship to her own writing: "When I'm tight / I write / To paint / I must be sober," or "Words are our enemies," or "Remain quiet — that doesn't pose any problems." Although she said that "what I write isn't literature," she went on to ask, "When you have things to say, what can you do?" The desperate ennui voiced in some poems such as "Voyage to the Moon" seemed to prefigure her suicide, as did the hopelessness embodied in her last paintings. It does not seem coincidental that her last volume of poems, published just months before her death, was entitled *Mordicus*, which translates as "with tooth and nail."

Sage's poetic motifs reflect images from her entire painted oeuvre, not only from those paintings that are contemporaneous with her writing. The futility of human endeavor expressed visually in the looming architectural shape in *Hyphen* (1954) is conceptualized verbally in a poem as the "ivory tower" that she has "built on despair" (1957). Likewise, the hollowed-out drapery that was a dominant visual motif from the mid-forties through the mid-fifties could have reached that state by virtue of the "tears that have made a hole on the inside" (1959). Holes recur as a theme in several of her poems, symbolic of life's emptiness. The sense of potential danger communicated in her painted landscapes was repeated verbally, in a poem such as "Acrobatics" — "When you walk on a tight-rope / at the least unexpected thing you break your neck." Sage expressed similar precariousness in her unpublished autobiography, "China Eggs," which begins: "I am walking very fast on a thin sheet of ice. I can either keep on walking or I can stop. If I stop, the ice will break." In this document, which she began the year that Tanguy died, Sage recounted her experiences before her move to Paris, a move that she described as the beginning of her "real" life. Like Marianne Werefkin in her "Letters to an Unknown," Sage created an alter ego, employing an unidentified "you," with whom she maintained a series of rambling conversations in the tense, wry voice of her poetry. The significance of the title "China Eggs" is somewhat ambiguous. Sage denied that the egg had any symbolic import, yet it recurs in her paintings and throughout the text of the autobiography. Many other women Surrealists used this motif, often as a symbol of feminine creativity and rebirth; however, eggs do not seem to have that meaning in Sage's personal iconography.

While the male gurus of Surrealism spoke bombastically from grandstands, Sage's voice was quiet and private. Her evocative images provided a chilling view of her interior state, one that was further corroborated in her poetry. Like Dali, she was uneasy in the world as it is, yet rather than expressing her alienation as he did through apocalyptic paranoia, she created a haunted landscape of unbuilt buildings and unpainted canvases.

SOURCES

Chadwick, Whitney. *Women Artists and the Surrealist Movement.* Boston: Little, Brown and Co., 1985.

Kay Sage, 1898-1963. Essay by Régine Tessier Krieger. Exhibition catalogue. Herbert F. Johnson Museum of Art, Cornell University, Ithaca, N. Y., 1977.

Miller, Stephen R. "The Surrealist Imagery of Kay Sage." In *Art International* 26:4 (1983), 32–47.

Sage, Kay. "China Eggs." Archives of American Art, Washington, D. C., 1955.
_____. *Demaine Monsieur Silber.* Paris: Pierre Seghers, 1957.
_____. *Faut Dire C'Qui Est.* Paris: Debressse-Poesie, 1959.
_____. *Mordicus.* Paris, 1962.
_____. *The More I Wonder.* New York: Bookman Associates, 1957.

KAY SAGE, EXCERPTS FROM "CHINA EGGS," 1955
(UNPUBLISHED AUTOBIOGRAPHY), ARCHIVES OF AMERICAN ART, WASHINGTON, D. C.

Introduction
"I am walking very fast on a thin sheet of ice. I can either keep on walking or I can stop. If I stop, the ice will break."

"Keep on walking. You could get to the other side."

"There is no other side."

"Don't think — don't think about anything at all. What is that on the pantry shelf?"

"I don't know."

"You've got to know. It wasn't there before so you must have put it there."

"I did not."

"Well. What is it?"

"A crumpled piece of paper."

"No."

"I don't know what it is. It doesn't look like anything I ever saw before."

"You've got to know what it is. You put it there."

"I didn't put it there."

"You must have. There isn't anyone else in the house except you and me and I didn't put it there. Go see what it is."

"No. I'd rather guess. A crumpled up piece of cardboard."

"No."

"Leave me alone. I don't give a goddamn what it is."

"My mother was a morphine addict. My father was an upright citizen. I wish somebody would write about what happened to me."

"Why don't you write about it yourself? You must know about it."

"I don't know about it. Besides I don't know how to write."

"You don't have to know how to write. You only have to know how to think."

"But you've been telling me not to think — not to think about anything at all."

"Oh be quiet."

❖

FROM BOOK 1, CHAPTER 1: There isn't going to be any story
My mother and father were divorced when I was ten. At least I think I was ten. Everything important that ever happened to me, I always think I was ten. I think I was ten when I went to Egypt. I think I was ten when a handsome young South American told me I would make my soul black if I kept on smoking dirty old pieces of Italian wrapping paper stuffed into the end of a bamboo stick and I think I was ten when I took the bullets out of my mother's revolver which she

had put, loaded, on her dressingtable. I think I was ten the first time she made me give her a hypodermic of morphine.

Anyway we were in a hotel when she told me about the divorce. I cried and cried because I thought it meant that my mother would be a widow dressed in black with a long black veil. I loved my mother passionately. As to her feelings for me, they were patently abnormal and surely sexual. I have no doubts that she liked men a lot but all her women friends were certainly most peculiar. She always kissed me on the mouth and told me I should kiss everyone else on the mouth. This did not seem strange to me at the time but it nearly got me into all sorts of trouble later on . . . .

❖

FROM CHAPTER 7: Morphine

One day when it was still the gilded period in New York, my mother had a terrible headache. I think I was ten, but I must have been eleven. She made me call the doctor and he gave her some morphine.

It is not difficult to imagine how easy life would be once you had discovered something which stopped all pain. Anything of such strength has unlimited power and therefore makes itself supreme. It must create pain in order to prove itself indispensable. There is no such thing as no pain. At best, you can detach yourself from it. You can do this by taking the pain out of yourself, setting it up as a monument and walking around it. I can talk about it because I have done it, I have walked through entire parks of pain, observing each monument as one would observe a piece of sculpture — seeing the form with its sharp or rounded edges, the planes and the terrible points — but being quite apart from it. If you learn to do this, you can stand physical pain. You can use the same system for mental pain but then you go crazy.

Anyway after that, my mother had a headache and morphine every month. Later, it happened more and more often. But she never took the morphine unless she had the pain. . . . She never took it in secret. She called a doctor when she could get one. When she couldn't she got a nurse to give it to her under doctor's orders. When she couldn't find a nurse she made me do it. She had to have a witness and she never failed to find a victim in me. Nor did she ever fail to persuade some doctor to give her a prescription. . . .

❖

FROM CHAPTER 8: Italy

. . . There were scorpions — the nice shiny brown ones that look like tiny lobsters — and we would shake out our bedroom slippers every evening just to be sure there wasn't one inside. We have often heard the story of these scorpions stinging themselves to death if they are encircled by fire. It is quite true. I have put one under a glass. He tries and tries to get out. When he has decided that there is absolutely no hope he turns up his tail and stings himself in the back. I would like to have the courage of a scorpion. . . .

❖

FROM CHAPTER 11: Ethics

"From the time that I was very young I had all the qualifications for making an excellent thief, beginning with my moral sense. I could see no wrong in anything as long as it didn't hurt anyone else. But don't misunderstand me. My standards were high and my ethics were unimpeachable."

"Who was to be the judge as to what would hurt someone else?"

"I, of course."

"How could you be sure?"

"There was one simple way. If they didn't know about it, it coudn't possibly hurt them. My father had a wonderful collection of bird's eggs which he kept on fine white sand in the drawers of a small cabinet. He had collected them from the bird's nests which was a nasty thing to do. I had quite a different reason for liking them. I didn't see why I shouldn't have the ones I particularly liked."

"Why didn't you ask him for them?"

"Because I knew he wouldn't have given them to me and it would only have made him think of them. He didn't even remember he had them. He didn't care anything about them but it was a collection and he had the kind of mind that would never have broken up a collection. That was the only interest he had in them. He never looked at them."

"How do you know?"

"Well you'll have to take my word for it that I did know. Anyhow, one by one, at various intervals I took the eggs I wanted. . . ."

❖

FROM CHAPTER 12: Graduation

The next winter my mother rented the house of her friends who had migrated elsewhere and I spent a wonderful year awakening to the call of sex. There has never been a community which contained a bigger bunch of devastatingly attractive good-for-nothing bastards than this one. They were all married men from fifteen to twenty years older than I and all bored with their wives. They had nothing else to do but ride around the countryside and call on any pretty girl they could find. . . . I loved all these men, each one in turn, and they completely spoiled me for all the eligible conventional young men who should have interested me. I had no thoughts whatever of marriage. I wanted to paint. All the eligible conventional young men wanted to marry me. I found this very tiresome and I preferred the reprobates who were not only more attractive but were good friends and were looking only for amusement. . . .

❖

FROM CHAPTER 13: Painting

"You keep talking about painting being the great interest in your life but you don't seem to have done much of it."

"Oh yes. I was painting all the time. Nothing of any importance until later but I was thinking about it. . . ."

"But you don't speak of your painting."

"It is difficult to speak about the things that matter most to you. They are the things which you know to be true. Never try to explain the truth." . . .

"What about inspiration then? And imagination?"

"There are no such things. Inspiration is remembering. Imagination is the direct result of observation." . . .

"Let's talk about writing."

"It is not at all the same as painting. Both are forms of exhibitionism but while the writer stands naked before the public, the painter dresses in a provocative manner. However, in either case the body must be beautiful."

"Nobody asked you to put your images on a sexual basis."

"Can you think of a better one?" . . .

". . . Then what makes an artist or writer good? Is it technique?"

"I will answer the first question first. If you really mean good, it is because he thinks right and lives right. If by good, you mean recognized, it is because he has had the good chance to have a good agent. As to technique, that is only the fine feathers. All the fine techniques in the world will not make a good painter or a good writer if he [has] nothing to say." . . .

". . . Let's talk about sculptors." "As long as there is an egg in the world what do we need of sculptors?" . . .

❖

CHAPTER 16: Rome of the Romans

. . . I started working in earnest at my painting. I drew from life at various Academies always staying away the days that the professor came to criticize and I met an artist called Onorato Carlandi who was to be my inspiration. He was old — old enough to have fought with Garibaldi — and I was inspired not by his painting but by his philosophy. His creed was liberty. *"E se tu sarai solo, tu sarai tutto tuo,"* he used to quote endlessly from Leonardo. He did not teach me to paint. He didn't even try to. But he taught me to think as I hadn't thought to think before. He was the head of a group known as " *I venticinque della Campagna Romana.*" Once a week they set out together by street-car, by train (third class) or by horse and cart, to some previously selected place in the campagna. There each one settled down and painted. The results were judged before lunch. The winner had to pay for the lunch which was in the nearest local "osteria." Once I paid it and was very proud. The lunches were always delicious. By the time I came along, the twenty-five had diminished to from three or four to ten at the outside. Carlandi took a fancy to me. I know in fact that he loved me very much. He invited me to come with them. I think that these were the happiest days of my life. I was the only woman in the group which was very dangerous among a bunch of Latins — but Carlandi watched me with a jealous eye and there was never anything except good-hearted fun as far as I was concerned. I had a passion for the Campagna and must not have minded the discomforts of getting there. The awakening at dawn to catch the street-car to the station, laden with heavy painting equipment, the jostling and the smells of the third-class compartments and sometimes the long rides in a two wheeled cart driven by some old peasant along stony and bumpy roads. I scarcely remember any of this. I only remember the hot sun after the mist had risen, the crystal air and the delicious meals of pasta, ricotta and sour Italian bread and still more sour wine. I made no friends in Rome outside of these. I saw no one except the people I worked with. I had even only one love affair but as this was not serious on my part, it is not worth mentioning. I think I was almost completely happy. . . .

I often wonder what would have happened if I had spent these years in Paris instead of in Rome and how much sooner I would have arrived at my subsequent way of thinking and painting. Rome was hopelessly academic and insular at that time. But then so, probably, was I. I doubt if I was ready yet for any revelations. In any case I simply drew and painted until I really knew how to draw and paint. I had not yet learned to think — that is I had not yet learned to think right. Still, I do not really believe that this academic background did me any harm. It only delayed me and I had to work equally hard to get rid of the enforced constraint. . . .

❖

BOOK III, FROM CHAPTER 24
(AFTER HER MARRIAGE TO PRINCE RANIERI DI SAN FAUSTINO)

. . . It was impossible for me to take up my old life again. I had closed the door behind me, quite unaware of having done so. It had not occurred to me that my friends would feel differently about me as a Princess. I though I was still me — and so I was — but there was no way of reconciling the two ways of living.

❖

FROM CHAPTER 27: The World is Not Round

"Let's talk about something else for a change. Let's talk about science. Did you know that they have just discovered the world is not round?"

"Yes I know. What does it matter?"

"It matters a lot to me. It makes me think much better of the world that it should be oval like an egg."

"That is not exact. You didn't listen well. It is not oval. It is pear-shaped."

"I would rather think of it as egg shaped. I don't like pears."

"I still can't see what difference it makes. It will always look flat to us and it is still the same world that we live in, or on."

"But it does make a lot of difference. It changes the whole outlook of man. Why has man always made round objects? Why is he always chasing balls? Isn't it because he thought the world was round?". . .

❖

FROM CHAPTER 29

". . . It depresses me to go back this way and to see how many years I threw away — just threw away to the crows. No reason, no purpose, nothing."

"Why are you always looking for a purpose and a reason? A lot of things happen that haven't necessarily any purpose."

"Then they shouldn't happen. That's just the point. There is no real purpose. Do you think it is acceptable for a man or a woman to work all their lives for no good reason?"

"But there is always a good reason. Ambition, money, fame and so on."

"None of these are valid. The only possible valid reason for working all one's life, other than having to eat, is to provide for children whom you have unnecessarily brought into the world as a result of your own pleasure. This, in itself, is a social crime as we know that one of the great troubles in the world today is over-population."

"Children apart, you do not then think that it is good to be constructive and to achieve something you have been striving for?"

"As I have said before, it is all right while you are doing the striving but even supposing you get to the greatest greatness you ever dreamed of, then what? Imagine that I had become the world's greatest artist — let us evaluate this. It would not necessarily mean that I had done anything greater than the first man who invented plumbing."

"But I thought you were always stressing the intellectual approach."

"I don't really know what I am stressing except that I like poetry as opposed to science — sometimes even science can be poetic but poetry will never be scientific. And I am speaking of poetry in the French — Universal sense."

❖

FROM CHAPTER 35: Non si sà mai

"I wasn't painting anymore. I had to do something so I began to learn Bridge . . . "

❖

FROM CHAPTER 36: Pebbles

Our marriage didn't go on the rocks, it just wore itself out on pebbles. It didn't take long — a year at the most — for me to be no longer in love with X. I never stopped loving him deeply but that is not the same. He was too immature or too overbred or too afraid of me to be a passionate lover, which, although I did not realize it at the time, was one of the things I needed. . . . X. was a child and I could do with him what I liked, all but one thing; I could not make him into a different person and I should never have tried nor wanted to. But I was still young and full of ideals so instead of accepting him with his charm and inability to cope with life, I resented the fact that he depended on me to do all the dirty work. I was a poet and a dreamer too. I did not want to face the difficulties of life any more than he did. He was neurotic. I would have liked to be neurotic myself. I had all the predispositions for it but I never had the time. I was always surrounded by people more neurotic than I whom I had to look after. I was forced to be practical which was in direct contrast to my nature. It was all immeasurably negative and frustrating. . . .

For a time, I saw quite a lot of Ezra Pound. I tried to get him to take an interest in my writing which was, at that time, replacing painting. I couldn't paint. I had turned one room into a sort of studio and thought I could take refuge there but it was utterly impossible. It didn't matter how much I told Gina I was not to be disturbed when I was there, she would knock discreetly and say someone wanted me on the telephone. Worse than that, X could not understand why he couldn't break in at any moment and never hesitated to do so. I gave up trying. Ezra took a look at my writing which, I am forced to admit, was not very good at the time, and told me write a sonnet a day. After I had written a hundred sonnets, he would discuss it with me. I applied myself seriously and wrote three sonnets which I thought, and still think, were very good especially considering the fact that I had never written a sonnet before. That was the end of the sonnets and I hope I will never have to write another one. I think he was wrong. I did not need discipline in writing any more than I needed discipline in anything else. When asked why he did not take more interest in my talents, his reply was that I was just one of those fish who swam to the top of the water every once in a while to get a breath of air, and then went right down to the bottom again. . . . I was very annoyed by his comment because I knew, by then, that whatever interest he had in me was not in my intellect. . . .

❖

BOOK III, FROM CHAPTER: Paris

As I had never really wanted to get married, I also passionately did not want children. I don't know why I never had any because I never thought to do anything about it. Just luck I guess. Possibly my subconscious warned me that the only children I could adequately bring into the world would be paint on canvas....

Extra

"Your story is very absorbing. Do you ever mean to publish it?"

"No. I couldn't possibly. There are too many other people and too many truths involved."

"But there isn't a word of truth in it."

"What do you mean by that? You mean that none of these things ever happened to me?"

"Yes, I mean exactly that. You only think they happened to you."

"Then, in that case, I wasn't there. You mean it was somebody else?"

"Yes, it was somebody else."

"And all the other people were other people?"

"Yes, all of them, including yourself, existed only in your imagination."

"Then who am I?"

"I don't know."

If you wind a clock too tight it will break the mainspring.

China Eggs — End

"Then you see, I put all my eggs in one basket — and I lost."

"I wouldn't have thought you had any eggs left."

"Oh yes, I had them all — intact."

"But you were forever putting eggs in baskets."

"I know, but those were only china eggs."

❖

SELECTED WRITINGS

In response to a letter from Edwin C. Rae of University of Illinois, Champaign/Urbana seeking information for catalogue of exhibition in which "Suspension Bridge for the Swallows" was included.

"... I have no comments to make about the arts of today and know nothing of the origins of 'Suspension Bridge for the Swallows' except that I painted it. I have no particular reason for painting anything except that I see it in my mind and have a desire to transfer it to canvas.

"As to the education of the artist, I am very much against it in any form, believing that if an artist is really an artist, he will learn alone by the simple process of drawing and painting.

"I am sorry that, as usual, I am not very communicative on these subjects...."

❖

Titles (poem)

Winter sleep

Why is the clock so slow?

The imperfect circle

Without any reason at all
Space thunder
Stand silent
You are cordially invited
One word
The birds of sadness
Inner space
Seven thousand, seven hundred seven miles away
The distance to the horizon
Chain fractions
Powers and roots
Chances multiples
Sunday, Monday or always.

❖

Poem, 1961

These are games without issue
some have been played
and are therefore static
others will be
and can still be
played
there are no rules
no one can win or lose
they are arbitrary
and irrelevant
but there is no reason why
anything should mean more
than its own statement
two and two
do not necessarily make four. . .

If that is a scientist at my door
please tell him
to go away.

❖

KAY SAGE, SELECTED POETRY

1. FROM *DEMAINE MONSIEUR SILBER* (PARIS: PIERRE SEGHERS, 1957)

The Tower
I have built a tower on despair
There you don't hear anything,
    there is nothing to see;
There is no response, when, black
    on black,
I scream, I scream in my
ivory tower.

La Tour
J'ai bâti une tour sur le
    désespoir,
on y entend rien, y a rien à voir;
Y a pas de réponse quand, noir
    sur noir,
je crie, je crie, dans ma tour
    d'ivoire

❖

Acrobatics
When you walk
on a tightrope
at the least unsuspected thing
you get your face knocked in;
Then leave me alone,
I'll find a way out of it
by myself.

Acrobatie
Quand on marche
sur une corde tendue,
à la moindre chose imprévue
on s'casse la guele;
Laissez-moi donc
me débrouiller
toute seule.

❖

My Speech
Words are our enemies,
A waste of time;
Me — I can say in one word
All that I think, all that
I feel . . .

I won't say it —
It's not elegant.

Ma parole
Les paroles sont nos enemies,
un gaspillage de temps;
moi, j'peux dire en un seul mot
tout c'que j'pense, tout c'que
j'sens . . .

Je le direai pas —
c'est pas élégant.

❖

Armour
I feel neither hot nor cold.
Good, bad — it's all the same
to me;
All that happens around me
Seems only like an image
on a screen.

The oyster has closed her shell
For good
with the pearl inside.

Armure
Je n'ai ni chaud ni froid.
Le bien, le mal — ça m'est
        indifférent;
tout c'qui se passe autour de moi,
ce n'est que des images sur un
        écran.

L'huître a fermé sa coquille
pour de bon,
avec la perle dedans.

❖

Monuments
A little girl decided
that she wanted to see
    a seed grow.
The seed
became a tree,
and the little girl became
a marble woman.

Monuments
Une petite fille
l'etait fixée
qu'elle voulait voir
une graine pousser.
La graine
l'est devenue un arbre,
et la petite fille,
une femme
en marbre.

❖

2. FROM *FAUT DIRE C'QUI EST* (PARIS: DEBRESSE-POÉSIE, 1959)

At the bottom of the letter
What I write

Au Pied de la Lettre
C'qu j'écris

is not literature.
My friends told me that,
I know it, of course;
I agree with them,
I'm of their opinion.
But then -
When you have things to say
what are you supposed to do?
Is it forbidden to write
    them down?
Must you hold you tongue?

c'est pas de la littérature.
Mes amis
me l'ont dit,
puis je le sais, bien sûr;
je suis d'accord,
je suis de leur avis.
Mais alors,
quand on a des choses à dire,
qu'est-c'qui faut faire?
C'est défendu de les inscrire?
Faut se taire?

❖

The Tears
Ended are the tears
that one has cried
they have dug a hole
on the inside

Les Larmes
Finies les larmes,
les larmes qu'on pleure —
Elles ont creusé un trou
à l'intérieur.

❖

Perfume
Unexpectedly, I smell
a delicious perfume —
a perfume full of memories,
of youth, of spring,
which seems to follow my smile,
the movement of my hands.

Parfum
Je sens, à l'improviste,
un délicieux parfum —
un parfum plein de souvenirs
de jeunesse, de printemps,
qui semble suivre mon sourire,
le mouvement de mes mains.

I search for it in vain.
I can't find
where it could be coming from
And then
in a flash, I've got it .. .
I know.
There!
That perfume
is the memory
of myself.

J'ai beau chercher
Je ne trouve pas
à quoi ça peut tenir . . .
Et puis
dans un éclar, j'y suis,
je sais.
    Voilà . . .
Ce parfum
c'est le souvenir
de moi.

❖

Fair
I went to the fair
and all that I bought
was a spool of black thread —
of darning thread.
Then,
needle and thread in hand
I patched up my life
with bits and pieces of chagrin
and moths.

Foire
J'suis allée à la foire,
et tout c'que j'ai acheté
c'est une bobine de fil noir
du fil à repriser.
Depuis,
aguille et fil en main,
j'ai rapiécé ma vie
avec des morceaux de chagrin
et des papillons de nuit.

❖

Repetition	**Répétition**
I am tired of doing the	J'suis fatiguée de faire
same things	sans arrêt
without stopping.	les mêmes choses.
I am tired of the perfume	J'suis fatiguée du parfum
of roses.	des roses.
I am tired of this bird	J'suis fatiguée de cet oiseau
who everyday, sits	qui, tous les jours, se pose
exactly there	exactement là
on the oak branch,	sur la branche du chêne,
chirping more beautifully in turn	criant de plus belle,
its same old story.	à tour de bras,
I am tired of seeing	sa même rengaine.
that same sun	J'suis fatiguée de voir
rise each morning	cet identique soleil
as if it had kept up all night.	se lever chaque matin
I am tired of the patter	comme il a fait la veille.
of scientists and experts;	J'suis faitguée des boniments
tired of a world in tears,	de scientistes et de savants;
of a laughing world.	fatiguée d'un monde en larmes,
	d'un monde riant.

I'm tired, what . . .	J'suis fatiguée, quoi . . .
Is it not my right ?	C'est pas mon droit?

❖

Voyage to the moon	**Voyage à la Lune**
When one doesn't know	Quand on sait pas
what to do	comment faire
to put things in order	pour mettre de l'ordre
at home	chez soi,
one goes away	on s'en va.

❖

Time switch	**Minuterie**
I am in the process	Je suis en train
of putting things in order	de mettre de l'ordre
in my thoughts	dans mes pensées,
in my drawers —	dans mes tiroirs —
Soon you will be able to turn	Tantôt vous pourrez tout
off all the lights;	éteindre;
I am no longer afraid of the dark.	Je n'ai plus peur du noir.

❖

3. FROM *THE MORE I WONDER* (NEW YORK: BOOKMAN ASSOCIATES, 1957)

An Observation
   The more I wonder,
   the longer I live,

how so much water
can stay in a sieve.

❖

The Window

My room has two doors
and one window
One door is red and the other is gray.
I cannot open the red door;
the gray door does not interest me.
Having no choice,
I shall lock them both
and look out of the window.

❖

Heroics

Because I run
it does not mean
I am not out of breath;
my courage comes from being scared to death.

❖

Illusions

There was an old woman
who hadn't a thing to wear
except holes.
So she sewed the holes together
and she dressed herslf with care;
but people passed her in the street
as though she were not there.

❖

Destiny

If I turn back
at least I shall not have the sun in my face.
But then there will always be
the long shadow of myself
before me.

❖

Literature

We were reading different books
all the time;
we never knew it
until you shut yours and I shut mine.

We were reading different books;
well, what of it?
You liked yours —
I *wrote* mine
and I love it.

❖

Occupations
　　When I'm tight
　　I write.
　　To paint,
　　I must be sober.
　　There might be something in this that I should think over.

❖

4. FROM *MORDICUS* (PARIS, DECEMBER 1962),
WITH TEN DRAWINGS BY JEAN DUBUFFET

weight it's heavy	**le poids** c'est lourd.
all that weighs is heavy.	tout c'qui pèse est lourd.
they have told us in vain that gravity doesn't exist above the earth. they're mistaken . . .	on a beau nous dire que le poids là-bas au dessus de la terre n'éxiste pas. on se goure . . .
in the heart and in the head all that weighs is heavy.	dans le coeur et dans la tête tout c'qui pèse est lourd.

❖

my bird and I I have a bird who has just perched on the bank of my lake This bird is mine — it is evident. it is sad it is silent it is large and high on its feet it does strictly nothing it doesn't move it is black and dull it is in mourning it observes the world tranquilly from the corner of its eye it's not an ordinary bird no, it's not all that. Don't breathe a word about it	**mon oiseau et moi** j'ai un oiseau qui vient se pôser au bord de mon étang. cet oiseau est à moi. c'est évident. il est triste il est silencieux il est grand et haut sur pattes. il ne fait strictement rien. il ne bouge pas il est noir et mat il est en deuil. il observe le monde tranquillement du coin de l'oeil. c'est pas un oiseau ordinaire non, c'est pas du tout ça. n'en soufflez pas un mot

but, I believe	mais je crois,
in the end	en fin de compte,
that bird	que cet oiseau
is me	c'est moi

❖

give

give me a station	donnez-moi une gâre
that is not busy with trains	qui s'occupe pas de trains.
give me a play on words	donnez-moi un jeu de mots
that comes to nothing	qui aboutisse en rien.
give me the question of the day	donnez-moi le point du jour
to replace an eye	pour remplacer un oeil.
give me a black picture	donnez-moi un tableau noir
to cheer up my mourning	pour égayer mon deuil.
give me the time that passes	donnez-moi le temps qui passe
to wear out the sages	pour avachir les sages.
give me a hyphen	donnez-moi un trait d'union
to figure out my age	pour déchiffrer mon âge.
give me a bateau-mouche	donnez-moi un bateau-mouche
to cross the fields	pour traverser les prés
give me a rubberband	donnez-moi un élastique
to hold my ideas together	pour boucler mes idées,
give me a cutting stone	donnez-moi une pierre de taille
an identity card.	comme carte d'identité.
give me and give me	donnez-moi et donnez-moi
for I can only take	car je ne fais que prendre
give me a rope	donnez-moi une corde
to hang myself.	pour me pendre.

donnez

Credit to John S. Monagan for permission to quote excerpts from "China Eggs" by Kay Sage.

Light is Gold, 1951. Gesso, plastic paint, acrylic, transparent lacquers on two panes of corrugated glass. 30" x 23". ©Addison Gallery of American Art, Phillips Academy, Andover, Massachusetts. All Rights Reserved.

IRENE RICE PEREIRA

1902–1971

IRENE RICE PEREIRA was a poet and a mystic as well as a painter, who sought to express the metaphysical potential of space and light in her paintings. Her passionate involvement with the transcendental nature of light and space grew from two experiences; the first, when still a child she saw God in a dewdrop; the second, her perception of light fading in the Sahara Desert when she was in her twenties. Pereira used complexly structured, abstract geometric forms as a vehicle to express the expansiveness of space and light; with the exception of some later drawings, all referential elements were eliminated from her art work. Intimate and passionate involvement with her aesthetic caused her to work often in a frenzy of inspiration, crying, neglecting food and sleep, beating out the rhythm of her work to herself.

Pereira was a prolific writer who explored her cosmology in philosophical discussions written over the last decades of her life. Unlike many artists included in this volume, Pereira *did* consider herself a writer, viewing her writings as an integral part of her creative oeuvre, another means of investigating the problems of representing space and light. Although she achieved a solid reputation during her lifetime, in the decade or so before her death it had fallen off; she died a bitter woman, convinced that her vision was unappreciated.

The oldest child of Hilda and Emmanuel Rice, Pereira was born near Boston and lived in several locations in western Massachusetts before her family finally settled in Brooklyn when she was about nine. She loved to read and write, and is said to have hoped to be a writer when she grew up. However, since her father died when she was in her teens and her mother was in ill health, Pereira had to support her mother and three younger siblings. She switched to the commercial curriculum in high school, and, within six months went to work as a stenographer. She was able to pursue her academic education in night classes at Washington Irving High School in New York City, however, where she also first studied drawing and painting. In 1927, she began a four-year course of study at the Art Students League. The cultural climate at the Arts Students League had changed since Georgia O'Keeffe's student days earlier in the century and the institution had shed some of its academic stodginess. Pereira was introduced to modernist aesthetics by her teachers Richard Lahey and Jan Matulka; David Smith and Burgoyne Diller were among her fellow students. According to her biographer, Karen Bearor, there is a discrepancy between the dates of birth on Pereira's birth certificate (1902) and passport (1907); Bearor suggests that perhaps Pereira "fibbed" in order to maintain her eligibility for "young artists" exhibitions, having started her career late by not beginning her art education until she was already in her twenties. (Bearor also points out some of Pereira's other fictions about her life, and, to some extent, her work.) In 1929, Pereira married the first of her three husbands, Humberto Pereira, a commercial artist.

Pereira began her "eastward journey," as she subsequently described the development of her artistic career, during the 1930s. In 1931 she went on a study trip to Europe, planning to attend the Académie Moderne in Paris, where Amédée Ozenfant was filling in for Fernand Léger. She was disappointed with its "old-fashioned" course of study and left Paris after several months, traveling in Italy and North Africa. While in the Sahara Desert she had a heightened experience of light, space, and vision whose metaphysical and cosmological force drove her artistic quest for the remainder of her life. When she returned to the United States in January 1932, Pereira began a series of nautical abstractions based on sketches of ships' parts made during her travels. Their machine aesthetic bears a visual resemblance to both the European Purists, whom she had encountered in Paris, and the American Precisionists. For Pereira, however, the use of machine parts had a distinct meaning in her artistic consciousness that she explored in depth in her autobiographical essay "Eastward Journey." She continued to work with the motif of "man in a machine world" until 1938, a turning point at which she "freed [her]self from the object," changing her focus from the machine to "the unknown white center." In the latter half of the thirties, Pereira supported herself by teaching, first in the Works Progress Administration's Design Laboratory, an experimental fusion of fine arts and design modeled on the Bauhaus, and then at Pratt Institute. In her teaching she stressed the importance of abstraction as a means of conveying inner content.

Pereira reached her first mature stylistic phase during the 1940s. Based on her work in the design laboratory, she began to experiment with the different textures produced by alternative media and surfaces, such as glyptal resin, glass, and parchment. She had already eliminated referential imagery from her work, using purely geometric forms "to find plastic equivalents for the revolutionary discoveries in mathematics, physics, biochemistry and radioactivity." In *White Lines* (1942) she created a deeply resonant space through overlapping geometric planes and vacillating, seemingly woven linear filaments. Slightly later works, such as *Bright Depth*, contain these elements, but also appear to be suffused by an intense glow, emanating from an infinite interior space. Pereira had begun to produce multilayered works in 1939, and by the mid-forties developed a series of works that were built up with several actual planes of materials, topped with corrugated glass. Pereira called these works her "shadow paintings" because they depended on actual cast shadows, as well as on painted illusions, to create images that were in perpetual motion. Such works as *Transversion* (1946) or *Light is Gold* (1951) seem to contain their own light within infinitely vacillating surfaces. Some critics believe that the shadow paintings represent Pereira's highest achievement. On the other hand, Pereira felt uneasy with the use of real shadows, perhaps because of her understanding that "everything that man cannot account for at the vanishing point turns back on him and his shadow." Nonetheless, the works are exceptionally evocative in their integration of poetry and geometry. Their experimentation with actual and implied visual motion predated such explorations by other artists by more than a decade.

The early 1950s mark a natural change in Pereira's stylistic development as well as the path of her career. By this time she had achieved an estimable reputation in the art world: her work had been purchased by several museums as well as by private patrons, and she had had numerous one-artist exhibitions culminating in a 1953 joint show with Loren MacIver, another woman abstract artist, at the Whitney Museum in New York. In her personal life Pereira had by that time divorced her second husband, George W. Brown, and married the poet George Reavey. In 1950, Pereira accompanied Reavey to Manchester, England, where he was a visiting professor. That experience turned out to be a crucial force in changing her artistic direction. She was overwhelmed by the perpetual drear and gloom of the city, which she described in her poem "The Black Night." Her strong response to the lack of light, however, enabled her to fully understand the importance of light as a humanizing principle. After her return to the United States in 1951, the content of the shadow paintings was "revealed" to her, leading her to abandon her multimedia approach in order to communicate unbroken illumination using only oil paint. Pereira considered the later works an improvement on her earlier ones in their sending light back to its source where it became color again, rather than returning to shadow. Her forms became more rectilinear and less diagonal and, rather than creating an infinite weave, she summarized them into ambiguously overlapping planes. Although initially her colors remained vibrant, by the 1960s she used softer ones, consistent with the more metaphysical titles of her later pieces, such as *Core of Substance* (1956) and *The Murmuring Reflections of Time Passed in the Rippling Waters* (1964). The works of this period imply a sense of landscape, a vast cosmic stretch of sea, land, and sky, activated by interpenetrating geometric planes, in which the contrast between the hard edges of the geometric forms and their roughly activated expressionist surfaces creates a dynamic tension.

Pereira's later works were never received as positively as the earlier ones, and the last twenty years of her life were marked by bitterness and disappointment, including the demise of her third marriage. In its dependence on geometric form, her work seemed almost in direct opposition to the Abstract Expressionism of the 1950s. Although some similarities existed between Pereira's aesthetic concerns and those of the Abstract Expressionists, Pereira had nothing but scorn for their popularity. By the early sixties, she had come to believe that her work was being deliberately suppressed by a monolithic, conspiratorial museum establishment; she even complained that her phone was tapped. Her diary entries indicate that she felt that her artistic self was dying in the United States, that "everything seemed frozen" and she needed to escape. Amost a decade after she had begun to express these feelings, Pereira finally left New York because of failing health and an imbroglio with her landlord. She spent the last month of her life on the Costa del Sol in Spain, where she died of emphysema in 1971, a bitter, disillusioned woman, convinced that her talent and life's work had been unappreciated and disrespected.

Pereira began to evolve her written theory of light, space and matter in response to the same revelation that initiated change in her artistic style. In *Light and the New Reality* (1951), she hypothesized a new approach to painting that would bring light back to its source. It was followed in 1955 by *The Paradox of Space and the Simultaneous Ever-Coming to Be*. In *The Nature of Space* (1956), she established the contributions of various cultures, from the ancient Egyptians to the present, in clarifying the concept of space. In numerous subsequent discourses on space, light, the nature of the universe, and the fourth dimension, Pereira discussed a "new optic," based on the idea that humans perceive solids in a dematerialized form that continuously activates light waves. The metaphysical nature of her quest is suggested by her books' titles, for instance, *The Transformation of "Nothing" and the Paradox of Space*, *The Finite and the Infinite*, and *The Transcendental Formal Logic of the Infinite: The Evolution of Cultural Forms*. Some of her most vivid and evocative writing is expressed as poetry, as in *The Crystal of the Rose* and *The Poetics of the Form of Space, Light and the Infinite*. Pereira's books, most published privately, elicited mixed responses and, in Pereira's opinion, her written works played a large role in her fall from critical grace. She believed that museum administrators were hostile to them and for that reason undermined her reputation; she was also distressed at the resistance to her writings that she perceived among her friends. The writings do prove difficult to penetrate, in some ways obfuscating rather than clarifying her life and work; Donald Miller describes them as "intensely explanative but non-self-revealing." These works do provide, however, the context and philosophical bases for her paintings and verify her manipulation of geometric form in order to make a cosmological statement. Abstraction had a very specific meaning for Pereira, affording contact with and expression of the "Absolute"; her writings serve to explain the "content" of her abstraction (much as Mondrian explains his in his essay "Plastic Art and Pure Plastic Art").

Pereira's private writings, voluminous notebooks and journals, also yield extremely important information concerning the artist and her work. In her notebooks, she grouped her paintings around metaphysical themes, such as the "sphering of light." Often she would list several relevant paintings at the top of a page on which a poem was written, indicating that the visual images and the verbal concepts had grown simultaneously. This confirmed her assertion that her writing and painting needed to be considered together. Pereira also kept detailed notes on her diverse metaphysical readings, including such subjects as theories of light and of the fourth dimension, Rosicrucianism, and alchemy. Her writings and paintings are, in fact, filled with alchemical symbols.

One other significant source of information about Pereira's imagery among her unpublished papers is her extensive dream journal, kept over several decades, in which she analyzed her dreams as one would explicate a literary text. They are distinguished by such Jungian and alchemical themes as keys, rocks, numbers, suffused illumination, and mystical impregnation, many of the same themes that she explores in her more formal writings. Her close attention to the content of her dreams and the motifs that recur within them demonstrate her profound belief in occult forces. In one of her published books, *The Lapis*, Pereira duplicates the process used for her dream journal of recording dream narratives and explicating their symbolism. In *The Lapis*, however, she also attempted to visually analyze the information in the dream, deliberately transforming the dream-images into the subject of her art.

Several historians have emphasized the dichotomies that characterized Pereira's work and life, particularly that of intellect versus intuition. Above and beyond such dualities, however, Pereira was a mystic. Like the sixteenth-century Theresa of Avila, who saw herself actually being pierced by divine light, Pereira's relationship to the concept of light was passionate and concrete. She clearly communicated the religious intensity of her involvement with light in "Eastward Journey," in her discussion of her stylistic development. Her conversion to Catholicism in 1963 may be seen as consistent with this sensibility. The poem which begins "Beauty nestles / in the arms / of the Absolute / awaiting 'your' grace . . ." and ends "Gloria in excelsis / inviolate / involute / evolute / and Absolute / I sphere 'Your' blazing name" expresses her intense, personal relationship with light, for her the primal material, and her perception of the godhead. Finding the means to depict this splendor was at the core of her artistic quest. Estella Lauter believes that Pereira's perception of a cosmos unified by light is related to a mythic pattern in art exhibited by other twentieth-century women. Pereira herself wrote, "Only a woman could have dealt with the irrational infinite and given it form — humanized it." In this regard it is interesting to read Pereira's comments about gender and art, made at a 1954 conference on "Women in the World of Man," particularly in light of her own works' representation of an unearthly plane.

Pereira's paintings were not "coldly geometric," as John Baur suggests; rather, they were suffused with warmly radiating light and intense emotion. Her pain at rejection was intensified by the personal nature of her relationship to the abstract concepts she expressed both verbally and visually. Like numerous other twentieth-century artists, she was profoundly moved by the hermetic tradition which she used as an artistic source. For her profound and poetic evocation of deep space and her experimental use of nontraditional media, Irene Rice Pereira deserves far greater renown than she has thus far received.

SOURCES

Baur, John I. H., ed. *Loren MacIver and I. Rice Pereira*. Exhibition catalogue. Whitney Museum of American Art, New York, 1953.

Bearor, Karen. *Irene Rice Pereira*. Austin: University of Texas Press, 1991.

Harithas, James. "I. Rice Pereira: American Painter-Writer with Bold Solutions to Old Problems." *Vogue* (June 1970): 128–29.

Hill, Martha, and John L. Brown. *Irene Rice Pereira's Library: A Metaphysical Journey*. Washington, D.C.: National Museum of Women in the Arts, 1988.

Lauter, Estella. *Women as Mythmakers: Poetry and Visual Art by Twentieth-Century Women*. Bloomington: Indiana University Press, 1984.

Miller, Donald. "The Timeless Landscapes of I. Rice Pereira." *Arts* 53 (October, 1978: 132–33).

Pereira, I. Rice. *Light and the New Reality*. New York, 1952.

_____. *The Nature of Space*. New York, 1956.

_____. *The Lapis*. New York, 1957. Reprint. Washington, D. C.: Corcoran Gallery of Art, 1968.

_____. *The Crystal of The Rose*. New York, 1959.

_____. *The Poetics of Form, Space, Light and the Infinite*. New York, 1968.

_____. "Eastward Journey." Archives of American Art (microfilm, roll D 223).

Schwartz, Therese. "Demystifying Pereira." *Art in America*, 6 (October 1979): 114–19.

Van Wagner, Judith K. "I. Rice Pereira: Vision Superseding Style." *Woman's Art Journal* 1:1 (Spring/Summer 1980): 33–38.

SELECTIONS FROM *THE LAPIS,* 1957

The Lapis is an interpretation of a dream of a lapis lazuli stone monument with a figure incised in the stone. I was surprised myself by it. I never knew what a philosopher's stone looked like.

The diagrams, pictures and text show the contradictions between the experience of an inner image and the optical illusions of visual representation. The diagrams and text are concerned with art optics and gravitational centers of mind energy in connection with world views.

In conclusion the study suggests that there is a serious discrepancy between structure and optics in the Renaissance and twentieth century world views resulting from the dilemma of the infinite and finite in Greek thought. Up to the twentieth century the optical visual perception of world-space has been different form the Euclidean geometry which describes it. The systems of thought for describing space are different from the visual and intuitive perception of space. Geometric systems of thought have avoided the infinite; whereas visual and intuitive perception involves the infinite.

❖

Dream of the Lapis

I crossed a bridge. The water was surging on both sides of the bridge. This made it very dangerous. The bridge was very close to the surging water, but it was a sturdy bridge so I crossed it safely.

Now I am in a place with many people. Someone is telling me about a dream and suggests that I paint it. I say, "I cannot paint someone else's dream, I can only paint what is really mine." Now I see the suggested picture. It is an image, quite beautiful, but it is not real because the image is lying flat.

Now as I contemplate the scene, I see the whole thing. The image is lying flat on a circular island, in the center of a most beautiful circular blue lake, surrounded by a verdant landscape of trees and an ethereal sky. It is beauty. It has a mystical quality of atmosphere in a spherical depth. But I am distanced because the image is lying flat.

Now as I look and contemplate this scene, the image of its own motion is lifted into a vertical position. I see it now. It is an oval stone, life-size, smooth and polished. It is about one foot in thickness and six, eight, or ten feet tall. The stone monument is polished lapis lazuli with a white figure carved or incised into it. It was really so very beautiful. The figure looked like Archaic Greek, or like an ancient prophet. What disappointed me was the fact that the reverse side of the Lapis Lazuli stone monument was unknown, i.e. it had no figure on it.

Now it is all clear to me. I see the picture of what I am supposed to paint. It comes into view. It is beautifully illuminated and alive and set in a spherical depth of illuminated ethereal atmosphere.

❖

"WOMAN IN THE WORLD OF MAN —
WOMAN AND DIMENSIONS IN ART"
LECTURE, UNIVERSITY OF MICHIGAN, JULY 21, 1954

When I first received the letter inviting me to speak on this program — "Woman in the World of Man" — I was startled. It brought back the first childhood picture I had of this world — my mother going about the endless menial family chores — the young children screaming about the house — while my father puffed himself off to the trotting races.

That women have always worked hard is obvious. The professional women [sic] of the 20th century works even harder; for she still has her household and parental duties to perform. Yet these women have distinguished themselves in practically every field with accomplishment — from ambassadors to scientists; anthropologists to cabinet ministers and so on. If man still lives in the conservative hope that women are only a flash in the pan — he is deluding himself. Women are here to stay and they certainly can match man's strength with endurance. However, I am only qualified to speak from the realm which I personally experience; namely, that territorry which is very little concerned with the factual world and only believes in the reality of the absolute and eternity. Nevertheless, no matter how remote that world may be from the physical and objective reality of things, one is constantly shocked into the realization that this inner world can only be preserved by understanding some of the problems that related to the social conditions of the present. Once a woman ventures outside the traditional preoccupation with a family, she is confronted with this masculine world of objective statements, facts, aggression, competition, thinking and logic. The role of this kind of a woman is very difficult and presents a dilemma; because while participating in the objective, masculine world, she still must preserve her femininity or her personality suffers from the conflict. Even in the more delicate and tenuous professions — such as poetry, painting and music the same problem exists. In painting, the male artist tolerates the woman who makes delicate feminine pictures; but should he sense ideas, masculine strength or force of conviction, he feels his masculine territory has been violated. The worst insult he can inflict on a woman is to suggest that she paints like a man as he indifferently shrugs his shoulders. However, it seems to me that the responsibility of the artist lies in the fact that whatever his inner need dictates he must be willing to support it; irrespective of HOW MUCH of this energy can be translated into the masculine or feminine sex.

In human life it takes both sexes to reproduce the "One" living thing of creation. Creative life as experienced in the human mind, makes a unity out of multiplicity; — one side cannot be sacrificed for the other. The artist is his *work* — and his conscious attitude is a responsibility to these children of creation. He must follow the dictates of his heart no matter where it may lead him. . . .

I am now going to read from a manuscript which I have called "Eastward Journey." "Eastward Journey" is the underlying symbolic experience of my paintings which after twenty years produced a metaphysic. In the text of "Eastward Journey" I have tried to record this excursion of the mind through the dimensions of space using the symbol to guide me. I have only completed the first ten years — 1932–1942; when the flat landscape of the tactile eye disappeared and the landscape behind and beyond the horizon become visible. I hope that these sections convey some of the feeling of that dark sea which one travels in the black night with only the beating of one's heart to guide them.

Eastward Journey

All I can say is that for the most part one's work is a mysterious process. Its conscious reality may remain a secret for a long time; maybe forever. Every step is a real experience — the greatest joy — the profoundest anguish and sorrow. It is a lonely road, sometimes quite desolate. One must possess courage and strength to fulfill those inner experiences so they become living realities with a life of their own. Sometimes it is all darkness; one does not know where the last step ends and the new one begins. Follow irrespective of the dangers encountered. The secret — the key — the treasure lies hidden in the darkness of creation — the black mass of white light.

From 1932 to 1937 my work is really a feeling process of man in a machine world and trying to establish his position or rather my own position. The work is both personal and impersonal because I had to anchor myself first, build the generator for energy, construct the ship to sail the seas, launch it and then dock it in a harbor. . . .

From my experience in the Sahara Desert, I learned in reality that there were deep and intense areas of feeling which had a very profound meaning and could not be interpreted through objects. These feelings were incomprehensible, profound and mysterious, like nature itself; trying to penetrate the depths of these feelings, the living core or the source of them was unfathomable. The impact of those mysterious forces left me stunned and shattered for many months. . . .

. . . I became aware of the possibilities of pigment. I realized that it could produce light and luminosity. It opened up a new arena for me. Previously, apart from such things as shape, relationship and other elements pertaining to pictorial construction, I seemed to have confined myself to the closed in space occupied by the object. It was mostly translating volume into planes so they would operate on a flat surface, and of organizing the surrounding space. . . .

But it was not until 1950 that I understood the real meaning of that journey. I had to find my way first. I had to explore the external world with my own machinery. After 1938 my world was no longer what the eye could see. It was what the eye could feel, and light and space took on a real meaning. At the same time I had released myself from machinery, and the inner pendulum was swinging out a rhythm with an intensity I had never felt before. The rhythm seemed like time itself. And from that point on, I have listened to its breathing. Light which always had a profound meaning for me, now took the form of dedication and I felt lightness, like the breath of a song. An unexplainable something had happened. The feeling was like having a key to a secret. . . .

. . . It was this fallacy of vision which later led me to the three dimensional paintings using transparent materials. I did have a very deep inner conviction for many years thereafter, which seemed to beat — "Somewhere" . . . " Sometime"! "Light! Light!" "There is the light of day!" "There is a light defining God!" I would seem to answer — "The way! Show me the way!" A mysterious something pursued me like an evil beast and its shadow. If I had previously felt that I had released myself from the object, a lie existed somewhere in the darkness between me and the truth. I was haunted by some strange beat which acted like a hungry child preventing me from sleeping. Somewhere between the light and the darkness lived this famished soul and accused me of misdemeanors. During this period I wrote myself very many hungry poems. What this was like is unexplainable because I never got an answer. I was living on a desert pursuing a mirage and never finding water. The tired feet and the burning heart just cried out in the wastelands of experience and I seemed destined to listen to that beating. Man is so small, the world so large and the universe overwhelming. Space seemed separated into two independent parts. . . . One part floating in space; the other dark, dense and underground. I was this ghost of the object, separated, alone, wandering between heaven and hell on this barren night desert of feeling. I may have thought that I had buried the machine system in its ancient home of logic because it had robbed man of feeling, but the space it once occupied had now to be filled with meaning; otherwise the gap was an arid abyss seething with "nothing" as the object.

Why from this period on, I have used geometric symbols, I cannot answer. They make themselves from an inner rhythm. I never plan a picture, I am simply the medium for communication. It is only later I sometimes fathom the riddle. I do know they are symbolic structural essences of experience. The feeling is like going into an unknown region. Sometimes I come up with an answer. But most always it is a perplexing problem for when the symbols change I must delve deeper. Sometimes one gets a glimpse of the bridge to Eternity before it disappears like a rainbow. Somewhere between exaltation and despair lies the answer. . . .

I was also doing a lot of experimenting with light and shadow. The first successful one was called *Shadow and Painting*. I used one surface of glass; I left open spaces surrounding the shapes so I was able to see through the picture and watch how the linear places and movements cast real shadows. . . . These pictures certainly conveyed to me the meaning of shadow, but in order to produce this phenomenon the light had to be on the same plane with the spectator. . . .

At this period — 1941 — it was quite clear to me that the shadow is the phenomenon which is produced when the object gets into the path of light and deflects it. The shadow expresses an illusion and distortion of things. The boundaries of man's physical world have been set within a framework of what is known and measurable. . . .When there is no longer something as a point of reference in the distance everything vanishes. At that point the shadow turns back and produces an overcast picture of a flat dimension. The vanishing point obliterates what man sees beyond it and doesn't allow his feelings to trespass the boundaries. Everything that man cannot account for at the vanishing point turns back on him as his shadow.

How I personally managed to work in those years I do not know. My life was plunged into that same sea of darkness. *Composition in White* was produced while a dearly loved sister was dying. How one carries on inspite of physical and mental sorrow is one of the most incomprehensible mysteries of being an artist. To me this sister was the personification of Classic Greek beauty. She had an austerity and purity of feeling like the breathless instant of dewdrop. A vapored essence of the earth's night journey, only to be swallowed up by the sun in the morning. This was a loss that stunned me. . . .

. . . .When the picture [*Red, Yellow, and Blue*, 1942] was complete, I saw at a glance its meaning. I had found it. I had come back with an answer! The white center represented the timeless and inexhaustible enigma. It was unknown, unknowable, unmeasurable, unfathomable and endless; the sensation of the infinite — the absolute! This area on the canvas I carefully guarded thereafter. It was the never ending place of timelessness; the unknown quality of space. The space with no boundaries; no place and all places. It was everything and nothing. The unknown duality of nature. It was the extent of one's experience on a flat surface; the canvas itself; space itself; solitary, alone and unidentified. . . . The gate had opened and a realm which was deeper, inward, onward, upward and forward was visible to me. It was the landscape behind and beyond the tactile lie of perspective. It was what the eye perceives when it looks inward and feels a firmament set with the jewelled constellations of the time that is man. . . .

Personally I had to pay to redeem myself from the shadow. When I returned to life after a severe illness parts of myself were gone. I had to start all over and learn to use my right arm. But I was now slowly and surely recovering . . . .

I would like to end this lecture with a poem which I have dedicated to the hand that paints the picture. I have called the poem "The Hand That Draws the Heart." [later published in *The Crystal of The Rose*]

Rain from the eye
Pours into the heart.
The hand clasps the message

And brings it to earth.

What can be divined
From my hungry soul?
What is the tiding
From my invisible host?

My hand guides me
to that unknown place.

What does my heart see
In that sacred face?
The bird's bosom ablaze
With the ruby jewel
Of the cloud ready
to burst into song.

Rain from the eye
Flows into the heart.
The palm of the hand listens . . . . .

❖

FROM IRENE RICE PEREIRA, "FOREWORD"
LIGHT AND THE NEW REALITY (NEW YORK, 1952)

As a painter, I have been concerned with light for many years. As a result
of my explorations I now feel I am able to clarify and define what is a new
approach to the problem of light in relation to painting. It is rather difficult to
summarize my paper "Light and the New Reality," but I am convinced that the
light flow in painting is the key to a continuity of experience between Man and
Universe.

Somehow, in our frantic tempo, rushing to express new ideas, we have forgotten the light and let it remain in the same position as the spectator — the
position assigned to it when perspective was promulgated. Light is constant
and continuous in nature. Light is the missing link in pictorial construction
which will make the synthesis between inner reality (what man feels about
light) and outer reality (what man knows about light); otherwise he cannot
sense dimensions in space and time. This discrepancy between FEELING and
THINKING has prevented him from *really* experiencing infinite dimensions.

The circulation of light transports the perceptions, otherwise they become
frozen from extension. When perceptions become frozen from extension man
loses his balance; he experiences panic, anxiety, chaos . . . "Nothing" . . . "End."
He feels "Void." The circulation of light transports the perceptions and insures
their safe return to earth.

The paintings which I do in a number of layers of glass, plastics, and other
materials had to contain their own inner light and spatial dimensions so they
would make a complete continuity and move without weight, that is, the light
created its own movements depending on the angle of vision. They also had to

contain their own inner and independent light. I achieved this by the use of color.

Although I have known for many years that the light source must be in the depth of the picture plane, it was only more recently that I was able to translate these dimensions completely on a flat surface (canvas). When I finally solved the pictorial construction the energy struck bottom. I made the journey and the whole system also defined itself in words, pouring out faster than I could write.

When light is placed in its proper position on a flat surface COLOR itself goes back to its own source and becomes light again. If we consciously change the source of light in painting, that is, if we remove it from its customary position in the foreplane (where we *think* it now exists) and transfer it to the depth of the painting, or somewhere in the back plane, we shall have the light coming toward us. The experience is similar to that produced by pre-renaissance painting, or the feeling we have of light filtered through the transparency of stained glass windows. Some artists today may have a sense of light being fluid, but the position of light must be a conscious reality. Then, and then only, will the artist experience space and time and be able to create a new language without losing his balance.

I know you will ask me how I discovered this discrepancy between what we feel and what we think about light. All I can say is that for the most part one's work is a mysterious process. Its conscious reality may remain a secret for a long time; maybe forever. Every step is a real experience — the greatest joy — the profoundest anguish and sorrow. It is a lonely road, sometimes quite desolate. One must possess courage and strength to fulfil those inner experiences so they become living realities with a life of their own. Sometimes it is all darkness; one does not know where the last step ends and the new one begins. But the light within glows a path of dedication — you follow irrespective of the dangers encountered. The secret — the key —the treasure lies hidden in the darkness of creation — the black mass of white light.

❖

EXCERPTS FROM IRENE RICE PEREIRA
THE NATURE OF SPACE (New York, 1956)

Man not only lives on a physical plane in a world of nature, but also in a world impregnated with profound and mysterious forces. These forces evoke deep feelings in the heart of man and ignite his soul with questions to which his intuition tries to provide the answers. These inquiries flame up into the light and bring with them the darkness before creation. Man's senses are aroused by these "unknowns." They challenge his imagination as though holding the key which may unlock his secret hopes, his desires, his aspirations; always leading him on in the quest for knowledge. These elements of Being partake of divine essence. They are veiled by their nature of being "unknowable." Inspired by his intuition from this deep spring of creative essence, man soars to the heights of exaltation in an ever-expanding endeavor to enlarge the small portion of space allotted to him as his share in creation. . . .

The energy of this ideal symbolic space relates man to the abstract, intangible, universal forces of his own existence. This space appeals to man's capacity to intellectualize, to abstract essences and to form symbols. The symbol is the reality representing the whole content of the substance of experience; and has within it the amount of energy to form the structure of space. The symbol is the mind's method for revealing the quality and quantity of illuminative power available for translating that portion of substance which has the power of becoming known to consciousness, and for transforming the remainder of the content into a new symbol. . . .

An idea is "nothing" unless it can be objectified and given a structure of space in space. If the idea cannot be externalized, it remains as an abstraction of something assumed to exist and can only be acted upon or speculated upon. It will never have reality, since it never had existence. If it does not have existence, it does not have dimensions. Without dimensions, the idea does not have extensions in space. If an idea is static in space, it can only be speculated upon.

The symbolic reference expresses the whole content of the substance of experience and is the authoritative source toward which the mind directs its energy. In this way, a space of contemplation is formed between the thought and what can be known about the thought. The participant, or the personification of the thought, is one's self as the mediator between the "unknown" and what can be known. The amount of energy activated by the thought, or idea, will form the structure of space in the mind to support the seed of the idea. . . .

❖

FROM IRENE RICE PEREIRA, *THE CRYSTAL OF THE ROSE* (1959)

EXCERPTS FROM "INTRODUCTION"

. . . It should not be necessary for an artist to have to explain or give reasons for the extracurricular activities of his spirit. The need of the spirit is unity and the absolute goal of its own perfection. Therefore, it is not unusual for this spirit to go on a philosophical excursion; embark on a rainbow; cross the sea's delight; and, becoming attached to a speck of cosmic dust, hitch a ride onward and upward to catch a glimpse of the infinity of time. . . .

An artist is committed to his destiny. Once he crosses the Rubicon he personally assumes the responsibility for his convictions. He has no choice but dedication to his work. The work must be kept free and moving, regardless of all obstacles. There is no either/or for the creative spirit. It is unconditioned. The spirit lives and grows and sustains itself in the light of day — above ground. . . . The spirit does not flourish in an atmosphere contaminated by the irrationality of the mindless; or the decadence of conformist tyranny. The bird that sings does not permit itself to be caught and caged for the amusement of its captors. The spirit flies above — in sight — but out of reach of those who do not make an effort to understand the heart of creative freedom.

❖

"Crystal of the Rose"
Part One
> We live together now
> You are alive
> inside of me.
> I shall always

treat you tenderly
and lovingly.
I now feel You.

You are the object.
You are the reality
of my feelings.
You are a bridge.
I can soar the heights
and swim the depths
because You are a bridge,
a gleaming suspension bridge.

You are a white stallion, too,
a brave, prancing stallion.
You are me,
You, me, bridge, stallion,
together we make
the dangerous crossing
over the rough turbulent waters.

We reach the other side.
I say to You,
There are rivers, too
but when they cannot
find their way to the sea
they become dry rivers
and dry rivers are sand.

In the center
is the diamond
and the rivers flow
and the brilliance
of the diamond
matches the radiance
of the sun.
Then all multiplicity
merges and becomes
One
because You are a bridge —
the reconciling structure.

Then what are You
in relation to me
that You have become
a bridge —
a shining silver structure

and your silver glory
matches the sun?

Now You become a
silver chalice
in the middle
of the sun.
And the molten chalice
becomes mercury.
You are now mercury
and when I feel You
You become a fluid.

Now I make
the dangerous voyage
to the sun
and back to earth
because You are
mercury.
Outside of me
your heels have wings
and when You flow
back inside of me
You are fluid.

February 14, 1950

❖

Speak to me eternity
eternally, eternally.
You are a light
I cannot see
you are a feeling light.
The eye inside told me so
an eye whose center
glistens gold,
an eye who sees a soul,
an eye who feels a rose. . . .

Grow Rose — Rose Grow!
In your diamond nest
crystal nest
of feelings jewels.
Now you shine
from within.
You are the radiance
of eternity
my feeling rose

of precious stones.
Eternally, eternity
it makes You.

Dewdrop
you contained
the secret of my love.
Is that why
you glisten there
with a rainbow
from above?
Now you told me
now I know.
I must now
transport you
to the sun.
To Thou on high
my secret goes.
Rainbow, dewdrop
dewdrop — Rose
rainbow — crystal
of the Rose.

February 20, 1950

❖

"The Lake's Dream"
The bird of light
and the wind of the sun
meet in the lake's dream.

The still face of the lake's dream
stirred by memories of the past
reflects time passed in its waters.

The earth of springs
marries them in a fountain.
The murmuring union of their love
ripples forever with laughter.

May 15, 1953

❖

EXCERPTS FROM IRENE RICE PEREIRA
THE POETICS OF FORM, SPACE, LIGHT AND THE INFINITE (1969)

"The Creative Light-giving Form"
THE CREATIVE LIGHT-GIVING FORM
having been impregnated

at its birth with an
eternal nuclear seed
of infinite and immutable power
that ever-conceives itself,
is ever-evolving
the FORM of itself.

CONSECRATED in the dim mist
of the unknown dark, the
unconditioned light-giving core,
has an affinity with,
a correspondence to
and a magnetic longing to
return to the primordial blaze
that was once the spring
of its own creative source.
Hence,
its movement is eternally
magnetically attracted toward
the Prime Source of its own Cause.

DORMANT, BUT INCUBATING,
pulsating and vibrating in
horizontal and vertical rays;
the creative light-giving Form
— the nuclear core of
the matter of the mind —
spheres itself as it informs itself
so as to release itself from
the immobilizing spell of
that which binds it to the inert
and concrete and free itself
so as to realize itself
and evolve the FORM of itself.

MAN BEARS THE SILENCE
of the majestic night
until the ringing light
bursts the inarticulate
impregnated shell
igniting the dark abyss
with the constellations
that illuminate and sphere
the unknown regions of
his own nature as the
light of consciousness
is Caused to reflect itself

on the undulating face
of the sparkling waters
as consciousness is informed. . . .

❖

"The Harmonics of Form"

Ultimately
man stands, as a subject and
participant in his own matter,
between the 'unknown' and
what can become 'known.'
Man is in the center of
the harmonics of the
sphere of the Whole;
in the center of
the throbbing heart of
his own nuclear core;
the same pulsating,
vibrating Cause that propagates
the light that illuminates;
gives life and FORM to all of nature;
the homogeneous Light of Reality;
the Cause of the Cosmic Reason
— the living harmonics of
                    LIGHT and FORM . . .

❖

"THE FORM OF BEAUTY"

Beauty nestles
        in the arms
        of the Absolute
        awaiting 'Your' grace.

Sphere the passion
        before the flame dies!
Gather the myriads
        of moistured spheres
        from the infinitudes
        of those majestic fields!

Trembling and drunk
        with the twinkling
        dizzy flight;
'Your' songs I see
        sown in the meadows
        of revolving celestial light.

Can one dare to suppose

what the throbbing heart
    already knows?

Furled
    in the wild trajectories
    of 'Your' rays
    I spin cross-cross the night
    punctuating day.

Now
    whirling homeward
    round the turn,
    A beam I sphere
    and cross the sun.

Gloria in excelsis
    inviolate
    involute
    evolute
    and Absolute
I sphere 'Your' blazing name.

February 9, 1963

❖

"The Birth of a Star"
    O, radiant portent —
deathless omen of
steepling exultation —
unhinge the powers!
Unlock the portals!
Pierce the silence!
Cascade the voice!

O, effluvia
of the Milky Way,
brim the big dipper
of Ursa Major's bowl!

Sweep the heavenly dome
with the lilting music of
the dizzy constellations'
burning gaze; breasts aflame
with the frenzied passion
of the primordial blaze!

Impregnate the haze!

Thunder,
bolt the breathless space!

O, there you are,
in gleaming lace,
Phosphor,
Phosphor,
Phosphor,
The Morning Star.

Courtesy of Djelloul Marbrook, nephew of the artist.

Curved Form with Inner Form (Anima), 1959. Bronze (edition of seven). 27¾" l.
Everson Museum of Art, Syracuse, N.Y., Gift of Mr. and Mrs. Robert C. Hosmer

BARBARA HEPWORTH

1903–1975

FROM THE TIME she was a child growing up in Yorkshire, England, Barbara Hepworth identified strongly with the surrounding landscape. As an artist, the major theme of her work was the close relationship between the human body and the earth, which she expressed through biomorphically abstract sculptural forms. To Hepworth, nature was a living, vibrating entity of which she was a part and from which she received her inspiration. Hepworth wrote about her method of working within a studio that was "a jumble of children, rocks, sculptures, trees, importunate flowers and washing," a work space that seems remarkably in tune with the organic quality of her sculpture. Like Käthe Kollwitz and Elizabeth Catlett, Hepworth provides a rare example of a woman artist whose artistic vision was nourished by life within a family. She was drawn to the relationship between people and the organic world, rather than to the interactions between humans. Hepworth expressed her deep involvement with nature in an abstract style, as did Emily Carr and Georgia O'Keeffe. But, unlike those two painters, she purged her work of practically all referential and descriptive elements. Although Hepworth was not a prolific writer, she lucidly articulated her thoughts concerning her art and life, and the intersections of the two, in several theoretical essays and an informal autobiography.

The oldest child of a land surveyor, Hepworth perceived her affinity for the landscape at an early age, when traveling through Yorkshire with her father as he made tours of inspection. Her penchant for the visual arts was encouraged when she attended the Wakefield Girls' High School, a lecture about Egyptian sculpture by her headmistress initially "fired [her] off" when she was seven. Throughout her life, Hepworth continued to be influenced by the simplified, organic, and volumetric aspects of non–Western sculptural styles, including the Cycladic and African as well as Egyptian. At sixteen she won a scholarship to the Leeds School of Art and, the following year, she was awarded another, to the Royal College of Art in London, for the study of sculpture. Henry Moore, five years her senior, was her fellow student, first at Leeds and then at the Royal College of Art, and the two became colleagues with similar aesthetic concerns. At the time they were students, the nineteenth-century attitude expressed by Harriet Hosmer, among others — that the creative aspect of sculpture was in the conception not the execution — still prevailed. Although only clay modeling was routinely taught, both Hepworth and Moore felt the need to seek instruction in methods of direct carving. Over the years, they developed a credo of "truth to materials," in which they attempted to preserve and articulate in the finished work the essential nature of the medium.

Upon graduation from the Royal College of Art, Hepworth received a grant from the Yorkshire County Council for a year of travel abroad. She headed for Italy, long a mecca for young artists, particularly sculptors, where she found the light at dawn "wonderful," especially after "three years of London smog." Although she produced no art for the Council (which she described as "unforgiveable"), the Italian landscape had an enduring impact on her work. It was typical of Hepworth's affinities that she was more moved by the land than by Italy's cultural artifacts. After almost a year in Italy, Hepworth married the English sculptor John Skeaping, who had been studying at the British School in Rome. They remained in Rome for two more years, until Skeaping's health necessitated a return home. During this time both studied marble carving and Hepworth learned the mechanics of moving weights at the famed quarries of Carrara. Whereas nineteenth-century sculptors had used the skill of Italian artisans to execute their pieces, Hepworth wanted to learn the nearly-lost art of carving from the artisans so that she could work directly in stone.

After her return to London late in 1926, Hepworth began to move into the early mature period of her artistic career. Her works from this stage are small-scale, organically abstracted figures that capture a general, universal gesture, typified by the 1929 wood carving of her infant son, Paul, raising his hands to his head. The first one-artist public exhibition of her works was held in 1927; she exhibited every few years for the rest of her career. After Hepworth's first marriage ended, she began her twenty-year association with the abstract painter Ben Nicholson, whom she married in 1931.

During the 1930s Hepworth was particularly productive and her sphere of influence broadened. With Nicholson she became closely associated with an international group of abstract artists, including not only her former schoolmate Henry Moore, but other major sculptural innovators of the early twentieth century, including Constantin Brancusi, Naum Gabo, Jean Arp and his wife the painter Sophie Taüber-Arp, and Piet Mondrian, who was their neighbor in London for two years preceding the war. All these artists used the common language of abstract form. Hepworth participated in several international exhibitions during this time and contributed to two publications in which the members of this artistic community presented their aesthetic theories: the 1934 manifesto entitled *Unit One*, edited by Herbert Read, and the 1937 *Circle*, edited by Nicholson, Gabo, and J. L. Martin.

In 1934, the Hepworth-Nicholson household was substantially augmented by the birth of triplets. The Second World War followed some years later and, although Hepworth was able to continue her work to a limited degree, the war interrupted the development of her career. In 1939, just before the war began, the family left London for St. Ives in Cornwall, a part of England long known for its community of artists. (Gabo, who had already fled Europe, moved with his family to Cornwall at roughly the same time.) During the war, most of Hepworth's daytime hours were devoted to survival, running a nursery for the children and cultivating a garden so they could all eat. Only at night was she able to draw. In 1943, after living for several years with friends, the family moved into their own house and Hepworth resumed sculpting, though she had no separate studio space. Although the move to Cornwall had been necessitated by adverse circumstances, its impact on Hepworth's work was extremely positive. Always sensitive to landscape, she discovered that the particular interrelationship of land, sea, and sky in Cornwall held a special resonance for her. It became her artistic subject and source for the remainder of her life.

After the war ended, Hepworth reached the height of her creative stride. In 1949 she was able to purchase the Trewyn studio in St. Ives that gave her room to work on the larger scale her sculptures had always suggested. The early 1950s also brought two upheavals in her personal life: separation from Ben Nicholson in 1951 and the death of her first son, a pilot with the Royal Air Force who crashed over Thailand in 1953. By 1954, the year of her major retrospective at the Whitechapel Gallery in London, she was moving toward even more creative growth despite these traumas. A trip to Greece that year had a significant impact on her future work. She responded profoundly to the landscape, which she saw reflected in the art and architecture of the Greeks, as can be seen in the notes that form her "Greek Diary." That year, too, she began to work in bronze.

During the last twenty years of her life, Hepworth remained professionally active, continuing to gain recognition and reaping some rewards for her achievements. She was awarded several honorary degrees including a doctorate from Oxford University, was made a Member of the British Empire in 1958, and a Bard of Cornwall in 1968, choosing "Gravyor" (sculptor) as her bardic name. In 1959 she won first prize at the São Paulo Biennial in Brazil. Tragically, she died in 1975 in a fire in her studio, trapped by her arthritic condition.

Hepworth's most dramatic period of stylistic development occurred during the 1930s. In *Pierced Form* (1931) she first broke a hole through a solid mass, creating a visual metaphor for the intrinsic connectedness of figure/ground and exterior/interior. As she explained, the pierced hole allowed the viewer bodily entry into the sculpture. This was a theme that she continued to develop for the remainder of her life. The birth of her triplets in 1934 had a notable impact on her style. When she resumed working about a month after their birth, she abandoned the naturalistic style that had characterized her work while pregnant, and which she had used to explore the mother-child relationship. Her works from the mid-thirties are more dependent on juxtapositions of pure geometric forms than on referential elements. Although subsequently her forms became more organic, only the most generally referential elements appeared from the mid-thirties on. The impact of Constructivism, via her close friendship with Naum Gabo, can be seen in Hepworth's work from the later 1930s. Her drawings from this period are characterized by a crystalline quality, the crystal with its multidirectional facets becoming an important artistic subject for her. Another of her stylistic innovations of this period, also related to constructivism, was the addition of painted colors and woven strings to her sculptures. These elements emphasized the hollowed complexity of the sculptures' interiors; rather than hiding the natural wood surface, the paint emphasized its grain. By the outbreak of the Second World War, Hepworth had begun to synthesize the fluidity that characterized her works from the 1920s with the geometric forms of her pieces from the later 1930s.

After the war Hepworth returned to many of her earlier themes, though they seemed more stylistically developed because she was finally able to execute her ideas in large scale. She also began experimenting with bronze-casting. Although the complexity of this process might have seemed to contradict her "truth to materials" aesthetic, she found a way of translating organic experience into her bronzes, so that their pocked surfaces appeared to have been subjected to the same process through which the sea and sun transform stones into sand. Bronze-casting allowed her to work on an even larger scale than before, and to explore the flow between the interior and exterior of forms with greater flexibility, as in *Curved Form: Anima* (1954), in which she created tension through a dynamic, multilayered series of enclosures.

Barbara Hepworth was a major artist who had a significant impact on the art of her own times, as an active participant in a group of abstract artists who built a modernist style from the aesthetic explorations of the early twentieth century. In the context of British modernism, she was a particularly pivotal figure and her revival of direct carving and the use of pierced forms were major contributions to twentieth-century sculpture. It is therefore disconcerting to encounter some sexist treatment of her achievements in art historical writings. Despite their parallel development, Hepworth's colleague Henry Moore is usually accorded a higher position than she: his achievements are discussed at greater length in most histories of British sculpture, and some critics have erroneously suggested that Hepworth was Moore's student. Furthermore, while it is clear that historian J. P. Hodin has great respect for Hepworth, his monograph on her work nonetheless claims that it is "remarkable" for a woman to have an impact on the art of her time, especially in what he refers to as "the most masculine" of arts, sculpture.

Hepworth did not deal directly with such issues, but her gender bore an important relationship to both the pattern of her life and the content of her art. Hepworth's life departed from the stereotype of artistic creation as a selfish, lonely process, with the artist sacrificing personal needs in order to succeed. In her writings and in taped conversations, Hepworth asserted that "a woman artist was not diminished by having children" and that the mundane aspects of daily life within a family were "nourishing . . . provided one always does some work each day." Only recently have such feminist critics as Ursula LeGuin accepted what Hepworth found to be true, and presented their own arguments that a woman artist's connection to life and its processes can enhance her art rather than detracting from it, that motherhood and, for example, authorhood can be two sides of the creative self.

Hepworth's method of sculpting and her reason for making art are consistent with her desire to live in touch with life's rhythms. Sculpting was a means of affirming her connection to the earth, for, as she said, "You can't make a sculpture without involving your body. You move and you feel and you breathe and you touch." Her art resonates with an organic quality, like the ebb and flow of tides. In fact, Hepworth saw her sculptures as "objects that came out of the land or the sea mysteriously." In a conversation in 1952 she said, "I am convinced that . . . we shall lose our capacity to live unless we feel at one with all the rocks and the timelessness of life, with perpetual movement and rebirth." Many of her carvings suggest the megaliths of prehistoric worship sites, reminiscent of the many sacred rock groupings found all over western Cornwall. She called several of her earlier pieces "menhirs" (ancient monumental standing stones), and one of her last works is a large group entitled *Conversation of Sacred Stones.* Throughout her life and art, Hepworth embodied a way of being and seeing that was rooted in the female experience of connectedness to humans, plants, earth, and sky, a mythic pattern recognized by Estella Lauter in twentieth-century women's art.

Hepworth did not use the written word as a form of creative exploration, as did some other artists included in this volume, but her writings nevertheless provide insight into her artwork. Some of her essays are consolidated in her *Pictorial Autobiography* (1970), an informal piece written in a down-to-earth, chatty style, and including photographic documentation. Though loose in structure, this autobiography follows the pattern of more formal ones in being a public statement in which the author puts her best foot, and her chosen view of herself, forward. (A more discursive exploration of her feelings than Hepworth elects to make, particularly those engendered by raising triplets or by losing her son, would have been welcome.) Excerpts in which Hepworth discusses her working method and way of life are included here.

Hepworth articulated her aesthetic theories in the pieces she wrote for *Unit One*, *Circle*, and *Studio Magazine.* In these writings, she was particularly convincing concerning her preference for abstraction, writing that she "did not want to make a stone horse that is trying to but cannot smell the air." Instead, she would rather "make exactly the right relation of masses, a living thing in stone" to express her love of natural forms and beings. She also described her method, in which she first searched for the right material to embody her idea, then allowed the material to assert itself while she responded with her bodily attention, describing her left hand as her "listening hand" which felt the pulse of the material as her right hand carved.

In the final analysis, her writings provide theoretical support for an interpretation of her works that stresses their life-affirming, biophilic aspects. On many occasions Hepworth expressed her visceral connection to certain landscapes — particularly Yorkshire, Cornwall, and Greece — a connection she viewed as a passionate, organic experience, common to all life. For Hepworth, the interrelationship between humans and the landscape they inhabit was central, primitive, magical, and sacred. Expressing that relationship was her purpose in making sculpture.

SOURCES

Alley, Ronald. *Barbara Hepworth, Exhibition at the Tate Gallery.* London: Lund, Humphries, 1968.

Hammacher, A. M. *The Sculpture of Barbara Hepworth.* New York: Harry N. Abrams, 1968.

Hepworth, Barbara. *A Pictorial Autobiography.* New York: Praeger Publishers, 1970.

_____ "Approach to Sculpture." *The Studio*, 132:643 (October 1946): 97–101.

_____. "Greek Diary." In *J. P. Hodin, European Critic*. Edited by Walter Kern. London: Cory, Adams and Mackay, 1965.

Hodin, J. P. *Barbara Hepworth*. Boston: Boston Book and Art Shop, 1961.

Lauter, Estella. *Women as Mythmakers: Poetry and Visual Art by Twentieth-Century Women*. Bloomington: Indiana University Press, 1984.

BARBARA HEPWORTH, EXCERPT FROM *UNIT ONE* (1934)

Carving is interrelated masses conveying an emotion; a perfect relationship between the mind and the colour, light and weight which is the stone, made by the hand which feels. It must be so essentially sculpture that it can exist in no other way, something completely the right size but which has growth, something still and yet having movement, so very quiet and yet with a real vitality. A thing so sculpturally good that the smallest section radiates the intensity of the whole and the spatial displacement is as lovely as the freed and living stone shape.

I do not want to make a stone horse that is trying to and cannot smell the air. How lovely is the horse's sensitive nose, the dog's moving ears and deep eyes; but to me these are not stone forms and the love of them and the emotion can only be expressed in more abstract terms. I do not want to make a machine that cannot fulfill its essential purpose; but to make exactly the right relation of masses, a living thing in stone, to express my awareness and thought of these things.

❖

"SCULPTURE"
FROM *CIRCLE*, 1937

Abstract is a word which is now most frequently used to express only the type of the outer form of a work of art; this makes it difficult to use it in relation to the spiritual vitality of inner life which is the real sculpture. Abstract sculptural qualities are found in good sculpture of all time, but it is significant that contemporary sculpture and painting have become abstract in thought and concept. As the sculptural idea is in itself unfettered and unlimited and can choose its own forms, the vital concept selects the form and substance of its expression quite unconsciously.

Contemporary constructive work does not lose by not having particular human interest, drama, fear or religious emotion. It moves us profoundly because it represents the whole of the artist's experience and vision, his whole sensibility to enduring ideas, his whole desire for a realization of these ideas in life and a complete rejection of the transitory and local forces of destruction. It is an absolute belief in man, in landscape and in the universal relationship of constructive ideas. . . .

A constructive work is an embodiment of freedom itself, and is unconsciously perceived even by those who are consciously against it. The desire to live is the strongest universal emotion, it springs from the depths of our unconscious sensibility — and the desire to give life is our most potent, constructive, conscious expression of this intuition.

❖

"APPROACH TO SCULPTURE"
FROM *THE STUDIO* 132: 643 (OCTOBER 1946)

I have always been interested in oval or ovoid shapes. The first carvings were simple realistic oval forms of the human head or of a bird. Gradually my interest grew in more abstract values — the weight, poise and curvature of the ovoid as a basic form. The carving and piercing of such a form seems to open up an infinite variety of continuous curves in the third dimension, changing in accordance with the contours of the original ovoid and with the degree of penetration of the material. Here is sufficient field for exploration to last a lifetime. . . . The satisfaction to be found in carving is in the pleasure of fresh impact of shape and in the joy of attack on different material.

I like to have a lot of material lying about the studio for a long time — even for years — so that I feel intimate with each piece. An idea comes and the right piece of wood or stone — the absolutely right piece — must be found for it, and it is the greatest hardship for a sculptor to be short of material.

Before I start carving the idea must be almost complete. I say "almost" because the really important thing seems to be the sculptor's ability to let his intuition guide him over the gap between conception and realization without comprominsg the integrity of the original idea; the point being that the material has vitality — it resists and makes demands. . . . I think a new discipline has to be discovered with each new sculpture, and that is why I do not feel in sympathy with any theories and disciplines imposed from outside. . . .

I do not like using mechanical devices or automatic tools. Even if the work was done ten times more easily I should miss the physical pleasure of direct contact with every part of the form from the beginning to the end.

I have been deeply interested during the last ten years in the use of colour with form. I have applied oil colour — white, grey, and blues of different degrees of tone. Except in two instances I have always used colour with concave forms. When applied to convex forms I have felt that the colour appeared to be "applied" instead of becoming inherent in the formal idea. I have been very influenced by the natural colour and luminosity in stones and woods and the change in colour as light travels over the surface contours. When I pierced the material right through a great change seemed to take place in the concavities from which direct light was excluded. From this experience my use of colour developed.

One can experience the colour change in nature in a cave, a forest or a pool and sense similar change in the emotional effect of all forms when the quantity and quality of light playing upon it changes. . . .

It is difficult to say how much time is spent in conceiving a project. I like to work all day and every day; the major part of the time is spent in actually carving, but all the time I am not working I am thinking about sculpture. Looking out of a window or walking down the road it is impossible not to be aware of form and colour. Then a new project suddenly appears, and demands realisation as a result of accumulated emotional experience. The carving process is a slow process and the conceiving of a project seems to spring more out of a general and sustained experience than one particular incident. Consequently the carrying out of one idea and the conception of new ideas usually run concurrently.

I have gained very great inspiration from the Cornish land- and sea-scape, the horizontal line of the sea and the quality of light and colour which reminds me of the Mediterranean light and colour which so excites one's sense of form; and first and last there is the human figure which in the country becomes a free and moving part of a greater whole. This relationship between figure and landscape is vitally important to me. I cannot feel it in a city.

❖

"A SCULPTOR'S LANDSCAPE"
FROM STUDIO INTERNATIONAL 171 (JUNE 1966)

I cannot write anything about landscape without writing about the human figure and the human spirit inhabiting the landscape. For me, the whole art of sculpture is the fusion of these two elements — the balance of sensation and the evocation of man in his universe.

Every work in sculpture is either a figure I see, or a sensation I have, whether in Yorkshire, Cornwall or Greece, or the Mediterranean.

Whenever I am embraced by land and seascape I draw ideas for new sculptures: new forms to touch and walk around, new people to embrace, with an exactitude of form that those without sight can hold and realize. For me it is the same as the touch of a child in health, not in sickness. The feel of a loved person who is strong and fierce and not tired and bowed down. This is not an aesthetic doctrine, nor is it a mystical idea. It is essentially practical and passionate.

Sculpture is to me an affirmative statement of our will to live: whether it be small, to rest in the hand; or larger, to be embraced; or larger still, to force us to move around it and establish our rhythm of life. Sculpture is, in the twentieth century, a wide field of experience, with many facets of symbol and material and individual calligraphy. But in all these varied and exciting extensions of our experience we always come back to the fact that we are human beings of such and such a size, biologically the same as primitive man, and that it is through drawing and observing, or observing and drawing, that we equate our bodies with our landscape.

❖

ON "CURVED FORM (TREVALGAN)"

This "Curved Form" was conceived on the hill called Trevalgan between St. Ives and Zenor where the land of Cornwall ends and cliffs divide as they touch the sea facing west.

At this point, facing the setting sun across the Atlantic, where sky and sea blend with hills and rocks, the forms seem to enfold the watcher and lift him towards the sky.

❖

FROM BARBARA HEPWORTH, "GREEK DIARY"
FROM J.P. HODIN, EUROPEAN CRITIC (LONDON: CORY, ADAMS, AND MACKAY, 1965)

GREECE
COLOURS
Indigo sea which when light reflects from cliffs, becomes

pure cerulean.
This indian red and pink hills — monastral purple mountains
at sunset which intensifies the greens to the wildest
vitality.

The Acropolis — the spaces between the columns — the depth
of flutings to touch — the breadth, weight and volume —
the magnificence of a single marble bole up-ended.
The passionate warm colour of the marble and all-pervading
philosophic proportion and space.

25.8.54

❖

DELOS

Ascended Kynthos alone, the cave of Apollo — half-way magnificent
and majestic. A pool with fine fig trees nearby full of giant
(sacred?) toads — leaping and barking. Also green frogs.

Went on alone up the last steep ascent but the wind was angry —
ferocious. I fell, my hair was nearly whisked off my head —
my clothes nearly torn off me. I bowed to the will of the gods
and descended.

Saw a magnificent Koros — tall, fierce and passionate bigger than
life size — in the Museum. A heavenly work — the back and buttocks
in relation to the hip and waist — an inspiration. I thought the
fragment of leg and calf (attached below the knee) was falsely
attributed. Fine Minoan ivories — especially the warrior with
double shield.

Delos was perturbed — an angry wind — making it difficult to return
to Miaoulis. . . .

26.8.54

❖

EXCERPTS FROM BARBARA HEPWORTH
A PICTORIAL AUTOBIOGRAPHY
(NEW YORK: PRAEGER PUBLISHERS, 1970)

ON HER CHILDHOOD IN YORKSHIRE

All my early memories are of forms and shapes and textures. Moving
through and over the West Riding landscape with my father in his car, the hills
were sculptures; the roads defined the form. Above all, there was the sensation
of moving physically over the contours of fulnesses and concavities, through
hollows and over peaks – feeling, touching, seeing, through mind and hand and
eye. This sensation has never left me. I, the sculptor, *am* the landscape. I am
the form and I am the hollow, the thrust and the contour.

Feelings about ideas and people and the world all about us struggle inside
me to find the evocative symbol affirming these early and secure sensations –
the feeling of the magic of man in a landscape, whether it be a pastoral image
or a miner squatting in the rectangle of his door or the 'Single form' of a mill-
girl moving against the wind, with her shawl wrapped round her head and

body. On the lonely hills a human figure has the vitality and the poignancy of all man's struggles in this universe.

ON THE COMPATIBILITY OF ART, MARRIAGE AND CHILDREN

This was a wonderfully happy time. My son Paul was born, and, with him in his cot, or on a rug at my feet, my carving developed and strengthened.

I did not see what was happening to us after our second show together at Tooths in New Bond Street. Quite suddenly we were out of orbit. I had an obsession for my work and my child and my home. John wanted to go free, and he bought a horse which used to breathe through my kitchen window!

There was no ill-feeling – we fell apart, and finally John remarried and had a country estate and three wonderful sons. John was always kind to me and still is; we keep in touch from time to time.

Friends and relations always said to me that it was impossible to be dedicated to any art and enjoy marriage and children. This is untrue, as I had nearly thirty years of wonderful family life; but I will confess that the dictates of work are as compelling for a woman as for a man. Not competitively, but as complementary, and this is only just being realised. . . .

This was a period of real maturity. I met Ben Nicholson, and as painter and sculptor each was the other's best critic. We visited Happisburgh and gathered stones to carve, and drew and painted. With us were Henry Moore and his wife Irena, Ivon Hitchens and my great friends Mary and Douglas Jenkins. Henry carved and I carved and my son Paul played on the beach. Work shaped up more and more strongly, and I prepared for my 1932 exhibition with Ben, and Herbert Read wrote my foreword. This was the beginning of a period of what the late Sir Herbert Read called 'a gentle nest of artists' through the 1930's in Hampstead. Sir Herbert was gentle, and I think we all were because we were free and totally and individually dedicated. They were hard times but so happy. . . .

These 'working holidays' at Happisburgh were wonderful. We talked and walked, we bathed and played cricket, then we worked and danced. I think this idea of a working holiday was established in my mind very early indeed. My father took us each year to Robin Hood's Bay to stay in a house on the lovely beach. At high tide the waves thumped on the house and spray fell all around us on the balconies. I was always in a state of great excitement. My room was the right hand attic and here I laid out my paints and general paraphernalia and crept out at dawn to collect stones, seaweeds and paint, and draw by myself before somebody organised me! This pattern was repeated in Norfolk, and later in Greece, and several times in the Isles of Scilly.

It made a firm foundation for my working life — and it formed my idea that a woman artist is not deprived by cooking and having children, nor by nursing children with measles (even in triplicate) — one is in fact nourished by this rich life, provided one always does some work each day; even a single half hour, so that the images grow in one's mind.

I detest a day of no work, no music, no poetry. . . .

My own work went well. Carving became increasingly rhythmical, and I was aware of the special pleasure that sculptors can have through carving, that of a complete unity of physical and mental rhythm. It seemed to be the most natural occupation in the world. It is perhaps strange that I should have become aware of this at the moment when the forms themselves had become the absolute reverse of all that was arbitrary – when there had developed a deliberate conception of form and relationship.

The children prospered and grew and laughed. They had a terrific sense of fun. The red-letter days were when Gabo or Calder, and later, Mondrian, came to share nursery tea. Three pairs of eyes would watch every movement, and three pairs of ears listen to every word.

Circle was published at last. Mondrian had made his studio opposite so very beautiful, and his company was always inspiring, as it had been in Paris when we used to visit him. After a while he really seemed to enjoy our domestic scene. His studio and Ben's were most austere, but my studio was a jumble of children, rocks, sculptures, trees, importunate flowers and washing.

❖

ON THE HUMAN FIGURE IN RELATION TO THE LANDSCAPE AND THE COSMOS

I am not scientifically minded; but the forces between the everchanging position of the sun and moon, and the effects upon sea and tide, and cloud and wind, which change the depth of shadow on forms have governed my life for a long time.

I began to get more and more turn-tables and to try to assess my own changing movements in relations to the sun.

Piercing through forms became dominant. Could I climb through and in what direction? Could I rest, lie or stand within the forms? Could I, at one and the same time, be the outside as well as the form within? . . .

. . . I would like to be an astronaut and go round the moon, and maybe remain in orbit for ever. But I would not like to land in case the light of the moon went out forever and all poetry die and deeper anguish descend on this anguished earth. But my son Paul once told me that there was a new aesthetic in flying and space and maybe these many brave men will guide us.

❖

The reason why people move differently and stand differently in direct response to changed surroundings; the unconscious grouping of people when they are working together, producing a spatial movement that approximates to the structure of spirals in shells or rhythms in crystal structure; the meaning of the spaces between forms, or the shape of the displacement of forms in space, which in themselves have a most precise significance. All these responses spring from a factual and tactile approach to the object — whether it be the feeling of landscape that one feels beneath one's feet or the sensitivity of the hand in carving, or in surgery, or music, and they have an organic and perceptual purpose.

All landscape needs a figure — and when a sculptor is the spectator he is aware that every landscape evokes a special image. In creating this image the artist tries to find a synthesis of his human experience and the quality of the land-scape. The forms and piercings, the weight and poise of the concrete image also become evocative – a fusion of experience and myth.

ON CONFRONTING THE WORK OF JEAN ARP AND PICASSO

We visited Meudon to see Jean Arp and though, to our disappointment, he was not there his wife, Sophie Taüber-Arp, showed us his studio. It was very quiet in the room so that one was aware of the movement in the forms. All the sculptures appeared to be in plaster, dead white, except for some early reliefs in wood painted white with sharp accents of black, and the next day, as we travelled on the train to Avignon, I thought about the poetic idea in Arp's sculptures. I had never had any first-hand knowledge of the Dadaist movement, so that seeing his work for the first time freed me of many inhibitions and this helped me to see the figure in landscape with new eyes. I stood in the corridor almost all the way looking out on the superb Rhone valley and thinking of the way Arp had fused landscape with the human form in so extraordinary a manner. Perhaps in freeing himself from material demands his idea transcended all possible limitations. I began to imagine the earth rising and becoming human. I speculated as to how I was to find my own identification, as a human being and a sculptor, with the landscape around me. . . .

ON HER TRIPLETS

On October 3rd Ben and I went to the cinema in Belsize Park, and my life–long friend Margaret Gardiner had supper with us. Ben had complained a little bit that I seemed withdrawn and concentrated over my pregnancy. But suddenly I said 'Oh dear,' and in next to no time I saw three small children at the foot of my bed – looking pretty determined and fairly belligerent. This was an event even my doctor did not suspect, and we had only a basement flat, no washing in the garden, and a kitchen–bathroom, and 20 in the bank and only one cot.

Ben was superb. The day before he had done a three–form white relief. At dawn he did another relief. He was a tower of strength, and rang round our immediate friends at dawn, who said 'Shut up Ben, this is no time for jokes.'

I, myself, knew fear for the first time in my life, as I was very weak, and wondered how on earth we were to support this family on white reliefs and the carving I was doing.

Ben was entirely right and, supported by his faith, our work strengthened in the right direction, and miraculously we made our way, due to the wonderful help given to us by our friends and patrons.

The children were an inspiration, each one giving us a very great joy.

❖

ON THE INTER-RELATIONSHIP BETWEEN MATERIAL AND FORM

In sculpture there must be a complete realisation of the structure and quality of the stone or wood which is being carved. But I do not think that this alone supplies the life and vitality of sculpture. I believe that the understanding of the material and the meaning of the form being carved must be in perfect equilibrium. There are fundamental shapes which speak at all times and periods in the language of sculpture.

It is difficult to describe in words the meaning of forms because it is precisely this emotion which is conveyed by sculpture alone. Our sense of touch is a fundamental sensibility which comes into action at birth — our stereognostic sense — the ability to feel weight and form and assess its significance. The forms which have had special meaning for me since childhood have been the standing form (which is the translation of my feeling towards the human being standing in landscape); the two forms (which is the tender relationship of one living thing beside another); and the closed form, such as the oval, spherical or pierced form (sometimes incorporating colour) which translates for me the association and meaning of gesture in landscape; in the repose of say a mother and child, or the feeling of the embrace of living things, either in nature or in the human spirit. In all these shapes the translation of what one feels about man and nature must be conveyed by the sculptor in terms of mass, inner tension and rhythm, scale in relation to our human size and the quality of surface which speaks through our hands and eyes.

I think that the necessary equilibrium between the material I carve and the form I want to make will always dictate an abstract interpretation in my sculpture — for there are essential stone shapes and essential wood shapes which are impossible for me to disregard. All my feeling has to be translated into this basic framework, for sculpture is the reaction of a *real object* which relates to our human body and spirit as well as to our visual appreciation of form and colour content.

ON THE IMPORTANCE OF LIGHT

The importance of light in relation to form will always interest me. In sculpture it seems to be an extension of the stereognostic sensibility, and through it I feel it ought to be possible to induce those evocative responses that seem to be part of primeval life, and which are a vital necessity to a full apprehension of space and volume.

There is an inside and an outside to every form. When they are in special accord, as for instance a nut in its shell or a child in the womb, or in the structure of shells or crystals, or when one senses the architecture of bones in the human figure, then I am most drawn to the effect of light. Every shadow cast by the sun from an ever-varying angle reveals the harmony of the inside and outside. Light gives full play to our tactile perceptions through the experience of our eyes, and the vitality of forms is revealed by the interplay between space and volume.

❖

ON THE TENSION BETWEEN THE REALISTIC AND THE ABSTRACT

The sculptor must search with passionate intensity for the underlying principle of the organisation of mass and tension — the meaning of gesture and the structure of rhythm.

In my search for these values I like to work both realistically and abstractly. In my drawing and painting I turn from one to the other as a necessity or impulse and not because of a preconceived design of action. When drawing what I see I am usually most conscious of the underlying principle of abstract form in human beings and their relationship one to the other. In making my abstract drawings I am most often aware of those human values which dominate the structure and meaning of abstract forms.

Sculpture is the fusion of these two attitudes and I like to be free as to the degree of abstraction and realism in carving.

The dominant feeling will always be the love of humanity and nature; and the love of sculpture for itself.

❖

ON HER WORKING METHOD

My left hand is my thinking hand. The right is only a motor hand. This holds the hammer. The left hand, the thinking hand, must be relaxed, sensitive. The rhythms of thought pass through the fingers and grip of this hand into the stone.

It is also a listening hand. It listens for basic weaknesses of flaws in the stone; for the possibility or imminence of fractures.

❖

Working realistically replenishes one's love for life, humanity and the earth. . . .

Working in the abstract way seems to release one's personality and sharpen the perceptions so that in the observation of humanity or landscape it is the wholeness of inner intention which moves one so profoundly. The components fall into place and one is no longer aware of the detail except as the necessary significance of wholeness and unity . . . a rhythm of form which has its roots in earth but reaches outwards towards the unknown experiences of the future. The thought underlying this form is, for me, the delicate balance the spirit of man maintains between his knowledge and the laws of the universe.

Barbara Hepworth writings and photographs Copyright Alan Bowness.

Self-Portrait with Cropped Hair, 1940. Oil on canvas. 15¾" x 11".
Collection, The Museum of Modern Art, New York. Gift of Edgar Kaufmann, Jr.

FRIDA KAHLO

1907–1954

IN HER INTENSE self-portraits Frida Kahlo used her own image to explore a range of poignant and painful emotions. She drew upon indigenous Mexican traditions as the source of her art in paintings characterized by their intimate size and private imagery. Central to Kahlo's life were the lasting effects of a streetcar accident that she was in as a teenager and that left her in a permanently weakened physical state, subject to acute pain. As a young woman, she became personally obsessed with the Mexican muralist Diego Rivera who shared her interest in Mexican culture and commitment to revolutionary causes; their mutual impact was profound. Kahlo was claimed as a Surrealist by André Breton, the arbiter of the Surrealist canon, who described her art as "a ribbon around a bomb," yet she, herself, denied having fantastic, dreamlike sources for her art, saying that she painted her own reality. In fact, most of her works are self-portraits, the use of her own image as an artistic subject corresponding to an interest in autobiography and self-representation evinced by other women artists and writers. Like many women, Kahlo responded to life's pressures by writing in a journal, and kept a diary for the last decade of her life. She used the diary to give voice to subconscious musings, both verbal and visual, rather than to record a narrative chronicle of events.

In both her art and biographical statements, Kahlo emphasized the two halves of her family background, European and Mexican. Her father, Guillermo, was a European Jew who had immigrated to Mexico at nineteen, working first in a jewelry store and then, by the time she was born, as a successful photographer. Her mother, Matilde Calderón, was a Mexican of Spanish and Indian extraction; she had urged her husband to learn photography, her own father's profession. Frida was the third of four daughters born to the couple; her father had two other daughters by his previous marriage, which had ended with his first wife's death. He suffered from epilepsy and was subject to intense moods. Kahlo described the atmosphere in her family as "one of the saddest I know."

Three circumstances of Kahlo's childhood had a continuing visual impact on her self-image and its representation in her work. During Kahlo's infancy her mother had been ill and the child had been suckled by an Indian wet nurse. In her self-portraits, a recurring motif was the expansion upon this experience with the metaphorical implication of having been nurtured by "Mexico." Kahlo's birth during the decade of the Mexican Revolution was also an important part of her later self-conceptualization, as a Communist and a revolutionary. In her diary she vividly recalled the street-fighting of the followers of Zapata and Carranza and, in an inscription on the wall of their house in Coyoacán (on the outskirts of Mexico City), she recorded her birth year incorrectly to make it coincide with the start of the revolution. Finally, Kahlo contracted polio when she was six; she had to be confined for about nine months and was left with one leg thinner than the other. It may have been during those months that she developed the imaginative resources that sustained her during later confinements.

At about fifteen Kahlo began to attend the National Preparatory School, perhaps the most elite secondary school in Mexico City. In response to the revolution, the school had begun to abandon its colonial influences and to develop a curriculum that stressed the indigenous Mexican culture, indirectly influencing the content of Kahlo's art. Kahlo was one of approximately thirty-five girls in a student body of over two thousand. She became closely involved with a group of seven boys and two girls, known as the "*Cachuchas*," reputed to be irreverent pranksters whose prime target was bourgeois stuffiness. Her special friend in the group was Alejandro Gómez Arias; she chronicled her growth from adolescent to young woman in a series of letters she addressed to him in the mid-1920s.

Kahlo's life was irrevocably changed in September 1925 when a trolley collided with the bus in which she and Arias were traveling. She was badly hurt in the crash: a broken handrail pierced her pelvic region, her foot was crushed, and her spine fractured in several locations. She was hospitalized for three months, but never really recovered completely. Complications arose within the year and she ultimately had over thirty operations that were in some way related to the injuries she had sustained in the accident. The injuries to her spine and pelvis left her incapable of bearing children, a source of great emotional distress to her.

Kahlo began painting during the process of recuperation. She had not had artistic aspirations before the crash; she had been following a premedical course at school, to which she never returned, although her medical training influenced her artistic imagery throughout her life. She apparently took several lessons with her father's friend, the commercial artist Fernando Fernandez, her only formal study of art besides two required classes at school. According to her own account, she painted her first self-portrait out of boredom, in 1926 when she was confined to bed, with oil paints that her father happened to have. Family and friends became her other early subjects. The role that painting played in her life when she first began — a means of articulating her loneliness, pain, and boredom — seems to have prevailed throughout her life.

In recounting her life's story, Kahlo often asserted that she suffered two catastrophic accidents: the bus crash and her meeting with Diego Rivera. The circumstances of the latter have been given in various accounts: they may have met at a party given by photographer and fellow communist Tina Modotti, although both Kahlo and Rivera chronicled other, earlier encounters. In any event, during 1928, Kahlo sought out Rivera to show him her work for his critiques. Rivera was quite favorably impressed with Kahlo's work and thought that she "had talent." Although Kahlo's artistic expression is clearly her own, Rivera's positive impact on her subsequent development should not be ignored, particularly since her career developed entirely after their relationship had begun. There are some parallels between their relationship and that of Alfred Stieglitz and Georgia O'Keeffe: Rivera nurtured Kahlo at a critical juncture when she was a relatively new painter and, as an established artist with many connections and a penchant for the limelight, he was able to open many doors that might otherwise have been closed. He also encouraged her to turn to her Mexican roots, both in her art and in her life-style and mode of dress, and as a vociferous socialist he supported her political radicalism. Rivera also respected her use of art as a means of exploring the depth of her emotions, proudly asserting that she was the "only artist who tore open her chest and heart to express the biological truth of feeling."

Kahlo and Rivera married for the first time in August 1929; they divorced ten years later but married again the following year. Their relationship was notoriously tumultuous. In her essay, "Portrait of Diego," Kahlo indicated her understanding that he could never really be married to anyone; his work was his first love, and he pursued it relentlessly. Throughout their married lives, Diego had sexual relationships with many other women. (Like Rodin and Picasso, he seemed to exemplify the stereotypical male artist whose sexuality and artistic energy are inextricably conflated.) Kahlo also had many extramarital sexual involvements (with both men and women), but her diary entries and paintings make clear how pained she was by Rivera's sexual infidelity.

Despite a dramatic and chaotic personal life, in the years that followed her marriage, Kahlo moved from being a beginner, the wife of the great artist, to being a recognized artist herself. In 1931, Rivera and Kahlo took an extended trip to the United States while he worked on several commissions, finally returning to in Mexico in 1934. When André Breton visited in 1938, he was sufficiently impressed with her paintings to offer to include them in an exhibit of Mexican art in Paris the following year. Also, in 1938, Kahlo had her first one-person exhibit, at the Julian Levy Gallery in New York. By this time she had already painted some of her most outstanding works, such as *A Few Small Nips*, produced in response to Diego's affair with her sister Cristina, the most devastating to her of his extramarital involvements, and *My Nurse and I*.

In the decade after Kahlo and Rivera's 1940 remarriage, her career solidified and her work was represented in various group exhibitions in the United States and Mexico. Her only one-person show in Mexico during her life, at the Galería

Arte Contemporaneo in Mexico City, did not occur until 1953. After her father's death in 1941 she returned to the house in Coyoacán and made that her permanent residence for the rest of her life. In 1943 she began teaching at the Ministry of Public Education's School of Painting and Sculpture, where Elizabeth Catlett was to teach a decade or so later. Many of her most stunning and mature works were painted in this period. However, she suffered increasingly from the deleterious effects of her accident twenty years earlier. Although she had experienced health crises during the 1930s, her situation deteriorated around 1946, when she went to New York to have several vertebrae fused. In 1950 she again needed to be hospitalized, this time for almost a year; in 1953, gangrene required that her foot be amputated, an operation which caused her severe mental anguish, as can be seen in her diary entries. She died only a year later, her health in an acute state of deterioration, dependent on drugs to ease her pain. Although it is certain that she had developed bronchial pneumonia, doubts have been raised concerning the specific cause of her death, which is listed on her death certificate as "pulmonary embolism."

Because Kahlo used her life as the almost exclusive subject for her art, it is quite tempting to read her biography from her works, a dangerous approach with any artist, and perhaps particularly so with Kahlo. It is, however, important and appropriate to assess the meanings she ascribed to the biographical elements she used to construct a personal iconography.

One recurring theme in both Kahlo's painting and writing was her relationship with Rivera. Her first visual treatment of this appeared in her wedding portrait, painted two years after their marriage, in which the contrast in their relative sizes is striking, Rivera looming beside Kahlo's diminutive figure. In subsequent images she conceptualized him as her child, as in *The Love Embrace of the Universe*, which shows him nestling on her lap. It has been suggested that this represented an aspect of their real-life relationship, a view supported by Rivera's depiction of Kahlo as his mother in his Hotel del Prado mural. Rivera acted as something of a muse for Kahlo, an inhabiting creative spirit. In *Thinking About Diego*, his image is placed in her forehead like a third eye, a position he holds in several other works. In *The Two Fridas*, the Mexican one who is not bleeding to death holds his image in her hand.

The mixed origins expressed in the *Two Fridas* were also an important artistic subject for Kahlo. She explored them in her painting *My Grandparents, My Parents and I* (1936), a painted genealogical chart showing chubby two-year-old Frida, standing in the "blue house" in Coyoacán, surrounded by portraits of her parents and both sets of grandparents, which she holds with a red ribbon, a kind of umbilical cord. Kahlo especially committed herself to asserting her "*Mexicanidad,*" her very mode of painting a deliberate attempt to identify with her Mexican origins. Based as it was on the style of ex-voto *retablos* derived from the popular religious culture, she always incorporated some aspect in her art, using bright colors, tin, or an inscription, and working in a naive style. The imagery that represents her ties to Mexico was expressed particularly strongly in such works as *The Love Embrace of the Universe*, and especially in *My Nurse and I*, where she shows herself with a baby's body and an adult's head, suckling at the breast of an indigenous deity. Another significant theme, that of being connected to the earth, Kahlo expressed in many works including *Roots* and *Self-Portrait with Cropped Hair*, in which the shorn locks of her cut hair seem to be growing into the earth. Kahlo's vision of cosmic and earthly interconnectedness extended beyond Mexico to the entire organic world. A generalized, yet rich and earthy, sexuality (mirrored in some of her writings) pervades many of her works as in her verbal description of penetration: "Only a mountain knows the inside of another mountain." In Kahlo's thought, Eros not only transcends the sexual, as Whitney Chadwick points out, it transcends the personal as well. "It is not love, nor tenderness, nor affection, it is the whole of life," she wrote. In her own life Kahlo surrounded herself with animals and painted her image with monkeys, dogs, birds, and lush tropical vegetation, embodying the earth's fertility. Kahlo's profound respect for the earth's fecundity heightened her perception of her own inability to bear children as a great tragedy.

By far, the most important issue to examine in Kahlo's work is her self-representation. In painting her own image more than fifty times, Kahlo was trying on and taking off masks, as she indicated directly in the title of *The Mask* (1945). The reality expressed in her works might well have been her own, as she asserted; however, no one image can be said to represent a single "true" reality. In some ways Kahlo's self-portraits are akin to the photographer Cindy Sherman's use of her own image to express multiple, simultaneous, and not-mutually-exclusive interpretations of "femininity." Kahlo's fascination with costume, both in her self-portraits and her actual dress, corroborate this desire to try on different personae. In *Self-Portrait with Cropped Hair*, for example, she paints the "rejected" Frida in masculine costume, stripped of her superficial femininity.

Perhaps the most significant aspect of Kahlo's self-representation was her ability to display her wounds, of which *The Broken Column* is the most outstanding example. *Wounded Deer*, *The Wounded Table*, *The Tree of Life*, and even *A Few Small Nips*, in which the bloodied female is not her own image, are only a few other instances where she externalized her pain so that it screamed at the viewer to be noticed. Sometimes this display specifically reflected her feelings about birth, as in *My Birth*, or her inability to have children, as in *Henry Ford Hospital*, referring to a miscarriage. Some historians have asserted that these works are autoerotic in their open display of pain and vulnerability. Certainly, they defy the conventions for depiction of the female body; in these images, "the mutilated body trespasses on the place of the classical nude." Although they create a distorted reality through exaggeration, they are so outrageous, so blunt, that they may be felt as true on a basic level where the unspeakable is finally articulated, made unmistakably palpable. For Kahlo, the female body was the seat of pain, not of pleasure.

Kahlo's diary, written during the last decade of her life, is unlike any other included in this volume. It is anything but the chronicle of a linear sequence of events, nor is it a series of self-analyses precipitated by or geared to actual occurrences, nor even, like Marianne Werefkin's journal, a step outside of herself to address an alter ego. Rather, Kahlo used her diary as another means of personal and artistic experimentation, of "trying on" personae, ideas, and thoughts. For that reason, Hayden Herrera considers it her most surrealistic work. Her writing method was consistent with the Surrealists' practice of using automatism to open up a stream of consciousness, in which both verbal and visual images flowed. Thus, the diary is filled with free associations, stimulated by words, by ink blots, by patterns. In this private document, Kahlo did not construct a coherent or controlled reality, nor did she attempt to make logical sense. Often, she wrote of her obsession with Rivera.

Kahlo took her own private vision and externalized it vividly, in a public language that could not be misunderstood. In so doing, she took a step in moving the experience of the female subject from its marginal cultural position toward the center.

SOURCES

Chadwick, Whitney. *Women Artists and the Surrealist Movement*. Boston: Little, Brown and Co., 1985.

Franco, Jean. *Plotting Women: Gender and Representation in Mexico*. New York: Columbia University Press, 1989.

Herrera, Hayden. *Frida: A Biography of Frida Kahlo*. New York: Harper and Row, 1983.

Mulvey, Laura, and Peter Wollen. *Frida Kahlo and Tina Modotti*. London: Whitechapel Art Gallery, 1982.

Tibol, Raquel. *Frida Kahlo: Crónica, Testimonios y Aproximaciones*. Mexico City: Editiones de Cultura Popular, S.A., 1977.

Zamora, Maria. *The Brush of Anguish*. San Francisco: Chronicle Books, 1990.

FRIDA KAHLO, EXCERPTS FROM THE DIARY, 1944–1954
(TRANSLATED BY HAYDEN HERRERA)

CHILDHOOD MEMORIES

I remember that I was four years old [actually she was five] when the "tragic ten days" took place. I witnessed with my own eyes Zapata's peasants' battle against the Carrancistas. My situation was very clear. My mother opened the windows on Allende Street. She gave access to the Zapatistas, seeing to it that the wounded and hungry jumped from the windows of my house into the "living room." She cured them and gave them thick tortillas, the only food that could be obtained in Coyoacán in those days. . . . We were four sisters: Matita, Adri, me (Frida) and Cristi, the chubby one.

❖

In 1914 bullets just hissed. I still hear their extraordinary sound. In the *tianguis* [market] of Coyoacán propaganda in favor of Zapata was made with *corridos* [revolutionary ballads] edited by [the printmaker José Guadalupe] Posada. On Friday these ballad sheets cost one centavo and, enclosed in a great wardrobe that smelled of walnut wood, Cristi and I sang them, while my mother and father watched out for us so that we could not fall into the hands of the guerrillas. I remember a wounded Carrancista running toward his stronghold [near] the river of Coyoacán. From the window I also spied [a] Zapatista with a bullet wound in his knee, squatting and putting on his sandals. [Here, Frida drew sketches of the Carrancista and the Zapatista.]

❖

I must have been 6 years old when I experienced intensely an imaginary friendship with a little girl more or less the same age as me. On the glass window of what at that time was my room, and which gave onto Allende Street, I breathed vapor onto one of the first panes. I let out a breath and with a finger I drew a "door." . . . [Here Frida drew the window of her room.]

Full of great joy and urgency, I went out in my imagination, through this "door." I crossed the whole plain that I saw in front of me until I arrived at the dairy called "Pinzón." . . . I entered by the "O" of Pinzón and I went down in great haste into the *interior of the earth*, where "my imaginary friend" was always waiting for me. I do not remember her image or her color. But I do know that she was gay — she laughed a lot. Without sounds. She was agile and she danced as if she weighed nothing at all. I followed her in all her movements and while she danced I told her my secret problems. Which ones? I do not remember. But from my voice she knew everything about me. . . . When I returned to the window I entered through the same door drawn on the glass pane. When? For how long had I been with her? I do not know. It could have been a second or thousands of years. . . . I was happy. I blurred the "door" with my hand and it "disappeared." I ran with my *secret* and my joy as far as the furthermost corner of the patio of my house, and always in the same place under a cedar tree, I cried out and laughed, surprised at being *alone* with my great happiness and with the so vivid memory of *the little girl*. Thirty-four years have passed since I experienced this magic friendship and every time that I remember it, it revives and becomes larger and larger inside of my world.

❖

CONCERNING DIEGO RIVERA
   To my child of the great occultist (December, 8, 1939)
   It is six in the morning
   and the turkeys are singing,
   heat of human tenderness
   Solitude accompanied —
   Never in all my life
   will I forget your presence
   You picked me up when I was destroyed
   and you made me whole again
   In this small earth
   Where will I direct my glance?
   So immense so profound!
   There is no longer any time, There is no longer anything.
   distance. There is only *reality*
   What was, was forever!
   What exists are roots
   that appear transparent
   transformed
   In the eternal fruit tree
   Your fruits give off their aromas
   your flowers give their color
   growing with the joy
   of the winds and the blossoms.
   Do not stop giving thirst

to the tree of which you are the sun, the tree
that treasured your seed
"Diego" is the name of love.

❖

. . . Diego: Nothing is comparable to your hands and nothing is equal to the
gold-green of your eyes. My body fills itself with you for days and days. You are
the mirror of the night. The violent light of lightning. The dampness of the
earth. Your armpit is my refuge. My fingertips touch your blood. All my joy is to
feel your life shoot forth from your fountain-flower which mine keeps in order
to fill all the paths of my nerves which belong to you.

❖

My Diego:
Mirror of the night.
Your green sword eyes inside my flesh. Waves between our hands. All you
in the space full of sounds — in shade and in light. You will be called AUX-
OCROMO — the one that attracts color. I CROMOFORO — the one that gives
color. You are all the combinations of number. life. My desire is to understand
line form movement. You fill and I receive. Your word crosses all the space and
reaches my cells that are my stars of many years retained in our body.
Enchained words that we could not say except in the lips of sleep. Everything
was surrounded by the vegetal miracle of the landscape of your body. Upon
your form, at my touch the cilia of flowers, the sounds of rivers respond. All the
fruits were in the juice of your lips, the blood of the pomegranate . . . of the
mammee and pure pineapple. I pressed you against my breast and the prodigy
of your form penetrated through all my blood through the tips of my fingers.
Odor of essence of oak, of the memory of walnut, of the green breath of ash.
Horizons and landscapes — that I crossed with a kiss. A forgetfulness of words
will form the exact idiom to understand the glances of our closed eyes.

You are present, intangible and you are all the universe that I form in the
space of my room. Your absence shoots forth trembling in the sound of the
clock, in the pulse of light; your breath through the mirror. From you to my
hands I go over all your body, and I am with you a minute and I am with you a
moment, and my blood is the miracle that travels in the veins of the air from
my heart to yours.
THE WOMAN

THE MAN
The vegetal miracle of my body's landscape is in you the whole of nature. I tra-
verse it in a flight that with my fingers caresses the round hills, the . . . valleys,
longing for possession and the embrace of the soft green fresh branches covers
me. I penetrate the sex of the whole earth, its heat embraces me and in my
body everything feels like the freshness of tender leaves. Its dew is the sweat of
an always new lover. It is not love, nor tenderness, nor affection, it is the whole
of life, mine that I found when I saw it in your hands, in your mouth and in your
breasts. In my mouth I have the almond taste of your lips. Our words have
never gone outside. Only a mountain knows the insides of another mountain.
At times your presence floats continuously as if wrapping all my being in an

anxious wait for morning. And I notice that I am with you. In this moment still full of sensations, my hands are plunged in oranges, and my body feels surrounded by you. . . .

❖

1947

I am the embryo, the germ, the first cell that — in potency — engendered *him* — I am *him* from the most primitive and the most ancient cells, which with 'time' became him. At every moment he is my child, my child born every *moment*, diary, from myself.

❖

ON SICKNESS AND DEATH

. . . I have been sick a year. . . . Dr. Farill saved me. He gave me back the joy of life. I am still in a wheelchair and I do not know if soon I will be able to walk again. I have a plaster cast, which, in spite of being a frightful bore, helps my spine feel better. I do not have pains. Only a weariness . . . and as is natural, often desperation. A desperation that no words can describe. Nevertheless, I want to live. I already have begun to paint the little painting that I am going to give to doctor Farill and that I am doing with all my affection for him. . . .

❖

I am DISINTEGRATION.

❖

POINTS OF SUPPORT

On my whole body there is only *one*; and I want two. In order to have two they have to cut *one*. It is the *one* that I do not have that I have to have in order to be able to walk, the other will already be dead! For me, wings are more than enough. Let them cut it and off I'll fly!!

❖

February 11, 1954

They amputated my leg six months ago, they have given me centuries of torture and at moments I almost lost my "reason." I keep on wanting to kill myself. Diego is the one who holds me back because of my vanity in thinking that he would miss me. He has told me so and I believe him. But never in my life have I suffered more. I will wait a little while.

❖

April 27, 1954
I have achieved a lot.
I will be able to walk
I will be able to paint
I love Diego more
than I love myself.
My will is great
My will remains
Thanks to the magnificent love of Diego, to the honorable and intelligent work of Dr. Farill. To the purpose, so honest and loving, of Dr. Ramon Parres [Frida's psychiatrist] and to the darling persons of my whole life [Dr.] David Glusker and Dr. Eloesser.

❖

Death is nothing but a process.

❖

I came out healthy — I made the promise and I will keep it never to go backwards. Thanks to Diego, thanks to my Tere [Teresa Proenza], thanks to Gracielita and to the little girl, thanks to Judith, thanks to Isaua Mino, thanks to Lupita Zuñiga, thanks to Dr. Farill, to Dr. Polo, to Dr. Armando Navarro, to Dr. Vargas. thanks to me myself and to my enormous will to live among all the people who love me and for all those whom I love. Long live *alegria*, life, Diego, Tere, my Judith and all the nurses I have I had in my life who have treated me so marvelously well. Thanks because I am a Communist and I have been all my life. Thanks to the Soviet people, to the Chinese, Czechoslovaks, and Polish people and to the people of Mexico, above all to the people of Coyoacán where my first cell was born, which was incubated in Oaxaca, in the womb of my mother, who had been born there, and married my father, Guillermo Kahlo — my mother Matilde Calderón, a brunette country girl form Oaxaca. Marvelous afternoon that we spent here at Coyoacán ; the room of Frida, Diego, Tere and me. Señorita Capulina, Señor Xolotl, Señora Kosti. [The last three are names of Frida's dogs.]

❖

We look for calm or peace because we anticipate death, since we die every moment.

❖

I hope the exit is joyful — and I hope never to come back — Frida. [Her last entry.]

❖

HER COSMOLOGY
1944
I sell everything for nothing. . . . I do not believe in illusion . . . the great vacillator. Nothing has a name. I do not look at forms . . . drowned spiders. Lives in alcohol. Children are the days and there is where I end.

❖

Now he comes, my hand, my red vision. larger. more yours. martyr of glass. The great unreason. Columns and valleys. the fingers of the wind. bleeding children. the micron mica. I do not know what my joking dream thinks. The ink, the spot. the form. the color. I am a bird. I am everything, without more confusion. All the bells, the rules. The lands. the great grove. the greatest tenderness. the immense tide. garbage. bathtub. letters of cardboard. dice, fingers duets weak hope of making construction. the cloths. the kings. so stupid. my nails. the thread and the hair. the playful nerve I'm going now with myself. An absent minute. You've been stolen from me and I'm leaving crying. He is a *vacilón.*

❖

Who would say that spots live and help one live?! Ink, blood smell. I do not know what ink I would use that would want to leave its track in such forms. I respect its wishes and I will do what I can to flee from myself worlds, Inked worlds — land free and mine. Far away suns that call me because I form a part of their nucleus. Foolishness . . . What would I do without the absurd and the fleeting?

❖

GREEN: warm and good light
REDDISH PURPLE: Aztec. Tlapali [Aztec word for "color" used for painting and
    drawing]. Old blood of prickly pear. The most alive and oldest.
BROWN: color of *mole*, of the leaf that goes. Earth.
YELLOW: madness, sickness, fear. Part of the sun and of joy.
COBALT BLUE: electricity and purity. Love.
BLACK: nothing is black, really *nothing*.
LEAF GREEN: leaves, sadness, science. The whole of Germany is this color.
GREENISH YELLOW: more madness and mystery. All the phantoms wear suits
    of this color . . . or at least underclothes.
DARK GREEN: color of bad news and good business.
NAVY BLUE: *distance*. Also tenderness can be of this blue.
MAGENTA: Blood? Well, who knows!

❖

. . . The revolution is harmony of form and of color and everything exists
and moves beneath only one law — life.

❖

November 4, 1952
Today as never before I am accompanied (25 years) I am now a Communist being. . . . I have read the history of my country and of almost all the
nations. I know their class conflicts and economics. I understand clearly the
materialistic dialectic of Marx, Engels, Lenin, Stalin and Mao Tse. I love them
as the pillars of the new Communist world. . . . I am only one cell of the complex revolutionary mechanism of the people for peace and of the new Soviet —
Chinese — Czechoslovakian — Polish people who are bound by blood to my
own person and to the indigenous peoples of Mexico. Amongst these large multitudes of Asiatic people there will always be my own faces — Mexican faces —
of dark skin and beautiful form, limitless elegance, also the blacks will be liber-
ated, they are so beautiful and brave.

❖

March 4, 1953
I lost my equilibrium with the loss (the passing) of STALIN — I always
wanted to know him personally but now it doesn't matter — Nothing stays
everything is revolutionized.

❖

1951
I am very worried about my painting. . . . Above all to transform it, so that it
will be something useful, since until now I have not painted anything but the
honest expression of my own self, but absolutely distant from what my painting
could do to serve the Party. I should struggle with all my strength for the little
that is positive that my health allows me to do in the direction of helping the
Revolution. The only real reason to live.

❖

For the first time in my life my painting tries to help the line traced by the
party.

❖

Tree of Hope.

La Vida callada . . .	The silent life . . .
dadora de mundos.	giver of worlds.
Venados heridos	Wounded deer
Ropas de tehuana	Tehuana clothes
Rayos, penas, Soles	Lightning flashes, pains, Suns
ritmos escondidos	hidden rhythms
"La niña Mariana"	"The little girl Mariana"
frutos ya muy vivos.	Fruits that are very much alive.
la muerte se aleja —	death keeps its distance —
lineas, formas. nidos	lines, forms. nests.
las manos construyen	hands build
los ojos abiertos	open eyes
los Diegos sentidos	the Diegos full of feeling
lágrimas enteras	whole tears
todas son muy claras	all are very clear
Cósmicas verdades	Cosmic truths
que viven sin ruidos	that live without sounds

Arbol de la Esperanza	Tree of Hope
mantente firme.	keep firm.

❖

FROM AN APPLICATION FOR A GUGGENHEIM GRANT, 1940

Professional Antecedents:

I began to paint twelve years ago, during convalescence from an automobile accident that forced me to stay in bed for almost a year. During all these years I have worked with the spontaneous impulse of my feeling. I have never followed any school or anyone's influence, I have not expected to get from my work more than the satisfaction of the fact of painting itself and of saying what I could not say in any other way.

❖

Work:

I have done portraits, figure compositions, also subjects in which landscape and still life take on great importance. I have been able to find, without being forced by any prejudice, a personal expression in painting. For twelve years my work consisted of eliminating everything that did not come from the internal lyrical motives that impelled me to paint.

Since my subjects have always been my sensations, my states of mind and the profound reactions that life has been producing in me, I have frequently objectified all this in figures of myself, which were the most sincere and real thing that I could do in order to express what I felt inside and outside of myself.

❖

FROM FRIDA KAHLO, *FRIDA KAHLO*
(TRANSLATED BY NANCY BRESLOW AND AMY WEISS NAREA)

PORTRAIT OF DIEGO

I warn you that I shall paint this portrait of Diego with colors that are unfamiliar to me: words, and for this reason, it will be poor. Moreover, I love Diego in a way that means I can't be a "spectator" to his life, but a part of it, for which reason — perhaps — I will exaggerate the positive aspects of his unique personality trying to remove that which, even remotely, could hurt him. It will not be a biographic statement; I consider it more sincere to write only about the Diego that I believe I have known a little in these twenty years that I have lived near him. I will not speak of Diego as "my husband" because it would be ridiculous; Diego never has been nor ever will be "husband" to anyone. Nor as a lover, because he embraces much more than the sexual limitations; and if I will speak of him as of a son, I would only describe or paint my own emotion, almost my self-portrait not that of Diego. With this warning, and with all honesty, I will try my truth: the truth, that his image sketches within my mind.

HIS FORM: With his Asiatic head above which his dark hair grows, so thin and fine that it seems to float in the air, Diego is a giant child, immense, of kind face and a slightly sad look. His bulging eyes, dark, very intelligent and huge, are constrained with difficulty — they are almost outside their orbits — because of swollen and protruding eyelids like a Bactrachian, very separate one from the other. Because of them his vision embraces a visual field much more ample, as if it were constructed especially for a painter of spaces and multitudes. Through these wide-set eyes invisible future events of Oriental wisdom can be foretold; only rarely does an ironic and tender smile disappear from his Buddha mouth of fleshy lips . . . a flower of his image.

Seeing him nude. one immediately thinks of a boy frog standing up on his hind legs. His skin is greenish-white, like an aquatic animal, but his hands and face are darker, because they are sunburned.

His childish shoulders, narrow and rounded, continue without angles into feminine arms, ending in wonderful hands, small and of fine design, sensitive and subtle like antennae that communicate with the entire universe. It is amazing that these hands serve to paint so much and still work tirelessly.

Of his chest one must say that if he had disembarked on the island governed by Sappho, he wouldn't be executed by her warrior women. The sensitivity of his wonderful breasts would have made him admissible. His virility, specific and strange, would also make him desirable in dominions of empresses covetous of masculine love.

His enormous belly, tender and smooth like a sphere, rests above his strong, beautiful, column-like legs that terminate in large feet. His feet open toward the outside in obtuse angles as if to take in the whole earth and sustain himself above it insurmountably, like an antediluvian being who would emerge from the water as an example for future humanity.

He sleeps in a fetal position. During his wakefulness, he moves with slow elegance. as if living inside a liquid medium. His movement expresses his sensitivity, making air seem denser than water.

The form of Diego is that of an affectionate monster, inspired by fear and hunger, created by the ancient concealer, a necessary and eternal element, the primal mother of men and all the gods that man invented in his delirium. WOMAN, among all of them — I — would always want to cradle him like a newborn child.

HIS CONTENT: Diego is marginal in all personal relations, limited and precise. Contradictory like all that moves life, he is, at the same time, an immense caress and a violent discharge of powerful and unique forces. On the inside he is like a seed that the earth treasures, and on the outside he is like the landscape. Some may hope from me a portrait of Diego that is personal, "feminine," anecdotal, amusing, full of complaints with a certain quantity of "decent" gossip, useful to the morbidly curious. Perhaps they hope to hear my laments of "how much one suffers" living with a man like Diego. But I cannot believe that the banks of a river are damaged by allowing it to run, nor the earth is damaged by the rain, nor the atom diminished by discharging its energy . . . for me, all has a natural compensation. In my role, difficult and dark. as ally of an extraordinary being, I have the reward that a green point has within a great amount of red: the reward of *balance*. the pains or joys that normalize life in this society are rotted with lies, but they are not mine. If I have prejudices and the actions of others wound me. even those of Diego Rivera, I am responsible for my inability to see with clarity. If I don't have these prejudices, I ought to admit that it is natural that the red globules struggle against the white and that this phenomenon only signifies health.

It will not be I who depreciates the fantastic personality of Diego, who I profoundly respect, saying stupidities about his life. On the contrary, I would love to express with the poetry that he deserves, but which I don't possess, that which in reality is Diego. . . .

There are three principal lines that I consider basic to his portrait: *First*, he is a constant revolutionary struggler: he is dynamic, extraordinarily sensitive and vital. He is an untiring worker in his craft, which he knows like few painters in his world; and he is always dissatisfied not to know more, to build more and to paint more. *Second*, he is eternally curious, and an untiring investigator of everything. *Third*, he absolutely lacks prejudice and, therefore, faith. because Diego accepts — like Montaigne — that "Stupidity begins where doubt ends." He who has faith admits to unconditional submission, without liberty to analyze or to vary the course of events. Because of his clear concept of reality, Diego is rebellious and knows marvelously the materialistic dialectic of life. Diego is revolutionary. Around this triangle, an enveloping atmosphere exists. This mobile atmosphere is love, love as foundation of vital beauty.

I imagine that the world where he would like to live, would be a great fiesta, in which all beings would take part, from men to rocks, from suns to shadows. It would be a fiesta of form, of color, of movement, of sound, of intelligence, of knowledge, of emotion. His earth would be an intelligent and loving spherical fiesta. In order to achieve this fiesta, he continually struggles and offers all that he has: his genius, his imagination, his words and his actions. Each instant he struggles to erase fear and stupidity in man. . . .

Since Diego is always working, he doesn't live a normal life. His capacity of energy breaks clocks and calendars. He generates and receives waves difficult to compare to others. His immense receptor and creator mechanisms make him insatiable. The images and the ideas flow in his brain with an uncommon rhythm and for this reason his desire to expand is uncontainable. This causes indecision. . . . But although he rarely makes up his mind to choose, he carries inside a vector–line that goes directly to the center of his will.

Being eternally curious, he is the eternal conversationalist. He can paint hours and days without resting, chattering while working. He speaks and discusses absolutely everything. Like Walt Whitman he enjoys speaking with all who want to hear him. His conversation is always interesting. He has sentences that amaze. wound. stir up emotions, but he never leaves those who hear him with the impression of idleness or emptiness. His words disturb because they are alive and true. The rawness of his concepts enervates those who listen because they do not agree with the established norms of conduct; they break the bark in order to give birth to the buds; they wound in order to allow new cells to grow. . . .

In the middle of the torment that clocks and calendars create for him he tries to do and let be done what he considers fair in life: working and creating. He never scorns the value of others, but he defends himself, because he knows that this signifies rhythm and proportion with the world of reality. In exchange for giving pleasure, he gives pleasure; in exchange for effort, he gives effort. Being more qualified than others, he gives much more quantity and quality of sensitivity asking only understanding. Many times not even this is forthcoming. Many of the conflicts that his superior personality causes in daily life arise form this natural discontrol that provokes his revolutionary concepts. The problems that could be called domestic, that various women have been close to Diego, consists of the same thing. . . .

With what arms can one struggle for or against a being who is nearer to reality? Naturally these weapons have to be amoral, rebels to what is already established or admitted as good or bad. I — with the fullness of my responsibili-ty — figure that I cannot be against Diego, and if I am not one of his best allies, I wish I were. From my attitude in this portrait essay many things can be deduced, depending upon who deduces them: but my truth, the only one that I can give about Diego is this. Pure, unmeasurable in *sincere–meters* [*Sincere-ometros* is a word Frida made up. It means both sincere–meters and without zero meters.] that don't exist, except in my conviction and my own experience.

No words will describe Diego's immense tenderness for things that have beauty; his affection for the beings who don't matter in the eyes of society; or his respect for those that are oppressed. He has special adoration for the Indi-ans who are bound to him by blood; he loves them deeply, for their elegance, for their beauty and for being the living flower of the American cultural tradi-tion. He loves children, all animals, with a predilection for Mexican hairless dogs and birds, plants and rocks. He loves all beings without being docile or neutral. He is very affectionate but never surrenders: for this, and because he hardly has time to dedicate himself to personal relations, they call him an ingrate. He is respectful and fine and nothing angers him more than abuse and the lack of respect of others. He cannot tolerate tricks or deceitful fraud or what in Mexico is called "pulling your leg." He would rather have intelligent ene-mies than stupid allies. He is rather merry by temperament, but it irritates him enormously when people waste his time while he is working. His amusement is his own work; he hates social reunions and he marvels at the truly popular fiestas. Sometimes he is shy, and as much as he is fascinated by conversation, he sometimes delights in being absolutely alone. He is never bored because everything interests him, studying, analyzing and being profound in all mani-festations of life. He is not sentimental but is intensely emotional and passion-ate. Inertia exasperates him because he is a continual current, live and potent.

He admires and appreciates all that contains beauty, whether it thrives in a woman or a mountain. Perfectly balanced in all his emotions, sensations and deeds, which are moved by dialectic materialism. precise and real, he will never submit. Like the cactus on his land, he grows strong and astonishing, whether in sand or in rock. He flowers with the most alive red, the most transparent white and sun yellow. Cloaked in thorns. he keeps his tenderness inside. He lives with his strong sap inside a ferocious medium, giving light alone, like the avenging sun on gray rock. His roots live despite being uprooted, surviving the anguish of solitude. sadness and all the weaknesses that cause others to yield. He rises with surprising force and. like no other plant. he flourishes and gives fruit.

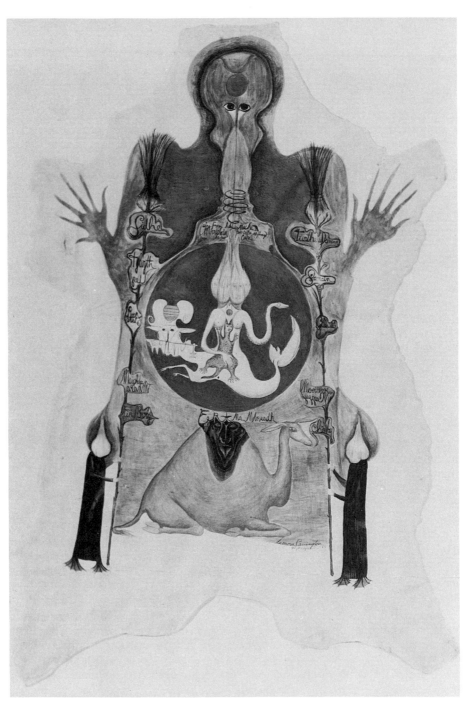

The Magic Witch, 1975. Gouache on vellum. 47¾" x 32⅜". The National Museum of Women in the Arts. Gift of Wallace and Wilhelmina Holladay. Copyright 1991 Leonora Carrington / ARS, N.Y.

LEONORA CARRINGTON

B. 1917

LEONORA CARRINGTON, OF the three women associated with Surrealism whose writings are included in this volume (the others are Kay Sage and Frida Kahlo), is the one most closely tied to the movement. Identifying herself as a Surrealist from early in her career, she participated in Surrealist exhibitions for many years and contributed to "the occultation of Surrealism," by using alchemical and hermetic motifs in her work. Her vision of women departed significantly from that of her male Surrealist colleagues, who celebrated the *femme-enfant*, the woman whose childlike lack of inhibitions played muse to their explorations of the unconscious. Like other women Surrealists, Carrington's perspective instead has validated and empowered women's active creative potential.

As a writer, Carrington uses words as a major creative outlet, exploring in her stories, essays, and plays many of the same themes that appear in her paintings. Like her male Surrealist colleagues, she wanted to use her art to "peel back the curtain." The vocabulary she developed to achieve this, however, is deeply rooted in a matriarchal consciousness. In her writings and her art, Carrington has made important contributions to women's search for a foundation that would enable them to take back the "mysteries [that were] violated, stolen or destroyed" by male dominance.

Carrington came from a privileged background, the only daughter and second child of four born to a wealthy English textile manufacturer and his wife. When she was three the family moved to Crookhey Hall, a large country house in Lancashire. Carrington depicts herself as a rebellious child who was expelled from two convent schools, and was sent to boarding schools in Paris and Florence to complete her education. At seventeen, she returned to England for the social season, during which she was presented at the royal court. Carrington's affluent background, like that of Kay Sage, may have given her the freedom to defy bourgeois expectations regarding appropriate female behavior; during her early Surrealist years she became notorious for thumbing her nose at decorum by committing outrageous acts, such as the time she removed her shoe at a fancy Parisian restaurant and smeared her foot with mustard.

Although she claims to have been "fascinated with drawing since the age of three," Carrington was nineteen before she persuaded her parents to allow her to enroll in the Amédée Ozenfant Academy in London. Art soon became the major focus of her life. She encountered Surrealist work for the first time at the First International Surrealist Exhibition, held at the Burlington Galleries in London that same year. In 1937, at the age of twenty, perhaps through Ozenfant, she met Max Ernst, an important voice in both the Dada and Surrealist movements, who was more than twice her age. Within the year, the two moved to France together to an old farmhouse in St. Martin d'Ardèche. In 1938, only two years after she first began her art studies, Carrington exhibited with the Surrealists in both Paris and Amsterdam. When Carrington met Ernst, she was an impressionable young student and he was a charismatic artist with an established reputation, able to facilitate her early access to an audience (as had Alfred Stieglitz for Georgia O'Keeffe, and Diego Rivera for Frida Kahlo).

The Second World War had a devastating impact on the course of Carrington's life. In 1939, Ernst was arrested (for the second time) as an illegal alien and Carrington panicked, convinced that as a foreigner, she too would be incarcerated unless she fled France. In an overwrought state, she sold the farmhouse for a bottle of brandy and began a frenetic trip via Andorra to Spain, ostensibly to acquire a passport in Madrid for Ernst. This journey and her subsequent confinement in an insane asylum in Santander, Spain, Carrington documented in *Down Below*, written in 1943. After her release from Santander, she made a marriage of convenience with a Mexican diplomat, Renato Leduc. They traveled to New York late in 1940, finally settling in Mexico City in 1942, where she remained for the next forty years. Carrington's marriage to Leduc ended soon after her arrival in Mexico; in 1946, she married Hungarian emigré photographer Emerico (Chiqui) Weisz. Also around that time, she first encountered Edward James, an English philanthropist and Surrealist writer, who became a major collector of her work.

During her first few years in Mexico Carrington painted very little, instead channeling her creative energies into writings which appeared in such Surrealist periodicals such as *VVV* and *View*. Although she had temporarily set painting aside, this period was quite important to her later artistic path due to her regular and influential contact with other "Surrealist exiles." Along with Remedios Varo, another painter, she was at the center of a group that included Weisz, Gunther Gerszo, Wolfgang Paalen and his wife Alice Rahon, and Varo's husband, poet Benjamin Peret. Carrington and Varo's relationship was especially close, leading them to explore together their creativity as women artists. During this period, Carrington gave up her male guides and began to depend, instead, upon a shared feminine sensibility as her creative source. Whitney Chadwick describes them as the first women Surrealists "to sever their work from male creative models and collaborate in developing a new pictorial language that spoke directly to their needs as women." Their private writings document how closely related their views were. Even after their personal paths diverged, their paintings reveal similar motifs — strange alchemical configurations and haunting elongated figures that they envisioned as a "new mythos" of female creativity.

In her earliest works, Carrington had begun to develop a personal iconography based on Celtic myths and childhood memories. Two of her most important symbols — a hyena, representative of sexuality and fecundity, and a white horse, a symbol of the creative spirit and based on one horse sacred to the Celtic tribe of Tuatha de Danaan — appear in her *Self-Portrait* of 1937. The white horse recurs in her portrait of Max Ernst, in which she depicted Ernst striding across a frozen landscape, cloaked in a purple, feathery robe wearing striped socks, and holding a lantern containing a frozen horse. This depiction is quite exceptional in combining the two roles that Ernst seemed to have played for Carrington, that of the male shaman, controlling events, and the creative spirit, so welcome to one who had had only one year of formal art education prior to their meeting.

A new awareness characterizes Carrington's works after 1945. She created magical worlds abounding with regenerative power, mysterious spaces inhabited by hybrid, wraithlike female forms derived from a fusion of symbols from alchemy, Celtic myth, other ancient legends and her childhood experiences. In *Tuesday* (1946), for example, a cat's head grows from the shoulders of a half-clothed female figure, a woman who is half-bird rides on a bird-like turtle, and a deer sprouts trees from its antlers and back. Like most of her paintings from this period, this work describes a mysterious natural ritual, here dramatically heightened by the full moon. Carrington used egg tempera for most of these works, a medium requiring a complex preparation process similar to much culinary activity (something that also interested Carrington). Tempera enabled her to suggest the archaic quality of fifteenth-century landscape paintings, which she further achieved through the inclusion of crumbling structures and disjunctive space, such as that created by tiny trees in the foreground corners. Like Hieronymous Bosch, whose work she had encountered in the Prado in Madrid before her breakdown, Carrington created vast landscapes filled with many small figures engaged in multiple activities. Also, like Bosch, she created a fluid sense of reality through the use of mutating hybrid figures. (It is interesting to note that Bosch and Carrington shared a fascination with the philosophical implications of alchemical transformation.)

During the next decades Carrington remained artistically active, painting and exhibiting regularly while raising her two sons. Her first one-artist exhibit was held at the Pierre Matisse Gallery in New York in 1948. In the early fifties, she experimented with sculpture, creating mythic figures from wood, whose surfaces were painted with images from her personal iconography, including birds, trees, and horned animals. These figures appear to be three-dimensional embodiments of those in her paintings; they have an oneiric quality, and seem almost to be archaeological relics from some ancient cult.

After the mid-1950s, Carrington's style shifted once more. She began to use oil paints, which changed the jewel-like effect on surfaces she had achieved in the earlier egg-tempera paintings. The works contain fewer, but larger, figures, and she continued to concentrate on evoking rituals grounded in a celebration of the earth, as in *The Garden of Paracelsus* (1957) and *Bird Seizes Jewel* (1969). In 1963 the National Museum of Anthropology in Mexico City commissioned her to paint a mural — *The Magic World of the Mayans*. To gain a deeper understanding of Mayan culture, Carrington lived for a time with the Indians in Chiapas, in southeastern Mexico, and based the mural on the symbolism of *Popol Vuh*, the Mayan creation story. Her later work was influenced as a result of this experience by the myths of that indigenous Mexican culture, as well as by her interest in Tibetan mysticism. Her most recent works also have an evocative quality that summons a magical sense of the earth and its forces, as in *The Magic Witch* (1975).

For the most part, Carrington's style and philosophy place her firmly among the Surrealists. She associated with Surrealist artists throughout her career, and was included by André Breton in his *Surrealism and Painting* as one of the inner circle. Typical of the Surrealist approach, her work attempts to visualize and temporarily stabilize elements of unconscious and subconscious knowing, often through jarringly unexpected juxtapositions. As did other Surrealist artists such as Salvador Dali and René Magritte, she creates dreamscapes, plausible but disturbing landscapes built with recurring elements of a personal iconography. Her very breakdown — her descent into madness — was a significant act in the Surrealist context, employing, in Rimbaud's nineteenth-century phrase, *le dérèglement de tous les sens* (disorder of all the senses) to achieve contact with the irrational. Furthermore (prior to her breakdown at least), Carrington epitomized the female ideal of the male Surrealists, the *femme-enfant*, the wild Bride of the Wind, as Ernst described her.

On the other hand, the orientation of Carrington's continuing quest brings her into direct opposition to the conception of women as handmaidens to male artistic creation. The mythic sources incorporated in her artistic vision celebrate the feminine principle for itself. Her verbal and visual imagery disaffirms any notion of patriarchal creative privilege, as when she claims that "the furies who have a sanctuary buried many fathoms under education and brainwashing have told Females they will return," and that "they must be taken back again, including the Mysteries which were violated, stolen or destroyed." Her paintings make unambiguous statements about the process of ritualistic reestablishment of female power, as in the image of a bird seizing — reclaiming — the jewel of women's wisdom.

Carrington began to write at about the same time that she began to paint, doing so in a variety of genres. Her first story, "House of Fear," was written in French and published in 1937 with an introduction and several illustrations by Ernst: it describes a young woman who is led by a horse into the "house" of her deeper self. In the next years she published numerous short stories, including "The Debutante" and "The Oval Lady," and in the late forties she wrote a play entitled *Penelope*, in which the heroine escapes from the realm of the fathers on a white hobby-horse named Tartar. The novel *The Hearing Trumpet* (1976), a revisionist grail quest, is one of Carrington's most ambitious written works. The protagonist, a ninety-two-year-old woman perceived as less than human by her son and his family, reclaims the grail — the feminine powers — and saves the earth. Most of Carrington's writings have been recently published as part of several newly translated collections.

Carrington's writings bear an especially important relationship to her own visual imagery and creative development, and to the history of women artists' ability to represent their experiences. The white horse, Tartar, simultaneously the spirit of her childhood rocking horse and the sacred Celtic symbol of creativity, and the hyena, representative of her sexual nature, are symbols that she explored in both her earliest writings and paintings. In "Fly, Pigeon," Célestin, with his white feathery robe and striped stockings, seems remarkably similar to the painted shamanic image of Ernst. The growing, transmuting forms that Eleanor describes in "Fly, Pigeon" inhabit many of Carrington's paintings. They relate as well to her more recent spiritual belief in Tibetan Buddhism's conception of a multiplicity of selves and her belief in an animal soul that inhabits humans. Comparison of the occult symbols in Carrington's earlier writings with those in *The Hearing Trumpet* and in her more recent paintings illustrate her shift to what Gloria Orenstein calls a "feminine matristic consciousness."

Perhaps Carrington's most personal work, *Down Below* is a classic story of a woman's quest for her true voice. Carrington described the process by which she went "down" into her inner consciousness, in an attempt to achieve psychic unity. She used "the language of alchemical lore" as a metaphor for the process of transmuting base materials into something more valuable, that is, transforming her self which looked for male guidance into one of psychic awareness. Before her breakdown, Ernst had been her Svengali; while "down below," Carrington learned to seek the power of strong women, such as Queen Elizabeth, and the androgynous power of Christ. The voice in *Down Below* differs from that of the rest of her writings: it is straightforward rather than obliquely encoded with occultisms.

Among the many women Surrealists, Carrington is one on whom the influence of her gender is overt (unlike either Kay Sage or Frida Kahlo). For Carrington writing and art-making have been inextricably linked to her spiritual quest; as did Marianne Werefkin and Irene Rice Pereira, Carrington sought identification with a cosmic force, pursuing her search through both the written word and the painted image.

SOURCES

Carrington, Leonora. *The Hearing Trumpet*. New York: St. Martin's Press, 1976.
_____. *The House of Fear: Notes From Down Below*. New York: E.P. Dutton, 1988.
_____. *The Seventh Horse and Other Tales*. New York: E.P. Dutton, 1988.
Chadwick, Whitney. "Leonora Carrington: Evolution of a Feminist Consciousness." *Woman's Art Journal* 7 (Spring/Summer 1986): 37–42.
_____. *Women Artists and the Surrealist Movement*. Boston: Little, Brown and Co., 1985.
Kaplan, Janet. *Unexpected Voyages: The Life and Art of Remedios Varos*. New York: Abbeville Press, 1988.
Leonora Carrington: A Retrospective Exhibition. Introduction by Edward James. Exhibition catalogue. New York: Center for Inter-American Relations, New York, 1976.
Leonora Carrington. Exhibition catalogue. Texts by Juan Garcia Ponce and Leonora Carrington. Mexico City, 1974.
Orenstein, Gloria Feman. "Leonora Carrington's Visionary Art for the New Age." *Chrysalis* 3 (1978): 65–77.
_____. *The Reflowering of the Goddess*. New York: Pergamon Press, 1990.

Rüegsegger, Anne. "Leonora Carrington: Ein Porträt zur Ausstellung 'La Femme et le Surréalisme" im Kunstmuseum Lausanne," *DU* (1988): 68–73, 92.
Suleiman, Susan Rubin. *Subversive Intent: Gender Politics and the Avant-Garde.* Cambridge: Harvard University Press, 1990.

FROM LEONORA CARRINGTON
THE HOUSE OF FEAR: NOTES FROM DOWN BELOW
(NEW YORK: E.P. DUTTON, 1988)

EXCERPTS FROM "DOWN BELOW"
Monday, August 23, 1943

Exactly three years ago, I was interned in Dr. Morales's sanatorium in Santander, Spain, Dr. Pardo, of Madrid, and the British Consul having pronounced me incurably insane. Since I fortuitously met you, whom I consider the most clear-sighted of all, I began gathering a week ago the threads which might have led me across the initial border of Knowledge. I must live through that experience all over again, because, by doing so, I believe that I may be of use to you, just as I believe that you will be of help in my journey beyond that frontier by keeping me lucid and by enabling me to put on and to take off at will the mask which will be my shield against the hostility of Conformism. Before taking up the actual facts of my experience, I want to say that the sentence passed on me by society at that particular time was probably, surely even, a godsend, for I was not aware of the importance of health, I mean of the absolute necessity of having a healthy body to avoid disaster in the liberation of the mind. More important yet, the necessity that others be with me that we may feed each other with our knowledge and thus constitute the Whole. I was not sufficiently conscious at the time of your philosophy to understand. *The time had not come for me to understand.* What I am going to endeavor to express here with the utmost fidelity was but an embryo of knowledge.

I begin therefore with the moment when Max was taken away to a concentration camp for the second time, under the escort of a gendarme who carried a rifle (May 1940). I was living in Saint-Martin-d'Ardèche. I wept for several hours, down in the village; then I went up again to my house where, for twenty-four hours, I indulged in voluntary vomitings induced by drinking orange blossom water and interrupted by a short nap. I hoped that my sorrow would be diminished by these spasms, which tore at my stomach like earthquakes. I know now that this was but one of the aspects of those vomitings: I had realised the injustice of society, I wanted first of all to cleanse myself, then go beyond its brutal ineptitude. My stomach was the seat of that society, but also the place in which I was united with all the elements of the earth. It was the *mirror* of the earth, the reflection of which is just as real as the person reflected. That mirror — my stomach — had to be rid of the thick layers of filth (the accepted formulas) in order properly, clearly, and faithfully to reflect the earth; and when I say "the earth," I mean of course all the earths, stars, suns in the sky and on the earth, as well as all the stars, suns, and earths of the microbes' solar system.

For three weeks I ate very sparingly, carefully eschewing meat, and drank wine and alcohol, feeding on potatoes and salad, at the rate perhaps of two potatoes a day. My impression is that I slept pretty well. I worked at my vines, astonishing the peasants by my strength. Saint John's Day was near at hand, the vines were beginning to blossom, they had to be sprayed often with sulphur. I also worked at my potatoes, and the more I sweated, the better I liked it, because this meant that I was getting purified. I took sunbaths, and my physical strength was such as I have never known before or afterwards.

Various events were taking place in the outside world: the collapse of Belgium, the entry of the Germans in France. All of this interested me very little and I had no fear whatsoever within me. The village was thronged with Belgians, and some soldiers who had entered my home accused me of being a spy and threatened to shoot me on the spot because someone had been looking for snails at night, with a lantern, near my house. Their threats impressed me very little indeed, for I knew that I was not destined to die.

After three solitary weeks, Catherine, an Englishwoman, a very old friend of mine, arrived, fleeing from Paris with Michel Lucas, a Hungarian. A week went by and I believe they noticed nothing abnormal in me. One day, however, Catherine, who had been for a long time under the care of psychoanalysts, persuaded me that my attitude betrayed an unconscious desire to get rid for the second time of my father: Max, whom I had to eliminate if I wanted to live. She begged me to cease punishing myself and to look for another lover. I think she was mistaken when she said I was torturing myself. I think that she interpreted me fragmentarily, which is worse than not to interpret at all. However, by doing so she restored me to sexual desire. I tried frantically to seduce two young men, but without success. They would have none of me. And I had to remain sadly chaste.

The Germans were approaching rapidly; Catherine frightened me and begged me to leave with her, saying that if I refused to do so, she too would remain. I accepted. I accepted above all because, in my evolution, Spain represented for me Discovery. I accepted because I expected to get a visa put in Max's passport in Madrid. I still felt bound to Max. This document, which bore his image, became an entity, as if I was taking Max with me. I accepted, somewhat touched by Catherine's arguments, which were distilling into me, hour after hour, a growing fear. For Catherine, the Germans meant rape. I was not afraid of that, I attached no importance to it. What caused panic to rise within me was the thought of robots, of thoughtless, fleshless beings. . . .

In Saint-Martin next morning, the schoolmistress gave me papers stamped by the town hall, which made it possible for us to depart. Catherine got the car ready. All my willpower strained towards that departure. I hurried my friends. I pushed Catherine toward the car; she took the wheel; I sat between her and Michel. The car started. I was confident in the success of the journey, but terribly anguished, fearing difficulties, which I thought inevitable. We were riding normally when twenty kilometres beyond Saint–Martin, the car stopped; the brakes had jammed. I heard Catherine say: "The brakes have jammed." "Jammed!" I, too, was jammed within, by forces foreign to my conscious will, which were also paralyzing the mechanism of the car. This was the first stage of my identification with the external world. I was the car. The car had jammed on account of me, because I, too, was jammed between Saint–Martin and Spain.

I was horrified by my own power. At that time, I was still limited to my own solar system, and was not aware of other people's systems, the importance of which I realise now. . . .

When we reached Andorra, I could not walk straight. I walked like a crab; I had lost control over my motions: an attempt at climbing stairs would again bring about a "jam." . . . My first steps in Andorra meant to me what the first steps on a tightrope must mean to an acrobat. At night, my exasperated nerves imitated the noise of the river, which flowed tirelessly over some rocks: hypnotizing, monotonous.

By day, we tried to walk about on the mountainside, but no sooner would I attempt to ascend the slightest slope than I would jam like Catherine's Fiat, and be compelled to climb down again. My anguish jammed me completely.

I realized that my anguish — my mind, if you prefer — was painfully trying to unite itself with my body; my mind would no longer manifest itself without producing an immediate effect on my body — on matter. Later it would exercise itself upon other objects. I was trying to understand this vertigo of mine: that my body no longer obeyed the formulas established in my mind, the formulas of old, limited Reason; that my will no longer meshed with my faculties of movement, and since my will no longer possessed any power, it was necessary first to liquidate my paralyzing anguish, then to seek an accord between the mountain, my mind, and my body. In order to be able to move around in this new world, I had recourse to my heritage of British diplomacy and set aside the strength of my will, seeking through gentleness an understanding between the mountain, my body, and my mind.

One day I went to the mountain alone. At first I could not climb; I lay flat on my face on the slope with the sensation that I was being completely absorbed by the earth. When I took the first steps up the slope, I had the physical sensation of walking with tremendous effort in some matter as thick as mud. Gradually, however, perceptibly and visibly, it all became easier, and in a few days I was able to negotiate jumps. I could climb vertical walls as easily as any goat. I very seldom got hurt, and I realised the possibility of a very subtle understanding which I had not perceived before. Finally, I managed to take no false steps and to wander around quite easily among the rocks.

It is obvious that, for the ordinary citizen, this must have taken on a strange and crazy aspect: a well–brought–up young Englishwoman jumping from one rock to another, amusing herself in so irrational a manner: this was wont to raise immediate suspicions as to my mental balance. I gave little thought to the effect my experiments might have on the humans by whom I was surrounded, and, in the end, they won. . . .

I was quite overwhelmed by my entry into Spain: I thought it was my kingdom; that the red earth was the dried blood of the Civil War. I was choked by the dead, by their thick presence in that lacerated countryside. I was in a great state of exaltation when we arrived in Barcelona that evening, convinced that we had to reach Madrid as speedily as possible. I therefore prevailed upon Catherine to leave the Fiat in Barcelona; the next day we boarded a train for Madrid.

The fact that I had to speak a language I was not acquainted with was crucial: I was not hindered by a preconceived idea of the words, and I but half understood their modern meaning. This made it possible for me to invest the most ordinary phrases with a hermetic significance.

In Madrid, we put up at the Hotel Internacional, near the railway station. . . .

We dined that first night on the roof; to be on a roof answered for me a profound need, for there I found myself in a euphoric state. In the political confusion and the torrid heat, I convinced myself that Madrid was the world's stomach and that I had been chosen for the task of restoring this digestive organ to health. I believed that all anguish had accumulated in me and would dissolve in the end, and this explained to me the force of my emotions. I believed that I was capable of bearing this dreadful weight and of drawing from it a solution for the world. The dysentery I suffered from later was nothing but the *illness* of Madrid taking shape in my intestinal tract. . . .

Alberto was handsome; I hastened to seduce him, for I said to myself: "Here is my brother, who has come to liberate me from the *fathers*." I had not enjoyed love since Max's departure and I wanted to very badly. Unfortunately Alberto, too, was a perfect fool and probably a scoundrel besides. In truth, I believe he was attracted to me, all the more so as he was aware of the power of Papa Carrington and his millions, as represented in Madrid by the ICI. Alberto would take me out, and once more I enjoyed some sort of temporary freedom. But not for long. . . .

After two or three days, the head of the ICI told me that Pardo and Alberto would take me to a beach at San Sebastán, where I would be absolutely free. I came out of the nursing home and got into a car bound for Santander. . . . On the way, I was given Luminal three times and an injection in the spine: systemic anesthesia. And I was handed over like a cadaver to Dr. Morales, in Santander.

❖

August 24, 1943

. . . This morning, the idea of the egg came again to my mind and I thought that I could use it as a crystal to look at Madrid in those days of July and August 1940 — for why should it not enclose my own experiences as well as the past and future history of the Universe? The egg is the macrocosm and the microcosm, the dividing line between the Big and the Small which makes it impossible to see the whole. To possess a telescope without its other essential half — the microscope — seems to me a symbol of the darkest incomprehension. The task of the right eye is to peer into the telescope, while the left eye peers into the microscope. . . .

I ceased menstruating at that time, a function which was to reappear but three months later, in Santander. I was transforming my blood into comprehensive energy — masculine and feminine, microcosmic and macrocosmic — and into a wine that was drunk by the moon and the sun. . . .

❖

August 26, 1943

. . . In the Sun Room I felt I was manipulating the firmament: I had found what was essential to solving the problem of Myself in relation to the Sun.

I believed that I was being put through purifying tortures so that I might attain Absolute Knowledge, at which point I could live Down Below. The pavilion with this name was for me the Earth, the Real World, Paradise, Eden, Jerusalem. Don Luis and Don Mariano were God and His Son. I thought they were Jewish; I thought that I, a Celtic and Saxon Aryan, was undergoing my sufferings to avenge the Jews for the persecutions they were being subjected to. Later, with full lucidity, I would go Down Below, as the third person of the Trinity. I felt that, through the agency of the Sun, I was an androgyne, the Moon, the Holy Ghost, a gypsy, an acrobat, Leonora Carrington, and a woman. I was also destined to be, later, Elizabeth of England. I was she who revealed religions and bore on her shoulders the freedom and the sins of the earth changed into Knowledge, the union of Man and Woman with God and the Cosmos, all equal between them. The lump on my left thigh no longer seemed to form part of my body and became a sun on the left side of the moon; all my dances and gyrations in the Sun Room used that lump as a pivot. It was no longer painful, for I felt integrated into the Sun. My hands, Eve (the left one) and Adam (the right one), understood each other, and their skill was thereby increased tenfold.

With a few pieces of paper and a pencil José had given me, I made calculations and deduced that the father was the planet Cosmos, represented by the sign of the planet Saturn. The son was the Sun and I the Moon, an essential element of the Trinity, with a microscopic knowledge of the earth, its plants and creatures. I knew that Christ was dead and done for, and that I had to take His place, because the Trinity, minus a woman and microscopic knowledge, had become dry and incomplete. Christ was replaced by the Sun. I was Christ on earth in the person of the Holy Ghost. . . .

❖

FROM LEONORA CARRINGTON
THE HOUSE OF FEAR: NOTES FROM DOWN BELOW
(NEW YORK: E.P. DUTTON, 1988)

EXCERPTS FROM "OVAL LADY"

A very tall thin lady was standing at the window. The window was very high and very thin too. The lady's face was pale and sad. She didn't move, and nothing moved in the window except the pheasant feather in her hair. My eyes kept being drawn to the quivering feather: it was so restless in the window, where nothing was moving! . . .

Before I knew exactly what I was doing, I had reached the entrance hall. The door closed quietly behind me, and for the first time in my life I found myself inside a stately home. . . . When we reached the third floor, we went into an enormous nursery where hundreds of dilapidated and broken toys lay all over the place. Lucretia went up to a wooden horse. In spite of its great age — certainly not much less than a hundred years — it was frozen in a gallop.

"Tartar is my favourite," she said, stroking the horse's muzzle. "He loathes my father."

Tartar rocked himself gracefully on his rockers, and I wondered to myself how he could move by himself. Lucretia looked at him thoughtfully, clasping her hands together.

"He'll travel a very long way like that," she said. "And when he comes back he'll tell me something interesting."

Looking out of doors, I noticed that it was snowing. It was very cold, but Lucretia didn't notice it. A slight sound at the window attracted her attention.

"It's Matilda," she said. "I ought to have left the window open. Anyway, it's stifling in here." With that she broke the windowpanes, and in came the snow with a magpie, which flew around the room three times.

"Matilda talks like this. It's ten years since I split her tongue in two. What a beautiful creature."

"Beautiful crrreature," screeched Matilda in a witch's voice. "Beeeautiful crrreature."

Matilda went and perched on Tartar's head. The horse was still galloping gently. He was covered in snow.

"Did you come to play with us?" enquired Lucretia. "I'm glad, because I get very bored here. Let's make believe that we're all horses. I'll turn myself into a horse; with some snow, it'll be more convincing. You be a horse too, Matilda."

"Horse, horse, horse," yelled Matilda, dancing hysterically on Tartar's head. Lucretia threw herself into the snow, which was already deep, and rolled in it, shouting, "We are all horses!"

When she emerged, the effect was extraordinary. If I hadn't known that it was Lucretia, I would have sworn that it was a horse. She was beautiful, a blinding white all over, with four legs as fine as needles, and a mane which fell around her long face like water. She laughed with joy and danced madly around in the snow.

"Gallop, gallop, Tartar, but I shall go faster than you." Tartar didn't change speed, but his eyes sparkled. One could only see his eyes, for he was covered in snow. Matilda cawed and struck her head against the walls. As for me, I danced a sort of polka so as not to die of cold.

Suddenly I noticed that the door was open, and that an old woman stood framed in the doorway. She had been there perhaps for a long time without my noticing her. She looked at Lucretia with a nasty stare.

"*Stop at once*," she cried, suddenly trembling with fury. "What's all this? Eh, my young ladies? Lucretia, you know this game has been strictly forbidden by your father. This ridiculous game. You aren't a child anymore."

Lucretia danced on, flinging out her four legs dangerously near the old woman; her laughter was piercing.

"*Stop, Lucretia!*"

Lucretia's voice became more and more shrill. She was doubled up with laughter.

"All right," said the old woman. "So you won't obey me, young lady? All right, you'll regret it. I'm going to take you to your father."

One of her hands was hidden behind her back but with astonishing speed for someone so old, she jumped on Lucretia's back and forced a bit between her teeth. Lucretia leapt into the air, neighing with rage, but the old woman held on. After that she caught each of us, me by my hair and Matilda by her head, and all four of us were hurled into a frenzied dance. In the corridor, Lucretia kicked out everywhere and smashed pictures and chairs and china. The old woman clung to her back like a limpet to a rock. I was covered in cuts and bruises, and thought Matilda must be dead, for she was fluttering sadly in the old woman's hand like a rag.

We arrived in the dining room in a veritable orgy of noise. Sitting at the end of a long table an old gentleman, looking more like a geometric figure than anything else, was finishing his meal. All at once complete silence fell in the room. Lucretia looked at her father with swollen eyes.

"So you're starting up your old tricks again," he said, cracking a hazelnut. "Mademoiselle de la Rochefroide did well to bring you here. It's exactly three years and three days since I forbade you to play at horses. This is the seventh time that I have had to punish you, and you are no doubt aware that in our family, seven is the last number. I'm afraid, my dear Lucretia, that this time I shall have to punish you pretty severely."

The girl, who had taken the appearance of a horse, did not move, but her nostrils quivered.

"What I'm going to do is purely for your own good, my dear." His voice was very gentle. "You're too old to play with Tartar. Tartar is for children. I am going to burn him myself, until there's nothing left of him."

Lucretia gave a terrible cry and fell to her knees.

"Not that, Papa, not that."

The old man smiled with great sweetness and cracked another hazelnut.

"It's the seventh time, my dear."

The tears ran from Lucretia's great horse's eyes and carved two channels in her cheeks of snow. She turned such a dazzling white that she shone like a star.

"Have pity, Papa, have pity. Don't burn Tartar."

Her shrill voice grew thinner and thinner, and she was soon kneeling in a pool of water. I was afraid that she was going to melt away.

"Mademoiselle de la Rochefroide, take Miss Lucretia outside," said her father, and the old woman took the poor creature, who had become all thin and trembling, out of the room. I don't think he had noticed I was there. I hid behind the door and heard the old man go up to the nursery. A little later I stopped my ears with my fingers, for the most frightful neighing sounded from above, as if an animal were suffering extreme torture.

❖

FROM LEONORA CARRINGTON
LEONORA CARRINGTON: A RETROSPECTIVE
(NEW YORK: CENTER FOR INTER-AMERICAN RELATIONS, 1976)

Commentary, 1975

The Cabbage is a rose; the Blue Rose, The Alchemical Rose, the Blue Deer (Peyote), and the eating of the God is ancient knowledge, but only recently known to "civilized occidental" Humans who have experienced many phenomena, and have recently written many books that give accounts of the changing worlds which these people have seen when they ate these plants. Although the properties of the cabbage are somewhat different, it also screams when dragged out of the earth and plunged into boiling water or grease — forgive us, cabbage.

Writing and painting are alike in that both arts — music as well — come out of fingers and into some receptive artifact. The result, of course, is read, heard or seen through the receptive organs of those who receive the art and are supposed to "Be" what all these different persons perceive differently. Therefore it seems that any introduction to art is fairly senseless since anybody can think or experience according to who he is. Very likely the introduction will not be read anyhow.

Once a dog barked at a mask I made; that was the most honourable comment I ever received.

The Furies, who have a sanctuary buried many fathoms under education and brain washing, have told Females they will return, return from under the fear, shame and, finally, through the crack in the prison door, Fury. I do not know of any religion that does not declare women to be feeble–minded, unclean, generally inferior creatures to males, although most Humans assume that we are the cream of all species. Women, alas; but, thank God, Homo Sapiens. . . !

Most of us, I hope, are now aware that a woman should not have to demand Rights. The Rights were there from the beginning; they must be Taken Back Again, including the Mysteries which were ours and which were violated, stolen or destroyed, leaving us with the thankless hope of pleasing a male animal, probably of one's own species. . . .

There are so many questions and so much Dogmaturd to clear aside before anything makes sense, and we are on the point of destroying the earth before we know anything at all. Perhaps a great virtue, curiosity can only be satisfied if the millennia of accumulated false data are turned upside down. Which means turning oneself inside out and to begin by despising no thing, ignoring no thing . . . and make some interior space for digestive purposes. Our machine-mentation still reacts to colossal absurdities with violence, pleasure, pain . . . automatically. Such as: I am, I am, I am. [Anything from an archbishop to a disregarded boot.] But is this so? Am I? Indigestion is imminent; there is too much of it. The Red Queen told Alice that we should walk backwards slowly in order to arrive there faster and faster.

The Sacred Deer is still worshipped in the desert here in Mexico.

The cabbage is still the alchemical Rose for any being able to see or taste.

Footprints are face to face with the firmament.

Old Father, the Story-teller, 1960
© Pablita Velarde

PABLITA VELARDE

B. 1918

BORN AND RAISED in the Santa Clara pueblo in New Mexico, Pablita Velarde has sought to establish a bond with her Native American ancestors and their teachings. She has seen herself and her work as bridge between the profound spirituality of her cultural tradition and the mundane world of twentieth-century existence. As a Native American artist of the Southwest, Velarde has achieved success, her work awarded numerous prizes and herself a figure of renown. In not attempting to enter the dominant world of western-European-inspired art, Velarde's orientation differs from that of other artists included in this volume. Like many of the others, however, she defined herself as an artist early in her life, has worked steadily at her art since that time, and has used the written word to express her vision. Writing, in fact, has been an important part of Velarde's creative endeavor and, while she has used the customs of her people as the subject of her art, their oral legends have formed the basis of her written work. Both her art and writings articulate the complexity of her multiple cultural allegiances. The revision of art history would do well to include her view from the margin, along with those in the mainstream.

Pablita Velarde was the third daughter born to farmers Herman and Marianita Velarde. She was called *Tse Tsan* (golden dawn) and as a child spoke only the Tewa language of the pueblo. When she was three, her mother died of tuberculosis, leaving behind by that time four daughters. Shortly thereafter Pablita and one of her sisters contracted a strange and undiagnosable eye ailment that kept them from being able to see for about two years. After their also unexplained recovery, when she was about six, the sisters began to attend St. Catherine's Indian School, a boarding school in Santa Fe, which Velarde attended from kindergarten through the sixth grade. With her arrival at St. Catherine's, Velarde began to learn about Anglo culture and acquire proficiency in the English language, to which she had not been previously exposed. (Although there are many accounts of Indian children forcibly taken from their families for "indoctrination" in an alien culture, this was not the case with the Velardes.) The Velarde sisters spent winters at the school and returned to the pueblo, where they helped with the farming chores during the summer months. It was during those summers that Velarde was first exposed to ancient Native American art when she would climb the Puye ruins above the Santa Clara pueblo, a cliff dwelling called "Pueblo of the Clouds," that was the ancient home of the Santa Clara people. Among the ruins the sisters found potshards, arrowheads, and flat rocks decorated with abstract pictures, and Velarde still vividly recalls her excitement at finding these "rock pictures."

After graduating from St. Catherine's in 1932, Velarde attended the United States Indian School, also in Santa Fe, run by the Bureau of Indian Affairs. During her first year there she encountered the teacher Dorothy Dunn, who had just come from Chicago to teach art. She encouraged her students to draw upon their tribal symbols and belief systems as artistic sources, and taught them basic technical painting skills, but not an academic way of seeing. Velarde was instantly receptive to Dunn's teaching method and, by the end of her first year of study, she began to gain recognition for her work. Before her graduation from the Indian School in 1936, Velarde had already exhibited a mural at the Century of Progress exhibit in Chicago and, along with other Native American students, had been hired by the federal government's art projects program to work on other murals depicting pueblo life. After graduation, Velarde returned to the pueblo where she taught arts and crafts at the day school, and helped her father and his new wife with their young children. In 1938, working as an au pair for the family of Ernest Seton, founder of the Boy Scouts of America, she traveled around the country as he gave lectures.

Velarde was only twenty-one when her career was effectively launched in 1939 by the receipt of two important commissions. The first, received through the efforts of Olive Rush, who had taken her work to the Century of Progress exhibit, involved several other young Native American artists who together painted a mural for the façade and open-air lobby of Maisels, a store that sold native crafts in Albuquerque. The second, the real breakthrough for her, came later that year, when Velarde was commissioned to make an extensive series of painted backdrops for display cases at the Bandelier National Monument in Frijoles Canyon, New Mexico. She drew upon her childhood memories in order to show scenes from pueblo life in the old days (the inhabitants of Frijoles Canyon had been cliff dwellers in the tradition of the ancient Santa Clarans). The thematic range of the cycle of images was extensive, depicting such everyday activities as growing, grinding, and cooking corn, hunting and preparing rabbits, ceremonial dances, and community government inside the ceremonial kiva. Although the purpose of these paintings was illustrative, Velarde's intention was to create each one as a work of art. Work on the project was interrupted in 1940 when government funding was redirected to the war effort; however, after the war was over, Velarde was rehired in 1946 to complete it.

During the period of the Second World War, Velarde's personal life underwent significant changes. When she was forced to stop work on the Bandelier project, she returned to Santa Clara where, contrary to traditional expectations, she remained unmarried, built her own house, and supported herself through the sale of craft items. She obtained a position as a telephone operator at the Bureau of Indian Affairs in Albuquerque, where, in 1941, she met Herbert Hardin, an Anglo whom she married shortly thereafter. Together they had a son and a daughter, who also became an artist. Hardin was drafted shortly after their marriage and their lives remained unsettled until he graduated in 1947 from the University of California and they returned to Albuquerque to live. They remained married until 1959. Velarde pursued her painting career throughout, drawing from themes inspired by her cultural heritage, and, over the years she received many awards and commissions. In 1954, along with Dorothy Dunn and several of Dunn's other students, Velarde received the Palmes des Académiques, a French Government award for artistic merit. The next year Velarde took the top prizes at the Intertribal Indian Ceremony in Gallup, New Mexico. In 1968 she received the Waite-Phillips trophy from the Philbrook Art Center in Tulsa, for "her outstanding contribution to Indian art in America." Two recent commissions include a set of panels for the Museum of New Mexico in Santa Fe and a large mural of the Herd Dance for the Indian Pueblo Cultural Center in Albuquerque.

During the mid-1950s, Velarde began work on a different sort of project, one that offered another means of exploring her connections to her cultural roots. She turned at that time to her family in the Santa Clara pueblo; although they had not been close since her childhood, she started to visit her father regularly, in order to hear once more the stories she remembered him telling in the community plaza. She collected these tales, and published them as *Old Father, the Story-teller* in 1960. In this book, each of the six traditional stories is accompanied by at least one original painting by Velarde. The volume begins with a magical depiction of Old Father, the Story-teller seated in the village square at night, the parade of constellations whose meaning he explains above him, the pueblo children seated around him, rapt with attention. This book contributed considerably to Velarde's public reputation. However, in writing down oral legends Velarde was going against tradition and when she returned during the 1960s to transcribe more Tewa folktales, she met resistance from both tribal officials and "unseen forces," sufficient to make her return to her life in Albuquerque.

One important way in which Velarde maintains a connection with traditional culture is through her choice of materials. Although her earliest works were watercolors, and she has used other media, such as oil and acrylic, Velarde is particularly interested in creating works that use pigments made from earth materials, as are "the ones on the kiva walls." She was originally introduced to the idea of grinding her own pigments in her teacher Dorothy Dunn's studio; however, for the most part, finding appropriate materials has been a process of trial and error. She says that for a time she gathered a wide assortment of all kinds of "rocks and dirt," that she "ground everything in sight" in her search for suitable earth-toned pigments. When Velarde is ready to paint, she mixes her powdered pigments with water and glue to achieve a desired "velvety appearance."

Dorothy Dunn's teachings influenced Velarde's style as well. When Dunn established her studio in Santa Fe, she did not want to teach an academic style of painting, but rather "to guide, encourage, discover, and discern" the rich Native American art tradition that was "very different from the heterogenous cultural background of the average American child." In order to help native children appreciate their "brilliant heritage" and use that as the basis of their art, instead of creating popularized distillations of academic style such as calendar and poster art, Dunn introduced her students to the collections of the Laboratory of Anthropology, in Santa Fe.

The resulting style as seen in Velarde's work is a somewhat problematic blend of diverse sources. In terms of her manipulation of formal elements, Velarde's style is definitely not academic. Even her most descriptive works contain elements of the principles of pictorial abstraction. Her colors are broad and flat, her figures devoid of modeling, and repeating patterns unify the picture surface. In *Koshares of Taos*, for example, she uses flat colors and repeating patterns to articulate her figures, rather than chiaroscuro or anatomical verism, and she creates a conceptual bilateral symmetry to structure her pictorial surface, rather than linear perspective. It is difficult to ascertain, however, to what extent an "Indian" quality resides in such a work, the aesthetics of which resemble those of many Anglo painters who were also not academically trained. Perhaps it is the high degree of narrative descriptiveness that makes her works seem more related to Anglo style than to indigenous forms. On the other hand, her work is so clearly Native American in content that her descriptive recordings of real-life activities have sometimes been read as ethnographic documents rather than as works of art.

Velarde's involvement with the content of her work rises beyond the purely narrative level to a greater spiritual dimension. For Velarde the use of subjects derived from observation of and experiences in the pueblo enables her to express her sense of profound connection with her heritage. The stories in *Old Father, the Story-teller* offer mythic answers to fundamental questions. In "The Stars," Old Father explains how the Santa Clarans came to their land. In "Sad Eyes," he tells about spiritual freedom through the metaphor of a boy raised by deer. "The First Twins" establishes the role of serious clowning in its ability to summon the supernatural and to banish evil. She referred to the period in her life when she began to work on the Bandolier paintings as the time "when I started to feed my soul with the old legends and hearsays." Through the process of immersing herself in cultural traditions, Velarde has brought herself to a deeper spiritual understanding, one that she has been able to share with others through writing and painting.

In traditional pueblo culture, women's creative abilities were greatly respected, but their art-making was limited to abstract design and pottery, with some women (notably Maria Martinez of San Ildefonso pueblo) achieving broad success as artists. As a painter of representational and narrative images, Velarde challenged the status quo. She acknowledges the painter Tonita Peña, the only earlier female narrative painter, as the inspiration that enabled her "to dare the men who put [her] in her place," and she has said that after she won the award from the Philbrook Art Center, "the boys didn't think that I belonged in the kitchen anymore because I was on their level."

Velarde's life and work have interwoven the values of both the Native American and Anglo cultures. Her own statement, "When I go back to sandy lake and

become a cloud person, the earth will remember me through my work," expresses the complexity of Velarde's endeavor: abiding respect for traditional values combined with recognition of her work in the public realm. The very communication
of her cultural tradition that has been a guiding principle of Velarde's art and life
has required her to change that tradition by being a woman who makes "male"
art and by recording the oral tradition in writing.

SOURCES

Wilt, Shirley (producer, director, writer). *Pablita Velarde*. National Park Service.
Videotape.
Nelson, Mary Carol. *Pablita Velarde*. Minneapolis: Dillon Press, 1971.
Silberman, Arthur. *100 Years of Native American Painting*. Oklahoma City: Okla-
homa Museum of Art, 1978.
Tanner, Clara Lee. *Southwest Indian Painting*. 2d ed. Tucson: University of Ari-
zona Press, 1973.
Velarde, Pablita *Old Father, the Story-teller*. Globe, Arizona: Dale Stuart King, 1960.
Reprint. Santa Fe: Clear Light Press, 1989.

SELECTIONS FROM PABLITA VELARDE
OLD FATHER, THE STORY-TELLER, 1960
(REPRINT. SANTA FE, NM: CLEAR LIGHT PRESS, 1989)

"THE STARS"

Many stars made bright holes in the clear, cold, autumn sky. In the village
plaza a fire danced and children danced around it. They were happy and excited because Old Father was in the village and would begin tonight to tell them
the winter's stories.

"Tell us a story, tell us a story." They loved Old Father and he loved them
and understood them. His kindness made a warmth like the fire. He laughed
and asked "What kind of a story?", and a tiny voice came tumbling, "Why are
some stars brighter than all the others? And why don't they ever fall where we
can find them?"

The children settled around the fire as Old Father gazed up at the stars
with a faraway smile. Pointing first toward Orion in the east, he said:

That is "Long Sash," the guide of our ancestors; he led our people to this
beautiful land where we now live. Our people followed him without question,
for he was a great warrior who had won many battles. He had grown tired of
seeing misery all around him, his own people suffering because of the cruel
ruler they had lived under for so many years. During his battles he had been in
distant lands, and when he told his people about these they asked him to take
them there. They were determined to end their suffering by going away to a
new land.

He tried to discourage them, telling them they had nothing to take along.
He warned them of the hardships, the sickness, and the deaths they would face,
but they were determined people, and in the end he could not refuse them.

They traveled with empty stomachs and scant clothing. Many died from
hunger and disease, but they continued on and on. Long Sash taught them to
hunt for their food, to make clothing from animal skins and bird feathers. After

a time he led them into a land where no man, not even he, had been. It was daylight all the time, and they rested only when they were too weary to travel any more. Many children were born, and some died, but the brave spirit of these people kept them going.

Old Father paused to look around him. He saw all the children were gazing upward as if the stars, gleaming like mica, had hypnotized them. Waving his hand across the sky Old Father raised the pitch of his voice, bringing the children out of their trance. They followed him, wide–eyed and open–mouthed.

"See that milky white belt across the middle of the sky?"

"Yes," they all answered at once.

"Well," continued Old Father, "that is the Endless Trail they were traveling on. In time, some of the people became doubtful and hard to reason with, and violence began to show itself here and there. Thereupon Long Sash decided that force was to be used on no one, that those who wished to follow him could come, and those who wanted to turn back could do so. In order to give every one an opportunity to rest and make his own decision, he had them camp on the spot. It was time for many of the women to bear their babies.

"See those two big bright stars (Gemini) to the north of Long Sash?" Old Father waited for an answer, but when none came he smiled and continued:

They are stars of decision. We must all make choices between forward and backward, good or bad. They mark the trail where Long Sash told his people, "If we choose to go forward, it will be a good choice, for the lives of the young stretch long before them. Choose the road back and you know what torture you will live. We have our signs ahead of us; let us not close our eyes, to see only the darkness!"

It did not take long for the people to decide to follow their leader. They all went on with lighter hearts and greater hopes. Long Sash sang loudly as he led his people on what seemed an endless journey. He hoped they would reach their destination soon, but he had prepared his people well, he had taught them patience, tolerance, and love for one another. Yet for some reason there was an emptiness in his own soul and he could not understand the reason why.

He himself was growing tired of the long wandering, and when he was by himself he wept in despair. He began to feel strange beings around him, and to hear unfamiliar voices. Not understanding these things, his first thought was that he must be losing his mind, but he was determined that he would lead his people to safety before anything happened to him. While he was resting he began talking aloud, and his people thought he was talking to them, and they gathered around him.

His voice was strange: "My fathers and my mothers, wherever you are, hear me, give me your guidance and give me strength to find our home. My people are tired now and I am not young as I once was. Give me wisdom and strength to decide for them, and give me an omen, give me an omen!"

The people looked at each other fearfully, feeling the need for someone stronger than Long Sash to depend upon. They looked at him, who was now asleep. They discussed what he had said and wondered about the unseen beings with whom he had spoken. They became afraid of him, and when he awoke he sensed that something was troubling his people, so he gathered them about him and told them he had had a dream with many omens in it. He told them the most difficult part of their journey was over; traveling would be easier for the rest of the trip. He told them of the unseen beings and the voices he had sensed, and commanded that they be addressed as "Fathers and Mothers," and that the people ask for their aid whenever the need for help was felt. "Always have faith in them, for they will answer you with their blessings. I am not sick of mind. Now my mind is clearer than it has ever been. I will leave my head-dress here as a symbol to all the others who may need a reminder of the greater spirits." . . .

After a long time they came into darkness and everyone was afraid again, but their leader kept on, following a bright light coming through a very small opening (Sipapu in Hopi; sipo–pede in Tewa). From somewhere they heard something digging and scratching. Still following the bright light they came closer to the noise, and when they reached the opening they found a little mole digging away. Long Sash thanked the small creature for helping them to find the opening, but the mole only replied, "Go and when you again find my sign, you will have found your home." They found a cord hanging and climbed toward the opening.

Through the opening Long Sash saw Old Spider Woman, busy weaving, and he asked permission to enter. Replied Old Spider Woman, "You are wel-come to pass through my house. Do not destroy anything and I will help you find your way out and show you the direction to take. When you see my sign again, you will have found your home." Long Sash thanked her, but he could not understand at the time what she meant.

Continuing on their way they came to a very cold, beautiful land to the north where they rested for many years. Some stayed to make their homes, for they were tired of moving. Long Sash told his people, " this is the land of ice and snow, and your helper is the bear, for he is big and powerful, as one must be in order to live here. Those who wish to continue I will lead, for we have not yet found any signs of the mole and spider." . . .

Long Sash called again for help from his spiritual ancestors, praying that they would again show him a sign. He felt low in spirit, but he taught his fol-lowers how to talk from their hearts, and how to find happiness in their misery, and how to read signs. From him they learned a new way of life, guided by a new belief. Many of our ancient ceremonials born of that belief are still with us, but many others have passed with time.

After Long Sash's communication with the spirits of his forefathers, a great bird flew overhead and circled the people four times before dropping two feathers from its tail. Falling to the ground, one feather pointed in the direction of the coyote, while the other pointed to the people. Long Sash then declared, "Here is our sign from our powerful messenger, the eagle. He tells us to follow in this direction!"

When they came to the new land they found it to have seasons wet and dry, hot and cold, with good soil and bad. There was game, but it was hard to get. Here and there they found little scratches or tracks, but they had not found the mole as they had expected to do. However, close to the banks of a muddy river they found an ugly creature with very rough skin and on his back a stone–like shell. He made the tracks of a mole, yet he was not a mole. Long Sash studied him for a long time before he exclaimed, "Look, he carries his home with him and is protected by it at all times because when he is drawn up inside it he looks and rolls like a rock. He travels slowly, as we have done. On his back we can see plainly that he carries the sign of the spider; and when he moves, his feet make tracks like those of the mole."

This made the people very happy, for now they were certain they had found their homeland here where we are today. We move about a little now and then but we will never leave this land, for this is where we belong.

❖

"Sad Eyes"

At sunrise a Deer Dance had begun, and most of the children had been awake since long before dawn. Still they chattered around the evening fire, asking Old Father endless questions about the day's exciting ceremony. Said Old Father,

Whenever you hear the early morning call of the Deer Dance ceremony you are hearing the echo of a song once sung to the deer by a boy who loved them.

It was pinyon harvesting time, and everyone in the village was camping on the high mesa near Puye. Men, women, and children started out early at dawn. A girl among them was expecting a child, and being young and inexperienced, she wandered deep into the woods, and there she bore her son. Frightened, she made her way back to camp but could not remember which direction she had taken, and although a search was made, the child could not be found.

A family of deer came down to the canyon to drink at evening time. Father deer was leading as usual, with mother following, then the young one. The old buck sensed something strange, and after sniffing the air he approached a clump of bushes, where he found the little human boy. He called the other two deer and they all sniffed the child and licked him with their tongues. Mother deer said she would nurse the boy, and while she fed him she began to love this little human child and made plans to carry him home. This she did by laying him across the father deer's antlers, and in this manner they carried him with them wherever they wandered.

As time went by the child grew and was happy with life. He was as wild as the animals and as swift-footed. He knew he was different but did not know how he came to be so. He understood the ways of the deer, for he was one of them. He knew the changes of the seasons and became aware of the dangers around him.

One year, when the leaves had changed and fallen, he was saddened for the first time in his life, because his deer brother whom he loved very much was missing. He went to look for his brother, and during his search he came near a camp where he saw beings like himself sitting around a fire, making noises. He could not understand why they sat so close to the fire, for to him fire was dangerous! He heard one of them lifting his voice above the others, and it made him want to do the same thing. He tried it, but he was heard and seen by the men, and soon he was running through the thicket to escape, which he did easily by outrunning his pursuers.

When he came back to the cave where he lived he told Father and Mother Deer what he had seen, and tried to sing the song. Although they did not understand him, they listened and approved. It became a familiar sound to them to hear the boy sing as he rode on the back of the father deer.

At the village there was excitement at the news the men told of seeing a wild boy in the woods. It was decided to hunt him down, as he might have been the cause of their many hunting failures the past few seasons. The first tries were disappointing; they could not locate the boy or even a deer. At last they encircled the water hole and sat in wait for the deer to come for their daily drink. They heard singing and saw a herd of deer coming, with the boy riding on the back of the biggest and oldest buck in the herd!

As the boy jumped off and lay flat on the ground to drink, the hunters closed in and captured him. They took him to the village and locked him in a room with a very small opening, and he was bewildered and very frightened.

He could not eat the food given him. All his life he had eaten roots, berries, and nuts and had drunk milk from mother deer with new fawns. His stomach pained, but still he would not eat. His eyes grew sadder every day.

One evening he heard voices as a woman outside his room begged the guard to allow her to see the boy. At first the guard would not listen, and became angry with her, and pushed her out of the way. She fell, and her eyes filled with tears. Her eyes had such sadness in them, the guard felt sorry he had been brutal, and he helped her up and let her enter the room, with a last warning that the boy was wild and might harm her.

As she entered she saw the boy crouching in a corner and she knelt beside him and studied his features. A deep feeling drew her to him, but when she lifted her hand to touch him he sprang out of reach. As they gazed steadily at one another, the sadness in his eyes seemed to be asking something of her. She knew the strange boy was miserable, and she smiled gently at him. His expression did not change, but after a time he did not seem to be afraid of her.

After that, the woman was allowed to stay with the boy. She made him sandals, and a kilt, and when she dressed him she was pleased to see he was a handsome young man. She showed him how to tan animal hides and to use the bone awl and sinews of animals for sewing. She made a quiver out of the skin of a lynx, taught him how to make arrows with flint tips, and brought him a bow. He even learned to say a few words, just as he had learned from the deer their way of talking.

He sometimes smiled at the woman now, but his eyes did not lose their sadness. Most of the day he stood at the small window humming his song, looking up at the fog clouds, the cloud flowers, on top of the mountain. Slowly the woman came to know he would never be happy with people. She thought of how she herself had often gone alone to the mountain and found peace there, feeling near to the Great One as she listened to the mountain's breathsound. She promised herself that when the time was right she would help the boy find his way back where he belonged.

In the mountains the deer had missed the boy, too. In dangerous attempts to find him some had lost their lives. As time passed they thought his life, too, must have been lost, and more sadness came into their eyes.

One day the woman was allowed to take the boy for a walk, the belief being that he had forgotten the deer. They walked toward the mountains, the boy's hand held tightly in hers, and when they turned to come back she saw the boy's eyes fill with tears. "Ahi, ahi, what can I do," she chanted softly, and she let his hand go. As he walked away from her he was singing his song, and the woman knew this time it was for her.

Now it is she who looks from her window up at the mountain, but her eyes are not sad. She has just finished a water jug, on it a new design, "The House of the Deer." To her it means the dwelling place of the spirit deer, a place where he has eternal freedom, and this brings her happiness for the strange boy.

As you know, we still use her design on ceremonial ollas.

"First Twins"

When the snows had gone Old Father came to the village to take part in the Thawing–out ceremony, and he told the children this story:

In another village a long time ago there lived an old couple. They had no children of their own, although they had prayed every day to the Great One for a child.

Early one morning as they returned home from giving offering to the Great Spirit they heard the weak crying of a baby. Both wondered if they had really heard the sound or if it were just wishful thinking. The old man walked toward the woodpile to gather some wood for the old woman's outdoor fireplace, toward which she had turned. As he bent over the woodpile he saw a tiny baby lying there! He called to the old woman, but to her own astonishment she had found in the ashes of the fireplace a tiny baby boy! They lifted the babies and turned at the same moment to show each other what they had found.

The sun was just rising over the mountains, and holding the babies toward it they silently prayed for care and protection of the children. The Grandfather went off to report the finding of the children to the men who governed the village, leaving Grandmother at home praying they would be allowed to keep the babies. In four days they would know, for, according to custom, if no one claimed the children in that time and no other family wanted them they might remain with the finders. . . .

As the years passed, the boys grew strong and happy. Grandfather taught them all the things young men should know —planting, harvesting and hunting — and they learned fast, and took over all of the old man's work. Grandmother taught them how to take care of their bodies and also how to avoid the evil ones. . . .

As they grew, so did their imaginations, and by the time they were adults some of their habits seemed strange to others and they were not invited to the other young men's activities. Grandfather advised them to change their ways, to be more serious with life; and because they were obedient boys who loved their parents they tried to heed his advice.

One morning one of the twins told the other of a dream he had had, but before he could finish, the other boy told him the rest of it. This happened many more times and, as they thought it strange, they told the old man about it. The old one told them parts of their dreams were of true things, matters they did not know about because they were not invited to village gatherings. He advised them to make a special visit to a shrine in the mountains, to fast and ask guidance. Grandmother made preparations for them, and gave the boys her blessing.

The old ones realized the meaning of the boys' dreams and felt that the twins should commune with the Spirit who was calling them. For a long time they had known that these children they had brought up were possessed with power beyond the natural. Now they could no longer protect them as children, but must let them realize their powers for themselves.

Over many years a wicked man in the village had gained complete control over the people. They were afraid of him, for he was an evil man who was known to have brought about such unexplainable happenings as illness which came suddenly, or even death in those families who resisted him. Fearful unhappiness hung over the whole village.

When the twins returned they told Grandfather what they must do, assuring him they had the protection of the Great One. Then they went to the wicked man and challenged him to a contest of powers. He accepted the challenge and demanded death to the loser!

The twins fasted and prayed, and when the day arrived everyone in the village gathered in the square to watch. The twins appeared in ridiculous costumes. Their bodies were painted in stripes of black and white, and corn husks were tied to their bodies and hair. Deer hoofs, fastened around their ankles, rattled as they walked. The people began to laugh at these good–natured boys, who went right along telling jokes and clowning. The people had not laughed so hard in a long time: they had been afraid to do so. This made the wizard angry, and he shouted that he was ready to begin the contest.

To frighten the people, he commanded the sacred serpent to appear and the Ava–yunn came out of the wall of his house! He ordered Ava–yunn, the Storm Serpent Old Man, keeper of all bodies of water, to spit out water into an olla set before him and this the serpent did. The wizard took the olla and had the water tested by the people. Then he shouted commands for corn stalks and squash plants to come forth, and the plants appeared! Now, he said, let the twins match his magic if they could.

With high praise for the wizard, the twins prepared to take their turn. They addressed each other as "Little Brother Before Me," explaining that they did not know which one had come first. The wizard, although flattered by their praise, shouted impatiently for them to get on with the contest. . . .

The twins grew more serious. They began talking in turns of something they could see far away, drawing ever nearer. With words they pictured cloud people approaching out of the distance along a rainbow. The listeners, absorbed and quiet, seemed to fall into a trance of expectancy as the twins talked, and burdens they had lived under for a long time were lifted from them.

At last one twin slapped his palms together and a puff of cloud arose. It flowered into a fog, and suddenly there was a roar of thunder and a flash of lightning. The people heard a singing of beautiful songs, mingled with the sound of raindrops. Through the mist they could see Kachinas dancing. They felt overwhelmed but at peace, and they threw sacred corn meal as an offering of their gratitude for this blessing. As the mist lifted, they saw the Kachinas go away as they had come, leaving with the people messages of hope and peace and happiness. The people knew, with hearts full of humility, that no one else would be blessed in this way.

Then they saw that the wizard was lying dead, struck by lightning, bringing to pass his own penalty of death to the loser!

The twins became great leaders in their village as the years went by. They were the first Koshares. That is why today the Koshares still call each other "Little Brother Before Me," as they appear at ceremonials in their black and white painted stripes, making the people laugh. But the Koshares also play a serious part, for they are summoners of the Kachinas — the supernatural ones, our ancestors. It is also true that the Pueblo Indians, among whom the birth of twins is rare, believed for many years that all such children had supernatural powers. They had customs concerning twins which, along with many of their sacred rites, they prefer not to have written down.

Homage to My Young Black Sisters, 1968 Cedar. 6' h.
Museo de Arte Moderno, Mexico City, Mexico
Used with permission of Elizabeth Catlett

ELIZABETH CATLETT

B. 1919

THE SCULPTOR AND printmaker Elizabeth Catlett may be considered the grande dame of African-American artists, even though she has lived in Mexico for most of her career. Like Käthe Kollwitz, to whom she has occasionally been compared, Catlett believes that art must be socially relevant in order to be effective. She is firmly committed to creating art that is "based on the needs of people," an art that both grows from and speaks to the experiences of ordinary people. For Catlett that especially means blacks, the poor, women, and Mexicans, people traditionally denied a voice and for whom her work speaks. The desire to give voice to the speechless she expresses in both her sculptures and prints, building with large forms that hover between the real and the abstract. Catlett has also empowered people through art in her career as a distinguished teacher who has influenced several generations of younger artists. She has spoken out in her writings regarding her artistic credo, particularly concerning her identification as a black artist and the importance for herself and other black artists of attending to their cultural heritage.

The death of Catlett's father, a former professor at Tuskegee Institute and at the time a mathematics teacher in the Washington, D.C., public schools, six months after her birth shaped Catlett's early life. Her mother, Mary, who had also trained as a teacher, was able to find only menial work to support Elizabeth and two older siblings, although she later became a truant officer for the Washington school system. Both of Catlett's maternal grandparents and her father's mother were freed slaves who spoke openly about their lives. Education was an abiding tradition in her family; although it had been illegal for a slave to be literate, her grandfather had been taught to read and write and, in turn, he educated all four of his children. Catlett has frequently acknowledged with respect and gratitude her grandparents' legacy and her debt to their struggle.

Catlett's interest in art began while she attended public school in Washington. Having decided to study art in college, she applied to Carnegie Institute in Pittsburgh where a cousin lived. Catlett experienced racism firsthand during the selection process: the only black applicant, she was denied admission despite the high quality of her work; she actually overheard a remark to the effect that it was "too bad" that she was black. She enrolled instead in the art department at Howard University in Washington, D. C., where she encountered her first artistic mentors — James Herring, the founder of the department; James Porter; James Wells; and Lois Mailou Jones. Porter was especially influential in introducing her to the work of the Mexican muralists and even helped get her a contract to paint murals for the Public Works Art Project, although by her own admission she did not take full advantage of this opportunity. During her time at Howard, she became increasingly committed to political activism. After graduating with honors, Catlett spent two years teaching art in Durham, N. C., where she continued her activism, fighting for equal pay for black teachers.

She further pursued her art studies in 1938, at the University of Iowa from which she received a Masters in Fine Arts two years later. She had chosen Iowa for two reasons: it offered free tuition for out-of-state students and the faculty included the American regionalist painter Grant Wood. Despite the obvious differences in their usual media, styles, and subject matter, Wood had a significant impact on the direction of Catlett's art. First, he presented her with an example of a rigorous and disciplined approach to work. Then, she was much impressed with his advice to "paint what you know," which Catlett understood to be her experience as a black woman. It was at Iowa that she seriously began to base her art on the content of that experience. Finally, Wood's encouragement led Catlett to first experiment with sculpture. Although as a graduate student she had initially concentrated in painting, her thesis project was a sculpture of a seated mother and child which won first prize at Chicago's Diamond Jubilee Exhibit of Negro Art later that year. Catlett was, in fact, the university's first recipient of an M.F.A. in sculpture. The positive educational aspects of her years at Iowa and her apparent success there are all the more remarkable since she had been forced to live in a racist environment where she had to seek off-campus housing in the "Negro" part of town, after being excluded from the segregated, all-white dormitory.

The next six or so years of Catlett's life were characterized by many changes, during which time she explored a variety of options. Her first major position after graduate school was as head of the art department at Dillard University, a black school in New Orleans, from 1940 to 1942. One of her most telling recollections of that period is of the clever subterfuge by which she snuck her class through a segregated park into a museum to see a Picasso exhibition. During the summer of 1941 she studied at the Art Institute of Chicago, where she met and married the printmaker Charles White. After spending a year in New Orleans, they moved to New York where they remained for the following five years.

Catlett found the atmosphere in New York stimulating to her artistic development and to her emerging identity as a black artist. She and White became part of a community of black intellectuals, including the artists Hale Woodruff, Romare Bearden and Jacob Lawrence, and the poets Gwendolyn Bennett and Langston Hughes. Catlett and some of these artistic leaders worked together on the faculty of the George Washington Carver School in Harlem, an experimental institution founded as a night school to expose ordinary working people to contemporary black figures in the arts. Catlett's experiences there were central to her understanding of and respect for the cultural needs of those she considered to be the audience for her work.

While in New York she encountered another of her artistic mentors, the French sculptor Ossip Zadkine. Zadkine held a quasi-Cubist approach to building form through the juxtaposition of positive and negative shapes and, although Catlett has asserted her belief that abstract art is not universally comprehensible, Zadkine's influence is clearly discernible in the large geometric shapes of which her sculptures are built. During these years, too, Catlett studied lithography at the Art Students League, which gave her access to an important creative outlet that could be more widely disseminated than sculpture.

In 1946, Catlett and her husband, Charles White, left New York for a visit to Mexico, a trip with major consequences for the future. Although she had made the trip with her husband, while in Mexico the failure of their marriage became evident, and they returned to the States for a divorce, after which Catlett went back alone to Mexico. Both Catlett and White had associated themselves with the Taller Grafica Popular, a socially oriented graphics collective. At the Taller, Catlett met her second husband, the artist Francisco Moro, whom she married in 1947 and with whom she had three sons. To escape political harassment, Catlett became a Mexican citizen in the early 1960s.

Catlett's return to Mexico after her divorce saw her professional life blossom. She became affiliated with the Taller and remained so for the next twenty years. She appreciated a structure in which artists produced works collectively, and its populist orientation conformed to her own developing consciousness that art had to be relevant to ordinary people. In Mexico, she studied at the School of Painting and Sculpture, where Frida Kahlo had taught a decade or so earlier. There she encountered two other important teachers, Francisco Zuñiga from whom she learned ancient methods of hand-building and José Ruiz with whom she studied wood-carving. While her sons were still young, Catlett concentrated her artistic energies on works in graphic-arts media, but by the late 1950s she had begun to sculpt once more as well. She became a professor of sculpture in 1958 at the National University of Mexico's School of Fine Arts, and was appointed shortly thereafter director of the school's sculpture division, a position she held until she retired in 1976.

Catlett's art has exhibited several styles simultaneously, moving between realism and abstraction over the years that she has worked in both graphic arts and sculpture. One can generalize to say that her prints have been more often realistically descriptive, perhaps because of their potential popular audience, than her sculptures, which have depended to a great extent on large, abstracted forms. However, even her most realistically conceived prints are characterized by a summary form — for example, the mother's head in *The Torture of Mothers* and the vivid, choppy use of contrast in *Harriet* — in each case, the abstraction helping to communicate the work's message more dramatically. Thalia Gouma-Peterson's suggestion that Catlett's sculpture after 1960 became more abstract than in the previous decades is valid in some cases. Earlier works, such as her master's degree project *Mother and Child* (1940) and *Tired* (1946), are built of more rounded forms with more descriptive features than such later works as her mother-and-child figures from the 1970s. However, even in the earlier supposedly more abstract pieces Catlett emphasized the relationship among broadly generalized volumes over descriptive depiction of trivial details, making her work seem monumental, regardless of its actual size.

As a sculptor Catlett is unacknowledged heir to the direct-carving approach pioneered by Barbara Hepworth and Henry Moore. Like Hepworth, Catlett uses the characteristic markings of a particular stone or the grain of a piece of wood as positive aesthetic elements in a finished work. This is especially visible in the way the curve of the wood grain articulates the swell of the cheek and the line of the jaw in *The Black Woman Speaks* (1970), or the way the curve of the buttocks of a figure in *Recognition* (1970) is indicated by the lines of discoloration in the onyx. Catlett takes advantage of the stimulating aspect of her materials and comments that she "might exaggerate the form [of a work] to bring out a little more of the grain of the wood." Again like Hepworth, Catlett occasionally creates works that explore the flow between exterior and interior forms, as in *Homage to My Young Black Sisters* (1968) with its prominent central core, and *Mask* (1970), perhaps her least representational work. Her work is notable for its inclusion of stylistic elements based outside the Western European tradition, a probable result of three influential sources: her work with Zuñiga on pre-Columbian methods; her early studies with Zadkine who, like many Cubists, looked to African sources; and, in the 1960s an introduction to African masks. Catlett herself has said, "Abstract art was born in Africa."

Catlett has carefully observed the gestures of maternity and the interactions between mothers and their children, and her works present many differing aspects of this complex relationship. Her earliest sculpture, *Mother and Child* (1940), was executed in a relatively realistic style and shows a baby burrowing into its mother's chest for comfort. The closeness of this relationship is further explored in a much later and more abstract version of the same theme (from 1972) where the baby's head seems to grow out of its mother's chest. She presents a more playful image in *Maternity* (1979), in which the mother's hollow body becomes a swing for the baby that it encloses and shelters. Catlett has commented on the fact that the baby figure in this work detaches "because children must be independent." On the other hand, Catlett has not shied away from presenting the potential pain of motherhood, as in her woodcut, *The Torture of Mothers*, that shows mothers, whose children have been murdered or persecuted under tyrannical governments, tortured by the pain of their children.

Women have been Catlett's most significant subject in both sculpture and graphic arts, from her earliest works until her most recent. Most of her images show women's strength, dignity, and courage, often revealing their essential humanity through the expressiveness of their faces. Her figures are clearly characterized by negroid features and, in fact, it would be more accurate to say that black women form Catlett's central subject. She produced one of her most important works between 1946 and 1947 (funded by a grant from the Rosenwald Foundation), a series of fifteen linocuts of *The Black Woman*. Strong and sympathetic, from the determination of Harriet Tubman who "helped hundreds to freedom" to the contemplative quality of *Blues*, originally titled *I Have Given the World My Songs*, these works and other earlier pieces show Catlett's early and persistent political consciousness. During the sixties and early seventies, the content of her work became more politically activist; like other black artists such as Betye Saar and Faith Ringgold, Catlett was moved by the intensification of the fight for civil rights in the United States. To that effect she remarked that art was necessary only "as an aid to survival" and important only in the way in which it "helped in the liberation of our people." Her large work, *Homage to My Young Black Sisters*, an image of a woman standing with an upturned face and an outstretched arm with clenched fist, is a remarkable synthesis of her concerns at that time. In other works of the period, she incorporated male protagonists, one recognizable as Malcolm X, another an unidentified male head framed by a gun's sight in *Target*, a chilling statement about the vulnerability of blacks in a racist society.

Because the point of view of Catlett's work is so consistently that of a strong and sensitive black woman, her art provides a radical challenge to traditional images in which such women are placed in marginal positions within a sexist and racist society. In Catlett's art, black women become central. It is their faces that represent *the* human face, their experiences that embody *the* human experience. As in the title of one of her sculptures, "the black woman speaks." Freida Tesfagiorgis calls Catlett an "Afrofemcentric artist," focused on the concerns of the black woman. In her lectures and written statements, Catlett has said that black artists need to seek their inspiration in black culture in order to make a cultural contribution that will transcend race.

Perhaps the most important view expressed in Catlett's writing is the fundamental belief that art needs to be socially relevant and that the artist cannot create in a vacuum cut off from his or her people. Catlett is similar in this to Käthe Kollwitz who said "I want to be effective in this time." Both women viewed art that was only aesthetically motivated as decadent, Kollwitz eschewing the popular expressionism of her time and Catlett, the pure abstraction of hers. It is interesting, too, that Catlett and Kollwitz worked with prints and sculpture, rather than with paint.

Not only did Catlett see art as an agent for social change, she also spoke eloquently concerning the need, the very hunger, for artistic expression in the lives of ordinary people. "Since prehistoric times . . . people have had this compulsive necessity to express themselves," she said. "There exists a fundamental need to create, to form an aesthetic something from raw materials." In her role as an educator Catlett put into practice her belief that art is for everyone, not just the privileged few. She touched the lives of her students and gave them the tools to embody their own artistic visions. For Elizabeth Catlett, art-making is a kind of sharing, and it is in this context that one must consider her artistic oeuvre, as well as her teaching.

SOURCES
Elizabeth Catlett Papers, Amistad Collection, Tulane University, New Orleans, La.
Fax, Elton. *17 Black Artists*. New York: Dodd, Mead & Co., 1971.

Goldman, Shifra. "Six Women Artists of Mexico." *Woman's Art Journal* 3:2 (Fall 1982/Winter 1983): 1–9.

Gouma-Peterson, Thalia. "Elizabeth Catlett: The Power of Human Feeling and of Art." *Woman's Art Journal* 4:1 (Spring/Summer 1983): 48–56.

Lewis, Samella. *Art: African-American.* New York: Harcourt, Brace Jovanovich, 1978.

_____. *The Art of Elizabeth Catlett.* Claremont, Cal.: Hancraft Studios, 1984.

Lewis, Samella, and Ruth Waddy. *Black Artists on Art*, vol. 2. Los Angeles: Contemporary Crafts, 1971.

Tesfagiorgis, Freida High. "Afrofemcentrism and Its Fruition in the Art of Elizabeth Catlett and Faith Ringgold." *SAGE*, 4:1 (Spring 1987): 25–32.

ELIZABETH CATLETT
EXCERPTS FROM "THE POWER OF HUMAN FEELING AND OF ART"
Public Lecture, November 10, 1981, Wooster College, Ohio

In spite of Dr._____'s glowing introduction I speak to you today as a very ordinary person, a member of four exploited groups — Blacks, Mexicans, women and poor people. . . .

I am not of the exceptional. I am rather of the fortunate. If all of us here would look back for a moment to our grandparents or our great grandparents, I dare to say that most of us would feel the same. We are not the exceptional. We are the fortunate. So let us not feel superior nor removed from our brothers and sisters of other races or other classes. Let us try to learn from them and deepen our concepts of what are basic life necessities.

I received a lesson that began a change in my life's direction when I taught in a people's school in Harlem in N.Y.C. back during World War II. About 350 of us were squeezed into a small room, sitting on a hot June night with the windows closed and the shades drawn — most uncomfortable, listening to Shostakovitch's 7th Symphony. A professor from Juilliard Music School had come to play this tape for our students who were mostly from Harlem's poor people — janitors, day workers, laundresses, cooks, elevator operators and so on — poor black people who served others.

When the first movement ended the professor explained that since the second movement was very long we would take a break to refresh ourselves with some cold punch. Our students politely refused. They said no. The break can wait. We want to hear it all together. Now. Ignorant me! I had thought they weren't interested in classical music.

I offer this as only the first of many subsequent experiences that have taught me the errors of many preconceived ideas about people. There was the janitor in Shrevesport Louisiana whose opinion of the best sculpture in my exhibition coincided with mine. I began to realize that uneducated people have the same cultural needs that we fortunate university people do. I began to work in my art so that they could always relate to something — subject, form, color, movement.

True art has always come from cultural necesssity. Since prehistoric times, since the earliest cave paintings, people have had this compulsive necessity to express themselves through painting, sculpture and engraving. We imagine that [is true of] music and dance as well. There exists a fundamental need to create, to form an aesthetic something from raw materials. When this creative urge is denied fulfillment, repression and frustration occur.

We black people know from experience of the material and spiritual deprivation existing in our communities of our and other ghettos. And we know of the resultant emotional and mental conflicts frequently leading to wasted lives. . . .

We who are in the arts and other professions should be the most sensitive elements in our cities. If we would make our professions relate more to the needs of the majority our lives could develop new directions and become more meaningful. We know as things are in our consumer society possessions are more important than people.

There is a strong wind blowing over the continents of the world, carrying freedom. It carries the determination that there will be no more hunger, no more curable sickness, no more nakedness, homelessness, no more ignorance, no more hate. But instead the right to walk head-high without fear; the right of nations to develop independently, and the right of human beings to develop as individuals to their full capacity.

Because we are more and more one world what happens in Asia, Africa, and Latin America affects you here and in Europe. Just as what happens here affects us in the Third World. Our responsibilities as the intelligentsia of America extend to these people too.

I would like to return to my starting point with a quotation from Sidney Bechet, the great jazz musician. He once wrote, "After emancipation . . . all those people who had been slaves, they needed the music more than ever now. It was like they were trying to find out in this music what they were supposed to do with freedom; playing the music and listening to it — waiting for it to express what they needed to learn, once they had learned it wasn't just white people the music had to reach out to . . . but straight out to life, and to what a man does with his life when it is finally his."

Some of us are still trying to find out what to do with our art, for in much of the world the lives of black men are still not their own. The big question for me as a black woman is how do I serve my people? What is my role? What form do I use, what content, what are my priorities?

A work of art may be spiritually, intellectually, or emotionally rewarding especially in the realm of what is real. It does not need revolution as its subject in order to be revolutionary. Up to now art has had little effect on political or social revolution. It does not even need to be public. It may be quite intimate, quite personal. Art will not create social change, but it can provoke thought and prepare us for change. Art can tell us what we do not see, sometimes what we do not want to see, what we may not realize about life, about sensitivity and crassness. What seems ordinary may be seen as spectacular. What seems ugly may appear quite beautiful and vice versa. What seems trivial may become important depending on how it is presented by the artist. . . .

I am not offering myself as an example for anyone to follow. I belong to another generation and was shaped under other conditions. I don't know what is right for anyone but myself.

We are all different and these differences between us should be respected and used as a way of enriching our lives. I only hope to stimulate your thinking and give you some insight as to the personal fulfillment that may be achieved through contributing to the betterment of other people's lives. Let me end with the words of Martin Luther King, Jr., in Atlanta at the Ebenezer Baptist church. "I just want to be there in love and in justice and in truth and commitment to others, so that we can make of this old world a better world."

❖

ELIZABETH CATLETT, PUBLIC LECTURE
STUDIO MUSEUM BANQUET, OCTOBER 1983 AND
UNIVERSITY OF MISSISSIPPI, OCTOBER 1984

I am here to tell you about my work and about myself. I am Black, a woman, a sculptor and a printmaker. I am also married, the mother of three sons and the grandmother of five little girls. I am a student and a teacher. Much of my life has been spent in learning and passing it on to other people. I was born in the United States and am now a citizen of Mexico having lived there since 1946. I believe that these states of being have influenced my work and made it what you see today; — so I will briefly elaborate to show what I think may be reason and result.

I am Black because my great great grandmother was kidnapped on the beach at Madagascar and brought to these United States to be sold as a slave. Both of my mother's parents and my father's mother were slaves. I have lived in ghettos all my life in the United States with the exceptions of Greenwich Village in New York and the French Quarter in New Orleans. So I am Black in culture, in music, in literature, in food, in family, in friends and in art.

Since I studied with the regionalist painter Grant Wood (who taught me at my most impressionable age to create from what I know best), I work with the subject matter of Black people, sometimes Mexican people. Because I am a woman and know how a woman feels in body and in mind, I sculpt, draw and print women. Many of my sculptures and prints deal with maternity for I am a mother and grandmother. Once in a while I do men because I love my husband and my sons; I share their sorrows and joys; and I fear for them in this chaotic world of today.

As a student I was strongly influenced by three artists, completely different: James Porter, at Howard University, painter, teacher and art historian, who first introduced me to the seriousness of art and the necessity for dedication; Grant Wood, at the State University of Iowa, from whom I also learned the planification and development of a work of art, and the necessary rigorous formal discipline; and Ossip Zadkine, the modern French sculptor, with whom I worked, studied and argued, learning again to keep my mind open and to experiment. He believed that art should go from the international to the national and so he sculpted harlequins and musicians. I reasoned that my art should go from the national to the international and so I sculpted Black women.

As a teacher I have had to learn much, including how to teach, in order to answer the questions and demonstrate for my ever-asking students. And from them — black, white, Mexican and Japanese, I have learned. . . .

I have known for some time that as a Black woman, fortunate enough to be a sculptor, I must work figuratively. Although abstract form interests me basically, I am limited to at least a recognizable figure by what I have chosen as the dues that I must pay, that I want to pay, that I am privileged to pay. This is a conscious limitation so that almost anyone may relate to something in my work; so that they can at least pass the barrier of "What is it supposed to be?" and move on from an interest in surface quality to form and space relations.

In 1946 on my first visit to the Fine Arts Palace in Mexico City to see an exhibition of the work of José Clemente Orozco, for many the greatest of the Mexican muralists, I was amazed to see lines of people in overalls or aprons, sandals, and even some barefooted, visiting the museum, as I was to see in Orozco's paintings. I realized he had painted people like them and their heros, their enemies — and the people stood looking for a good long while — very moved as I could see. In this day of many exhibitions of non-objective abstract, or conceptual art, I no longer see them there, but they visit the Museum of Anthropology every Sunday — the working people of Mexico.

My interest in working so that Black people would find something of empathy in my art was reinforced when I went to Mexico and worked with the printmakers in the Taller de Grafica Popular. One of their principal stated aims was to make their art serve the people of Mexico. So my basic aim was broadened to include Mexicans and all people who have a need for art as the audience I wish to reach. That means just about everybody.

For the last ten years I have exhibited for Black people in colleges, small galleries, cultural centers and even provisional spaces in churches. The interaction between me and these working people, students and a few collectors sprinkled in has contributed to my development enormously.

I do know that I have followed an alternate path as an artist. I was not interested in making money and becoming famous. I was, and still am, interested in bringing art to people who for one reason or another have little opportunity to see art or understand what it can do for them. I was surprised in 1983 by an invitation to exhibit in the New Orleans Museum of Art. When I lived in New Orleans back in the 1940's black people were not able to visit the museum because it was in a city park, off limits to us. . . . So you can see how I was surprised by the same museum's invitation to *a black woman* to exhibit there.

I believe that I am successful in my attempts to reach people on many levels. At the exhibition that I had in the New Orleans Museum, every one was excited, from the black security force, men and women, to the museum director and the New Orleans art critics.

Sculpture for me is a way of life. I must make time almost daily for modeling or carving or drawing out an idea. To express my ideas creatively through this three-dimensional form is a necessity. I learn all I can about technique. I continually search for new tools with which to work more effectively. I seek new experience. I learn from many perople.

But I work from dual necessities — social as well as aesthetic, political as well as physical, emotional as well as intellectual. Sculpture is my connection between nature and society. When I physically transform a raw material —

wood, clay, or stone — into an aesthetic expression of the life of my people, I feel complete as a human being.

❖

EXCERPTS FROM ELIZABETH CATLETT
"THE NEGRO PEOPLE AND AMERICAN ART AT MID–CENTURY"
A SPEECH PRESENTED TO THE NATIONAL CONFERENCE OF NEGRO ARTISTS, APRIL 1961

. . . The group activity of Negro students in the South has made changes in two years that we have not seen in more than fifty. We need to exchange ideas and experiences and tactics so that we may be better prepared to make the contribution as Negro artists that our heritage demands of us.

The artists who live in the big cities of the North are less isolated. They live in the atmosphere of art schools, art galleries, art critics, and art patrons, and there are more opportunities for exhibiting and selling. But they experience a frustrating denial of opportunity to exhibit as Negro artists and so they are strongly tempted to lose their identity in the mass of American artists, who following the prevailing mode say nothing socially, or even realistically. The result is a rationalization of their non–objectivity; they are accepted; they are no longer Negro, they are American; they are now equal.

And what is this great goal of being an accepted artist in the art movement of the United States? Of the hundreds of millions of human beings in our world, who reaps the cultural benefits of United States' art in 1961? We all know who reaps the economic benefits. But what is the great United States' contribution in the graphic and plastic arts to world culture? This question must be investigated and answered before the Negro artist can make his decision. Otherwise he is doomed to a minor position in a minor contribution that is of little importance to our changing world. Art is, and always has been, an expression of the historic conditions of people and should be a part of humanity's cultural wealth. We cannot afford to waste our artistic lives on petty aspirations which, even if reached, offer us no more than a very limited fame and thirty silver coins.

Are we here to communicate? Are we here for cultural interchange? Then let us not be narrow. Let us not be small and selfish. Let us aspire to be as great in our communication as were the forefathers of our people, whose struggles made our being here possible. Let us be as unselfish as the Mississippi students who were jailed on Monday for sitting down in a public library. Let us do something for ourselves for a change and communicate with the great audience of the Negro people in America. Let us take our paintings and prints and sculpture not only to Atlanta University, to the art galleries, and to patrons of the arts who have money to buy them; let us exhibit where Negro people meet — in the churches, in the schools and universities, in the associations and clubs and trade unions.

Then let us seek inspiration in the Negro people — a principal and never-ending source. What have we, as artists, said to the world, or even to our own people, about our heroes in the United States? Have we told them of the inspiringly heroic life of Frederick Douglass? Do Negroes know the face of Harriet

Tubman because of our efforts? Are we ourselves familiar with our people so that we may express their desires and inspirations and ambitions? When we are, it will be possible for us to offer the world a Negro visual expression that will approximate the sincere and profound cultural contribution of Negro music.

It is more difficult than you may imagine to change a way of thinking. It is hard for a New Orleans mother, reared in an atmosphere of white supremacy, to accept a Negro schoolmate for her child. But she has to change! The new determination for equality and freedom that is cleansing our world of the filth of discrimination will force her to change. It is equally hard for an artist, conditioned to his dependence on art critics and galleries and dealers, to think of the art he produces objectively, to think of his individual position in a historic period of time. We need to re-valuate and determine what is trivial and what is vital. We live in an environment that emphasizes material possessions, that reduces living and life to a level of minor importance. I want my children to grow up in a world where mathematics and sculpture are more important than comic books and fashionable clothes, where art is not judged by monetary values. . . .

❖

FROM ELIZABETH CATLETT, "STATEMENT"
BLACK ARTISTS ON ART (1972)

Within the past few years I have gradually reached the conclusion that art is important only to the extent that it helps in the liberation of our people. It is necessary only at this moment as an aid to our survival. It has to be a means of communication between artists and people. I have now rejected "International Art" (European Art) except to use those of its techniques that may help me make the messages clearer to my folks. If my work at the moment seems contradictory in its form, I hope it is clear in content and that the form will clarify itself.

I have come to believe that only work is important. Our self–indulgence is a waste of time that we do not have. Our work can help us in the changes that we must make in this world in order to survive.

Art for me now must develop from a necessity within my people. It must answer a question, or wake somebody up, or give a shove in the right direction — our liberation.

❖

EXCERPTS FROM ELIZABETH CATLETT
"THE ROLE OF THE BLACK ARTIST"
THE BLACK SCHOLAR, JUNE 1975

. . . Black artists are more recognized and have more opportunities today than ever in the past. There are national exhibitions, national slide collections, books published on black art, films on black art and individual artists. Some have one man exhibitions in major U.S. museums — The Modern, the Metropolitan. Dealers are interested in having us in their galleries — we sell, money can be made from us. There are grants to study, at home or abroad; there are funds to exhibit, and jobs in important universities with big salaries, as teachers or artists in residence.

The why of this situation so advantageous to black artists needs to be well understood in order to be well utilized. . . .

A work of art may be spiritually, emotionally, or intellectually rewarding especially in the realm of the real/ordinary/popular. It does not need revolution as its subject in order to be revolutionary. Up to now it has had little effect on political or social revolution. It will not create authentic social change, but it can provoke thought and prepare us for change, even helping its achievement. For art can tell us what we do not see consciously, what we may not realize, and that there are other ways of seeing things — maybe opposite ways. What seems ugly may be seen as beautiful and vice versa; what seems important may be trivial as presented by the artist.

Only the liberation of black people will make the real development of black art possible. Therefore it is to our advantage as artists as well as blacks to lend all our strength to the struggle. As culture reperesents only one aspect of a people the artist must make his production an integral part of the totality of black people.

Are we a part of the movement for black liberation? Or are we comfortably settled as educators, miseducating future black creators or perpetuating the art myths of racist America? Are we concerned first with ourselves (as part of the American way of life), with mutual admiration organizations, concerned with self–esteem and self–enrichment, vainglorious in our self–praise as artists that we are interpreting black life? Or are we so sure that *all* black is beautiful that we no longer strive for learning, for more understanding of ourselves, for technical excellence, for new means of expression? Painting the color is not sufficient. We must produce the *best* for our brothers and sisters. . . .

❖

FROM SAMELLA LEWIS, *ELIZABETH CATLETT*
(CLAREMONT, CA: HANCRAFT STUDIO, 1984)

EXCERPTS FROM STATEMENTS

Work

Combining realism and abstract art is very interesting to me. People always try to separate them and say that you are either abstract or you are realistic, either you are abstract or you are figurative. And I don't believe it. I think that any good figurative artist relies strongly on abstractions.

I try to use form as expression. For example, people associate certain things with certain kinds of lines and certain kinds of shapes. So I try to use form symbolically in order to express different ideas.

I work intuitively once I get started. I start out intellectually, then I am guided by the work — back and forth. Sometimes I create by accident and then develop the work intentionally. I have an idea and I begin to work on a print or a sculpture. I proceed and ask myself what I can do to strengthen my original feeling. . . .

When I work on a project I think about it — sometimes before I go to sleep. Solutions come to me because I am able to free my mind and to allow my thoughts to come forth. I am able to solve problems that would not be solved if I were forcing myself to continue to work on the problem physically.

When I begin a sculpture, I have an idea of what I want to do. I make sketches that are sometimes based on the shape of the material that I am going to use. When I began my work on *Recognition*, I knew that I wanted to use a triangular piece of onyx that I had in my studio. Even though I had the stone and could envision the shape of the work, I preferred to make a small model. When I am carving stone, I get involved and so work very slowly. However, if I have a model, I can rough out quickly. Then I chart out the angles and planes. Using this method, I can work faster and in a more direct way.

I usually develop pencil sketches or make small plaster sketches [models] to be used as references for larger works. There are times when I already have in mind studies to be used in developing new works. Whenever there are ideas, concepts, or feelings that are being considered, it is necessary to think simultaneously of the appropriate materials to be used in executing the works.

When I carve, I am guided by the beauty and by the configuration of the material. When I use wood, for example, I might exaggerate the form to bring out a little more of the grain of the wood. I like to finish sculpture to the maximum beauty attainable from the material from which it is created. . . .

On occasions, I use technicians when I am doing sculpture. Sometimes I have technicians who help me with large pieces of wood — the roughing–out with chain saws — based on models that I make. Frequently I do this work myself but it is difficult, hard, physical labor. I always involve technicians in the physically and technically demanding work required for casting a large piece in metal. Whenever and however I use a technician, I am always present so that I can experience each proceeding and make any necessary changes or decisions. . . .

Art must be realistic for me, whether it's sculpture or printmaking, and this, if anything, is responsible for my long–standing conflict with style. You see, I've always wanted to be an abstract artist. I've wanted to be able to work purely with form. But I've shied away from abstract work with the excuse that what my audience wants to see is more important than what I want to do. I don't know, but the idea probably came from the Taller. You know — a popular audience has to have a popular style and modern art is strictly for the sophisticated set. The truth is that the need for realism in art is actually a part of me and I don't need to excuse it with the idea that my audience isn't "ready" for anything more "modern." They are accepting works of pure form. After all, abstract art was born in Africa. . . .

❖

The focus of women

I'm a feminist, but I get the same feeling about the feminist movement that I get when I hear the very sad problems that middle–class women in the U.S. have in their need to express themselves. When I put it beside what is going on in the Black ghetto and the Chicano ghetto and in countries in Latin America and Africa — especially South Africa — and the Far East, middle–class feminism doesn't get to be that important to me. . . .

I am interested in women's liberation for the fulfillment of women; not just for jobs and equality with men and so on, but for what they can contribute to enrich the world, humanity. Their contributions have been denied them. It's the same thing that happens to Black people. . . .

Does this suggest that there's a women's aestheticism different from the traditional male aestheticism? Would you like an informed critic who knew nothing about you, on seeing one of your works, to identify it immediately as female–produced? I would be very happy. I have nothing against being identified as a woman or a female artist. I think there is definitely a woman's aestheticism, different from the traditional male aestheticism. I think that the male is aggressive and he has a male–supremacist idea in his head, at least in the United States and Mexico. We need to know more about women. I like to interpret women: women's ideas, women's feelings. The female aestheticism is more sensitive, and I'm happy to be a part of it.

❖

Teaching

I learned from Diego [Rivera] that the more you know about anything, the greater an artist you are. So I think the depth of what you know about everything — especially about yourself, where you came from, what you're doing — is much more important than knowing what's going on in the galleries of Paris.

When I was teaching at the university, students would come to me (as the head of the department) and say they can't learn anything from one teacher or another. "He does that naturalistic stuff, and I'm an abstract artist. There's nothing he could teach me." But there isn't anyone who can't teach you something — if only you will learn. "Since you're required to take that class from that teacher," I would tell these students, "why don't you just learn what he knows and add that to your store of knowledge? At the very least, it will give you a broader perspective of art."

I learned technique from traditional, establishment schools, and it took me a long time to realize that technique was the main thing to learn from them. But technique is so important! It's the difference between art and ineptitude. . . . You can't make a statement if you can't speak the language; here it's the language of the people, the language of art. . . .

Courtesy of Elizabeth Catlett.

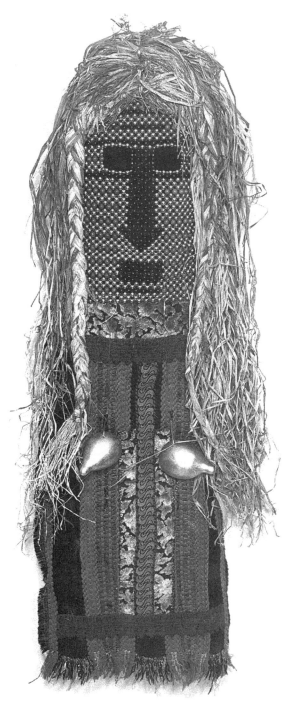

Women's Liberation Talking Mask, Witch Series #1, 1973. Mixed media, beads, raffia, cloth, gourds. 42" h. Courtesy Bernice Steinbaum Gallery, New York City

FAITH RINGGOLD

B. 1930

IN HER PAINTINGS, sculptures and particularly her recent story quilts, Faith Ringgold successfully merges the Western art tradition in which she was trained with the pictorial and narrative traditions of her African-American heritage. Ringgold has asserted that she did not want to achieve artistic success at the expense of "one iota of my blackness, or my femaleness, or my humanity," all aspects of her personhood that she has successfully balanced in her work. As affirmed by the title of her autobiography, "Being My Own Woman," her independence has been important to the development of both her art and her personal life. She began writing her autobiography in 1977 in an effort to fill her need to tell her story in her own words. Over the years, that need to give voice to her visions expanded, resulting in her creation of text-and-image story quilts for which she writes original narratives. Words are of central importance to Ringgold in the achievement of her art.

Born and brought up in Harlem, Ringgold has extraordinarily positive recollections of her early experiences, and still spends half the year in the neighborhood in which she was raised. Her father, Andrew Louis Jones, drove a truck for the city's sanitation department; her mother, Willi Posey, took care of their three children and, by the 1940s, began a career as a clothing designer. She started by making Eisenhower jackets for the army and went on to study pattern design at the Fashion Institute of Technology. Ringgold and her mother collaborated on some artistic projects later, and she credits her mother as a role model for her own life. She remembers the Harlem of her childhood as a very rich community, both culturally and personally. Living close to her extended family (many of whom had migrated from Florida at the turn of the century), she heard fascinating stories and reminiscences that they traded back and forth. Their neighbors and friends in the elegant Sugar Hill section were among the most distinguished black political and cultural figures of the generation, such as educator and writer W. E. B. Dubois, and musicians Duke Ellington and Sonny Rollins. As a child, Ringgold was frequently bedridden with asthma and artistic creation became one of her favorite escapes from the boredom of illness. She claims to have been aware in her early teens of her special talent (but does not believe that it was especially nurtured by her teachers) and by her senior year in high school, had decided that she wanted to become an artist.

Ringgold's formal study of art came in 1950 when she enrolled in New York's City College as an art education major, specializing in painting. That year, too, she married her first husband, jazz pianist Robert Earl Wallace, and had two daughters, eleven months apart, before the year was out. She graduated from City College in 1955 with a bachelor's degree in art education, and began an eighteen-year career teaching art in the New York City public schools. By 1959 she had earned a master's degree in art, also from City College. Ringgold did not begin to define herself as an artist, however, until the early 1960s. After completing her master's degree, she rejected her uncle's advice to pursue a doctorate, deciding instead that a trip to Europe to see art would be more helpful to her artistic education than further academic study. Upon her return to the United States, she claimed her former dining room as studio space, an important gesture establishing art-making as a major priority in her life. Shortly thereafter, her first marriage having ended, she married her second husband, Burdette Ringgold, in 1962.

It was at this time that Ringgold began to work toward finding a way to create images of black people that were acceptable to her. She felt that she had to go beyond her education, which taught art through copying the "masters" art of the Western tradition, and that the art with which she had thus far worked with was dead. She began to seek models that would allow her to create more vital images to effectively express her intent, and found inspiration in Cubism and African art. "Instead of looking to Greece, I looked to Africa," she once said. Her quest to create an art that expressed her ethnicity was technical as well as spiritual. She has described how her teachers were unable to show her the mechanics of painting blacks' skin color, and how they persisted in thinking of all painted figures as white, one of the barriers to her making art that was true to her own vision. These technical problems actually led to the development of her aesthetic. Because of the difficulty of contrasting the darkness of black people's flesh tones with the darker tones of shadow, she stopped trying to paint chiaroscuro in the late sixties. Instead, she experimented with using flat, contrasting colors to indicate shadow, a technique she had observed in some African masks. She also tried out the use of proximate dark tones. She decided also not to use perspective because it does not allow activation of the entire picture surface or, in her words, it distorts the "all-overness" of a painting.

By the later 1960s Ringgold had developed a mature style characterized by bold flat colors and abstracted forms. This style is evident in works belonging to her American People series and most particularly in several very strong paintings from that time, such as *The Flag Is Bleeding* and *Die*. In their accessible imagery, the American flag, for instance, these works bear a resemblance to works of the Pop Art movement that was in its heyday at that time. However, as Lowery Sims points out, Ringgold and other black artists imbued the popular icons with meaning, in contrast to Pop artists' "deadpan" use of similar items. Ringgold first used her art as political commentary in 1963, after which it became a significant aspect of her style. The two works mentioned above, for example, vividly present the violence of race relations in the United States. During these years Ringgold actively tried to gain gallery representation and to establish contact with other black artists. Although success in neither endeavor was immediately forthcoming, in 1966 she became affiliated (for several years) with the Spectrum gallery in New York, and over the next years she met such distinguished black artists as Romare Bearden, Hale Woodruff, and Jacob Lawrence. She became a political activist, campaigning for both black people's civil rights and women's rights. In 1971 she helped to found "Where We At," an organization of black artists.

During the next decade, inspired by two non-Western sources — African masks and Tibetan *tankas*, religious paintings, often on fabric — Ringgold began to work with three-dimensional forms executed in fabric. After seeing an exhibition of tankas in Amsterdam, she decided to mount her paintings on "soft frames" to make them easier to transport. (The problems she had experienced carrying a fourteen-foot mural down her studio stairs made portability a real concern.) She also began a series called the Family of Woman, fiercely haunting masks, their mouths open to allow them to speak, of mixed media, animated with fabric bodies, and based on people she had known and encountered growing up in Harlem. She collaborated with her mother, Willi Posey, by then a fabric designer, while working on these pieces. Ringgold recounts that she had taught African crafts, such as beading and mask-making, at the Bank Street School of Education for some time before she realized that she could use these techniques in her own work. Giving herself permission to deviate from the traditions she had learned, by incorporating in her own work elements from her African cultural heritage and her mother's art, enabled Ringgold to take an important step closer to her goal of expressing her inner vision. By the mid-seventies, Ringgold was animating the characters she created, at first stuffing the bodies to give them greater dimension, as in her "bag" couple, *Zora and Fish*. She then moved to creating environmental performance pieces, employing characters she created. *The Wake and Resurrection of the Bi-Centennial Nigger* (1976), for example, dealt with the devastating impact of drugs on black people's lives. In these performances she collaborated with her daughter, the writer Michele Wallace, bringing together three generations in her art. She continued to create figures in three-dimensions, freestanding soft sculptures, and even doll kits. Ringgold took a further significant step in 1973 when she resigned from her teaching position in the New York City schools in order to devote her energies exclusively to her artistic career.

In the 1980s, Ringgold achieved a breakthrough to perhaps her greatest artistic achievement to date, in the conception of the "story quilt." Her first quilt was created for a project conceived by Charlotte Robinson, entitled "The Artist and the Quilt," which brought together quilts made by eighteen women artists who usually worked in "high art" media, such as painting or sculpture. Ringgold collaborated with her mother on *Echoes of Harlem*, portraying in paint the faces of people she had known, while Posey used traditional quilting techniques to sew the finished piece. Although this was their last collaboration (Posey died in 1981), the work provided the catalyst for Ringgold's subsequent artistic development. During the next decade, Ringgold executed numerous story quilts: at first, she made single works, such as *Who's Afraid of Aunt Jemima*, but later went on to make multiple-quilt series that elaborated intricately plotted stories, such as her five-quilt sequence, *Bitter Nest*. As she herself has noted, the story quilts were a vehicle for bringing together the characters she had created in her earlier masks and performance pieces.

The narratives embedded in the quilts carry their own significance. Each quilt is narrated by a woman, articulating a point of view that is decidedly female. Their scenarios and characters are diverse — a slave born on the crossing from Africa to America, a pious woman from the South, an affluent black alumna of Williams College in Massachusetts, as well as many voices from Harlem. Many speak with the inflections of black English. Ringgold wrote all the stories for her quilts herself, with the exception of the narrative material on *The Purple Quilt*, which is derived from Alice Walker's book *The Color Purple* and dedicated to all "US women [and men] who survived to tell-the-story." Their narrative structure derives from her family's oral tradition of story-telling, which Ringgold has claimed as a major influence in her life. Although the content of all her quilt narratives derives from her own background, the only directly autobiographical one is *Change: Faith Ringgold's Over 100 Pound Weight-Loss Story Quilt*, the title of which is self-explanatory. Thalia Gouma-Peterson has suggested that some of Ringgold's quilt stories are related to the African "dilemma tale" in which a problem is posed but inconclusively resolved. For example, in *Who's Afraid of Aunt Jemima*, the protagonists die and their less than exemplary children inherit Jemima's business. The narrative ends with a question, "Now, who's afraid of Aunt Jemima?," forcing the viewer/reader to confront ambiguity.

Ringgold's use of the quilting medium is a deliberate statement of her identity as a woman of African-American heritage. Her awareness of the relationship of the quilts' relationship to traditional African quilting methods and her sensitivity to the significance that quilts have had in women's lives underlines their appropriateness as vehicles for telling black women's stories. Several critics have called the nature of the quilts and the stories that they tell subversive. In the stories, Ringgold allows black women to speak with authority about their lives in their own voices, bypassing the stereotypes of the dominant culture, thus giving them power and centrality. Her autobiographical quilt, *Change*, for example, narrates her own power as she gained control over her own body and life, and defined herself in her own terms. Freida High Tesfagiorgis has described Ringgold as an "Afro-femcentrist," because her art consistently and centrally shows black, female subjects and conveys black women's realities.

Perhaps the greatest significance of the story quilts is the challenge that they present to the assumptions regarding the traditionally separate realms of crafts and fine art. Since the nineteenth century, women have used quilts to express the truths about their lives, whether through the vaguely referential symbolic language of pattern (as in a pattern called "Underground Railroad") or through more directly representative means (as through biblical narratives like Harriet Powers's "Bible Quilt"). The very fabrics used for quilts often have meaning to their makers, and quilts are used to mark events of importance, such as engagements and births. Like those quilts produced from within the crafts tradition, Ringgold's quilts maintain those connections to women's lives. Yet Ringgold is an artist trained in the fine-art tradition; she exhibits her quilts in art galleries, not at craft fairs, and they are bought by museums. The quilts thus cross the borders between cultural and artistic traditions; as objects and in the stories they tell, they have many meanings.

Extracts that show the wide range of voices Ringgold has brought to her writings have been selected for this volume. Excerpts from her autobiography "Being My Own Woman," reveal her own process of self-validation, and they speak to her aesthetic and political satisfaction at working on her Black Light paintings, and to the special tensions and joys involved in being a black woman who balances motherhood and artisthood. One expects that Ringgold's art will continue to develop and evolve, yet, based on her achievements to date, she has already made her mark by eloquently expressing in art and words her position as a black American woman.

SOURCES

Faith Ringgold, Change: Painted Story Quilts. Exhibition catalogue. Bernice Steinbaum Gallery, New York, 1987.

Faith Ringgold: A Twenty-five Year Survey. Exhibition catalogue. Fine Arts Museum of Long Island, Hempstead, New York, 1990.

Fax, Elton. *17 Black Artists.* New York: Dodd, Mead, and Co., 1971.

Munro, Eleanor. *Originals: American Women Artists.* New York: Simon and Schuster, 1979.

Ringgold, Faith. *Tar Beach.* New York: Crown Publishers, Inc., 1991.

Sims, Lowery. "Aspects of Performance in the Works of Black American Women Artists." In *Feminist Art Criticism,* edited by Arlene Raven, Cassandra Langer, and Joanna Frueh, 207–25. Ann Arbor, Mich., and London: UMI Research Press, 1988.

Tesfagiorgis, Freida High. "Afrofemcentrism and Its Fruition in the Art of Elizabeth Catlett and Faith Ringgold," *SAGE,* 4:1 (Spring 1987): 25–32.

Wallace, Michele, and Lowery Sims, eds. *Faith Ringgold: Twenty Years of Painting, Sculpture and Performance (1963–1983).* Exhibition catalogue. Studio Museum in Harlem, New York, 1984.

FROM FAITH RINGGOLD, *STORY QUILTS*

"WHO'S AFRAID OF AUNT JEMIMA," 1983

Jemima Blakey didn't come from no ordinary people. Her Granma and Granpa bought they freedom out a slavery in New Orleans. Granma Jemima Blakey — they called her Aunt Jemima too — made cakes and catered fine parties for them plantation owners in Louisiana. And Granpa Blakey was a first–class tailor too. From memory he could make a suit of clothes fit like a glove. They was sure smart people, them Blakeys. And Jemima was just like 'em, hard–working, and God–fearing till the day she died.

Jemima could do anything she set her mind to. When Ma Tillie and Pa Blakey, Jemima's Ma and Pa, forbid her to marry Big Rufus Cook on account a they wanted her to marry a preacher. Jemima up and married Big Rufus anyway, and they run off to Tampa, Florida to work for Ole Man and Ole Lady Prophet cookin, cleanin and takin care a they chirrun somethin Jemima never had to do livin in her Ma and Pa's comfortable home in New Orleans.

Ole Man Prophet used to joke that Jemima was his heir. "Jemima keep my house and family like they hers. I reckon I'll leave 'em to her when I die," he used to tell Ole Lady Prophet. "Over my dead body," she used to say. Well as God would have it, lightning struck they house one night whilst the servants was away and burnt it to the ground. Ain nar' a one of them Prophets survive. And, praise God, she was.

Jemima & Rufus was rich now. They come to New York with they chirrun Georgia and Lil Rufus and opened a restaurant and catering business in Harlem. Big Rufus was a fine chef too, and could tailor clothes out this world just like Granpa Blakey. He looked like white, and couldn't see nobody but Jemima, black as she was. No — never did. "Where you get that fine–looking man from Jemima?" folks used to ask her. "Where I get you from asking me that question?" she'd say, laughing.

Now Lil Rufus, Jemima's baby, handsome as a Greek god, took color after Jemima's side a the family. Jemima likena died when he married a white gal, name a Margo he picked up in Germany, of all places, during that Korean War. Brought her home too, to live in Jemima's house in Harlem. They had three girls: Jemmie, JoAnn and Julia. They look just like Jemima. They ain look nothin like they Ma, Margo, she was a scrawny little ole white gal. Love the ground Lil Rufus walk on.

Georgia, Jemima's daughter, was high yaller likena her pa, Big Rufus, and had green eyes and long straight hair she could sit on. Only thing she took after Jemima was her shape. Georgia was real big up top and had skinny legs and big feet.

Jemima'd blow up like a balloon when folks say'd she was Georgia's maid. Georgia'd laugh and call her ma Aunt Jemima. Jemima'd take that piss tail gal over her knee and whoop her till she quit. "You ain no more'n your ma," Jemima'd tell her, and Georgia'd screw up her lil' horse face an holler.

Jemima was some proud at Georgia's wedding to Dr. Jones. But Ma Tillie said, "Jemima, that's a evil ole ugly black man, you'll see."

Tillie Blakey, Jemima's Ma, was half Indian. A real beauty in her youth, she was coal black with long braids and keen features. They say she ran a bad house for white men in New Orleans. All's I know she was a good church–going woman owned a fine house and left plenty money to the church when she died. Pa Blakey called it penance money from the devil. He swore he'd never touch it. Much as he loved Georgia and her struggling doctor husband, and they two chirrun Peter and Annabelle, he never give em a cent of Ma Tillie's money.

After Pa Blakey died, Jemima and Big Rufus give they restaurant business in Harlem to Lil Rufus and his German wife Margo, and moved to New Orleans. There they opened another restaurant near Georgia's house.

But Jemima ain never see her grand chirrun, Peter and Annabelle. "My Pa don't want you in our house," they told her one day. And then Peter kicked Jemima in her bad knee and he and Annabelle ran off. The next day before Dr.

Jones could leave for his office, Lil Rufus was there, and he was mad as hell. When Dr. Jones saw him, he jumped in the pool fully dressed, bag an all.

That same morning Jemima and Big Rufus had a fatal car accident on the way to open they restaurant. God rest they souls. Lil Rufus brought they bodies back to Harlem, and give 'em an African funeral — Praise God! Dressed Jemima in an African gown and braided her hair with cowrie shells. Put Big Rufus in a gold dashiki. They looked nice though, peaceful, like they was home.

Georgia, her doctor husband, and them two worthless chirrun a hers got Jemima's restaurant business and Ma Tillie's big fine house in New Orleans. Now, who's afraid of Aunt Jemima?

❖

"Slave Rape Quilt," 1985

Mama was 8 months gone when he raped her. When she fought back he whipped her so bad she just lay there on the deck of that stinkin vessel too weak to fight no more. When the water come gushing out of her privacy she crawled over to the side of the vessel and squatted down on her haunches. She give out a grunt like the roar of a lion and I was born right there on the slave-ship Carriolle en route to South Carolina to be a slave in America.

The drunken sailor came over to look at me. "It's a girl," he said, "I guess the negress done quit fightin me. She dead." He reached out to touch me. Without a warning Mama was up, and had him. With her last gust of strength she plunged over the side of the vessel into the deep dark water and took him with her. Ain neither one of 'em come up out that water not once. That was on March 22, 1846. I grew up listening to Cap'n Carriolle tell that story in his garden, as I lay in the bushes nearby. Missus and all the guests be drinkin and laughin and he'd start to tell bout "the drunken son of a bitch who couldn't even tame a slave woman–with–child. Went to hell with a negress hanging round his neck." I was 6 years old when I figured out it was *my* Mama drowned her rapist the day I was born. Bullet and Lacey was the only family I had. They was house slaves on the Carriolle Plantation. Bullet was a prize fighter too. He could hit hard and fast like his name. Cap'n Carriolle matched him up with slaves from plantations all over South Carolina. And Bullet always won. Bullet gave the money he made to Cap'n Carriolle to pay for his own and Lacey's freedom. Now Bullet was paying for my freedom too.

Missus Grace and Cap'n Carriolle had two sons, Winter and Luke. Lacey was Missus maid, but she nursed the whole family when they was sick. Lacey knew more bout healin than the doctor. She'd pick roots and plants from the ground and boil up a tea heal anything. And if she had a mind to she'd bring them on a misery last 'em for weeks. But ain nobody know that but me an Bullet. By the time I was 8 years old I was Missus Grace's maid. Lacey taught me everything to do for Missus. Even doctoring. I could heal just like Lacey. Lacey took the old cook's job in the kitchen, and I helped Lacey when Missus Grace didn't need me. Lacey warned me 'bout Winter and Luke. Say they was queer and I should stay way from em. "Don't say nothin to Bullet," she told me, "he a crazy Negro, he kill em ifn they touch you. An that Luke — we didn't know if'n he was a boy or a girl when he come here." . . .

One night a man name a Yankee came to dinner at the Carriolle Mansion. He come to buy slaves. "These is my prize house slaves," Cap'n Carriolle told him, talking bout Lacey and Bullet. "They gonna be free niggers soon. If'n Bullet keep fightin an knockin niggers out. An I'd have to kill Bullet if'n I sold Beata. Yeah she's a black beauty. Pure African. But she ain for sale either. My wife is ailing an she depends on Beata. It'd kill her if'n I sold her now. In the morning I'll show you some slaves you can buy."

That night I ran down to the Old Plantation to talk to Mama. Tell her how Yankee want to buy me, Bullet and Lacey. On the way there, somebody threw me on the ground an covered my mouth. It was Lacey. "Yankee was gonna buy us . . . " "Shut up he ain no slaver, he a abolitionist from the North, he come here to get us some money for guns and food for the trip North. We goin tonight on the underground railroad," Lacey said. "I ain gonna leave my Mama," I screamed. "Your mama's dead girl," she screamed back at me. "Well, I ain gonna leave her down here even if'n she dead," I told her, "I gonna stay right here till I gets my freedom." Lacey was cryin now. She told me that Cap'n Carriolle wasnt never gonna give us our freedom no matter how much money Bullet give him. She said Bullet his son an that he ain want him to leave here. They was leavin now and that they would send back fo me later. "I ain gonna never leave, me an my mama stayin," I said. "God take care of us."

The next morning Yankee, Bullet and Lacey were gone. The Carriolle safe was robbed of money an jewelry. I ran down to old plantation an hid in the old house under the bed an lay still. I could hear footsteps crossin the dry grass in the garden. "Beata, I know you here. Better let me find you 'fore the others come. You know Bullet an Lacey gone. Come on out!" Cap'n Carriolle yelled, "I ain gonna hurt you." I came from under the bed. I could hear him searching the rooms. Now he was in the door, lookin dead at me with those scary green eyes. Bullet did look like him and he had green eyes too. I never seen a Negro with light skin, straight hair an green eyes before. Cap'n Carriolle began rubbin his belly like I was something good to eat. "I'll kill you, you old white headed drunken sot. Wanna rape me like you raped my Mama? I'll kill you if its the last thing I do." I screamed, searching the room with my eyes for something to hit him with. Now I was praying out loud and cryin. "Oh God Mama, I'm gonna die. He gonna kill me for sure and I ain ready to die." Cap'n Carriolle started talkin to me real slow an strange, like he really meant it. Say:

"I gonna free my slaves, an give 'em this land an share the crops, give em a house an live stock an some money. They been workin free long enough. The war bout over, the South done lost. The union army just bout here. Bullet and Lacey done run off. Yankee, a lying thief, stole my money an slaves an Missus Grace is dying. I'm old an sick an I got two sons ain worth a damn just waitin for they Ma an me to die."

All he wanted to do was look at my young body and rub my breasts and between my legs. He was too old an weak to force me. "You ain gonna make me?" I asked, "No," he said and I pulled his old body on top of me, and put my arms around him. "Did you rape my mama too?" He just broke down and wept like a baby.

I hated him now more than ever. But I could hear my freedom ringing in my ears so loud Mama's voice could hardly be heard: "Get outa there Beata, run!" But where? This time Mama, I ain gonna listen. Ain nobody to love. Hate's all I know bout and I can't live that way, Mama.

Missus Grace died the day before my baby was born. I named her Rebecca Lucretia Carriolle. Rebecca had the Carriolle's green eyes, honey brown skin and curly hair, but she looked like me. Rebecca an me was living at Old Plantation now. Cap'n Carriolle give us the house there and was makin good his promise to free his slaves. One night Mama told me to go get Rebecca and hide here in the shrine. . . .

. . . "Mama," I said, "I ain gonna never leave you. Bullet an Lacey say we don't belong here in this plantation. We don't belong nowhere Mama. But we stayin Mama. Rebecca an me ain gonna have to die like you Mama. We gonna live an be free."

❖

"CHANGE: FAITH RINGGOLD'S OVER 100 LB. WEIGHT–LOSS PERFORMANCE STORY QUILT," 1986

January 1, 1986

In this year, 1986, I will lose 128 pounds. By January 1, 1987 I will weigh 130 pounds, or I'll eat your hat. Mine I've already eaten. Faith, you have been trying to lose weight since the sixties. For the last twenty, twenty–five years you've been putting yourself on diets, charting your lack of progress and gaining weight. For the next six months you'll be in California, away from everybody, the perfect place to make the CHANGE.

You always lose weight when you're away from them. They lose weight when you're away from them, too. There's a message in this. Never mind — you just know what *you* need. Peace of cake — I mean mind. It's as simple as that. Aggravation makes you hungry. You are overcontrolling. Admit it! You took the test and passed — high. But you can CHANGE that, too. Mommy can exchange her 100 pound of burden for some peace and a life of her own. Whatever it takes to do it. It's a first place pie–oriety — I mean priority.

Use art to document the CHANGE: this quilt, a performance and a video of the entire weight loss process. Now you tell me how you're going to explain not losing weight this time? I'll say, "Well you see, there was this cute little pig moved in next door. Used to come over all cooked, ready to eat. I couldn't keep my hands off his ribs." No, Faith — there are no excuses. You can't gain it back. We're talking total change this time: good nutrition, behavior modification, daily exercise, and *hunger*.

I know you don't want to admit it. When it comes to food you lack self–esteem. Like everything else you probably ate it, and can't even remember what it tasted like. Let's face it. You're quite good at eating large portions of food and the weight gain is over. But can we talk? Yes. I am out to prove something right here and now. I can change. I can do it. I can do it. I can CHANGE, I can CHANGE. Now.

❖

1930–1939

In the 1930's folks had fried chicken and greens for Sunday dinner, and fried fish and potato salad on Friday. Your family had leg of mutton on Sunday, and fried fish on Saturday. Fried fish was the only food your mother fried when you were a kid 'cause nobody ever heard of porgies cooked any other way. Because you had asthma and were allergic, you were on a health food diet of steamed vegetables, fresh fruit, lamb, chicken, veal, skimmed milk, corn meal gruel, and homemade lemon ice cream made with skimmed milk that tasted awful. . . .

Your mother never allowed you to eat between meals. The kitchen was closed every evening after supper till breakfast the next morning. Years later you developed a fascination for late night eating by the light of the open refrigerator door. You thought those calories didn't count. But what about the tell–tale evidence they left behind and in front?

❖

1940–1949

By the 1940's we all had to clean up our plates for the starving children. That of course, was right up your alley since you never left anything anyway. It was in those years that you discovered chocolate candy bars. They were a nickel then and as big as the ones that cost 50¢ today. All you really thought about in those years were chocolate candy bars, boys, make–up, and clothes. . . .

❖

1950–1959

Women in the 1950's had to get married to leave home. Barbara was married first. Her wedding was beautiful; however, both of your marriages were terrible mistakes. You were still in college when you and your two daughters moved in with your mother after your divorce. All through the 1950's you were scantily clothed in tight, revealing dresses with matching 3" heels, a size too small; and you often amazed onlookers by falling down whole flights of stairs without injury. . . .

❖

1960–69

In 1961 you discovered French bread & cheese, and wine-with-your-meals in Europe though you were brought up to believe that people who drank wine were winos. The French, however, carried their wine well — that is, everywhere — they drank it like water. In Italy you acquired a refined taste for pasta, veal parmigiana, olive oil, and more wine. Cafe dining on the Via Veneto in Rome stimulated your palette and enlarged your waistline. Eating was fun but it was also therapeutic.

In the 1960's you found a lot of things to eat about. You were married again, had two teenaged daughters, developed a mature style of political art, began looking for a gallery, found one on 57th Street, and had your first one person show. It was then that you began promising to lose weight. Pork was now a political issue. "Baby don't eat no pig; it'll kill you!" the brothers said. But you did. . . .

❖

1970–79

In the 1970's food was a feminist issue and you were a fat feminist. Always looking for a quasi politically correct reason to eat. And of course you found plenty of them. In the sixties it was being a wife and mother, the rejection of being a black artist and other oppressions. In the seventies it was all that and being a woman too. . . .

❖

1980–1985

. . . It was now time for a CHANGE. No more gimmicky diets. Let your *body* tell you what you need. After all that pasta you needed protein so you went on a fried chicken meal plan. It was health food, as you recall, since the chicken was fried in corn oil. This time you tipped the scale at a whopping 258 pounds, and broke it. The scale was tired. That same day, Baby Faith came running out of your room screaming, "Gran ma your scale says I weigh 258 pounds." It is time for a CHANGE.

January – October 1986

. . . It is September 27, 1986, and though I have 40 pounds yet to lose I have lost 88 pounds. Today I am thinner than I have been in the last twenty years. I eat fresh fruit and vegetables instead of pasta and pork chops, and I exercise almost everyday. I am out to prove something right here and now. I can CHANGE. I can do it. I can do it. I can CHANGE, I can CHANGE. Now.

COMMENTARY ON "THE BITTER NEST"

"The Bitter Nest" was written as a performance piece, not a story quilt in that I tried to piece together music, dance, art, and story telling; and to highlight the twenties — the romantic period of the Harlem Renaissance.

In the forties when the kids would assemble at my house to talk, invariably someone would tell things they'd heard about the twenties and how fabulous life was in Harlem then. Men used to stroll down 7th Avenue on their way to church on Sunday dressed in top hats, spats, and sporting a cane. The women were beautiful in their flowered hats and matching outfits. We often talked about the romantic figures of the times who were in their hey day then: Langston Hughes, Aaron Douglass, WEB Dubois, etc. Those are the people who inspired the faces on *Echoes of Harlem*, the first quilt mother and I made back in 1980. Those faces are how I imagined the people looked in the twenties. My mother belonged to a club called the "Aristocratic Eight"; membership was limited because it wouldn't be swanky if it was too big. Somehow all that snobbery made us feel like we had something to look forward to; as if that time would come again and we would be a part of it when it did.

In dynamic contrast to the Harlem Renaissance and the life of Dr. Celia Marcum Prince and her eccentric artistic mother, Cee Cee; was Celie, brought up in the rural environment of "The Color Purple," the novel written by Alice Walker. The stories are very similar in that the pathetic character Celie in "The Color Purple" and Cee Cee in "The Bitter Nest" both rise to greater independence and strength through developing their own individual talents. Both made sewn things: quilts and clothes with their hands. I was inspired by that story Alice wrote. So much so, that in 1986, I created a quilt of the characters about which Alice's words are written. This quilt, *The Purple Quilt* is a tribute to Alice Walker for her wonderful story telling and for elevating the victim to the level of heroine, and for upholding the family.

EXCERPTS FROM "THE BITTER NEST," 1988

PART 1: LOVE IN THE SCHOOLYARD

Once upon a time there was a young black woman doctor named Celia Cleopatra Prince. Her father, Dr. Percel Trombone Prince, was a socially prominent black dentist in the Harlem of the twenties. Celia's mother, Cee Cee Markum Prince, a loving wife and mother, was a marvelous cook and home-maker. Cee Cee was known for her unusually decorated home and the unique pieced and quilted bags she filled it with.

People came to the Prince home as much for the social atmosphere the dentist venerated as Cee Cee's food and dancing, which she performed against an environment of her own colorful bags, coverlets, and wall hangings.

Celia learned early to dislike her mother's uniqueness, not only because she made odd looking things and dressed up in strange costumes, wore masks and danced to music only she could hear, but because she was deaf. Since Celia's birth, Cee Cee had not spoken and, although she could read lips and make sign language, she chose not to communicate with anyone except the dentist, and Celia, who chose not to communicate with her.

Celia's family lived in a large townhouse on Harlem's Striver's Row, a tree–lined street famous for its beautiful brownstones owned by the most prominent of Harlem's fashionable 400.

In line with her family's wishes, Celia went off to Howard University and graduated first in her class with a degree in medicine. Her office was set up in the family brownstone and many of the dentist's patients were now Celia's patients too. Though her career as a doctor was successful, her personal life always had that strange taste of bittersweet.

The dentist, already an old man by the time Celia was born, was lonely after the death of his first wife. He first saw Cee Cee in the yard of the Junior High School not far from his office. She was carrying a large bookcase which she dropped, spilling the contents on the sidewalk. The dentist gathered up the books and placed them back in the torn bookcase and offered Cee Cee a lift home. Noticing the brand new Oldsmobile the dentist had parked at the curb, she decided it was safe to take up his offer. After that first day, the dentist came every day at dismissal time to drive Cee Cee home. The other girls gathered around to see the impressive dentist driving such an expensive car. Cee Cee told them he was her uncle. No one questioned that. Before long, the dentist invited Cee Cee to his house, and she went. She went every day after school to prepare dinner for him and straighten up. She had a key to the house so that she could come and go. And then she got pregnant for the dentist. . . .

The baby was a beautiful girl. They named her Celia. After giving birth, Cee Cee developed a deafness in both ears. . . .

❖

PART 2: HARLEM RENAISSANCE PARTY

Cee Cee was meticulous about the house. Everything had a place. Cee Cee collected boxes and empty containers to put things in. Her mother sent her hand–woven and hand–dyed fabrics from Africa which inspired her to sew an endless array of bags which she now used as containers for everything. Her method of working was always the same. First she selected colors and patterns of the brightly dyed fabrics and cut them into squares. And then she sewed the strips together to form large lengths of fabric out of which she made the bags, covers, drapes, costumes, et cetera.

Celia was very disturbed by Cee Cee's odd looking patterns. She learned in drawing to match colors tastefully and to select one pattern and repeat it in some way to create a balanced harmonious design. Cee Cee had not gone further than the eighth grade in school when she married the dentist. Her education in the subtleties of refined coloration and design was cut short or was never learned. At any rate Cee Cee, shall we say, turned a "deaf ear" to any talk that her bags were "tacky," as they said in those days, and that she was a "tasteless, low class hussy to clutter up the dentist's fine house with all that 'Mammy–made' stuff."

From the time Celia was a little girl, she took on the responsibility to keep a conversation going at the dinner table. . . . Cee Cee's roast duck, and fricasseed chicken, macaroni and cheese, candied sweets, peach cobbler and at Christmas time, Cee Cee's fruit cake, drenched in 200 proof Jamaican Rum you could set fire to were unsurpassed in Southern cooking. . . .

After dinner, Cee Cee put on a show of sorts that topped off the evening and put the conversation of such frequent visitors as Alaine Locke, Countee Cullen, Langston Hughes and Aaron Douglass at a standstill. Dressed in her oddly pieced and quilted costumes, masks and headresses of her making, she moved among the illustrious guests to music only she could hear. Strange as it seemed, they looked forward to Cee Cee's unusual presentations and thought of her as an eccentric undiscovered original. The times pressed the artists of the Harlem Renaissance into a regiment of social and political propaganda for the elevation of Race People. But what was Cee Cee doing? Was this art? No one dared ask that question knowing full well that the interrogator would only look like a fool and the one who answered would be one. And furthermore, no one wanted to offend the dentist or Cee Cee.

Celia sat through these performances like an old man at a church tea. She hated Cee Cee's unusual display and made it a point to let the guests and Cee Cee know it. "My mother is a family disgrace. The only hope I have of not becoming the laughing stock of everybody is to get out of here and follow in my father's footsteps and become a doctor. I cannot relate to her. As far as I am concerned, she is crazy like her quilts." The dentist accepted Cee Cee's shows as a peculiarity associated with her deafness. "Cee Cee is just trying out something to express herself," he'd say, "she will be going for sewing lessons soon as Celia is older and off to college and she can get out of the house."

Celia got older and went off to college and came home a doctor and Cee Cee was still right there making bags and dancing to music only she could hear.

❖

"TAR BEACH," 1988

I will always remember when the stars fell down around me and lifted me up above the George Washington Bridge. I could see our tiny roof top with

Mommy and Daddy and Mr. and Mrs. Honey, our next–door neighbors, still playing cards as if nothing was going on, and Be Be, my baby brother, laying real still on the mattress, just like I told him to, his eyes like huge flood lights tracking me through the sky.

Sleeping on Tar Beach was magical. Laying on the roof in the night with stars and skyscraper buildings all around me made me feel rich, like I owned all that I could see. The bridge was my most prized possession. Daddy said the George Washington Bridge was the longest and most beautiful bridge in the world and that it opened in 1931 on the very day I was born. Daddy worked on that bridge hoisting cables. Since then, I wanted that bridge to be mine.

Now I have claimed it. All I had to do was fly over it for it to be mine forever. I can wear it like a giant diamond necklace, or just fly above it and marvel at its sparkling beauty. I can fly, yes fly. Me, Cassie Louise Lightfoot, only eight years old and in the third grade and I can fly. That means I am free to go wherever I want to for the rest of my life.

Daddy took me to see the new union building he is working on. He can walk on steel girders high up in the sky and not fall. They call him The Cat. But still he can't join the union because Grandpa wasn't a member. Well Daddy is going to own that building cause I'm gonna fly over it and give it to him. Then it won't matter that he's not in their ole union or whether he's colored or a half–breed Indian like they say. He'll be rich and won't have to stand on 24 story high girders and look down. He can look up at his building going up. And Mommy won't cry all winter when Daddy goes to look for work and doesn't come home. And Mommy can laugh and sleep late like Mrs. Honey and we can have ice cream every night for dessert. Next I'm going to fly over the ice cream factory just to make sure we do. Tonight we're going up to Tar Beach. Mommy is roasting peanuts and frying chicken and Daddy will bring home a watermelon. Mr. and Mrs. Honey will bring the beer and their old green card table. And then the stars will fall around me and I will fly to the union building. I'll take Be Be with me. He has threatened to tell Mommy and Daddy if I leave him behind.

I have told him it's very easy, anyone can fly. All you need is somewhere to go that you can't get to any other way. The next thing you know, you're flying among the stars.

❖

FROM *BEING MY OWN WOMAN,* 1977

I found myself longing to paint come the summer of 1969. I had developed a new light in my painting, which I called Black Light, a way of looking at us that came out of our new "black is beautiful" sense of ourselves. My palette was all dark colors. Placed on a white ground they appeared to be only black. But next to each other the dark tones of reds, greens, blues, browns, and grays came alive, no matter how subtle the nuance. It was magic. Ad Rinehardt had done it but I could not find out what method he had used. And, furthermore, he did *abstract* black paintings. Mine were black paintings of black people. I had trouble with the glazes. They produced too much glare, or they made the surface quality of the paint too fragile. I needed time to experiment. My second one–woman show was scheduled for January 1970. The summer would be my only real chance to paint. I had a lot of ideas for new paintings. The subjects taunted me: mask faces, dancing figures of black life, a dark flag with the letters D–I–E in the stars and the letters N–I–G–G–E–R in the stripes. But there was no telling what the summer would produce with two troublesome teenagers stalking my every move. I had to solve that problem first.

The girls, aged sixteen and seventeen, were into rebellion by then. People who didn't have children thought the youth of the day would be our salvation.

"The young people's rebellion is revolutionary," they would say. Revolutionary was a word they used for defiant, youthful, modern, anything for which you could be condemned as too old if you didn't agree with it. Revolutionary could mean practically anything but *a revolution*. They were just doing their thing was another popular explanation for youthful rebellion. That one was more like it. But whose thing was it really?

What made me so upset was that my girls seemed more like they were into doing someone else's thing. They were more the doees than the doers. And as their mother and an older woman in her thirties, I was the target for all the rage they felt for giving up so much for so little. It was as if their brains froze over at the mere sight of a man.

Stokely Carmichael echoed the sentiments they seemed to embrace: "The only position of women . . . is prone."

"But how do you feel about this?" I asked them, trying not to reveal to them the horror I felt that they could repeat this statement without feeling some of the rage they just normally aimed at me. Michele was objective about her feelings: this was his point of view; it had nothing to do with how she felt. Barbara had not been present at the theater group when Stokely spoke so she couldn't really comment. . . .

"Please don't allow yourselves to be used by anyone, male or female," I said. "If you lay your heart out there, it is sure that some creep will come along and step on it. Don't just let life happen to you. Defy *his* ideas as you do mine. Don't just let life happen to you."

But Michele had a super crush on Stokely Carmichael, and Barbara was excited just to hear that she had met him.

"What's he like?" she asked. It was obvious no one heard a word I said.

They had already been told by all the movements that Mother is the undisputed enemy of all revolutionary ideas. Contradictions didn't matter.

"Have a baby for the Revolution!"

Would they then be revolutionary mothers or just more of the old breed, mere women with the added burden of a child to bring up, possibly alone?

Birdie, my husband, was very expressive on the baby issue.

"We don't want a baby, Barbara and Michele. If we did we could have one ourselves. Your mother and I are not as old as we seem. Hold those boys off. The Revolution my ass! All they want to do is fuck and run."

"But, Daddy," said Barbara, "you don't know the boys of today. They are honest. We're not into the lies of your generation."

"We who? You better speak for yourself. You don't know what those little motherfuckers are into!" . . .

. . . I got an idea for a vacation they would like: summer study abroad at the University of Mexico in Mexico City. Barbara could study her favorite subjects, Spanish and Portuguese, and Michele could study hers, art and literature. They could live in a student house where they could be on their own with other young people. A sense of freedom was apparently what they yearned for. . . .

Though Mother disapproved of my allowing the girls to go to Mexico by themselves, she admitted that they really had enjoyed studying French at the Alliance Française when she had taken them to Paris in the summer of 1967. It was what saved the trip from total disaster, because they had presented quite a discipline problem to Mother. That summer was a great success for me. Back in New York I had painted my three murals: *The Flag is Bleeding*, *U.S. Postage Stamp Commemorating the Advent of Black Power*, and my riot mural, *Die*. Had it not been for Mother taking the girls to Europe *that* summer, I would not have been able to complete those paintings for my first one–woman show.

Birdie and I had been separated since then, since 1967. We had had to have some time away from each other. There was just too much going on: the girls, the art, teaching, and then the house. That was why I walked out the summer Mother took the girls to Europe. I didn't want to spend my summer cleaning the house and cooking, so I moved into Mother's apartment and spent my days at the gallery painting till well into the.night. At the end of the summer when the girls and Mother came home from Europe, Birdie had left. Who could blame him? So we had been living apart since then. I needed him, but I needed my freedom too. Maybe later we could get back together again, after things calmed down and we could have some time for ourselves. But if I called him now he would just say, "Don't let those girls go away alone. Keep them with you. Give up the art. Postpone the show. They'll be back at school in a few months anyhow." But then so would I.

They left for Mexico after a thorough briefing: remember to lock your door; be careful when you meet strangers; stay together; and most of all look out for each other. Michele was the oldest by eleven months. She was responsible for Barbara. Kelly, the man I was seeing then, was fluent in Spanish and he knew Mexico City. He contributed to the planning of the trip and he took the girls to the airport to see them off, while I finished my last days of teaching for the year. Right away I began to assemble my canvases and paints and set about perfecting the glaze formulas I needed to prevent glare on my Black Light paintings. For the first day or two I did nothing but work. Kelly was busy too, catching up with the time he had lost in editing his magazine with helping the girls to get ready to go to Mexico. We talked on the phone and the girls called. They were in Mexico and starting school the next day. Everything was perfect.

Thereafter Kelly came evenings for dinner, and remained with me well into the early morning. I had to stop painting at 4 P.M. to shop and cook in preparation for his nightly visits. He was taking too much time from my work. He argued that I had the summer, but I worried about "the best laid plans" and the "mice" and the girls, not to mention "the men." I told him so. He began to bring the food each night and cook it himself.

The very next evening after our conversation, Kelly arrived early with a package of groceries. I greeted him and returned to my studio. Soon after he called me to eat. But I was right in the middle of a breakthrough, the attainment of a gorgeous metallic blackness. What glazes had I mixed? I was in heaven. My paintings were talking to me. I wanted to share this with Kelly as he had shared with me his writing and his other successes.

"Kelly, let's eat in the studio so I can show you my painting," I said. "I've got something interesting to show you here."

He appeared at the door of my studio wearing my ruffled apron over his shirt, tie, and the pants of his three piece suit. Kelly was a very serious, highly intelligent man with not much of a sense of humor. I could rarely look at him without wanting to laugh. For one thing he had an afro that was more than twice the size it should have been, and for another he wore horn–rimmed glasses. They were just exactly the sort of glasses that someone would wear who had far more brains than brawn. I wasn't laughing this time though.

"See," I said to his impassive face, "you have to look at it from the side. There is a kind of metallic sheen on this black here and it is because I've mixed certain glazes, and I am trying to find out what the underpainting is . . ."

His eyes remained expressionless, two beads in the center of huge horn rims. I tried to go on, "The underpainting is . . ."

He sucked his teeth.

". . . the paint that . . ."

He sucked his teeth again and turned to leave the studio.

"Come outside and eat," he commanded. "Your food is getting cold."

Story Quilts, Faith Ringgold © 1986.
"Being My Own Woman," by Faith Ringgold an excerpt from an unpublished autobiography.

This is a print made from the center drawing of the Rejection Quintet, five works originally inspired by several experiences I had in Chicago; one with a male dealer, the other with a male collector, both of whom made me feel rejected and diminished as a woman. I decided to deal with my feelings of rejection and in so doing confronted the fact that I was still hiding the real subject matter of my art behind a geometric structure as I was afraid that if I revealed my true self, I would be rejected. In the first drawings I asked: "How does it feel to be rejected?" and answered: "It's like having your flower split open." In the last drawing I asked: "How does it feel to erase your real identity?" and answered: "It's like opening your flower and no longer being afraid it will be rejected". In this, the transitional image, I "peeled back" the structure to reveal the formerly hidden form. What a relief to finally say: "Here I am, a woman, with a woman's body and a woman's point of view.

Print from: Female Rejection Drawing, #3. Lithograph. 23" x 29".
©Judy Chicago, 1984

JUDY CHICAGO

B. 1939

JUDY **CHICAGO, LIKE** many male artists, made her professional commitment to art early in life and has adamantly pursued that chosen path without wavering. Her work, however, has been anything but conventional and her achievement of her goal, to find a visual language through which she could express her "femininity" in her art through her use of so-called "vaginal iconography," has been both applauded and attacked. Chicago established a deliberate dialogue with the historical tradition in which the achievements of women have been slighted, challenging its assumptions about iconography, materials and means of production. She is also important as one of the most outspoken feminist artists of the 1970s, a controversial figure whose strong media presence contributed to public awareness of the feminist revision of art and its history. Her autobiography, *Through the Flower*, is an articulate discussion of the struggle involved in her own artistic development, raising questions regarding the process of self-conceptualization relevant to many other women artists.

Judy Chicago was born Judy Cohen in Chicago, the first child of a working couple. Her father worked as a union organizer until the conservatism of the McCarthy era forced him to abandon that career and begin anew as an insurance salesman. Although Chicago says that her mother, who had wanted to be a dancer, understood her artistic inclinations better than her father, it is he who was really her role model in life, the most important influence in her development as an achiever in the world. Like other women artists throughout history, Chicago's strong identification with her father enabled her to internalize his authority and to become an active, powerful agent on her own behalf. Chicago's father assumed an even more mythic role in her life due to his unexpected death while she was still a teenager. The fact that they had argued shortly before he died made her fear her own power and mistrust her strength, an issue with which she had to come to terms in order to achieve artistic maturity.

As a child, Chicago was able to carve out a special place for herself through art, a theme that appears in many artists' biographies. From the time she was eight through her high school years, she took art classes at the Art Institute of Chicago, where the permanent collection had a strong impact on her as well. After graduation from high school, she continued her art studies at the University of California in Los Angeles (UCLA), where she settled on working in sculpture. In 1961 she married Jerry Gerowitz (with whom she had been involved since her sophomore year in college), who died in a car crash a year later, an event she describes as being particularly traumatic since it reopened the pain she had experienced at her father's death. Characteristically, her response to Gerowitz's death was to plunge herself into her work, which she accomplished as a graduate student at UCLA. In recounting her own life, his death marks the end of the chapter concerned with her childhood; it is only afterward that she describes the process of "making a professional life."

Over the next ten years Chicago struggled to discover her true vision and a suitable means of expressing it. During the same time she attempted to achieve recognition in the art world. Her search for deeper content was thwarted by pressure from her teachers and mentors, whom she describes as reacting negatively to the biomorphic shapes that she explored in her first works after Gerowitz's death. Wanting to be accepted "by the boys," when she finished at UCLA she attended auto-body school to learn spray painting, in order to be able to create the hard, metallic finishes characteristic of the Minimalist aesthetic that dominated the art world at that time. Chicago's sculpture in the mid-sixties was consistent with the then-current interpretation of artistic validity. In such works as *Rainbow Picket* (1965), a series of uniformly finished slabs of wood, whose pastel colors give the only hint of her later painterly concerns, her surfaces were hard-edged, her personal content was suppressed. In spite of her attempts to conform, she writes that she was "continually made to feel by men in the art world that there was something 'wrong' with me."

By 1968, however, Chicago began to identify the cultural denial of her sexual identity with the sense of denial she had been experiencing as a woman artist. Her resulting decision to make her concealed content more overt marked a turning point in her artistic development. Three series of works from the late sixties spoke directly to this issue. The first, large Plexiglas domes, forms which she believed expressed fecundity, were spray-painted in luminescent layered colors, which she saw as metaphors for her own hidden depths. In the second, *Atmospheres*, environmental works in which she used fireworks, she allowed the multicolored air that had been imprisoned in the domes to escape. Finally, in the *Pasadena Lifesavers* series, she used specific color combinations to work out her feelings about masculinity and femininity, adopting at the same time the centralized form that characterized her later work. Another important transition occurred when the domes and lifesavers were exhibited in late 1969 at the art gallery at California State University in Fullerton. She decided at that time to change her name from Judy Gerowitz to Judy Chicago as "an act of identifying [her]self as an independent woman." By naming herself she indicated that she refused to accept limitations predetermined by a patriarchal society.

From this point on Chicago followed the lead of the "mothers" rather than that of the "fathers" in merging form and content in her work. In the early 1970s she began to teach and to develop programs in feminist art education, first at California State University at Fresno and then at the California Institute of the Arts (Cal Arts) in Los Angeles. These experiences had a major impact on the subsequent direction of her own art, on her work's environmental nature and feminist content, and her participation in communal production. Chicago coordinated with Miriam Schapiro the transformation of a dilapidated old house in Los Angeles into "Womanhouse," a joint project with her class in which each student created a particular room to visually express the identification of women with their domestic spaces. Some of the visual metaphors were brilliant articulations of that relationship, such as Vicki Hodgett, Robin Weltsch, and Susan Frazier's *Nurturant Kitchen*, whose pink walls were bedecked with eggs that became breasts and Sandra Orgel's *Linen Closet*, in which a woman emerged from the shelves and the sheets. Chicago's own *Menstruation Bathroom* effectively communicated the contrast between the bloodiness of women's monthly cycles and society's desire to suppress all traces of those cycles. Additionally, the group explored the cultural oppression of women through performance pieces that emphasized the repetitive nature of the activities of women in Western culture, such as doing housework, applying make-up, and waiting. Also during the seventies, Chicago married again, this time to the sculptor Lloyd Hamrol. Although they attempted to negotiate the conflicting demands of marriage and art by maintaining separate living and working quarters, by the end of the decade the marriage had ended.

Although the work on Womanhouse lasted only a year, it dramatically affected Chicago's later artistic development. Its influence is seen particularly clearly in her major work to date, *The Dinner Party*, a monumental environmental sculpture celebrating the achievement of women from prehistoric through contemporary times. In this work, 39 historical and mythical figures are placed around a triangular table, each woman represented by a place setting consisting of custom-designed ceramic plates and needlework runners and standardized cups and silverware. The names of 999 more women are inscribed on the triangular tiles of the "dedication floor." The work was inspired by historical research Chicago began in the early seventies in search of achievements by artistic and intellectual foremothers. She first explored her interest in female historical figures in works such as *Reincarnation Triptych* or *Compresssed Women Who Yearned to Be Butterflies*. In these, and in her series of Rejection Drawings, Chicago conceptualized the formal structure that formed the basis of *The Dinner Party* plates, the "central core imagery" that she believed characterized art by women. The environmental nature of *The Dinner Party* and the collaborative aspect of its production (many workers contributed to its realization, although Chicago was its singular creator), also emerged from her experiences working in a group at Cal Arts and on Womanhouse. As in

Womanhouse, *The Dinner Party* employed materials not in the high art repertoire, and celebrated needlework and ceramics, two crafts that have been devalued for being primarily of women's sphere.

Chicago used needlework again as the foundation of her next major piece, *The Birth Project*, also a collaborative work, comprising a large number of tapestry panels that could be seen in varying combinations. She has explained that she chose the theme of birth specifically to redress its lack of depiction in Western art. Many of the images in the series exhibited a more broadly conceived development of the central core structure of her earlier works. After having worked with female imagery for more than a decade, in 1982, Chicago concluded that she "couldn't make images of women any more"; her two most recent works, *Powerplay* and *The Holocaust Project,* focus on images of men.

Chicago's autobiography, *Through the Flower,* is an extremely rich document. It is an excellent example of an artist's biography, a genre whose conventions were developed during the Renaissance, in which Chicago vividly articulates the process, relevant to all artists regardless of gender, of finding the artistic means to express one's internal vision. Chicago conceptualized her quest as a specifically feminist one, how to be both a woman and an artist in a society that has considered them mutually exclusive. *Through the Flower* speaks to the plight of women artists within a patriarchal culture in which, as Chicago writes, "simply by being a woman and an artist one challenges assumptions of male dominance." She resolved the conflict through the content of her art and although Chicago's solutions may not be universally applicable, the struggle that she identified between being an artist and being a woman was experienced to some degree by all the artists whose writings are included in this volume. It is interesting that, despite the feminist journey that she chronicled, Chicago's path to successful realization of her artistic potential followed a route more typical of men than of women. In spite of the importance and her awareness of historical foremothers, Chicago accepted for herself the patriarchal concept of the artist-hero who sacrifices all to his (or her) art. Käthe Kollwitz, Barbara Hepworth, and Elizabeth Catlett are three artists discussed in this book whose journeys to artistic success followed alternate paths.

The process of writing *Through the Flower* helped Chicago to develop the female-centered motif on which she based her mature artistic style. "Moving through the flower is a process that is available to all of us, a process that can lead us to a place where we can express our humanity and values as women through our work," she wrote at the conclusion of the book. She alludes to both blooming and passage in her use of this metaphor. She also wrote that she used the flower "as the symbol of femininity" but that "the petals of the flower are parting to reveal an inviting but undefined space, the space beyond the confines of our own femininity. These works symbolized my longing for transcendence and personal growth." Chicago asserted that the opening flower was often the hidden content of the work of many women artists who frequently used "central images . . . sometimes surrounded by folds or undulations, as in the structure of the vagina." Her central core structure has been criticized as reductionist (Karin Woodley claimed that "the representation of each group of women by a plate beautifully crafted as a vagina conjures up the same old misconception of women's sexuality"), as have many of the assumptions Chicago has made about female sexuality and identity, especially in regard to a particularly female style.

Chicago remains a controversial figure in other ways as well. Some have suggested that her emphasis on needlecraft and household arts could be seen as celebrating women's oppression. Her obvious personal strength, particularly her dominant role in cooperative projects, has brought about negative comments, an attitude that reinforces her assessment of the cultural bias against strong women.

Chicago, however, has made great strides toward a woman-centered artistic vision. Her use of performance art, workshop production, useful crafts such as embroidery and ceramics, and the creation of a dinner party itself are all ways in which she challenges traditional definitions of artistic acceptability. To show that women have created art under adverse circumstances celebrates the art, not the adversity. Her central imagery is overwhelmingly lush, sensual, and unabashedly sexual. Its power, rather than limiting women's potential, allows contemporary viewers to reconsider the cultural negativism concerning women's sexuality. Although Chicago has received a certain amount of media notoriety, there is a gap between her artistic achievement and the acknowledgment she has received. *The Dinner Party*'s "disappearance" from the public eye is an illustration that women are still punished for speaking the truths about their lives in their art.

The selections included here from Chicago's autobiography concern the process by which she "thought back through her mothers" to find her artistic vision. Her explication of *The Dinner Party* discusses the evolution of her concept, and a passage written on the bottom of *Female Rejection Drawing, #3* has also been reprinted for its effective explanation of her use of vaginal imagery.

Chicago has been willing to engage in active debate with the art historical tradition. Both her life and her work have taken place in an overtly feminist context, and their consideration provides an appropriate conclusion to this discussion of ways in which women artists have articulated, validated, and expressed their visions.

SOURCES

Brown, Betty Ann, and Arlene Raven. *Exposures: Women and Their Art.* Pasadena, Calif.: New Sage Press, 1989.

Chicago, Judy. *The Birth Project.* Garden City, N. Y.: Doubleday and Co., 1985.

_____. *The Dinner Party, A Symbol of Our Heritage.* Garden City, N. Y..: Doubleday and Co., 1979.

_____. *Through the Flower: My Struggle as a Woman Artist.* Garden City, N.Y.: Doubleday and Co., 1974.

Witzling, Mara. "*Through the Flower*: Judy Chicago's Conflict Between a Woman-Centered Vision and the Male Artist Hero." In *Writing the Woman Artist*, edited by Suzanne Jones. Philadelphia: University of Pennsylvania Press, 1991.

Woodley, Karin. "The Inner Sanctum: The Dinner Party." In *Visibly Female*, edited by Hilary Robinson. New York: Universe Books, 1988.

SELECTIONS FROM JUDY CHICAGO, *THROUGH THE FLOWER*
(GARDEN CITY, NY: DOUBLEDAY AND CO., 1974)

FROM CHAPTER 7, "FINDING MY WAY AND DISCOVERING WOMEN'S ART"

Early in the fall of 1971, shortly after my return from Fresno, I went to visit AnaïsNin. I met Anaïs at a social gathering and she told me that she had read and liked one of the articles I wrote for the *Everywoman* issue on the Fresno program. . . .

. . . After a while I got over my awe of her, but the visit had a big impact on me. We discussed the confusion I felt about what direction I wanted to pursue in my work. I explained that I felt as if all these new possibilities had opened up for me as a result of the women's movement. Since I had become involved in the movement, I had, in addition to painting and teaching, lectured, started working in performance, and made some films. I told her that I felt as if my art was not reflecting my whole self and that I thought that the best thing I could do would be to give up painting and become involved in some other artmaking method.

She suggested that I use writing to "try out" all the various paths I could see myself taking and as a method of exploring the many directions for the arts that feminist consciousness seemed to suggest. She said that writing allowed one to "act out" what one could not actually live out. I went home determined to work on a book based upon my experiences and struggles. But I was frightened at the prospect. People in the past had told me that I *could* write, but I never believed them. I think that I had difficulty absorbing the idea of being able to write along with being able to paint. An "artist," I had learned, was generally mute and inarticulate. It was difficult to put together the fact that I was visually talented, could "direct," perform, organize, speak publicly, teach, and now, according to Anaïs, write, too. But I figured if anyone should know if someone could write, she should. However, just trying to be an artist had resulted in men saying I couldn't be an artist and a woman too. How could I be an artist and a writer and an organizer and a performer/director, a teacher, a politically active person, and a woman also? Was it all right to be all those things, I wondered? And how could I either integrate my talents or choose among them?

Working on the book helped me to organize my thoughts and ideas and to examine the experiences I had been having. While I was writing it, I also began experimenting with overtly feminist visual images. About the same time that I visited Anaïs, I started working at a print shop owned by a well–established male artist. He had always been very supportive of me and had offered me a chance to make a lithograph. . . .

The lithograph I made was inspired by a conversation I had had at a friend's house. Four of us, all women in our early thirties, were discussing menstruation. Suddenly we realized that none of us had ever openly discussed that subject in any depth before. As we were all involved in art, that realization led us to a conversation about the absence of menstruation images in art and literature made by women. I decided to do a menstruation lithograph, called "Red Flag." It was an image of a woman's hand pulling a bloody Tampax out of her vagina. I tried to make the image as overt as I could, and even then some people interpreted the Tampax as a bloody penis, a testament to the damage done to our perceptual powers by the absence of images of female reality.

Working on the print was a real experience. I was very nervous when I brought the photograph to the litho shop, where I was to work with a male printer. I didn't know how he would react, and I was still extremely uncomfortable about exposing my point of view as a woman around men. Working on the print helped me considerably. The printer and I calmly talked about adjusting the blood color and making sure that the Tampax looked like it was really emerging from the vagina. I made the print for two reasons: first, I wanted to validate female subject matter by using a "high art" process, which is what hand lithography is, and second, I think I was trying to test male reaction to overt female subject matter. In fact, as I think back about the eight months after I returned from Fresno, I can see that I was actively testing my limits and my talents, was searching for a method of integrating my art and my feminism, and was also trying to gauge the potential response of the established art community to the new work I was making. Having internalized so many taboos throughout the years, I was sure that people would have violent reactions to the print. However, if the printer or people in the shop had any difficulty in dealing with the image, their professionalism never let them demonstrate it. I can see now that I was slowly developing the confidence that I could, in fact, reveal my real feelings in my work and that nothing terrible would happen. . . .

By the time Womanhouse closed, I had finished the first draft of my book, seen the positive responses to both Womanhouse and my print, and in the process developed greater ease about expressing my own point of view. I realized that the reason I had thought about doing performance was that I wanted my work to have the same *impact* on values that performance seemed able to produce. Trying it helped me see that even though performance did offer the opportunity to express female subject matter more directly than did abstract art, I was a sophisticated artist. This meant that I would only be satisfied if I could do "high quality theater" and that would require that I develop a whole range of skills which I did not have. It would be quite different to develop a real feminist theater than to do simple and relatively uncomplicated performance pieces.

I had been drawing and painting since I was three years old. All those years had been spent developing keen visual abilities. I would have to start all over again if I were to do theater. Suddenly, that struck me as ridiculous. Why should I relinquish the skills I already had? I discovered then that I didn't *want* to repudiate the aesthetic tradition in which I was raised, albeit male, or pretend that my skills and sophistication were something to be devalued and discarded as "male," "elitist," or "bourgeois." Rather, I wanted to wed my skills to my real ideas and to aspire to the making of art that could clearly reveal my vision and point of view as a woman. . . .

I decided, in that spring of 1972, to go back to my studio to begin a series of drawings, to find a way back to myself and my life as an artist that I had had to interrupt for eight months. Starting to work again was a revelation, for I had changed and grown in that time away from my studio. I now knew what my goal was: to make my form language reflect my real feelings as a woman, a goal that I am now, in 1974, beginning to realize. Then, I slowly and haltingly began to try to make my subject matter clearer. I used the form language I had spent ten years in developing to express my longing to grow and my acceptance that my childhood was over — childhood, the time when all things are possible because one is still unformed.

In the spring of 1972, another event occurred that forced me to face the end of my childish dreams of escaping responsibility, being twenty again, and being "taken care of" by a mother figure. After a series of unfortunate misunderstandings between us, Mimi decided to withdraw from most of our activities together. . . . I felt rejected. I felt punished and again, when I didn't know where else to go with my feelings, I went deeper into my studio life.

I made a series of drawings structured on a grid that Mimi had used. I guess that by adopting her format, I tried to hold onto her a little longer. Even while I was going through the feelings, I knew that they were out of proportion to reality. All that had happened was that a friend of mine had, for her own reasons, decided to change certain aspects of her life. In so doing, she changed our relationship, which I didn't like. But for me it had mythic meaning, in the sense that she had represented the "mother" who would love me for being independent, something that I wanted as much as any student in the program or woman in the society. That want, which, in my estimation, most women share, is not a function of having had "bad" mothering. Rather it is a result of growing up in a male–dominated society, in which women condition their daughters toward behavior that is "safe" and therefore unchallenging to male domination. To have a mother who loves you for being independent is to have a mother who fosters rebellion in your heart and revolution in your bones. And that can only come to pass in a feminist community. . . .

All through the spring, I had struggled with my feelings about the split with Mimi in a series of works based upon that grid structure. Her images were closed. The spaces inside my grids opened up. You could see into them; they held a beautiful and peaceful space. But you could not enter those spaces. One's way was barred by a series of flesh beams. It was the human condition that prevented one from re–entering "Childhood." These images led me to another series, one that represented the place I felt myself to be at that moment — moving through the limits of female role. I used the flower as the symbol of femininity, as O'Keeffe had done. But in my images the petals of the flower are parting to reveal an inviting but undefined space, the space beyond the confines of our own femininity. These works symbolized my longing for transcendence and personal growth. They were my first steps in being able to make clear, abstract images of my point of view as a woman. . . .

Once I began to examine women's work independently from men's, it became obvious that what some women had been trying to say about themselves as women in their art actually *constituted a challenge to male perception* of women and exposed male art as only a *partial*, rather than a universal, perception of reality. The same question about what it means to be a woman that informed the work of many abstract artists was present in women's representational work as well. In subject matter, if not in style, Hepworth and Cassatt, O'Keeffe and Kollwitz, St. Phalle and Bontecou, all confronted a similar dilemma in their development as artists. Their self–images did not correspond to society's definition of women. Asserting their own self–definitions was an implicit step toward challenging the culture and demanding that it adjust its definition of women to correspond to the reality of women's lives, a demand that was not even apprehended, much less met. . . .

Investigating women's art helped me see my circumstances and frustration as an artist as a social and political dilemma that could only be solved by a fundamental change in the nature of society. Being denied the recognition I deserved, being rejected by the male art community, and having my achievements and point of view as an artist denied and diminished were all symptoms of my situation as a woman in a male–dominated culture.

FROM CHAPTER 9, "GETTING IT TOGETHER"

. . . Anaïs' comments about the quality of transparency in women's work had helped me identify and validate one of my own impulses. My ability to see "through form" and recognize content had always embarrassed me because I could "read" not only art content, but also the meaning of human behavior. Seeing "the transparency of the psyche" in other women's work, relating to it, liking it, helped me accept that this ability was part of my gift as a woman. I decided to "expose" my perceptions by writing them down on my paintings — writing whatever I was feeling while I was making the work, so that my process and my image became "transparent" and understandable to others.

My readings, my studies of women's art, and the developing female art community were combining to make me feel more comfortable about myself, to feel confident about exposing my real feelings, and to relax and feel less anxious about myself. I was also emerging from seeing myself through the limiting stereotypes available to women in male culture. In my efforts to avoid being considered a "dumb cunt," I had accepted being seen in terms of another stereotype, that of the "superwoman." To protect myself, I had learned to hide my needs and to get what I needed through giving to others. In the context of the growing female community, I was experiencing myself in a new way. Some women perceived me as men did: strong, invulnerable, defensive, manipulative. But there were others who were able to see me as I really was: strong but vulnerable, powerful but accessible, strong–minded but open. As I saw my own perceptions of myself reflected in their views of me, I was able to expose more and more of my softness, my shyness, my fears, and my needs. This process had a profound effect on my work. . . .

It took several days to install the show (at the Woman's Building in Los Angeles) and do the writing. On one wall of the exhibition, I wrote these words:

The Great Ladies — begun in the Fall of 1972, completed in the Summer of 1973; these women represent themselves, aspects of myself, and various ways in which women have accommodated themselves to the constraints of their circumstances. Some years ago, I began to read women's literature, study women's art, and examine the lives of women who lived before me. I wanted to find role models, to discover how my predecessors had dealt with their oppression as women. I was also searching for clues in their work — clues that could aid me in my art. I wanted to speak out of my femaleness, to make art out of the very thing that made me the "other" in male society. I developed an increasing identification with other women, both those who lived before me and those who, like me, felt the need for a female support community. Together, we built an alternative art institution — the Woman's Building. My paintings can only be fully understood in this new context we have made. I want to thank all those who helped me install my show. This was the first time I've received such remarkable support and I feel honored to be a part of the reappearance of the Woman's Building, 80 years after it was first established in my home town.

For a solid month before the opening, I suffered from depressions, anxiety attacks, even rashes. I felt that the opening of the building and the exhibition of my new work truly revealed my commitment, my ideas, and my values, and I was afraid that they would be rejected. Five thousand people attended the opening. I could hardly believe the crowds when I arrived. I walked up to the gallery that housed my show, and people embraced me and cried and told me how moved they were by what I'd done. I couldn't believe it. I was being myself — really myself — and not only was nothing terrible happening, but I was receiving the acknowledgment I had been deprived of for so long. . . .

. . . Working to build the female art community in Los Angeles helped me to expand my own self–image, to experience myself in ways that are simply not possible within the present structure of male–dominated society, where women's power is seen, if not negatively, then certainly stereotypically. In fact, male society makes women feel as if their power is *not needed or valued*, whereas in the female community, women's power is essential. This drastically changes the way one experiences oneself as woman, as one is valued for the *development* of one's capacities, rather than for the repression of them. . . .

The existence of the Woman's Building, . . . my experiences over the years in building a female community all combined to make me feel considerably more comfortable about being and expressing myself as a woman in my life and in my art. Finally, in the spring of 1974, I made a real breakthrough in my work. I found a way to convey clearly the content that was still hidden in my earlier images. This made me realize that I had been involved in a process, a process which had allowed me first to experience myself, then express myself fully, a process that has rarely been available to women and which, in my estimation, is simply not possible in a male–dominated situation. Once I could actually be myself and express my point of view, both personally and professionally, I recognized that *through my art*, I could contribute my values and attitudes as a woman to the culture in such a way that I could *affect* the society. Because, as women, we actually have access to the mechanisms of society and because we are more than one half the population, we *can change and mold our environment*, but only if we can be ourselves and express our real points of view. Moving "through the flower" is a process that is available to all of us, a process that can lead us to a place where we can express our humanity and values as women *through our work* and in our lives and in so doing, perhaps we can also reach across the great gulf between masculine and feminine and gently, tenderly, but firmly heal it.

❖

EXCERPTS FROM JUDY CHICAGO, *THE DINNER PARTY*
(GARDEN CITY, NY: DOUBLEDAY AND CO., 1979)

FROM "CREATING A WORK OF ART: FIVE YEARS OF MY LIFE"

... I remember one particularly poignant experience of visiting a china-painter's house and seeing, as Virginia Woolf once said, that the very bricks were permeated with her creative energy. All the chairs had needlepoint cushions; all the beds were covered with quilts; all the pillowcases were hand–embroidered; all the walls were covered with oil paintings; all the plates were painted with flowers; and the garden was planted with the kinds of flowers that were painted on the plates. This woman had done all that work, trying as best she could to fit her creative drive — which could probably have expanded into mural–size paintings or monumental sculptures — into the confined space of her house, which could hardly have held another piece of work. The china-painting world, and the household objects the woman painted, seemed to be a perfect metaphor for women's domesticated and trivialized circumstances. It was an excruciating experience to watch enormously gifted women squander their creative talents on teacups. I wanted to honor the women who had preserved this technique, and, by making china–painting visible through my work, I hoped to stimulate interest in theirs. I was planning thirteen plate settings, with the name of each woman embroidered on the tablecloth along with a phrase indicating what she had achieved. It became evident, however, that thirteen plates were not enough to represent the various stages of Western civilization, and therefore the number tripled. I arrived at the idea of an open triangular table, equilateral in structure, which would reflect the goal of feminism — an equalized world. (Also, the triangle was one of the earliest symbols of the feminine.) But there was something wrong with the image of this large table without a context: the concept of an isolated woman "pulling herself up by her bootstraps" simply did not stand up to the evidence of history. Rather, women's achievements took place against a background of societies in which women either had equal rights or were predominant to begin with or, later, enjoyed expanded opportunities, agitated for their rights, or built support networks among themselves.

To convey this idea, I decided to place the triangular table on a floor inscribed with the names of additional women of achievement besides those represented by place settings. This would suggest that the women at the table had risen from a foundation provided by other women's accomplishments, and each plate would then symbolize not only a particular woman but also the tradition from which she emerged. The floor would be porcelain, like the plates, and the women's names would be painted on triangular tiles in gold china–paint with a luster overglaze. This would make the names appear and disappear as the viewer walked around the table — a fitting metaphor for women's history. . . .

. . . I began to think about the piece as a reinterpretation of the Last Supper from the point of view of women, who, throughout history, had prepared the meals and set the table. In my "Last Supper," however, the women would be the honored guests. Their representation in the form of plates set on the table would express the way women had been confined, and the piece would thus reflect both women's achievements and their oppression.

There were thirteen men present at the Last Supper. There were also thirteen members in a witches' coven, and witches were always associated with feminine evil. The fact that the same number had both a positive and a negative connotation seemed perfect for the dual meaning of the piece; the idea of twenty–five plates therefore gave way to thirteen.

But the Last Supper existed within the context of the Bible, which was a history of a people. So my *Dinner Party* would also be a people's history — the history of women in Western civilization. . . . as long as women's achievements were excluded from our understanding of the past, we would continue to feel as if we had *never* done anything worthwhile. This absence of any sense of our tradition as women seemed to cripple us psychologically. I wanted to change that, and I wanted to do it through art. . . .

❖

FROM "THE DINNER PARTY TABLE: THIRTY–NINE GUESTS"

The women represented at the *Dinner Party* table are either historical or mythological figures. I chose them for their actual accomplishments and/or their spiritual or legendary powers. I have brought these women together — invited them to dinner, so to speak — in order that we might hear what they have to say and see the range and beauty of our heritage, a heritage we have not yet had an opportunity to know.

These guests, whether they are real women or goddess figures, have all been transformed in *The Dinner Party* into symbolic images — images that stand for the whole range of women's achievements and yet also embody women's containment. Each woman is herself, but through her can be seen the lives of thousands of other women — some famous, some anonymous, but all struggling, as the women on the table struggled, to have some sense of their own worth through five thousand years of a civilization dominated by men. The images on the plates are not literal, but rather a blending of historical facts, iconographical sources, symbolic meanings, and imagination. I fashioned them from my sense of the woman (or, if a goddess, what she represented); the artistic style of the time (when it interested me or seemed to have a potential to express something about the figure I was portraying); and my own imagery.

When I began working on the *Dinner Party* plates, I developed an iconography using the butterfly to symbolize liberation and the yearning to be free. The butterfly form undergoes various stages of metamorphosis as the piece unfolds. Sometimes she is pinned down; sometimes she is trying to move from a larva to an adult state; sometimes she is nearly unrecognizable as a butterfly; and sometimes she is almost transformed into an unconstrained being. . . .

There is a strong narrative aspect to the piece that grew out of the history uncovered in our research and underlying the entire conception of *The Dinner Party*. This historical narrative is divided into three parts, corresponding to the three wings of the table. The first table begins with pre–history and ends with the point in time when Greco–Roman culture was diminishing. The second wing stretches from the beginning of Christianity to the Reformation, and the third table includes the seventeenth to the twentieth centuries. Beginning with pre–patriarchal society, *The Dinner Party* demonstrates the development of goddess worship, which represents a time when women had social and political control (clearly reflected in the goddess imagery common to the early stages of almost every society in the world). The piece then suggests the gradual destruction of these female–oriented societies and the eventual domination of women by men, tracing the institutionalizing of that oppression and women's response to it.

During the Renaissance, the male–dominated Church — built in large part with the help of women — and the newly emerged, male–controlled State joined hands. They began to eliminate all who resisted their power — the heretics who held onto pre–Christian, generally female–oriented religions; the lay healers who continued to practice medicine in the face of increasing restrictions by the emerging medical profession; the political dissenters who challenged the corruption of the Church; the women who refused to submit to their husbands, to their fathers, and to the priests; those who insisted on administering the drug ergot to relieve the suffering of women in labor; those who helped women abort themselves; those who wished to practice sexual freedom; those who wanted to continue preaching or healing or leading social groups and religious groups; and all who resented and resisted the steady but inevitable destruction of what was left of female power. These women were harassed, intimidated, and — worst of all — burned, in a persecution whose real meaning has completely evaded the history taught to us today.

By the time of the Reformation, when the convents were dissolved, women's education — formerly available through the Church — was ended. Women were barred from the universities, the guilds, and the professions; women's property and inheritance rights, slowly eroded over centuries, were totally eliminated; and women's role was restricted to domestic duties. Opportunities were more severely limited than in pre–Renaissance society. The progress we have all been educated to associate with the Renaissance took place for men at the expense of women. By the time of the Industrial Revolution women's lives were so narrow, their options so few, there is little wonder that a new revolution began — a revolution that has remained hidden by a society that has not heard the voices raised in protest by women (as well as by some men) throughout the centuries.

The women represented in *The Dinner Party* tried to make themselves heard, fought to retain their influence, attempted to implement or extend the power that was theirs, and endeavored to do what they wanted. They wanted to exercise the rights to which they were entitled by virtue of their birth, their talent, their genius, and their desire, but they were prohibited from doing so — were ridiculed, ignored, and maligned by historians for attempting to do so — because they were women. . . .

❖

JUDY CHICAGO, FROM *FEMALE REJECTION DRAWING*, #3, 1974

In trying to "peel back" the structure I have used in my work because I felt that I had to "hide" the real content, I found myself making a vaginal form. I was not so interested in drawing a cunt but there is a big gap between my feelings as a woman and the visual language of the male culture. Whenever I want to deal with the issue of vulnerability, emotional exposure or primitive feelings, the only image I can think of is a vagina, probably because those aspects of the human experience have been relegated to the sphere of the "feminine" and then deprecated. My struggle has been and is to find a way to let the female experience be represented in such a way that it can stand for the areas of human experience that male society denies, thus challenging the prevailing values. I don't know how to do that yet. Neither does anyone else. It is the major problem those of us face who are trying to forge a new language, one that is relevant to women's experiences. Recently, I was criticized for the gap that exists between my "rhetoric" and my work. On one level, the criticism was justified and helped me to begin to "peel back" the structure that I had imposed upon my real content in order to make an identity as an artist in the world. But, in another way, the criticism makes me angry because it implies that it is my failure as an artist that creates the gap, and that is simply not true. Whatever gap exists grows out of the fact that I have been trying to bridge a gap that exists in the world — the gap between my feminist consciousness and sophisticated art language. In the years I was studying to be an artist, I was consistently rejected as a woman and even more violently rejected if my womanhood was reflected in my art. Does anyone really understand what it means to have to suppress your femaleness in order to be able to express your artistness — or what it does to you? I was not willing to be an artist in a closet and now I am not willing to be a woman in a closet. I've chosen to take on the struggle to be myself in the fear of society's rejection in the hope that by so doing, my work will help change society. So now I'm put down because I haven't got it all together. Even my husband who loves me and understands my work and my struggle, rejected the image of my hidden femaleness in this drawing. How many people in this world can stand up to the consistent rejection male culture subjects women to? How many husbands are willing to struggle with their feelings like my husband did, in order to embrace the drawing? How many women are willing to face rejection and rejection and rejection and rejection and rejection and rejection and rejection and still insist on exposing their femaleness?

INDEX

Berthe Morisot
Reprinted from *Berthe Morisot: Correspondence*, edited by Denis Rouart, published by Moyer Bell Limited.

Mary Cassatt (1844–1926)
Letter to Bertha Potter Palmer, courtesy The Art Institute of Chicago.
Letters to Theodate Pope, courtesy the Hill-stead Museum Archives.
Letter to Eugenie Heller, Thomas J. Watson Library, The Metropolitan Museum of Art.
Lettters to John W. Beatty, Homer St. Gaudens and William Ivins, Archives of American Art, Smithsonian Institution.
Letters to Eliza Haldeman, Emily Sartain, Harrision Morris, Pennsylvania Academy of Fine Arts, Archives.
Letters to Lois Cassatt and Alexander Cassatt, Philadelphia Museum of Art Archives: Archives of American Art/ Carl Zigrosser Collection.
Letters to Louisine Havemeyer, Metropolitan Museum of Art, Courtesy the Estate of Lois Cassatt Thayer.

Cecilia Beaux
Estate of Cecilia Beaux.

Marianne Werefkin
Used with permission of the Fondazione Marianne Werefkin, Museo Communale d'Arte Moderna, Ascona.

Käthe Kollwitz
Käthe Kollwitz, *The Diaries and Letters of Käthe Kollwitz*, edited by Hans Kollwitz, translated by Richard and Clara Winston. Copyright © 1988, Northwestern University Press, Evanston, Illinois. First published 1955 by the Henry Regnery Co. Reprinted by permission of Northwestern University Press.

Emily Carr
Selections from *Growing Pains*, *Hundreds and Thousands*, and *Heart of a Peacock* reproduced with the permission of Stoddart Publishing Co. Limited, 34 Lesmill Rd., Don Mills, Ontario, Canada.

Paula Modersohn-Becker
Paula Modersohn-Becker: The Letters and Journals, edited by Günter Busch and Liselotte S. Wensinger and Carole Clew Hoey. English translation © 1983, Taplinger Publishing Co. Republished in 1990 by Northwestern University Press in arrangement with S. Fischer Verlag. Reprinted by permission of Northwestern University Press.

Georgia O'Keeffe
Letter to William Milliken © 1991 The Cleveland Museum of Art.
Letters to Anita Pollitzer, Alfred Stieglitz, Mabel Dodge Luhan, copyright © 1990 The Georgia O'Keeffe Foundation, from *Georgia O'Keeffe: Art and Letters*, © National Gallery of Art, Washington, D.C.
Letters to Ettie Stettheimer, William Howard Schubart and Eleanor Roosevelt, by permission of The Georgia O'Keeffe Foundation.
Excerpts from Georgia O'Keeffe, *Georgia O'Keeffe*, copyright © 1987 Juan Hamilton.

Kay Sage
Credit to John S. Monagan for permission to quote excerpts from "China Eggs" by Kay Sage.
Other writings by Kay Sage used with permission of Henry Sage Goodwin.

Irene Rice Pereira
Courtesy of Djelloul Marbrook, nephew of the artist.

Barbara Hepworth
Barbara Hepworth writings and photographs, copyright © Alan Bowness.

Frida Kahlo
Translation of diary entries reprinted by permission of Sterling Lord Literistic, Inc. Copyright © by Hayden Herrera. Used with permission of Sra. Dolores Olmedo-Patino.

Leonora Carrington (b. 1917)
"Commentary" reprinted with permission of the author. Copyright © 1976 by Leonora Carrington.
"Down Below" and "The Oval Lady," from *The House of Fear* by Leonora Carrington, translated by Leonora Carrington. Translation copyright © 1988 by Leonora Carrington. Used by permission of the publisher, Dutton, an imprint of New American Library, a division of Penguin Books USA Inc.

Pablita Velarde
© Pablita Velarde. Excerpted from *Old Father, the Story-Teller*. Published by: Clear Light Publishers, Santa Fe, NM, 1989. ISBN # 0-940666-10-3.

Elizabeth Catlett
Courtesy of Elizabeth Catlett.

Faith Ringgold (b.1930)
Story Quilts, Faith Ringgold © 1986
"Being My Own Woman," by Faith Ringgold, an excerpt from an unpublished autobiography. Used with permission of Faith Ringgold.

Judy Chicago
© Judy Chicago, *The Dinner Party: A Symbol of Our Heritage*, New York: Anchor/Doubleday, 1974.
© Judy Chicago, *Through the Flower*, New York: Anchor Press, 1977.